Labors Lost

LABORS LOST

Women's Work and the Early Modern English Stage

NATASHA KORDA

PENN

UNIVERSITY OF PENNSYLVANIA PRESS

PHILADELPHIA

Copyright © 2011 University of Pennsylvania Press

All rights reserved. Except for brief quotations used for purposes of review or scholarly citation, none of this book may be reproduced in any form by any means without written permission from the publisher.

Published by
University of Pennsylvania Press
Philadelphia, Pennsylvania 19104-4112
www.upenn.edu/pennpress

Printed in the United States of America on acid-free paper

10 9 8 7 6 5 4 3 2 1

Library of Congress Cataloging-in-Publication Data

Korda, Natasha.
 Labors lost : women's work and the early modern English stage / Natasha Korda. — 1st ed.
    p. cm.
  Includes bibliographical references and index.
  ISBN 978-0-8122-4344-4 (hardcover : alk. paper)
   1. Women in the theater—England—History—16th century.
2. Women in the theater—England—History—17th century.
3. Women—Employment—England—History—16th century.
4. Women—Employment—England—History—17th century.
5. Theater—England—History—16th century. 6. Theater—England—History—17th century. 7. English drama—Early modern and Elizabethan, 1500–1600—History and criticism. 8. English drama—17th century—History and criticism. 9. Theater and society—England—History—16th century. 10. Theater and society—England—History—17th century. I. Title.
PN2582.W65K67 2011
792.0820942—dc22

2011011211

For Alex

Contents

Note on Spelling and Dates   ix

Prologue   1

Chapter 1. Labors Lost   15

Chapter 2. Dame Usury   54

Chapter 3. Froes and Rebatos   93

Chapter 4. Cries and Oysterwives   144

Chapter 5. False Wares   174

Epilogue   212

Notes   219

Bibliography   269

Index   313

Acknowledgments   331

Note on Spelling and Dates

ALTHOUGH I HAVE adhered to the original spelling of the early modern texts cited in this book, to make these citations legible to a wider audience of readers, I have silently expanded contractions, occasionally emended punctuation, given the modern equivalents of obsolete letters, and transliterated i/j and u/v. Unless otherwise indicated, dates of plays given parenthetically refer to estimated year (or date range) of first performance found in Alfred Harbage, *Annals of English Drama, 975–1700: An Analytical Record of All Plays, Extant or Lost, Chronologically Arranged and Indexed by Authors, Titles, Dramatic Companies, &c.*, rev. Samuel Schoenbaum, 3rd ed., rev. Sylvia Stoler Wagonheim (London and New York: Routledge, 1989). Publication dates of texts cited may be found in the bibliography of printed sources at the end of this book.

Prologue

SCHOLARS HAVE LONG sought to explain the anomaly of the all-male stage in Shakespeare's time but have failed to consider working women's contributions to theatrical production behind the scenes. Situating the commercial playhouses within the broader economic landscape of early modern London, this book argues that the rise of the professional stage relied on the labor, wares, ingenuity, and capital of women of all stripes, including ordinary crafts- and tradeswomen who supplied costumes, properties, and comestibles; wealthy heiresses and widows who provided much-needed capital and credit; wives, daughters, and widows of theater people who worked actively alongside their male kin; and immigrant women who fueled the fashion-driven stage with a range of newfangled skills and commodities. Marshaling a broad range of evidence on these and other women who worked in and around London's public and private playhouses, *Labors Lost* seeks to recover this lost history by detailing the diverse ways in which women participated in the work of theatrical production and the ways in which male playwrights and players in turn helped shape the cultural meanings of women's work.

At stake in the representation of working women on the early modern stage was the status and legitimacy of playing itself as profession. The parameters of legitimate trade underwent tremendous pressure in late sixteenth- and early seventeenth-century London due to exponential population growth, an influx of migrant and immigrant labor, and a rapidly expanding informal economy. Women, whose labor was often proscribed or restricted within the formal economy regulated by guilds and civic authorities, predominated in the informal networks of trade that flourished in the suburbs and liberties where the commercial theaters were located. The players relied on such trade, creating new opportunities for working women—who furnished costumes, properties, credit, and a hand in the theaters' day-to-day operations—while at the same time excluding women from the visible workspace of the stage itself in an effort to define "playing" as legitimate, manly work. Far from a marginal phenomenon, the gendered division of theatrical labor was thus crucial to the rise of the professional theater in England and provides an apt context within which to understand the dramatic tropes, figures, forms, fashions, goods, gestures, and sounds used by male players to depict working women onstage.

Women's work was not only represented by male actors on the stage, it was woven into the fabric of players' costumes, congealed in the folds of their starched ruffs, set into the curls of their perukes, arranged in the petticoats of boy-actors, calculated on the companies' balance sheets, and inscribed in the terms of their bonds. Female "gatherers" collected entrance fees at the doors of theaters, while the cries of female hawkers echoed inside and outside their walls and the wares they sold were consumed in the pit, in the galleries, and on the stage. Understanding the varied roles women played behind the scenes of theatrical production imbues early modern dramatic texts with new significance while offering a new perspective on the textures and textiles of plays in performance. The work of historical recovery that grounds this understanding is of necessity an interdisciplinary endeavor that will lead the reader through multiple forms of evidence, surveying dramatic and other cultural texts, documents of theater history, and women's social and economic history, as well as prints, paintings, and a diverse array of material ephemera associated with women's work in theatrical production and commerce.

Dress pins, hooks, buttons, costume wires, cosmetic implements, silk lace, spangles, drinking vessels, money pots, and nut and oyster shells are among the diverse, ephemeral artifacts relating to female crafts and trades unearthed in archaeological excavations of the sites upon which early modern English playhouses once stood. Although traces of women's work were everywhere in the professional theater, as they were within the culture at large, then as now, they often went unnoticed or unacknowledged. A handful of glass beads found at the site of the Rose theater may serve as an illustrative example. Each bead measures an average of just two millimeters in diameter. These "tiny objects," in the words of archaeologists Julian Bowsher and Pat Miller, would ordinarily have escaped the field of vision, being "too small to spot" even by trained eyes. They were discovered only while processing soil samples that were taken to look for other remains.[1] Such minutiae, all too easily disregarded, may seem scant evidence upon which to ground a history of women's offstage work. Yet contextualized in relation to theatrical records regarding female "spanglers" of costumes, these tiny, gleaming artifacts help illuminate the unseen labors necessary to produce theatrical spectacle, as well as the gendered division of theatrical work. For the work of spangling—or sewing beads and sequins onto costumes to make them appear more lustrous—like that of spinning, silk winding, needlework, lace making, ruff starching, and other occupations relating to luxury cloth and clothing manufacture, often fell to women precisely because they involved minute manipulations best performed by "small" fingers or tedious toil accorded to the underpaid. Of scant interest in and of themselves, these miniscule bits of glass point to a substantial workforce of women who labored in the informal networks of artisanal production and trade that gave rise to the professional stage.

The hollow, fragile, and seemingly insignificant glass beads unearthed in the remains of the public theaters serve as an apt metaphor for the scattered traces of women's work that remain in archives and museum collections, and for the sleuthing—and sometimes simple serendipity—that leads to their detection. Deciphering these scattered traces often requires laboriously collecting many shards or fragments of evidence that would remain, when viewed in isolation, indecipherable. Like beads, they take on significance or value only relationally, when strung or stitched together to form a pattern. The work of scholarship on women's labor history and its cultural meanings in this sense parallels that of early modern women themselves, requiring flexibility, ingenuity, and at times mere drudgery. The countless women who stitched, wove, washed, starched, spun, and spangled the fabric of early modern culture, sold its commodities, and financed its commercial ventures, often remain anonymous in historical records, their labor unrecorded. The historical invisibility of women's work in early modern English culture—its relegation behind the scenes of both theatrical and craft production to a "shadow" or informal economy—was produced by innumerable cultural forces and mechanisms of erasure. Women's luxury textile manufacture, for example, was often dismissed as the devil's work. Puritan diatribes against the incessant production and consumption of ornament were frequently aimed at women, decrying such attires as false or insubstantial. Similar attacks were mounted by guildsmen who sought to stigmatize female labor in unguilded occupations as shoddy or unskilled. The meager evidence that remains about such work thus often appears in literature and legislation attempting to proscribe it.

If early modern women's theatrical labors have been "lost," as the title of this book suggests, it is thus not because they were ever fully present in the past and can therefore simply be "found." Rather, such labors were commonly dismissed, devalued, and delegitimized in their own time. Since the early modern period, it has been a cultural commonplace that "women's work is never done."[2] An early seventeenth-century broadside ballad first formulated this familiar refrain in the form of a complaint voiced by a wife, who recounts her domestic drudgery in detail.[3] Her "woful Fate" includes rising before and going to bed after the rest of her family, who are therefore unaware of her toils—giving rise to her need to recount them. Countering this lack of acknowledgment with the repeated refrain, "a Womans work is never done," she insists that this is "a thing to be thought upon." Yet the ballad offers no solution to the dilemma it reveals, concluding where it began: "And thus to end my Song as I began, / You know a Womans work is never done." The knowledge it imparts thus fails to undo the defining conundrum of women's work: unending and ever-present, it is nonetheless placed under cultural erasure, as though it had never been done.

Feminist scholars and activists have had varied responses to this ostensibly transhistorical commonplace. Second-wave feminists appropriated the slogan as a form of political critique when Joyce Stevens included it in her Women's Liberation Broadsheet for International Woman's Day in 1975 ("Because woman's work is never done and is underpaid or unpaid or boring or repetitious and . . . for lots and lots of other reasons we are part of the women's liberation movement").[4] In this form it was reprinted on posters, postcards, and T-shirts and became a rallying cry for civil rights–era working women. In adopting the refrain of a seventeenth-century ballad, these women intimated that "the patriarchy" hadn't changed much since then, at least with respect to gendered restrictions on employment and wage differentials. Grappling with these troubling continuities, feminist historians of the 1980s sought to elaborate a more nuanced account of how women's working lives had changed since the premodern or early modern period. In an influential 1988 review essay on this body of scholarship, entitled "History That Stands Still," Judith Bennett acknowledged the continuum ("women who worked in medieval towns encountered some basic problems still characteristic of today's female work force; they clustered in low-status 'female' jobs that were low skilled and low paid")[5] while nonetheless insisting that "these continuities in women's work do not mean that there is no history to be written" because the "particular constraints and boundaries that framed women's work have varied over time in important ways that need to be reconstructed and analyzed." These "historical changes in the circumstances and meaning of work," she maintained, warrant careful scrutiny.[6] Pursuing this line of inquiry in the mid-1990s, Daryl M. Hafter called for a "semiotics of women's work" grounded in the recognition that its significance emerges only from its historical contexts and the cultural discourses that shape it.[7] Hafter argued for the importance of language and representation in organizing the social reality of work, as well as giving it expression, an insight that is crucial to the present study. The language of labor divides the social world into hierarchies—male/female, skilled/unskilled, paid/unpaid, licit/illicit, and so forth—which in turn confer value, meaning, and legitimacy on different categories of work and workers. These hierarchies are historically variable and culturally contingent, shifting in response to changing social and economic conditions.

The momentous historical upheavals that took place in England in the late sixteenth and early seventeenth centuries had a profound impact on the material forms and cultural meanings of women's work, yet the significance of this impact has by no means been agreed upon by historians. The thesis of a steady decline in women's economic status brought about by "capitalistic industry," first advanced in Alice Clark's groundbreaking *Working Life of Women in the Seventeenth Century* (1919), has been subject to debate, critique, and refinement in more recent studies, as discussed in Chapter 1.[8] Although it is generally agreed, for example, that the formal economy regulated by the guilds or livery companies placed increasing restrictions on women's work in the early modern period, these restrictions did not result in a wholesale exclusion of women from the labor force; rather, they helped institute a gendered division of labor that relegated women's work to an expanding informal economy of female creditors, moneylenders, pawnbrokers, frippers, victuallers, alewives, street hawkers, textile workers, and a wide range of other occupations unrepresented by guilds or livery companies. Urban women were particularly likely to work outside the home, generating their own incomes by providing services, lending money at interest, earning rent from lodgers or rental properties, and/or selling drink, food, cloth and clothing, and a diverse array of newly available consumer goods.[9] *Labors Lost* builds on such scholarship by investigating the ways in which women's work in these varied occupations contributed to theatrical commerce and production in London. Insofar as the professional stage was one of the most visible and successful of these new industries, whose legitimacy was hotly debated, it was at the frontlines of the contemporary controversy regarding what constituted "honest" "workmanship" and as such participated in shaping the cultural meanings and gendered division of labor within the broader culture.

In examining women's offstage contributions to the professional theater and the ways in which their work was represented (and absented) onstage, *Labors Lost* complements several recent studies of the cultural significance of work in early modern England. Tom Rutter's *Work and Play on the Shakespearean Stage* (2008) studies changing conceptions of male labor in the drama and, like the present study, considers the theater "inextricably implicated in contemporary debates over what constituted legitimate forms of work and recreation."[10] Yet Rutter devotes just a few pages of his study to women's work.[11] Michelle Dowd's *Women's Work in Early Modern English Literature and Culture* (2009) analyzes literary and dramatic renderings of female service, wet-nursing, and huswifery but does not consider female labor in occupations that contributed to theatrical production. In contrast to Dowd's focus on women's domestic and unpaid labor, this book concentrates on women's work in a wide range of paid occupations in and around the commercial theaters. Finally, Laurie Ellinghausen's *Labor and Writing in Early Modern England, 1567–1667* (2008) explores professional authorship as a vocation open to non-aristocratic men and women, including playwrights like Ben Jonson, an analysis upon which the present study builds in Chapter 5 by exploring its gendered dimension.

Recent scholarship on women's contributions to theatrical culture in pre-Restoration England has hitherto concentrated primarily on female "players" or performers, including aristocratic women's performances in court and household entertainments and itinerant women performers in the provinces, and has thereby left largely intact the paradigm of the "all-male" professional theater in London.[12] *Labors Lost* seeks to revise this paradigm by revealing the participation of ordinary working women in theatrical culture and commerce at the center of England as well as on the periphery. The analyses of women's work in the networks of commerce surrounding the public and private theaters in London and their dramatic renderings found in this book likewise contribute to recent work on the staged city. Jean Howard's important study of the emergent genre of city comedy and its varied progeny in *Theater of a City: The Places of London Comedy, 1598–1642* (2007), like her broader corpus of work, has contributed to our understanding of the ways in which the theater made sense of an expanding city and the new forms of gendered subjectivity to which it gave rise.[13] While city comedies feature prominently in several chapters of the present study, I also consider dramatic genres not ordinarily associated with urban commerce, suggesting that they, too, were influenced by the presence of working women in and around the theaters.[14]

Another area of research to which this book contributes is the growing body of scholarship on early modern material culture and its gendered meanings, by attending to the way in which stage properties and costumes, as well as play texts, evoke and/or elide the political economies that shape their pre-histories of production.[15] The plays produced in England's first commercial theaters were spectacular commodities in their own right, whose successful performance often relied on an appearance of effortlessness or sprezzatura and thus on the erasure or concealment of toil that took place behind the scenes.[16] In Shakespeare's time as in our own, the theater undoubtedly functioned for many as a vehicle of escape from the world of work.[17] Indeed, opponents of the stage insisted that it did so quite literally by luring artisans and apprentices away from their trades into "nurseries of idleness." From this perspective, the myriad labors that contribute to theatrical production might seem irrelevant to the finished product of plays in performance. Yet as Tom Rutter observes, Elizabethan and Jacobean dramatic literature was "very much concerned with the topic of work," as playwrights responded to anti-theatrical attacks against playing as a form of idleness by "emphasizing the industriousness and skill of professional actors."[18] Laurie Ellinghausen further demonstrates that the "embrace of writing as work" by professional playwrights in Shakespeare's time represented "a challenge to aristocratic literary culture" and in particular to its valorization of sprezzatura.[19] Playwrights deployed the "language of labor," she maintains, in an effort to depict writing for the stage "as a vocation—a 'mystery' of a new kind."[20] Yet they did so not only by foregrounding their own "workmanship," as Ellinghausen claims, but also at times by revealing the myriad labors that took place offstage in the pit and galleries, and behind the scenes of theatrical production. In so doing, they held a mirror up to financiers, playing companies, theater personnel, and, more broadly, an entire workforce that contributed to the rise of the professional stage. Over time, however, as players and playwrights sought to elevate their own status above that of the "rude mechanicals" who toiled offstage, such "metatheatrical" reflections grew more vexed and ambivalent, and sometimes hostile and satirical, particularly when referencing women's offstage work. Plays therefore have a great deal to tell us about changing conceptions of theatrical labor and theater *as* labor, as these conceptions were shaped by gender and status hierarchies.

Although plays and other cultural texts often reveal a great deal about contemporary perceptions of women's work, they do not offer self-evident data about the material forms of such work, theatrical or otherwise. To understand how dramatic representations of female labor relate to material practice, we must read plays in relation to other forms of evidence, which are equally in need of interpretation. Records of women's work in the archives are often opaque and always partial—both fragmentary and shaped by particular perspectives or biases. Typically, the problem is one of sheer invisibility: working women simply don't appear under ordinary circumstances in many sources documenting the lives of those who labored in the formal economy. Indeed, such sources often seem "to have been deliberately framed to withhold from us the answers to our questions about women's lives."[21] Historical records pertaining to women's work during the "long sixteenth century" (c. 1480–1620) are notoriously scarce.[22] When working women do appear in records from this period, it is often in documents aimed at controlling or proscribing their labor, or in court records concerning their infringement of labor restrictions or disputes stemming from their work. Scholars interested in the history of early modern women's working lives have consequently developed techniques of "reading against the grain," using traditional sources in innovative ways and identifying new sources.[23]

Attending to the roles of ordinary, working women in theatrical production likewise requires an expansive, flexible methodology that extends the traditional disciplinary boundaries of theater history beyond the walls of the playhouses to include the heterogeneous forms of commerce that lent them support. The scattered traces of women that appear in theatrical records take on new significance when read within the broader context of their work within the economy at large. For this reason, the phrase "in and around the theaters" appears frequently in this book to describe the commercial networks that surrounded the playhouses and directly or indirectly contributed to theatrical production. These networks are the focus of Chapter 1, which examines evidence of women's offstage work in traditional sources of theater history (e.g., theatrical inventories and account books) while supplementing these with documents pertaining to women's social and economic history, in particular those concerned with regulating an unruly, informal, female workforce. The chapter begins by surveying existing feminist scholarship on women's participation in theatrical culture broadly construed, which has hitherto been divided between those who take the absence of women to be the defining condition of the professional stage in Shakespeare's time and those who have uncovered women's presence in other types or areas of performance. This absence/presence dichotomy, I argue, is insufficiently nuanced to account for women's ubiquitous, yet often unacknowledged, labors in the informal economy and their contributions to theatrical production behind the scenes. Drawing on recent scholarship on women's work in the informal sector developed by economic historians and political economists, this chapter seeks to understand the gendered division of labor that gave rise to the all-male stage in relation to that of the economy at large. It then surveys the many forms of women's offstage work in theatrical production and commerce, including the participation of theater wives and widows in their husbands' business affairs; women who worked in the luxury textile trades and their contribution to the production of theatrical spectacle both at court and in plays performed in the commercial theaters; the influence of the newfangled attires manufactured by immigrant tirewomen on the material cultural of the stage and their service as theatrical dressers for boy-actors; women's work in the secondhand clothing and pawnbroking trades upon which the professional playing companies relied; and women's broader contributions to the day-to-day business of theatrical production and commerce as moneylenders, gatherers, sempsters, starchers, laundresses, and hawkers of wares in the theaters.

To what extent were early modern theatergoers made aware of the offstage contributions of laboring women to the *work* of playing? Under what circumstances, and for what purposes, did the staging of props and costumes point to their pre- or offstage histories of manufacture, and their status as worked upon by women? How were audiences encouraged to view women who worked in and around the theaters, at the door, in the pit and galleries, and behind the scenes of theatrical production? As these questions suggest, unfolding a cultural history of women's offstage work is not simply a matter of retrieving its penumbral presence but of deciphering the ways in which it was both represented and absented, figured and disfigured, onstage. In Chapters 2 through 5, I thus turn my attention to dramatic "ciphers" that evoked the unending and ever-present, yet in varying ways elided, labors of women onstage. In early modern England, the cipher or zero was used to figure absence in general, and female absence (including the so-called "nothing" of female sexuality) in particular. Because the cipher had the power to increase or decrease the value of other figures, it was used to represent absences that were perceived to be productive and presences that were perceived to be false or illusory. Thus, for example, it might be employed to evoke the productive, yet invisible presence of working women in early modern culture but also to stigmatize the products of their labor as insubstantial, insignificant, or deceptive. The remaining chapters analyze exemplary, dramatic ciphers of female labor in early modern dramatic literature and performance, including the ciphering of female usurers; the ephemeral and illusory substance of starched ruffs and other attires manufactured by immigrant tirewomen; the haunting, yet inarticulate cries of female hawkers; and the trashing of market women's "false" wares on the stage. Through these ciphers of absent presence and present absence, I argue, the elusive, yet ubiquitous labors of women behind the scenes of the "all-male" professional stage in Shakespeare's time were figured as never done.

Chapter 2 focuses on the poetics of the cipher or zero itself, which is deployed in Shakespeare's Sonnets and *The Merchant of Venice* to figure the work of counting and accounting practiced by female moneylenders in the networks of credit surrounding the commercial theaters. The wills of theater people reflect women's involvement in these credit networks, as do equity court records of debt litigation. Yet usury was considered to be the very antithesis of "honest," manly work in early modern England and was often described in gendered terms as an unnatural reproduction of wealth that circumvented productive labor. Female usurers epitomized this gendered threat by making money breed money. Although recent historical research has revealed that women were among the most prominent lenders of money at interest in Shakespeare's time, there has been no discussion of female creditors' contributions to theatrical finance or of their depiction in dramatic literature. This chapter examines women's moneylending within the broader economy to help make sense of their appearance in theatrical documents and surveys contemporary attitudes toward their lending and accounting practices in a wide array of cultural texts, including plays, pamphlets, prints, paintings, ballads, conduct books, and sermons on usury. Female creditors were variously represented as objects of desire, seduction, and courtship by men who had designs on their wealth, while being subjected to sexual slander by a society prone to view commercially active women as prostitutes. Married women who set aside separate assets during coverture and who loaned money at interest to their husbands and other male relatives were viewed as important, yet often resented, sources of business capital. Read within this context, Portia's positioning of trust and credit at the center of the marriage "bond" in *The Merchant of Venice*, her provision of capital to pay off her husband's debts, and the skill and exactitude with which she wages law in the trial scene are strongly evocative of emergent discourses surrounding the figure of the female creditor. In both the Sonnets and *The Merchant of Venice*, I argue, Shakespeare deploys the poetics of the cipher or zero to figure the "nothing" in which the usuress breeds her ever-multiplying profits and the newly exact methods of "noting," or counting and accounting, through which female creditors calculated their gains. The trope of the cipher thus aptly figures the productive, yet effaced role of women in financing bonds of credit between men, including those of the all-male playing companies. The chapter concludes with an analysis of the pivotal props staged in *The Merchant of Venice* (the rings, caskets, and scales) and the dramatic tension they create as symbols of avarice, vanity, and usury, on the one hand, and temperance, moderation, and just reckoning, on the other. In staging this tension, I argue, the play draws on an iconographic tradition featured in prints and portraits depicting women moneylenders and their (ac)counting practices. Such images were produced throughout Europe during the sixteenth and seventeenth centuries but were particularly popular in the Netherlands, where women played an especially active role in the world of work and commerce. This analysis serves as a segue to Chapter 3, which focuses on the role played by immigrant craftswomen from the Low Countries in producing the material culture of the English stage and the depiction of commercially active "Dutch" women in plays and other cultural texts of the period.

The Returns of Aliens living in London contain a wealth of evidence about such women and help shed light on immigrant women's work as starchers, laundresses, and tirewomen in and around the commercial theaters. The introduction of starching techniques to England by craftswomen from the Low Countries during Elizabeth's reign had a profound influence on fashion trends and, consequently, on the material culture of the apparel-driven stage. There is perhaps no icon of fashion more readily associated with the stage in Shakespeare's time than the starched, linen ruff. Yet we tend to forget the labor that was congealed in this most fetishized of commodities. The exquisite delicacy, pristine whiteness, and fragile shape of these starched attires distance the body of the wearer and the mind of the spectator from the world of soil and toil. Yet insofar as the very labor-obliterating form of ruffs required the extraordinary and ongoing labor of women to be produced and maintained, they perfectly exemplify the status of women's work as never done. As material ciphers of women's work on the Shakespearean stage, ruffs and other starched linen attires further exemplify the way in which the defining attribute of that stage as "all-male" depended upon the erasure or forgetting of female labor that took place behind the scenes. This chapter seeks to decipher the extent to which the staging of starched attires recollected their pre- or offstage histories of manufacture and to what ends, focusing in particular on two plays performed in the aftermath of the immigrant influx, Thomas Dekker, Henry Chettle, and William Haughton's *Patient Grissil* (1600) and the anonymous *The London Prodigall* (1603–5). The staging of immigrant tirewomen's starched ruffs, rebatos, and head-attires can only be fully understood, I argue, within the broader landscape of gender, labor, immigration, and national identity that shaped the cultural significance of these seemingly trivial fashion accessories.

In the next two chapters, I consider how the staging of women's offstage work was influenced by players' and playwrights' ongoing quest to legitimize playing as a profession during two particularly tense moments in this history of professionalization. Chapter 4 examines the visible, vocal, yet often unwanted and decried presence of female street-criers in and around the commercial theaters and their shaping influence on the staging of "cries" in dramatic literature during the so-called War of the Theaters (c. 1599–1602). The fleeting, fugitive performances of these itinerant, petty retailers, who made their living outside or on the fringes of the formal marketplace, has enjoyed a remarkably durable presence in a wide array of both popular and elite cultural forms, including plays, masques, prints, ballads, and court music. This rich vein of cultural production is matched by an abundant mine of evidence regarding street hawkers and their wares in contemporary civic legislation, court records, and recent archaeological excavations. Although the players themselves had once been classified among itinerant peddlers in vagabond legislation, as their reputation grew and they established a permanent home in the purpose-built theaters of early modern London, they increasingly sought to elevate the status of their profession by crafting a distinct performance idiom and elevating that idiom above those of amateurs. Framed by a reading of Hamlet's advice to the players—which seeks to differentiate the professional player from the crier while the play's soundscape simultaneously draws upon the crier's vocal idiom—this chapter argues that the representation of criers in dramatic literature shifted with the players' rise in status. Jonson, Marston, Chapman, and Shakespeare all deploy the figure of the crier as a foil against which to define the profession of playing and as a means of stigmatizing rival playwrights. The cries of female hawkers in particular were construed as rude, inarticulate ciphers of sound and as such were opposed to the skilled eloquence of the professional, male players. At the same time, however, they provided a performance idiom to which the professional players and playwrights made strategic recourse for both low-comic and high-tragic ends.

Chapter 5 pursues this line of inquiry a decade later, during an equally pivotal moment in the professional stage's quest for legitimacy. This chapter argues that this aim was accomplished by stigmatizing not only the voices but also the wares of market women through the staged destruction of their purportedly false, insubstantial, or adulterated products. Focusing on Thomas

Middleton's *A Chaste Maid in Cheapside* (1613) and Ben Jonson's *Bartholomew Fair* (1614), both written during a particularly tense period of contestation over the boundary between legitimate and illegitimate work, this chapter analyzes the gendering of this boundary and the moralizing discourse through which it was policed. At stake in the staging of market women's wares in these plays, I argue, was the definition of virtuous, civic masculinity—an ideal to which the professional players aspired but from which they had long been excluded. Goods manufactured outside the masculine fellowship of the urban guilds by foreigners, aliens, and women were by definition not good, in a moral as well as economic sense, and were deemed evil, insubstantial, "unworkmanly," unwholesome, false, and deceitful. When vicious objects were discovered in workshops or for sale in London's markets, they were ritually destroyed in quasi-judicial proceedings that were directed as much at the inanimate object as at its maker. Market women were punished with the same apparatuses used to discipline prostitutes, adulteresses, scolds, and shrews, symbolically linking their informal commercial activities and "adulterated" wares to female sexual, verbal, and moral incontinence. The false wares produced by women were construed as mere "trash," or insubstantial "nothings," to be destroyed as soon as they were identified, and as such functioned as ciphers of the absent-presence of women's work. The staging of false wares in the commercial playhouses, like that of the cries of female vendors, had implications that bore on the status and legitimacy of playing as a profession, insofar as the charge that players counterfeited legitimate trades often centered on their own trafficking in false wares. Anti-theatrical polemics focused their invectives on the deceptive props and costumes staged in public playhouses. In staging the controversy over unlicensed trade, professional players and playwrights thus sought to defend their own skilled workmanship by distinguishing it from the deceitful practices of market women, whose wares were reduced, quite literally, to trash.

For centuries critics have written about the "all-male" theater of Shakespeare's time. As this book seeks to demonstrate, this construct is in important ways a myth. It is true only if we confine our definition of the theater to the onstage activities of the professional playing companies in London and divorce these activities from the larger apparatuses of theatrical production and the varied commercial practices that contributed to the business of playing. In revising this paradigm, *Labors Lost* seeks to open a new conversation about the nature and significance of the female labors upon which the professional stage relied and against which it sought to define itself, inviting critics and scholars to reconsider the period's drama in their light. It is my hope that the shaping influence of working women on early modern theatrical production and dramatic literature will be of interest not only to specialists in the field but to a broad range of readers and theatergoers, and to theater people of our own time, who know firsthand the importance of all that takes place behind the scenes.

Chapter 1

Labors Lost

FEMINIST SCHOLARSHIP ON women's role in the pre-Restoration theater has hitherto been characterized by two divergent approaches, the first claiming that the professional stage in London simply excluded women and the second demonstrating that women participated in theatrical activity in a variety of ways outside its purview. Dympna Callaghan's provocatively titled book, *Shakespeare Without Women*, exemplifies the former approach by arguing that "there were no women on Shakespeare's stage" and that this exclusion was an important index of early modern women's oppression.[1] Callaghan makes a strong claim that the paradigm of the "all-male theater" is not in itself anti-feminist and that we must look unflinchingly at "the exclusion of women from the Renaissance stage as the determinate material condition of the theater's production and representation of femininity" if we are to grasp the implications of "what was rather than what should or might have been."[2] The "absence of women" from the professional theater is from this perspective quite simply historical fact—"what *was*" rather than what should or might have been.[3] Contrary or qualifying examples of female theatrical activity are considered exceptions that prove the rule, futile attempts to mitigate the harsh reality of women's absence from the stage.[4]

Like all "facts," however, the historical paradigm of the "all-male theater" is a product of perspective—of the disciplinary parameters scholars have used to define the proper objects of theater history. If we shift this perspective, alter these established parameters, things begin to look rather different. Revisionist scholarship detailing women's participation in theatrical activity beyond the purview of London's professional stage has done just this. Phyllis Rackin's *Shakespeare and Women* sums up this perspective, arguing that "there were many women among the itinerant musicians, acrobats, and other performers who toured the English countryside" and that women also performed in "guild plays, May games, and civic entertainments that were regular features of village life."[5] In an effort to displace the paradigm of the all-male Shakespearean stage, this strain of scholarship has redefined our most basic understanding of what constitutes a "stage"—or for that matter, a player, playhouse, or performance—and, in so doing, has unearthed a growing body of evidence detailing women's presence in a diverse array of performance practices. The title of Rackin's book nicely summarizes this shift in paradigms from absence to presence by countering the bluntly privative preposition *without* in Callaghan's title with the equally bluntly affirmative conjunction *and*.

What distinguishes these two historical accounts is not so much a disagreement over the facts as a difference of emphasis and perspective. Thus, scholarship emphasizing female absence has tended to confine its definition of the theater to the onstage activities of the professional playing companies in London and to minimize the significance of women's participation in theatrical activity beyond this purview, branding such activity as exceptional or of lesser significance. Conversely, scholarship asserting female presence has tended to minimize the significance of women's absence from the professional stage in an effort to shift critical attention from the center (London) to the periphery, from professional to amateur performers, from England to the Continent, from city to court, and so on.

Scholars in both camps agree that women were active theatergoers but disagree as to the significance of female spectatorship. Advocates of female presence argue that women "constituted a sizeable proportion of the paying customers in the public playhouses" and that "the offstage presence of women would have exerted a powerful influence upon playscripts."[6] Those who emphasize female absence, by contrast, maintain that women's role as spectators exemplifies their status as "the consumers of the very representations they could not produce, and by extension, [as] the bearers, not the makers, of meaning."[7] Female spectatorship is from this perspective yet another instance of women's secondary status and exclusion from the stage. Even if one defines female spectators' presence as productive, Callaghan asserts, "the productions of the audience are not equivalent to the production on the stage."[8] This claim is grounded in the long-held assumption that women were "not represented at the production end" of the theater industry.[9]

Advocates of female presence have begun to put pressure on the latter assumption, arguing that if we broaden our conception of what constitutes theatrical production beyond the onstage activities of the professional playing companies in London's commercial theaters, we find that women participated in various sorts of theatrical activity as playwrights, patrons, and performers. Female playwrights such as Mary Sidney, Elizabeth Cary, and Mary Wroth wrote "closet dramas."[10] Elite women, including monarchs, aristocrats, and heiresses, supported theatrical activity as patrons.[11] Queen Elizabeth I and Anne of Denmark retained troupes of actors and minstrels and sponsored plays, masques, and other entertainments at court.[12] Aristocratic women mounted dramatic entertainments at their country estates and entertained monarchs with lavish spectacles during royal progresses.[13] Non-aristocratic women of means likewise patronized a variety of players and itinerant performers in the provinces. One such woman, Joyce Jefferies, was a wealthy seventeenth-century heiress who never married, supported herself by lending money at interest, and paid a variety of entertainers (including traveling players, dancers, musicians, and singers) to perform at her home in Hereford in the West Midlands.[14] Ordinary women offered material support to dramatic activity that took place in inns and alehouses. Of the four London inns that served as playhouses during Shakespeare's time, David Kathman has demonstrated, three (the Bell Savage, the Cross Keys, and the Bull) were owned or leased by women.[15]

The bulk of recent scholarship on women's contributions to theatrical production outside the domain of London's professional theaters has been devoted to deepening our knowledge of a broad array of female performance practices and may be subdivided into three main avenues of research.[16] The first of these focuses on the ways in which female performers on the Continent, who traveled to England in itinerant troupes, influenced female roles and performance styles in England.[17] The second focuses on English women who performed as amateur or itinerant entertainers. This category may be further subdivided into scholarship on elite women who performed in court masques and country house entertainments;[18] women of the middling sort who performed in parish drama and festive pageantry in both rural and urban settings;[19] poor women who performed as itinerant entertainers in streets, alehouses, and market squares;[20] and finally women at all social levels who engaged in theatrical behavior broadly construed, from the public proclamations of queens to the bawdy jests and billingsgate of "queans" (prostitutes).[21] A third area of research focuses on the very rare instances of women, the primary and only uncontested example being Mary Frith, who are known to have performed in the commercial theaters in London.[22] This multifaceted yet "relatively hidden tradition of female performance," in the view of scholars emphasizing female presence, "does not support any blanket claim that women were excluded from the stages of Renaissance England."[23] From the vantage of those emphasizing female absence, however, such scholarship fails to undermine the paradigm of the all-male, *professional* London stage: "Exclusion from the stage" defined in these terms, in Callaghan's view, "is not remedied by those rare instances of female performance" that occurred beyond its purview.[24]

This brief survey illustrates, I hope, that scholarship on female absence from the professional stage and presence in other arenas or types of performance are equally important to our understanding of early modern English theater history. The polarization of these two perspectives, however, has hitherto occluded analysis of this gendered differential itself. While the paradigm of the "all-male stage" had long rendered the activities catalogued above invisible, scholarship emphasizing female participation in other arenas of theatrical activity has focused almost entirely on detailing the forms of this participation rather than on understanding the gendered division of theatrical labor it has thereby revealed. Stephen Orgel's *Impersonations* was something of an exception, in that it set out to explore *both* the anomaly of women's exclusion from the professional stage *and* the robust tradition of female performance elsewhere (both in England and on the Continent) in an effort to address the question: "Why did only the English public theater resist the introduction of women on the stage?"[25] Orgel states his reluctance, however, to venture a response to the question thus posed: "As I have indicated, any attempt to answer this question by simply producing an explanation, whether social, religious, or political, will only close off the ramifications of the question. But the context within which the issue can be understood must have to do with culture-specific attitudes toward women, and toward sexuality."[26] Orgel quite rightly suggests that any attempt to solve the puzzle of women's exclusion from the professional stage (and, concomitantly, of their inclusion in other spheres of theatrical activity) must consider the broader terrain of the early modern sex/gender system (i.e., its "culture-specific attitudes" toward gender and sexuality). As Orgel's book unfolds, however, it becomes clear that his primary concern is with how the former (the gendered division of theatrical labor) illuminates the latter (the sex/gender system), rather than vice versa.

Michael Shapiro likewise considers the question of why women were excluded from the professional playing companies in spite of the fact that "[t]here was never . . . any legal statute prohibiting the appearance of women onstage."[27] He departs from Orgel's focus on the early modern English sex/gender system, however, arguing that similar attitudes toward women existed in France, Italy, and Spain, where professional actresses were employed as early as the 1560s. For this reason, he directs his inquiry "away from cultural attitudes toward gender and toward the economics of the English commercial theater."[28] Although Shapiro purports to privilege questions of economy over attitudes toward gender, the argument he proposes makes clear that the two are not so easily separable: "Perhaps the strongest reason for the continued exclusion of women from the stage," he maintains, "was a desire on the part of male actors to preserve the profession of acting as a site for male employment."[29] Shapiro thus views women's exclusion from the professional stage as an extension of their exclusion from employment within the economy at large. Citing no specific evidence to support this assertion, he observes that "[f]or most of the sixteenth century, women were being pushed out of economic niches they had occupied earlier."[30] This claim, first put forth in Alice Clark's groundbreaking *Working Life of Women in the Seventeenth Century* and taken up in relation to London's citizenry in Steve Rappaport's *Worlds Within Worlds*, has been subject to qualification and critique in a number of important ways by more recent scholarship on women's social and economic history. As we shall see, a more nuanced understanding of the gendered division of labor in the broader economy will help shed light on that found in the professional theater.

Clark's book remains "the leading exposition of the pessimistic view that capitalist industry seriously eroded women's status, which had been higher in the pre-capitalist and pre-industrial past."[31] Recent studies have revised Clark's sweeping thesis and revealed a more complex picture, finding that women's exclusion from certain crafts, trades, and occupations did not follow a strictly linear development but occurred unevenly in different occupations and regions and fluctuated in response to economic conditions such as labor shortages.[32] Like Clark, Rappaport cites examples of restrictions placed on female labor by livery companies, such as the Clothworkers' Company, which in 1548 warned every company member not to "suffer either his wife or any of his maiden servants to work openly either in his shop or at his tenters [i.e., wooden frames on which cloth was stretched to dry]." The order was repeated four months later in even stronger terms: "no man shall suffer nor set to work any maiden or womankind to the handicraft in any shop, tenter, or other open place."[33] The intermittent appearance of such orders should not, however, be taken as proof of women's wholesale exclusion from the artisanal labor force. Indeed, the very necessity of such orders and of their repetition point to female participation in commercial activities that were, over the course of the sixteenth and early seventeenth centuries and in accordance with other economic factors, curtailed, hidden, or proscribed in various ways. It is clear from the heading written in the margin by the Clothworkers' Company clerk, moreover, that the above orders were aimed not at women working in the craft *per se* but rather, as the heading puts it, at "women working *openly.*"[34] Rappaport himself acknowledges that proscriptions on women's work by London's livery companies "should not be construed as evidence that most women did not participate directly in the city's economy." He further argues that "it is likely that in the early modern period most women were actively engaged in the production and distribution of goods and services."[35] The *form* of women's participation in the economy, however, differed from that of men. In order to grasp the significance of this difference, and how it may have influenced the gendered division of theatrical labor, we must therefore develop a more complex understanding of the gendered division of labor within the economy at large.

The Clothworkers' Company's restrictions on "women working openly" provide an important insight into the particular form of women's economic activity in suggesting that it often took place behind the scenes. This was particularly true of married women and "maids" (or never-married women), as widows of freemen had special rights and privileges allowing them to work openly in ways that were often proscribed for other women. Thus, for example, a Weavers' Company ordinance of 1596 stipulated "no woman or mayd shall use or exercise the Arte of weaving upon any Loome, Sapyn or Benche excepte she be the widowe of one of the same Guilde."[36] Although crafts- and tradesmen's wives and daughters often worked actively alongside their male kin, either in manual labor or taking charge of the financial end of the family business (receiving payments, acting as buyers, and so forth), their labor was unremunerated and therefore largely unrecorded. As such, it belonged to a hidden, yet nonetheless crucial "shadow" economy.[37] Never-married women, who are variously estimated to have comprised 20 to 30 percent of all adult women in seventeenth-century England,[38] had little opportunity to participate in the formal economy regulated by the guilds or livery companies, unless they were the daughters of guildsmen.[39] They and other women whose work was restricted by the guilds, and who could not find work as domestic servants, were forced to enter an informal economy of petty retailers, itinerant vendors, unlicensed alewives and victuallers, keepers of lodgers, pawnbrokers, secondhand clothing dealers, providers of services such as laundering and starching, wage-earning textile workers (e.g., sempsters, spinners, spanglers, etc.), and a host of other new and unguilded industries. As a result, much of the work performed by the employed women of early modern London was, in Peter Earle's words, "*of a casual nature and none of it organized by guilds or livery companies.*"[40]

Although this informal commercial activity was disapproved of by guilds and civic authorities, historical evaluation should look beyond the guildsman's assessment. For as Beverly Lemire has argued, these "'disorderly' commercial practices were as common as they were reviled" and "must be integrated into our concepts of the market"—and, I would add, of the theater.[41] To effect such integration, however, we must be willing to traverse disciplinary boundaries and take a fresh look at theater history in light of recent research on the many different types of commercial activity in which urban women were engaged. A dichotomous view of female absence versus presence is insufficient to account for women's work in the informal sector, which was present yet often hidden, unacknowledged, undervalued, stigmatized, or otherwise placed under cultural erasure. Precisely how to define women's "informal" commerce, however, remains a difficult question. The blurred contours of this sector of the market have given rise to a host of descriptive terms—irregular, black, hidden, shadow, parallel, secondary—that serve to reinforce its marginal status. More recently, political economists have focused instead on the relational aspect of what they term "informality," arguing that it is not so much a static or bounded sector of the economy as "a specific form of relationship of production" whose contours or boundaries are in constant flux with respect to the formal economy, varying in accordance with the vicissitudes of politico-economic regulations.[42] Hence, forms of labor that are considered illegitimate and curtailed in one commercial setting or historical context may be perfectly legal in another, and the same economic activities may continually shift their relative location across the formal/informal divide.[43]

Conceived in this way, informality is hardly a marginal phenomenon but rather "a fundamental politico-economic process at the core of many societies," often serving to "fill in where the conventional economy falls short or fails."[44] Participants in the informal economy likewise vary, incorporating a broad range of economic agents, from those who have been excluded from the formal economy and who may have no other means of survival (e.g., the poor, women, immigrants) to informal entrepreneurs seeking ways to profit from the economic dynamism of unregulated commerce. Because informality "cut[s] across the whole social structure," encompassing a broad range of heterogeneous economic activities and agents, it may simultaneously incorporate relations of production that are progressive and exploitative, and work that is highly paid and underpaid.[45] As such, it provides a useful framework within which to comprehend the contributions of a diverse range of female participants in the networks of commerce surrounding the theaters—from impoverished hawkers and hucksters to skilled, immigrant textile workers to wealthy widow moneylenders. It will also help illuminate how the gendered division of labor within the nascent entertainment industry was shaped by shifting definitions of what constituted legitimate and illegitimate work.

The concept of informality renders visible a wide array of commercial activities occluded by the "apparently all-pervasive" formal economy, which in early modern England was regulated by both guilds or livery companies and civic officials.[46] In the networks of commerce surrounding the London theaters, these activities might include the labor of theater wives, widows, daughters, and maidservants; the informal lending practices of petty pawnbrokers upon which theater people relied; the sale of secondhand clothing by female frippers to actors and theater managers;[47] the sale and maintenance of luxury attires for the stage by immigrant and native tirewomen, starchers, and laundresses; the provision of ale, tobacco, nuts, fruit, and other comestibles by female hawkers to spectators; the sex work of prostitutes, bawds, and brothel keepers in the environs of the theaters;[48] and even the activities of petty female criminals, such as dealers in stolen goods.[49] As the diversity of such activities makes clear, the concept of informality challenges our very definition of the market and "demands a new understanding of what constitutes work" as well as "play."[50] Indeed, the very instability of the boundary between what counts as work or as non-work (a category variously defined as play, pastime, leisure, game, sport, or, more pejoratively, as idleness, sloth, or outright crime) in a given historical context makes it essential that we consider the two categories relationally.

Historians generally agree that London's informal economy expanded rapidly during the late sixteenth and early seventeenth centuries, when the city's population grew exponentially.[51] Increasing immigration to the city, and in particular to its extramural suburbs, resulted in large numbers of impoverished migrants taking up occupations outside guild control.[52] The flourishing of such informal commerce in London's suburbs and liberties may be attributed as well to the limited capacity of civic authorities and livery company officials to enforce labor standards and market regulations there.[53] City authorities nonetheless tried to curb the expansion of such unruly commerce through numerous legislative initiatives. Those who made a living in the informal sector were often accused of "framing themselves to lead a more easie lyfe than by labor" and of "findinge thereby . . . a more idle and easier kinde of Trade of livinge, and . . . a more readie[,] more greate[,] more profitable[,] and speedier Advantage and Gaine."[54] As the language of such legislation makes clear, work in the informal sector was not only considered illegitimate by civic officials, it was not considered work at all. Unguilded labor was routinely relegated to the status of mere idleness. The frequency of such legislative initiatives during the late sixteenth and early seventeenth centuries, together with their repeated assertions that the population of unguilded laborers was "greate & excessive" and growing, rather than abating,[55] echoes other evidence suggesting that efforts to rein in the rising tide of informal commerce met with little success. Contemporary legislation and court records likewise suggest that in the early modern period, as in the present, the informal sector was female dominated.[56] Guild restrictions on female labor, rather than excluding women from the workforce entirely, thus gave rise to "unregulated interstices into which women visibly and eagerly entered."[57] Although we may never know the precise extent of women's informal commercial activity in early modern London, it is clear that "any analysis of women's contribution to work that does not take account of such commercial activity will be seriously flawed."[58]

Although recent scholarship on the formal economy and civic culture presided over by London's livery companies has contributed greatly to our understanding of the rights and privileges of citizenship (conferred on those who obtained the "freedom" of the City), it has had less to say about Londoners who were excluded from the citizenry, such as foreigners (migrants from other parts of England), aliens (immigrants from other countries), and women. Although Rappaport's influential *Worlds Within Worlds* estimated that the freedom was enjoyed by roughly three-quarters of London's adult male population in the 1550s, this represented only one-fifth of the city's total population.[59] London's formal economy and civic culture underwent dramatic transformation during the latter half of the sixteenth century, which saw a "loosening of the Guild system" as the guilds "were breaking away from the purpose for which they were originally founded, and were taking part in pursuits and industries alien to their primary functions."[60] This loosening occurred partly as a result of London's population growth (and the resulting pressure of external competition from non-citizen laborers) and partly as a result of internal competition from crafts- and tradesmen who had served apprenticeships and earned the freedom in one trade but were practicing another.

The latter phenomenon took on unprecedented proportions as guildsmen began to take advantage of a custom of the City whereby "every Citizen and

Freeman of London, which hath been an Apprentice in London unto any trade by the space of seven years, may lawfully and well relinquish that trade and exercise any other trade at his will and pleasure."[61] Originally intended to apply only to those engaged in wholesaling, rather than in craft production and retailing, by the later sixteenth century the custom was invoked by crafts- and tradesmen all over London as justification for the pursuit of occupations other than those for which they had served apprenticeships.[62] Although the Statute of Artificers of 1562 had attempted to reassert the necessity of apprenticeship in the particular industry the person intended to pursue, it ultimately failed to accomplish its aim due to the difficulty of enforcement, and the loosening of the guild system continued apace.[63] Examples of the growing numbers of crafts- and tradesmen taking advantage of this custom abound. During Elizabeth's reign members of the Drapers' Company were pursuing occupations as diverse as embroiderer, upholsterer, felt maker, silk weaver, wine seller, grocer, apothecary, barber-surgeon, smith, gunner, pewterer, salter, woadmonger, painter-stainer, printer, bookbinder, bookseller, and stationer.[64]

By the early seventeenth century, "the trades and companies within the city were almost inextricably tangled."[65] Commenting on this state of affairs, George Wither includes an impresa in his *Collection of Emblemes* (pub. 1635) depicting an "honest Carpenter" under the title, "When each man keepes unto his Trade, Then, all things better will be made." Reproving those who "love to meddle" in trades other than their own, Wither laments that "most are now exceeding cunning growne / In ev'ry mans affaires, except their owne" and warns "if these Customes, last a few more Ages, / All Countries will be nothing els, but Stages / Of evill-acted, and mistaken parts; / Or Gallemaufries, of imperfect Arts."[66] Wither's comparison of artisans who meddle in trades other than those in which they have been trained to actors who play "mistaken parts" on the stage was not far-fetched. Many actors (and others involved in the professional stage) were freemen of livery companies who had opted to leave their traditional occupational backgrounds to earn a living by playing.[67] In doing so, they took opportunistic advantage of the custom of London that allowed them to retain the privileges of the companies in which they had served apprenticeships while pursuing an unguilded occupation. These men effectively kept one foot firmly planted in the security of the formal economy while taking a giant step with the other into the risks and benefits of informal commerce.[68]

It is no accident that the rise of the commercial theaters coincided with the loosening of the guild system and the expansion of the informal sector, nor that the new, purpose-built theaters were located in the very same suburbs and liberties of London in which unregulated commerce thrived. The professional playing companies and the entrepreneurs who backed them took maximum advantage of the flexible forms of economic activity that characterized these precincts.[69] Certain aspects of the older economic structures were imported into the new, such as the apprenticeship system.[70] Yet there were important differences between the playing companies and the livery companies, for the players had "no central organization, no court system, and no regulations that governed all of them . . . and [they] certainly did not have the social prestige of the ancient guilds, like the Goldsmiths or the Mercers."[71] By retaining structural aspects of the guild system in their new economic ventures, the players "relat[ed] the work of acting to the crafts and professions, and thereby implicitly la[id] claim to their rights and privileges."[72] The professional playing companies were, in this sense, transitional economic formations that in certain respects retained the residual structure of guilds while at the same time assuming the emergent form of innovative capital ventures.[73] Situated on the cusp of the formal and informal economies, they enjoyed a hybrid status that allowed them to take opportunistic advantage of both.

How, then, did the commercial theaters' hybrid status influence female participation in the nascent entertainment industry? In the remainder of this chapter, I will survey the diverse forms of female labor in the networks of commerce that contributed to theatrical production. These networks reveal that what took place "behind the scenes" was by no means confined within the walls of the tiring-house or playhouse. The commercial theaters were thoroughly imbricated in the broader commercial nexus of unguilded crafts, trades, and new industries in London's suburbs and liberties. The business transactions of theater people with the city's wider workforce continually traversed the walls of playhouses, bringing theater companies into contact with a diverse range of working women. The overview that follows is not meant to be exhaustive but rather to offer a broad account of the gendered division of theatrical labor, which I hope will provide a framework for ongoing research. In the succeeding chapters, I take a more in-depth approach to particular aspects of women's work in and around the theaters and its shaping influence on early modern dramatic literature.

Not surprisingly, the gendered division of theatrical labor in early modern England in many ways reflected that of the economy at large. The wives of theater people, like the wives of crafts- and tradesmen, at times worked actively alongside their husbands, participated in the financial end of their husbands' business ventures, and continued to work in these capacities, at least for a time, into their widowhoods. Margaret Brayne, for example, collaborated with her husband, John Brayne, in the building of The Theatre in Shoreditch, the first successful purpose-built theater in London, in 1576. Previous accounts of Margaret Brayne's contribution to theater history have been limited to her financial dealings and litigation with James Burbage following the death of her husband, John, who was Burbage's partner. According to Robert Miles's testimony in the litigation with Burbage, John Brayne, who was the primary investor in the project, although a financially successful grocer, was soon overwhelmed by the building expenses and forced to sell his house and stock, give up his trade as a grocer, pawn his own clothes and Margaret's, and "to r[u]n in debt to many for the money to fynishe the said Playe housse / & so to ymploye himselfe onlye up*p*on that matter / . . . / to his utter undoing / ffor . . . in the latter end of the fynishing therof / the said Braynes and his Wyfe . . . were dryven to labo^r in the said wo^rkes / for saving some of the charge / in place of ij° laborers."[74] While the once wealthy Brayne and his wife were clearly driven to this arrangement by the extremity of the situation, the testimony suggests a pattern of collaboration between husband and wife that may have carried over from the Braynes' years as grocers.[75] The Braynes provide an example of the kind of flexibility and improvisation required of crafts- and tradesmen and women in launching these new theatrical enterprises.

Theater wives and widows, like the wives of crafts- and tradesmen, also participated in the financial end of their husbands' business affairs. Christopher Beeston, an actor and theater entrepreneur who owned the Cockpit theater, appointed his wife, Elizabeth Hutchinson, "full and sole executrix" of his estate "by reason I doe owe many greate deb*t*es, and am engaged for greate som*m*es of money, w*h*ich noe one but my wife understand*es*, where or how to receave pay or take in." Beeston's will indicates that his wife was involved not only in his credit activities but in the procurement of costumes as well, as it directs "that my said executrix shall . . . provide and finde for the said Companie [the King's and Queen's Young company], a sufficyent and good stock of app*a*rell fitting for their use."[76] It seems unlikely that Beeston would have entrusted his wife with this task if she had had no prior experience procuring costumes for the stage. Agnes Henslowe, the wife of theater entrepreneur Philip Henslowe, also appears to have been involved in her husband's financial affairs, as she is listed numerous times in his account book lending money to actors as well as friends, family, and other employees.[77] Henslowe apparently owed the initial investment capital for his business and theatrical ventures largely to his provident marriage to Agnes, who had been his former master's widow, so it is not surprising that she should have taken an active interest, and even played an active role, in his business affairs.[78] The involvement of Agnes Henslowe and Elizabeth Hutchinson in their husbands' credit activities reflects women's active role in credit networks within the broader economy as moneylenders, pawnbrokers, and purveyors of shop credit, a subject explored in greater depth in Chapter 2.

It seems likely that theater people's daughters and unmarried female kin were apprenticed or informally trained in crafts and trades that contributed to theatrical production, although evidence of such involvement is scarce.[79] The apprenticeship of Philip Henslowe's niece Mary, mentioned in his account book, provides an intriguing example. Having assumed responsibility for the upbringing of the orphaned children of his brother Edmund, Henslowe brought them to London in February 1595 and several months later apprenticed his nephew John to a dyer named Newman for forty shillings. In June 1595, he apprenticed his niece Mary to John Griggs for seven years for the sum of £5 "to Learne to sowe al maner of workes & to Lerne bonelace."[80] The term "workes" here refers to needlework and embroidery. "Bonelace," manufactured with bobbins made of bone, was used to adorn clothing and linen attires, such as ruffs, cuffs, and bands. Although bonelace varied in quality and price depending on its complexity and the thread with which it was made, at the high end, when made of gold and silver thread, it might cost as much as seven shillings per yard.[81] The skills Mary was to learn were thus potentially a valuable property of skill. It is not clear from whom Mary was to learn these skills. It seems unlikely that it would have been from Griggs himself, who is listed in the deed of partnership between Henslowe and Cholmley for the building of the Rose theater as the carpenter responsible for erecting "the saide playhouse wth all furniture therunto belonginge."[82] It is more likely that Mary was apprenticed to Griggs's wife. The couple were close friends of both the Henslowes and Alleyns (Griggs was also involved in building the Alleyns' house).[83] Alice Clark cites numerous instances of girls apprenticed to the wives of guildsmen, including carpenters, to learn needlework.[84] An engraving depicting midday work circa 1595 depicts a similar gendered division of labor: two carpenters are shown sawing and leveling, while two women sit at work, one of them making bonelace (see Figure 1).

In general, as we have seen, there was a great deal of fluidity in the crafts practiced by guildsmen and their wives. Griggs, who practiced the craft of carpentry, describes himself in a loan agreement with Henslowe as "John griggs cyttezin and Butcher of London."[85] This fluidity played a crucial role in the

Figure 1. After Hendrik Goltzius, engraving of midday work from a series entitled *Four Times of Day*, c. 1595. Two male carpenters sawing and leveling, as their female kin engage in women's work, one making bonelace. The caption ("It is a good day for work, and hard toil; those who make an all-out effort will be thoroughly worn out") may serve as a caution to the two women, who gossip as they work. © The Trustees of the British Museum.

rise of the commercial theaters and professional playing companies in London, allowing traditional artisans the flexibility to adapt their skills to new commercial enterprises. This may be precisely what Henslowe had in mind in apprenticing his niece: given the exorbitant sums of money laid out in his account book for making up new and adapting old costumes, and for the purchase of various types of lace to adorn them, Mary's skill as a sempstress and lace maker would have been a valuable asset in Henslowe's theatrical ventures. A roughly contemporaneous apprenticeship agreement, dated September 1597, in which a young girl named Margaret Davis was apprenticed to one "Josine Graunger of London widdowe," illustrates the variety of skills employed during the period by sempstresses (or seamstresses, also called "needlewomen" or "workwomen"), stipulating that she is to learn "to woorke all manner of Cuttworke Bonelaces Needlewoorke edginge And allso all manner of Blackwoorkes And allso to woorke w'th goulde and silke and all manner of playne woorkes and whatsoever elles belongeth to a woorkewoman."[86] Henslowe's payments to the "lace man" and "cope [i.e., copper] lace man" date from 1598 to 1603 (around the time Mary would have completed her apprenticeship) and are mainly for the purchase of copper lace in bulk. The lace men in question were thus most likely retailers as lace was commonly manufactured by women and children.[87] We can only speculate as to whether Mary's skills in sewing "al maner of workes" and in the manufacture of bonelace were put to use in the mending or adorning of costumes for the stage between 1602/3 or earlier and 1605, when she "felle sicke of a dead pallsey."[88] More work needs to be done on women's participation in the theatrical affairs of male kin, including in-depth case studies of individual theater families. An understanding of women's roles in the broader workforce is crucial to understanding such participation, and serves as an important reminder that the lace, silkwork, and other trimmings that adorned players' garments were commonly manufactured by female hands.

Because women worked actively in the textile and clothing trades, they often appear in theatrical records relating to the manufacture and adornment of costumes and other accessories. Evidence regarding women's work in the manufacture of luxury attire is particularly plentiful in the account books kept by the Office of Revels concerning plays, masques, and other entertainments staged at court, both because court entertainments made abundant use of them and because the Revels Office kept meticulous records of its expenditures. Although masques were far more lavish and expensive than plays performed in the public theaters, the evidence they afford is pertinent to the professional stage insofar as the attires used in them were typically handed down to the professional players as payment for court performances when they were no longer deemed "serviceable" for the latter.[89] The ornate costumes passed down to the playing companies by the Revels Office would have provided attire for actors playing elite (or would-be elite) characters and for the staging of masques in plays, which became increasingly popular during the early seventeenth century.[90] The recycling of aristocratic attire was characteristic of the clothing economy more broadly: it was common knowledge, and the butt of many a satirical jibe, that aristocrats brought their cast-off apparel "to the theatre to sell."[91] According to Thomas Platter, "it is the English usage for eminent lords or Knights at their decease to bequeath and leave almost the best of their clothes to their serving men, which it is unseemly for the latter to wear, so that they offer them then for sale for a small sum to the actors."[92] The luxury attires manufactured by women for aristocratic clients and court entertainments thus found their way into the tiring-houses of the commercial theaters through the secondhand clothing market (in which women worked actively) and, when the players were able to afford it, through the purchase of bespoke items from female artisans, as discussed below.

There is no way of telling precisely how many female artisans and tradeswomen worked for the Revels Office, since many entries of payments to crafts- and tradespeople who worked outside the office do not indicate their gender.[93] However, the accounts do include a number of named female artisans and tradeswomen who worked outside the office, supplying a range of textile wares. One of the primary suppliers of canvas (used in the manufacture of large properties) to the Revels Office, for example, was a linen draper named Mistress Dane. One entry of a payment to her reads: "The Lynnen drap*er* M*ist*ris Dane for Canvas to paynte for howses for the players & for other properties as Monsters, greate hollow trees & suche other."[94] A number of entries reveal that artisans' wives, daughters, and widows participated in the retail and manufacture of textile work done outside the office, such as a payment of eleven shillings six pence "To Clatterbook*es* dawghter for cloth for Ruffs[,] apornes[,] Neckerchers & Rayles [i.e., white linen neckerchiefs] for Eldertons playe" and an additional twelve pence "for making them."[95] The entry suggests that the daughter of Thomas Clatterbook, a tailor who worked for the office, may have contributed to the "making"—the sewing, adorning, and starching—of these linen attires, a female occupation discussed at greater length below and in Chapter 3. In the case of work done outside the office, however, we cannot be sure whether the women listed were merely delivering the goods or had a hand in making them.

In entries regarding work done inside the office and at court, however, it is clear that the participation of female artisans in the manufacture of costumes and properties was not at all unusual. Two such women, "Anne prynne" and "Ales Tayler," were hired independently by the office to work as "Imbroderers & Habberdashers."[96] A number of craftsmen also regularly brought their wives into the office to work beside them. William Pilkington, an embroiderer, property maker, and haberdasher, thus brought his wife, Joan, into the office to assist him in manufacturing "apparell properties & headpeeces," including "strange hattes & garnishinges." She was paid twelve pence per day, as against her husband's wage of twenty pence per day, and sometimes worked there for months at a time.[97] Other craftsmen's wives who worked in the office alongside their husbands manufacturing costumes, properties, and head-attires were Awdrey Moorer, wife of Richard Moorer, Ellin Morgan, wife of William Morgan, and the unnamed wife of John Bettes, who was paid eighteen pence per day for "spangling" (or sewing gold and silver sequins and beads onto) head-attires.[98] Mrs. Bettes may have brought female assistants into the office to work with her as there is an additional payment to "ij Maides" (who were paid twelve pence per day) directly following the payment to her.[99] Spangling was painstaking, meticulous work and was one of the many unguilded forms of textile work in which women specialized. On one occasion, the Revels Office hired twenty-six unnamed "Women spanglers" to work together in the office spangling costumes for court entertainments.[100] Such entries suggest the existence of a workforce of female spanglers at the ready when called upon by the office.[101] An example of the spangler's craft may be seen in an elaborately embroidered woman's jacket in the Victoria and Albert collection dating from the early seventeenth century, to which beads and spangles appear to have been added when the jacket was used as a masque costume (see Figure 2).

Another fascinating and hitherto unacknowledged female occupation in luxury textile manufacture that contributed to theatrical production was that of the tiremaker or tirewoman. Such women appear in the Revels Office accounts, as well as in theatrical records pertaining to the commercial theaters, reflecting their active involvement in this industry within the broader economy, a topic discussed at greater length in Chapter 3.[102] Tirewomen specialized in the manufacture, adornment, and arrangement of head-attires—as distinct from hats and caps, which were generally manufactured by men—as well as perukes, periwigs, false hairpieces (such as "roules," or rolls of hair, and curls), and other luxury accessories, including ruffs, cuffs, bands (and the wires used to support them), points, laces, and fans. These attires became

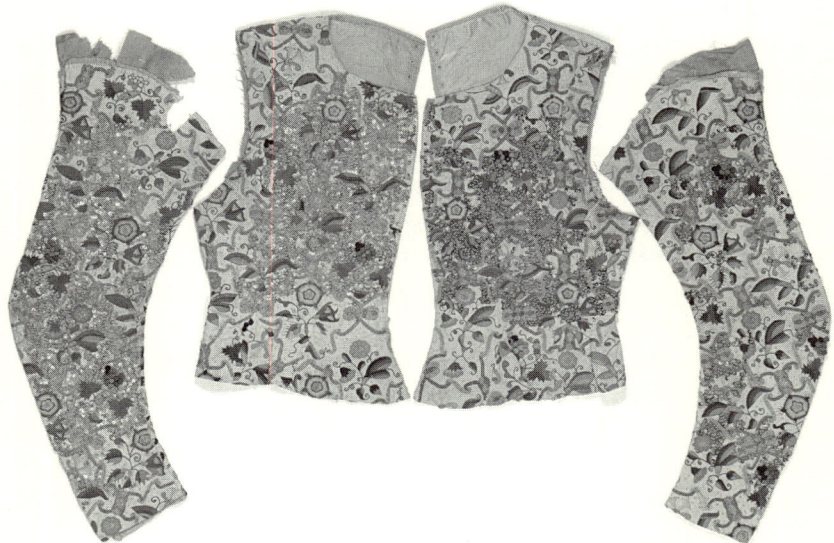

Figure 2. Spangled jacket, Great Britain, 1600–1620. Linen and silk, hand sewn with silk and linen threads and embroidered with silk, silver, and silver-gilt threads, silver-gilt spangles, and glass beads. The beads and sequins appear to have been added at a later date to "translate" the jacket into a masque costume. © The Victoria and Albert Museum.

highly fashionable among elite and would-be elite women during Elizabeth's reign and were worn onstage by female masquers in court entertainments, as well as by boy-actors playing female roles on the commercial stage.

Puritan sermons and treatises attacking spectacle and ornament frequently focused their invective on tirewomen and their wares, construing their occupation as an illegitimate calling that meddled with God's own "workmanship" by attempting to beautify his creatures. Philip Stubbes begins a section of his *Anatomie of Abuses* devoted to the "Abuses of Womens apparell" by claiming that women who wear fashionable attires and artificially embellish themselves "adulterate the Lord his woorkmanship," and demanding "Yf an Artificer, or Craftsman shoulde make any thing belonging to his art or science & a cobler should presume to correct the same: would not the other think him self abused, and judge him worthy of reprehension? And thinkest thou (oh Woman) to escape the Judgement of God, who hath fashioned thee . . . ?"[103] In likening the "Abuses of Womens apparell," and in particular the manufacture of luxury attires, to the work of a cobbler, Stubbes denies the work of the tirewoman artisanal legitimacy. Cobblers were prohibited from making shoes by the Worshipful Company of Cordwainers and were permitted only to repair old shoes, although like others who worked in the informal sector they were wont to breach these restrictions (the verb "to cobble" thus came to mean clumsy or faulty mending or fabrication [*OED*, "cobble, *v*.¹" 1, 2]). God's punishment of women for this "offence" is akin in Stubbes's view to that of the legitimate "Artificer, or Craftsman" who fines unguilded laborers for manufacturing "false wares," a phenomenon discussed in Chapter 5.

Stubbes goes on to decry, and in the process to describe in great detail, what he considers the most egregious abuses in female apparel, both of which belong to the tirewoman's trade: the monstrous fashion of ruffs and the "Attiring of womens heades in England." The description of head-attires is particularly copious and worth citing at length to convey a sense of the work and wares in which theatrical tirewomen specialized:

> Then followeth the trimming and tricking of their heades, in laying out their hair to the shew, which of force must be curled, frizled and crisped, laide out, (a worlde to see). . . . And least it should fall down it is underpropped with forks, wiers, and I can not tel what. . . . Then on the edges of their bolstered heir . . . there is laide great wreathes of gold and silver curiously wrought, and cunning[ly] applyed to the temples of their heads. And . . . at their haire thus wreathed and crested, are hanged Bugles [i.e., cylindrical beads], (I dare not say Bables), Ouches [i.e., brooches or gems], Ringes, Gold, silver, glasses, and such other gewgawes, and foolish trinkets besides, which for that they be innumerable, and I unskilfull in womens tearmes, I can not easily recompt. . . . If curling, and laying out their owne naturall haire were all . . . it were the lesse matter, but they are not simplie contente with their own haire, but buy other haire. . . . And this they weare . . . as though it were their owne natural haire: and upon the other side, if any have haire of her owne naturall growing, which is not faire ynough, then will they die it in divers collours. . . . Than on toppes of these stately turrets (I meane their goodly heades . . .) stand their other capitall ornaments, as French-hood, Hatte, Cappe, Kercher, and suche like, wherof some be of Velvet, some of this fashion, some of that, according to the variable fantasies of their serpentine mindes. And to such excesse is it growen, as every Artificers wife, almost, will not stick to goe in her

hat of Velvet every day, every Marchants wife, and meane Gentlewomen, in her french-hood, and everye poore Cottagers Daughter, in her Taffeta hat, or els of Wooll at least, well lined with Silk, Velvet or Taffeta . . . . They have also other ornaments besides these to furnish foorth their ingenious heades, which they call (as I remember) Cawles [i.e., close-fitting caps or nets], made Netwise to the end, as I think, that the cloth of golde, cloth of Silver, or els Tinsel (for that is the worst[)] wherwith their heads are covered and attired under their Cawles, may the better appeare, and shew it selfe in the bravest maner. So that a man that seeth them (there heads glister and shine in suche sort) he would think them to have golden heads.[104]

Stubbes's dilation on the "Bugles," "Ouches," "French-hood[s]," "Cappe[s]," "Kercher[s]," "wreathes," "Cawles," and other "gewgawes" with which women adorn their heads and on the varied labors and techniques (trimming, tricking, curling, frizzling, crisping, underpropping, dyeing, wig-making) used to embellish their hair belies his claim that the tirewoman's trade is unskilled and that he is himself "unskilfull" in the "tearmes" of their mystery, a claim that serves the rhetorical purpose of casting the accoutrements of head-attiring as "innumerable" and beyond "recompt." He links these incessant labors to the everchanging, "variable fantasies" (the designs and desires) of those who produce and consume them. Although his assertion that such attires are worn by "everye poore Cottagers Daughter" is most likely an exaggeration, it nonetheless suggests that by the 1580s–90s, the fashion had begun to trickle down to the middling and (in more modest form) to the lower sort. In spite of his condemnation of ornate head-attires, his allowance that they are "a worlde to see" and that they "glister and shine in suche sort" that one would think those who wore them had "golden heads" gives some sense of the spectacular effect they would have produced both on- and offstage.

Tirewomen specialized not only in the fabrication of such attires but in styling the elite and would-be elite women and boy-actors who wore them. Among the elite, the job of head-dressing often fell to female waiting-women and servants, but there are records of professional tirewomen working in London as well. Queen Elizabeth's head-attires were mostly fabricated and arranged by her Ladies and Gentlewomen of the Bedchamber and Privy Chamber,[105] but she also purchased head-attires from two professional tirewomen, Ellin Webbe and Margaret Schetz, née Barney (who provided "Whoddes [i.e., French hoods]," "Cornettes [i.e., a type of coif]," "habilliamentes," "Crippens," "Cawles," and "Rolles"),[106] and from her silkwomen, Alice Mountague and Dorothy Speckard (who provided "Attiers" as well as "perewigges of heaire").[107] Mountague, as we shall see, also sold her wares to the Revels Office. There are numerous Elizabethan and Jacobean portraits of aristocratic women wearing the head-attires used in masques, such as a portrait miniature of an unknown woman wearing an elaborate, bejeweled head-tire by Isaac Oliver (c. 1609) in the Victoria and Albert collection (see Figure 3).

The professional tirewomen who worked for the Revels Office sometimes worked in the office or at court and were paid by the day, and sometimes out of their own workshops, in which case they were paid by the piece. The latter was the case with "Mistris Swegoo," who in 1572 was paid by the piece "to garnishe ix heades and ix skarfes for the .ix. Muzes owte thoffice" with "Spanish silke of sundry cullers."[108] The extravagant scarves she fabricated were made of "Lawne [i.e., a type of fine linen]," "White Sipers [i.e., cypress, a fine silk]," and "ffrenge of golde." On several occasions, immigrant tirewomen, who were in particularly high demand for their knowledge of foreign fashions and manufacturing techniques, were hired by the Revels Office to provide head-attires for boy-actors, whom they accompanied to destinations such as Hampton Court and Richmond, where they also served as theatrical dressers. On Shrove Monday in 1573/4, the Revels accounts list "An Italian Woman &c. to dresse theier heades."[109] The "&c." may refer to the Italian woman's servants or assistants, since the next record makes clear that she was not working alone: "Lodging, ffyer, & vittells for the children [of the Merchant Taylor's School] & Women [tha]t wayted tattyer them" for a masque staged on Shrove Tuesday at Hampton Court. We know the identity of one of the women who accompanied the Italian head-dresser, since a later record for "hier of the womens heares for the Children" refers to her daughter: "To the Italian women & her dawght*er* for Lending the Heares &c. & for theier se*r*vice & attendaunc*es*."[110] In 1574/5, there is a similar entry concerning another foreign tirewoman and her daughter, this time French, who provided perukes and dressed the heads of the Children of the Chapel for a play staged at Richmond. Under the heading "The Hyer of Heares for headd*es*," the accounts list a payment "To the french woman for her paynes and her Dawghters paynes that went to Richemond & there attended . . . [the] Children & dressed theier head*es* &c. when they played before her Magestye."[111] These records provide a fascinating example of foreign tirewomen working independently behind the scenes of theatrical

Figure 3. Isaac Oliver, portrait miniature of an unknown woman in a masque costume with ornate head-tire, c. 1609. © The Victoria and Albert Museum, presented by The Art Fund.

entertainments staged by children's companies at court, possibly with hired employees and certainly with daughters whom they had trained in their craft. The records make clear that tirewomen not only fabricated perukes and head-attires for boy-actors but served as theatrical dressers as well.

Tirewomen also manufactured head-attires for the professional stage. Henslowe's accounts list three separate payments to two different named tirewomen for the purchase of head-attires, including a payment of twelve shillings in December 1601 "at the apoyntment of the compan*e* [the Admiral's Men] unto m^{rs} gosen for a head tyer," a second payment of the same amount in February 1601/2 "to m^{rs} go*ossen* for a headtyer," and a loan of ten shillings in January 1602/3 to John Thare, a member of the Earl of Worcester's Men, "to geve unto m^{rs} calle for ij curenets for hed tyers" for a performance at court.[112] There are numerous other payments for the purchase of similar attires, including one to "steven the tyerman for to delyver unto the company for to bey a headtier & a Rebata & other thinges."[113] The latter entry makes clear that such luxury head- and neck-attires were not fabricated by the company's tireman, and were in all likelihood purchased from the skilled, mostly female artisans who specialized in their manufacture, such as Mistresses Gossen and Calle. The Articles of Agreement made in 1607/8 concerning Whitefriars theater, then home of the Children of the King's Revels company, reveals that tirewomen sometimes worked in the tiring-houses of private theaters dressing the heads of boy-actors, as its list of theater personnel includes "the gatherers, . . . the booke keeper [i.e., prompter], tyreman, [and] tyrewoman."[114] We can only speculate as to the precise role this "tyrewoman" played in the acquisition, manufacture, and maintenance of the "apparrell which laie then in the said [tiring] howse," which was purportedly worth "fower hundred pounds."[115]

The inclusion of *both* a tireman and tirewoman in the Whitefriars' playhouse personnel, however, would seem to indicate a gendered division of labor within the trade of theatrical attiring. Although it is unclear precisely where the line between these two specialties was drawn, the evidence discussed above and in Chapter 3 suggests that tirewomen specialized not only in the manufacture of female attires but also in dressing boy-actors playing female roles. The plays performed by the Children of the King's Revels at Whitefriars, and those staged by other children's companies, contain numerous female roles for boys who had to be dressed in the elaborate head- and neck-attires in which tirewomen specialized. The plays frequently call attention to these attires, suggesting that they were an attraction for audiences (providing an added incentive to keep a tirewoman on the payroll). In the first play licensed for the company,

Edward Sharpham's *Cupids Whirligig* (1607), for example, Lady Troublesome, Peg (her kinswoman), and Nan (a merchant's daughter) enter adjusting their head-attires for a wedding masque: "Doth my Tyre sit well Nan?" the Lady asks, to which Nan replies, "Passing well, ile assure you Madame."[116] In Lewis Machin and Gervase Markham's *The Dumb Knight* (1607–8), another play written for the King's Revels, Lollia, wife of Prat the Orator, is obsessed with gentlewomen's attires: "the tire, O the tire," she sighs, "made castell upon castell, jewell upon jewell, knot upon knot, crownes, garlands, gardins, and what not? the hood, the rebato, the french fall, the loose bodyed gowne, the pinne in the haire, . . . and every day change." When her friend Mistress Colloquintada enters, she admires her neck-attire: "You have a pretty ruffe, how deep is it?" she asks. Colloquintada replies, "Nay this is but shallow, marry I have a ruffe is a quarter deep, measured by the yeard," and then returns the compliment: "you have a pretty set too, how big is the steele you set with?"[117] The sexual innuendo of such comments, which make punning reference to the boy-actor's "yard" (i.e., penis), suggests that the allure of the boy's body beneath these attires was an added attraction to theatergoers who patronized their plays.[118] It was the tirewoman who worked for the King's Revels who would have been responsible for acquiring such attires, setting the boys' ruffs, and making sure their head-attires "sat" well.

Other children's company plays likewise call attention to boy-actors' attires, make frequent reference to tirewomen and their wares, or contain tirewomen as characters. In Jonson's *Cynthia's Revels; or, The Fountain of Self-Love* (1600–1601), first performed at Blackfriars by the Children of the Chapel, the fashion-crazed ladies of Cynthia's court, Philautia (self-love), Phantaste (fancy or light wittiness), Argurion (money), and Moria (folly), continually change and compliment one another on their attires to reassure themselves they are of the latest fashion.[119] Phantaste enters at the beginning of act 2, scene 4 and immediately exits again to "change [her] fan" (l. 1). In the meanwhile, Moria compliments Philautia: "Is that your new ruff, sweet ladybird? By my truth, 'tis most intricately rare" (ll. 6–7). When Phantaste returns, she has changed not only her fan but her "head-tire" and explains, "Yes, faith, the other was so near the common: it had no extraordinary grace; besides, I had worn it almost a day" (ll. 59–61). Praising the Italian design of the head-tire, Philautia complains: "we cannot have a new peculiar court-tire but these [entertainers] will have it" (ll. 68–69), to which Phantaste replies, "Oh, aye, they do most pitifully imitate" (l. 71). The 1616 Folio's substitution of the term "entertainers" for the 1601 Quarto's "retainers" emphasizes in metatheatrical terms that the fashion of head- and neck-attires was being imitated not only by servants of the elite but by the players themselves—a substitution that merely makes explicit what spectators could see with their own eyes.

In Middleton's *Michaelmas Term* (1604–6), performed by the Children of Paul's, a professional "tirewoman" named Mistress Comings (with a pun on "combings" and perhaps also on her lucrative earnings or "comings-in" and sexual commerce) collaborates with a male tailor on the transformation of a "Northamptonshire lass" into a courtesan by arranging her "loose-bodied gown . . . wires and tires, bents and bums [i.e., bumrolls or bustles], felts and falls [i.e., felt hats and falling collars]" (1.3.13–16).[120] Sexual innuendo (e.g., loose-bodied, falling, bending, feeling, bums) again refers to the body beneath the attire, whether that of the fictive courtesan or the boy-actor playing her part. Her pander, Hellgill, insists that the "finest" women are "begot [i.e., conceived/dressed] between tirewomen and tailors" (3.1.5–6). He further suggests that the tirewoman's trade involved educating her customers in the latest foreign fashions and the proper manner in which to wear them, promising the country wench, "I'll bring thee where thou shalt be taught to dress thee" (ll. 58–59). At the beginning of act 3 the wench enters with the tirewoman, who is "*busy about her head*" (3.1.s.d.), performing the labor of attiring onstage. Mistress Comings fulfills her educative function while she arranges the wench's head-attire, commenting, "Say what you will, this wire becomes you best" (ll. 8–9).[121] As she leaves, the tirewoman is paid for this "head-counsel" (l. 67) by the courtesan. As the above examples attest, the staging of tirewomen's wares in children's plays satirizes the constantly changing fashions of female attire and the incessant labor or busy-ness that fuels it, while at the same time capitalizing on their sexual and sartorial allure.

Dressing and undressing those who wore these attires, both onstage and off, was laborious work that required training in the skills of starching, pinning, lacing, hairdressing, and so forth. Some sense of the sheer scale of such work at the court of Elizabeth may be gleaned from her wardrobe accounts: in one six-month period in 1565 the queen ordered 18,000 "great verthingale pynnes," 20,000 "myddle verthingale pynnes," 25,000 "great Velvet Pynnes," 39,000 "smale Velvet Pynnes," and 19,000 "Small hed Pynnes," which were used to pin deep tucks in farthingales, make flounces, fasten foreparts, arrange pleats, affix the decorations provided by silkwomen, and attach ruffs, cuffs, veils, and so forth.[122] The time constraints of a stage performance would have demanded particularly swift and dexterous dressing and undressing, pinning and unpinning, by tirewomen behind the scenes. The difficulty of attiring boy-actors for the stage and the exigency of accomplishing such work quickly are lampooned in Thomas Tomkis's play *Lingua; or, The Combat of the Tongue, and the Five Senses for Superiority: A Pleasant Comœdie*, performed at Trinity College, Cambridge, between 1602 and 1607, in which each of the senses puts on a show to prove its preeminence. When Tactus (or Touch) is summoned to stage his show, he arrives unprepared and explains the delay as follows:

> Who would by toyl'd with wenches in a shew. . . . Thus 'tis, five houres agoe I set a douzen maides to attire a boy like a nize Gentlewoman: but there is such doing with their looking-glasses, pinning, unpinning, setting, unsetting, formings and conformings painting blew vaines, and cheekes, such stirre with Stickes [i.e., setting sticks used to starch ruffs] and Combes, Cascanets, Dressings, Purles [i.e., looped edging, made of gold or silver thread], Falles, Squares [i.e., fabric covering the bosom], Buskes [i.e., whalebone stay used to stiffen corsets], Bodies [i.e., bodices], Scarffes, Neck laces, Carcanets [i.e., bejeweled, ornamental attires worn on the head or around the neck], Rebatoes, Borders, Tires, Fannes, Palizadoes [i.e., wires supporting the hair], Puffes [i.e., gatherings of fabric or ribbons], Ruffes, Cuffes, Muffes, Pussles [a nonce word playing on pucelle?], Fussles [a nonce word playing on fuss?], Partsets [i.e., partlets, worn to cover a décolletage], Frislets [i.e., small ruffles], Bandlets, Fillets, Croslets, Pendulets, Amulets, Annulets, Bracelets, and so many lets, that yet shee is scarse drest to the girdle.[123]

Tactus's description of the "many lets" or hindrances of female attire reveals the potential pitfalls posed by pinning and fussing with "Puffes, Ruffes, Cuffes" and other intricate ornaments in the tiring-house and suggests that this difficulty was exacerbated by the diminutive size of the boy-actor, who wears a kirt*let* instead of a kirtle, a band*let* instead of a band, and so on. It also makes clear that the work of attiring the boy-actor for his "shew" is done by "maides" who specialize in such attires. Their incessant, interminable labor is once again emphasized: though they have been toiling for "five houres," the boy-actor playing the "Gentlewoman" is "scarse drest to the girdle."

The many dress pins, hooks, buttons, chapes (or aglets used to bind the ends of the "points" or laces that held together parts or articles of clothing), costume wires (used to support ruffs, rebatos, and head-attires), and cosmetic implements found in excavations of the Rose and Globe theater sites, as well as references to women's head-and-neck-attires worn as costumes in plays performed by the adult companies, lend further support to the evidence found in theatrical documents that such attires were worn in plays staged in the public theaters as well and that they, too, may have used skilled tirewomen as dressers for their boy-actors.[124] That some of these minute dress accessories were undoubtedly lost during costume changes in the tiring-house attests to the economic incentive adult playing companies would have had to hire experienced tirewomen to dress the boy-actors who wore them, and increasingly so in the early seventeenth century, as their plays began to emulate the staging practices of masques and to function as arenas for advertising the latest court fashions to the middling sort.

The skills and fabrics associated with such head- and neck-attires were imported to England during Elizabeth's reign by female artisans from the Netherlands, France, and elsewhere in Europe, as discussed in Chapter 3. The Revels Office frequently drew on the skills of immigrant craftswomen, such as the French and Italian tirewomen discussed above, or "Joyce ffrolick," who was hired as a scene painter to paint canvas for "howses for the plaies" both "in thoffice & at the Coorte." She was paid sixteen pence per day and worked alongside male assistants (who were paid the same wage as she) and master painters (who were paid a slightly higher wage of twenty pence per day).[125] It seems that Joyce was one of the more highly skilled of the painters' assistants, as on one occasion she was hired to work for thirty days and ten nights, while the seven male assistants were hired for an average of only eleven days each.[126] Joyce was probably Dutch or Flemish, as Netherlandish painters, male and female, were highly skilled and sought-after.[127]

Women who worked in the silk industry likewise appear in the Revels Office accounts, as silk was the preferred fabric used in the manufacture of costumes, head-attires, and other fashionable attires for court masques. The silkwomen, as Marion K. Dale has shown, had a virtual monopoly, beginning in the fourteenth century and extending at least into the mid- to late sixteenth century, on the manufacture and sale of narrow silk wares such as woven ribbons and bands, and silk lace and fringe. The term "silkwoman," according to Dale, was used to describe women "who were in any way interested in the production or sale of the commodity" and whose stock-in-trade covered a "whole range of goods, from colored silks or gold and silver thread sold by the ounce, to the more elaborate decorative articles or ribbons and similar woven silks," to "articles of clothing" that "came sometimes from their own workshops."[128] Although the London silkwomen had no guild, Dale demonstrates that in many respects they modeled their industry along the lines of a craft guild, practicing their craft independently, taking on apprentices, and employing workers.

During the second half of the sixteenth century, the London Weavers' Company attempted to assert its prerogative over the production of silk wares and as part of this process began to levy fines against company members who were caught "tak[ing] any woman to his apprentice."[129] A 1577 ordinance thus stipulated: "No Silke weaver to take any woman prentice to that Art."[130] It is clear from the frequent fines levied against freemen of the company who disobeyed its ordinances throughout the sixteenth and seventeenth centuries, however, that women continued to be employed as silk weavers and as ancillary workers, such as silk winders and throwsters.[131] Moreover, throughout this period widows were exempt from these restrictions entirely.[132] An ordinance of 1596 thus states: "Item no woman or mayd shall use or exercise the Arte of weaving upon any Loome, Sapyn or Benche excepte she be the widowe of one of the same Guilde."[133] During the late sixteenth and early seventeenth centuries, the London Weavers' Company struggled to control the proliferation of immigrant silk workers in London, who emigrated in large numbers from the southern Netherlands (mainly from the Walloon provinces, Flanders and Brabant),[134] introducing new techniques in silk weaving to the native population.[135] From 1571 to 1593, the number of male and female immigrant silk workers in London rose from 932 to 1,800.[136] The Returns of Aliens living in London make clear that Netherlandish craftswomen worked actively during this period in all aspects of silk production in London, as discussed in Chapter 3. Their craft is illustrated in a Flemish engraving by Philips Galle, after Jan van der Straet, in the British Museum dated circa 1590–1600 of an all-female workshop of Flemish silk spinners (see Figure 4).

This was a period of intense competition between native and alien silk workers in London, particularly during the economic "crisis" of the 1590s, when the Weavers' Company sought government protections against the aliens.[137] A complaint lodged by the yeomen of the company in 1595 makes clear that they perceived immigrant silkwomen to be a threat to their trade, for it includes the accusation that the alien silk workers "sett Wooemen and Maydes at worke."[138] In the early seventeenth century the company further accused the immigrants of employing "Wooemen Broakers to sell for them," who went daily "from shop to shop . . . from one end of the City to the other, and all other out places."[139] It seems likely that some of the unnamed silk-women employed by the Revels Office and at court during this period were

Figure 4. Women of various ages in a vaulted room spinning silk, from a series of prints by Philips Galle (after Jan van der Straet) entitled *Vermis Sericus*, c. 1590–1600. Engraving. © The Trustees of the British Museum.

immigrants.[140] The (mostly unnamed) silkwomen listed in the Revels accounts during Elizabeth's reign provided a diverse range of silk products, including buttons, fringe, tassels, lace, and various types of silk fabric for the manufacture of head-attires, adornment of costumes, and fabrication of small properties.[141] The named silkwomen who worked for the office include a "silkweaver" named Joan Bowll, a "sylkwoman" named Mistris Wyett, and the queen's own silkwoman, Alice Mountague, from whom the office purchased "Bone Lace wrowght w*ith* sylver and spangells" and "Lawne of fine white Netwoorke," and who provided the tirewoman Mistress Swegoo (mentioned above) with "Lawne," "White Sipers [i.e., cypress, a delicate, transparent fabric resembling cobweb lawn]," "ffrenge of golde twisted," "Bone Lace cheyne ffrenge & edging lace of golde & silv*er* with spangles," "Poynting Ribbon of golde and sylke," "Ribon of penny brode silke," "parchement Lace of watchett and sylver," "Laces of Crymsen," and "Spanish Lace & white heare lacyng" to fabricate head-attires and scarves for a masque of ".ix. Muzes."[142]

The "dyverse Sortes" of trimmings in which tirewomen, silkwomen and female embroiderers and spanglers specialized were crucial in the process of "translating" or renovating old costumes to make them appear new. This process was one of the Revels Office's primary preoccupations, since costumes were only supposed to be worn once for performances at court. The cost of making up each garment new from scratch would have been prohibitive, however, so the office chose instead to take apart older garments and remake them in a new form or simply to "garnish" older costumes to give them a new look with silk ribbon, fringe, spangles, and so forth. An example of the spectacular effect produced by this process may be glimpsed in the embroidered woman's jacket in the Victoria and Albert collection mentioned above (see Figure 2). The linen ground of the jacket is covered with gilt spangles, each topped with a tiny bead, added to the original embroidery to make the jacket appear more opulent in the candlelight of a masque.[143] Garments embellished in this way in and for the Revels Office underwent several "translations" before being retired, when they were passed down to the professional players.[144]

The professional playing companies used similar techniques to translate and adorn costumes as needed, albeit within their far more modest means. Typically, players' costumes on the commercial stage were embellished with inexpensive copper lace, remains of which were found at the site of the Rose theater. Yet there are numerous examples in Henslowe's accounts and playhouse inventories of costumes adorned with gold, silver, silk lace, and fringe as well.[145] A list of playing apparel in the hand of Edward Alleyn, compiled circa 1602, includes many items adorned with gold, silver, and other expensive trimmings.[146] These silk- and tirewomen's wares are likewise among the artifacts uncovered in the excavations of the Rose and Globe theaters. "The variety of fashionable passementerie (a collective term for decorative trimmings) from the Rose," according to archaeologists Julian Bowsher and Pat Miller, "is particularly impressive in such a small assemblage."[147] Examples of trimmings found in the Rose excavation include silk tablet-woven bands, woven silks cut into strips, and velvet bands of the type used to adorn the costumes in Alleyn's inventory. Also notable among the artifacts found at the Rose in the area below the stage, as well as that of the galleries, are the large number of glass beads, both round and cylindrical (bugles).[148] Such beads and bugles, as we have seen, were typically sewn onto costumes by groups of women spanglers. Alleyn's inventory includes many beaded and spangled costumes.[149] These ornate costumes may have been passed down to Alleyn by the Revels Office as "fees" for performances at court or acquired from a secondhand "fripper" (an occupation in which women likewise worked actively).

The professional players frequently relied on the secondhand clothing trade for costumes.[150] As Susan Cerasano has argued, "players kept costs to a manageable level by buying second-hand garments and purchasing new costumes for only the major actors (or the unusual characters . . .) for each production."[151] Elizabeth Hutchinson, mentioned above, probably relied on the secondhand clothing trade to "provide and finde" the "stock of apparell" requested in her husband's will for the King's and Queen's Young company. There are many entries in Henslowe's accounts detailing loans to the Admiral's Men for the purchase of secondhand costumes and of his selling them used costumes himself.[152] Yet even the costumes that were made up new by male tailors, such as those made by "the littell tayller Radford" and "dover the tayller" in Henslowe's accounts, were likely to have been worked upon by women's hands, as tailors ordinarily executed the laying out and cutting of fabric but hired semptresses to stitch them together.[153]

Evidence of women's involvement in the secondhand clothing trade in and around the commercial theaters may be found in Henslowe's account book, some thirty pages of which are devoted to records of a pawnbroking business he managed between 1593 and 1596.[154] Sir Walter Greg was the first to have noted that Henslowe's pawnbroking business would have been "likely to form a useful adjunct to dramatic management, since the articles deposited were in many cases rich stuffs and apparel, which if unredeemed would prove of value in the company wardrobe."[155] Henslowe's pawn accounts reflect the active involvement of women in both the pawnbroking and secondhand clothing trades. The great majority of customers listed in the accounts are women: of the 312 loans in which the debtor's identity is given, 78 percent were to women and only 22 percent to men.[156] The accounts provide a fascinating glimpse into the day-to-day economic activities of working women in the environs of the commercial theaters and help remind us that the commercial networks in which the theaters were intertwined, and upon which they relied, were hardly "all-male" preserves. The high incidence of women in the accounts may be attributed not only to the needs of market women to find ready cash or of housewives to make ends meet but to the financial interest some of the women appear to have had in Henslowe's business. A "goody Watson" is listed fifty-three times in Henslowe's accounts, often pledging more than one and sometimes up to five bundles in a single day. In the four-month period between September 1594 and January 1595, she is listed forty-eight times—or once every two and a half days, on average. During this period, in the series of accounts in which she figures, there are only eight loans made to people other than Goody Watson. It thus seems certain that she was herself a broker or fripper who was hired by Henslowe as an agent or as a partner in his business.[157] Two other female intermediaries seem to have assisted Henslowe in his pawnbroking business: one set of accounts begins with the heading "m^{rs} grantes Recknynge 1593[/4]," indicating a female agent who kept a reckoning of loans and interest payments, while another set from the same period includes over forty loans made to an "Anne Nokes."[158] Male pawnbrokers like Henslowe relied on such female intermediaries because of their expertise in assessing the value of pawned goods and attire, and because of their knowledge of the community of female borrowers, knowledge that enabled them to assess a borrower's credit.[159]

If Henslowe appropriated unredeemed pledges, as Greg conjectures, or made even more extensive use of the articles of apparel and other goods he kept in pawn, he would not have been out of the ordinary.[160] There is a great deal of evidence that this kind of activity was common practice among pawnbrokers of the period.[161] The illegal use, renting out, and appropriation of pledges were among the most common offenses for which early modern pawnbrokers were taken to task in contemporary court records, legislation, and popular literature.[162] In 1596, Elizabeth Crowcher claimed that she had borrowed twenty-four shillings from John Cleaborough, who like Henslowe was a Southwark pawnbroker, "upon a gown and taffety apron" and that "when she came to redeem her goods her apron was worn out for which she refused to receive her goods."[163] In 1610, a pawnbroker named Thomas Warwicke claimed to be within his rights in renting out the female attire and other goods pawned by a widow named Anne Lee because they had not agreed upon a fixed date for repayment of her loan, accusing her of "impudent and shameless boldness" for expecting her pawned goods to be in his shop when she returned for them. Other cases reflect disagreements over the length of time a pawnbroker was required to keep pawns before being allowed to sell them and over goods delivered as pawns being confused with those intended for resale.[164] If Henslowe used the garments and other pawned goods left in his storage "Rome" prior to their redemption or appropriated unredeemed pledges for use on the stage, it would help explain the dearth of female costumes and small properties in the Admiral's Men's inventory of 1598. This absence may have been supplied by the many sumptuous female gowns (a number of which were left unredeemed), linens, and tableware listed in the pawn accounts.[165]

The evidence surveyed above suggests that the gendered division of theatrical labor in many ways reflected that of the economy at large, where women were also active in the manufacture and retail of cloth, clothing, and luxury attire, in the secondhand clothing and pawnbroking trades, and in the provision of credit. Yet the theaters also created new employment opportunities for working women. Certain of these opportunities were relatively unique, simply because the purpose-built theaters were themselves relatively unique. Thus, for example, women worked in the financial end of the theater business as gatherers, who collected the penny fee for general admission and further fees for entrance to the interior galleries where, according to Thomas Platter, "one s[at] better and more pleasantly and on that account pa[id] more."[166] There is evidence that "not a few of the gatherers were women."[167] Margaret Brayne worked as a gatherer at The Theatre in Shoreditch (which she herself had helped to build) in the late 1580s after the death of her husband, John.[168] Mary Phillips was paid a "stipend" by Thomas Greene, the leading actor of Queen Anne's Men, and his fellows in the winter of 1606/7 "for keeping the gallarie dores of the [Boar's Head] playhowse."[169] Joan Hewes and Mary Phillipps worked as gatherers at the Red Bull playhouse in 1607, and Hewes is also recorded as a gatherer there in 1618.[170] In 1612 Robert Browne wrote to Edward Alleyn on behalf of a "Mr Rose," an impoverished hireling of Prince Henry's Men, "to p[ro]cure him but a gathering place for his wife" at the Fortune theater.[171] The Globe and Blackfriars playhouses had at least one female gatherer in 1627, according to the will of Henry Condell (an actor and manager of the King's Men, and housekeeper in the two theaters), which bequeaths to his "old servant Elizabeth Wheaton . . . that place or privilege which she nowe exerciseth and enjoyeth in the houses of the Blackfriars London and the Globe on the Banckside for and during all the terme of her naturall life yf my estate shall soe long continue in the premises."[172] Material remains of the gatherer's trade may be found in the forty-seven "money boxes" or pots—cheaply produced ceramic containers that were smashed to obtain daily collections—discovered in the excavation of the Rose theater site.[173]

There is some evidence that the role of gatherers was not always limited to the collection of entrance fees. An undated letter from William Birde to Edward Alleyn (c. 1617) suggests that gatherers performed a variety of functions, being reassigned as "nessessary atendaunt[s] on the stage" or "to mend [players'] garments" as needed.[174] Birde's letter likewise conveys the sense that the gatherer's role was taken quite seriously, which should come as no surprise given that the safekeeping and proper allocation of the nightly takings was essential to the financial well-being of company sharers and theater "housekeepers." The demonstrated trustworthiness of the gatherer was a central concern in her or his appointment. Browne's letter testifies of Mrs. Rose, "she shall so carry her self in that place as they shall think it well bestowed by reason of her upright dealing in that nature."[175] It was not simply the honesty of gatherers that was at stake in their assignment but their allegiance as well. For the gatherers effectively functioned as agents or representatives of diverse financial interests in a given theatrical enterprise. The deed of partnership in the Rose theater, for example, allows each of the partners, Henslowe and Cholmely, if they cannot be "there present" as door keepers themselves, to "appoynte theire sufficiente debutyes or assignes . . . at theire Choyse to Coleckte gather and receave all suche some and somes of moneye of every personne & personnes resortinge and Cominge to the saide playe howse."[176] When disputes between various financial interests arose, the allegiance of these deputized gatherers was crucial.[177]

The flexibility of theatrical personnel at times blurred the boundary between offstage workers and players: several extant dramatic plots or "platts" consisting of entrances, exits, and other stage directions indicate that gatherers and other stage attendants were used as "mutes" (i.e., non-speaking parts) onstage.[178] The plot of *Frederick and Basilea* performed by the Admiral's Men at the Rose in 1597 includes a number of entrances and other stage directions for "Gatherers."[179] We do not know whether female gatherers were ever called upon to do so, nor will I dwell on such a possibility here, as my subject is not exceptional instances of female performance on the professional stage but women's day-to-day participation in the offstage work of theatrical production. The visible and vocal presence of working women in and around the theaters may have been a more significant aspect of the playgoer's theatrical experience, moreover, than would the occasional female "mute" onstage. Given that most forms of marketing in early modern London involved vocal solicitation or "cries," the role of door keepers may have involved such advertisement in addition to the collection of entrance fees, particularly given that not all theatergoers were literate and able to read playbills. Several early modern plays contain scenes in which gatherers "cry" plays, such as Marston's *Histrio-Mastix* (a scene discussed in Chapter 4) and the puppet show gatherers in *Bartholomew Fair*, Filcher and Sharkwell (whose names suggest they might not be quite so upright in their dealings), who cry out to the passersby: "Twopence apiece, gentlemen, an excellent motion" (5.4.20), prompting the prospective customer (Knockem) to ask, "Shall we have fine fireworks and good vapours?" (l. 21).[180]

Knockem's reference to "vapours" or tobacco smoke reminds us that plays were not the only commodities that customers consumed in theaters. It has long been known that a variety of other comestibles and wares were "carried around" and vended to audiences before, during, and after performances in the public amphitheaters and in the intervals between performances in the private theaters,[181] including gingerbread,[182] pippins,[183] nuts,[184] ale, and even cheap print: William Fennor in 1616 speaks of pamphlets that "will hap into your hands before a Play begin, with the importunate clamour of 'Buy a new Booke!' by some needy companion that will be glad to furnish you with worke for a turned tester."[185] Recent archaeological evidence suggests a much broader range of comestibles were sold in playhouses than previously imagined, including foodstuffs typically sold by female vendors, as discussed at length in Chapter 4. There is evidence that such concessions generated significant revenue: the third of the Articles of Agreement concerning the Whitefriars theater speaks of the "gaine or profit [that] canne or maye be made in the said howse either by wine, beere, ale, tobacco . . . or any such commoditie."[186] As the reference to the sale of wine, beer, and ale reminds us, "Every Elizabethan theater had, as a necessary and profitable side-show, a tavern attached," and "Drinks could be had in the theatre itself or in the theatre tavern, before, during, or after the performances."[187] Although by the late sixteenth century men predominated in the upper echelons of the brewing business, the service end of the business and the hawking of beer, ale, and tobacco in the streets continued to be women's work.[188]

The varied forms of women's work in and around the commercial theaters in London described above do not change the general "fact" of their exclusion from the professional stage itself. To the extent that the male playing companies retained structural aspects of the guilds in an effort to buttress the status of playing as a legitimate profession, they may well have been motivated to exclude women from the stage as the most visible workspace of that profession and to distinguish their own performance practices from those of female amateurs.[189] It is well-known that civic authorities and puritan preachers who inveighed against the legitimacy of the professional theater accused the players of effeminacy and of effeminizing their audiences. The gendered form of such attacks has most often been understood to refer to the practice of cross-dressing, as at times it explicitly did.[190] Yet the accusation of effeminacy was also frequently linked to the charge that playing was an illegitimate or "idle occupation."[191] The stigma of idleness and its gendered dimension take on new significance within the broader context of the City's preoccupation with the rise of informal commerce in the suburbs, known colloquially as the "Skirtes of the Cittye."[192]

In the eyes of the theater's opponents, playing was considered the antithesis of work.[193] Tom Rutter has traced the emergent discourse linking playing to idleness through civic legislation and anti-theatrical literature of the late sixteenth century.[194] Beginning in the 1580s, he demonstrates, civic officials began to advance the argument that plays lured artisans and apprentices away from the "honest exercises" of their crafts and trades and "maintaine[d] idleness in such persons as have no vocation."[195] Rutter argues that this development derived, "ironically enough, from the fact that playing was becoming more like other forms of labor in London: repetitive, geographically fixed, carried out on weekdays."[196] This irony disappears, however, if we read the Corporation of London's response to playing in relation to its attempts to control other unguilded crafts, trades, and new industries proliferating in the suburbs and liberties. The language used by city authorities and anti-theatrical writers to stigmatize the professional players was identical to that deployed against petty brokers, botchers, frippers, hawkers, hucksters, gamesters, and so forth who plied their trades in the informal sector: players were parasites or "Caterpillers of a Commonwealth"[197] who sought "a more idle and easier kinde of Trade of livinge . . . [than] manuall Labours and Trades did or coulde bring them."[198] "Most of the Players," according to Stephen Gosson, are "men of occupations, which they have forsaken to lyve by playing."[199]

The language of idleness and parasitism used to discredit those who made their living in the informal sector (or who stretched the boundaries of the formal economy beyond its accustomed limits) took its ideological justification from the Protestant doctrine of vocations or callings, which redefined labor as a positive means to salvation rather than a punishment for sin.[200] A calling was a divinely "appointed charge, and manner of life, in some *honest* worke."[201] The terms "honest" and "lawful" commonly appear in elaborations of the doctrine to qualify what counts as a true calling and are defined with reference to Genesis 3:10, "In the sweate of thy browes thou shalt eate thy bread," and Ephesians 4:28: "let him labour, working with his hands the thing which is good."[202] As interpreted by Protestant divines, these two passages enjoined one to live on the fruits of one's own labor rather than the labor of others and so benefit the commonwealth. By contrast, those who labored in dishonest callings were thought to "live of[f] the labours of other men, and themselves take no paines or travaile, do no good in the world, benefite not humane societie" and to be "but unprofitable burthens."[203] Playing frequently appears as one of the dishonest callings enumerated in sermons and treatises such as William Perkins's *Treatise of the Vocations; or, Callings of Men* (pub. 1603):

> [M]any perswading themselves of their callings, have for all this no calling at all: As for example, such as live by usury, by carding, and dicing, by mainteining houses of gaming; by plaies and such like: for god is the author of every lawfull calling; but these and all such miserable courses of living, are either against the word of God, or else are not grounded thereupon. And therefore are not callings or vocations but avocations from God and his waies.[204]

It was the duty of parents to ensure that their children were trained up in honest callings, although many, according to William Gouge, failed in this endeavor. Among these reprobates, Gouge lists parents who "bring up their children in unwarrantable and unlawfull callings, as . . . to be stage-plaiers" who are nothing but "very drones, and caterpillars in the common wealth."[205] Stage players were held to epitomize idleness not only because "they lyve by playing," rather than working, in Gosson's terms, but because they lured others away from their legitimate occupations as well.[206]

The claims that playing was a dishonest calling and that the commercial theater was a "nurserie of idelnesse"[207] were frequently cast in gendered terms that linked idleness to effeminacy. According to Gosson, players lead "a softe, a silken, a Courting kind of life, fitter for women than for men," and as such are "unfit for manly discipline."[208] Thomas Beard similarly argues that playing serves "to no other purpose but to make the people idle, effeminate, and voluptuous."[209] The link between idleness and effeminacy found further justification in contemporary humoral discourse. In his treatise against dicing, dancing, and "Vaine Playes or Enterluds," John Northbrooke claims that idle pastimes, such as plays, are like sleep in that they "ingendreth much humiditie and rawe humours in the bodie," allowing "all the moystures and humors of the bodie, with the naturall heate, [to] retire to the extreme parts therof," thereby making those who engage in such pastimes "slouthfull, weake, and *effeminate with overmuche ydlenesse*."[210] The purported idleness of players makes them cold, damp and effeminate, while "good true labourers in the Common wealth" make their living "with their owne handes, in the sweate of their face" like "honest men."[211] A decade later, William Rankins similarly asserts that players' "idlenesse weakeneth the sences and members of men, that they shall never be able to profit their countrie."[212]

To counter such claims, defenders of the stage sought to establish its legitimacy as a "manly discipline" and "honest" profession. They did this in part, as we have seen, by modeling the playing companies on the livery companies. Professional playing, in the words of the actor Nathan Field, was a trade just like that of "the mercer, draper, goldsmith, or a hundred trades and mysteries that at this day are lawful."[213] Defenders of the stage likewise sought to refute the humoral argument that playing dissipated the heat and manliness of both the natural body and the body politic. In his *Apologie for Poetrie*, Sir Philip Sidney mocks the "imputations" of effeminacy "laid to the poore Poets" by mocking the claim that "before Poets did soften us, we were . . . the pillars of manlyke libertye & not lulled a sleepe in shady idlenes with Poets pastimes." To the contrary, he argues, poetry is "an Art . . . not of effeminatenes, but of notable stirring of courage."[214] Although Sidney is not referring here to dramatic poesy per se, similar arguments were used by defenders of the stage. In his *Apology for Actors*, Thomas Heywood defends playing as a "worthy imployment" by countering the humoral argument of the anti-theatricalists with one of his own.[215] Far from engendering "rawe humours," he argues, theater serves "to recreate such as are wholly devoted to Mellancholly, which corrupts the bloud," and to "refresh such weary spirits as are tired with labour, or study, to moderate the cares and heavinesse of the minde, that they may returne to their trades and faculties with more zeale and earnestnesse."[216] Instead of impeding honest labor or posing a threat to the commonwealth, he suggests, the recreation of theater instead allows the worker to apply himself to his calling with renewed zeal. Plays of the period, such Thomas Dekker's *The Shoemakers' Holiday*, Rutter argues, stage a similar sentiment in depicting diligent workers taking time off to recreate.[217]

Although none of the forms of female employment in and around the theaters discussed in this chapter and those to follow changes the "fact" of women's exclusion from the visible workspace of the professional stage, they allow us to understand this exclusion within the broader context of the gendered division of labor within the economy at large, where women's work was likewise relegated behind the scenes of production to a "shadow" economy that was nonetheless crucial. The all-male playing companies relied on women who made their living in the informal economy, even as they sought to legitimate their profession as an "honest," "manly" calling. Situated on the cusp of the formal and informal sectors, the commercial theaters thus worked to women's advantage *and* disadvantage, opening new employment opportunities for women while at the same time excluding them from the most visible or open workspace of the theater, the stage itself, in an effort to define the play that took place there as legitimate work.

Although relegated offstage, behind the scenes of theatrical production, women's work nonetheless had a shaping influence on dramatic literature and its staging in Shakespeare's time, as I demonstrate in the chapters to follow. This influence appears not only in the representation of working women in play texts but also in the staging of properties and costumes manufactured by female hands and in the performance idioms of the professional players, who borrowed from the vocal and gestural repertoire of working women, just as they patronized their wares. Perhaps the most invisible form of female labor behind the scenes of theatrical production was that of women moneylenders and creditors, insofar as their labor created no tangible product (a charge often leveled at the players themselves), only the empty ciphers inscribed in their account books. Yet the ciphering of usuresses thereby created value in the form of capital, which could be used to fund theatrical ventures. In so doing, they created something out of nothing, much like theater professionals themselves, who responded to the female creditors to whom they were indebted, as we shall see, with a mixture of gratitude and resentment.

Chapter 2

Dame Usury

USURY IN EARLY modern England was construed as the antithesis of "honest" work, or in Aristotelian/Thomistic terms, as an unnatural reproduction of wealth that circumvented productive labor.¹ Instead of working, usurers put money itself to work—and their money never stopped working, even on the Sabbath.² Usury thus had an unfair advantage over and led to the decay of legitimate trades. The Preacher in Thomas Wilson's 1572 *Discourse Uppon Usurye* warns that if usury is allowed, men will cease to labor in their "lawful vocacion[s]":

> The plough man will no more turne up the ground for uncertayne gayne, when hee maye make an assured profite of hys money, that lieth by hym. The artificer wil leve hys woorkynge. The clothier will cease hys makynge of clothes, because these trades are paynefull and chargeable: yea all men will geve themselves wholie to lyve an idle lyfe . . . fewe men will woorke, and most will play, and men livyng without labor and doinge nothing, wil loyter and wallow in the ease of usury.³

Unlike honest artificers who labor to produce "holsome wares," usurers do nothing but "wallow in the ease of usury" and produce nothing but ever-increasing gains.⁴ The labor of financial management undertaken by those who worked in England's expanding credit economy—counting and accounting, keeping track of credit and debt, calculating rates of interest, and so forth—was not considered work but rather a form of sloth, idleness, or play. Clearly, usurers had no legitimate calling, it was circularly reasoned, since they had no guild or livery company.⁵

Like players and others who made their living from unguilded or "idle occupations," usurers were stigmatized as effeminate. In the case of usury, however, the charge of effeminacy was grounded not only in idleness—the "Mother of all vices"—but in the Greek term for usury, *tokos*, derived from the verb *tiktein*, "which signifieth to beget, or to bring foorth," as in the "chylding or generacion [of money]."[6] In reproducing wealth without producing wholesome, substantial wares the usurer "maketh idlenes it selfe fruitfull," for "he taketh no paines himselfe, but onely expecteth the time when his interest will come in, like the belly which doth no worke, & yet eateth all the meate."[7] The common image of the usurer with a swollen belly was linked not only to excessive greed and consumption but to conception, for usurers make "a barren thing (as monie is) to bring foorth as it were children, that is to say, pence and shillinges."[8] Unnaturally applying God's injunction to "increase & multiply" to the reproduction of wealth instead of human offspring, they beget "a monstrous birth" and in so doing "*ex nihilo nihil fit*," make "something out of nothing."[9] Usury's unceasing generation or engendering of wealth was figured as monstrously excessive, as in *The Winter's Tale* where Autolycus advertises a "doleful" ballad about "a usurer's wife [who] was brought to bed of twenty money-bags at a burthen" (4.4.263–65).[10] It thus represented a twofold transgression, simultaneously perverting God's injunction to "increase and multiply" (Gen. 1:28) by breeding coins instead of children and evading Adam's curse (Gen. 3:19): "In the sweat of your face shall you eat your bread."[11]

English polemics against usury during the late sixteenth and early seventeenth centuries nonetheless acknowledged its pervasiveness in practice, frequently commenting on the proliferation and diversification of its forms and practitioners.[12] In 1572, Thomas Wilson thus observed: "I do not knowe anye place in christendome, so muche subjecte to thys foule syne of usurie, as the whole realme of Englande ys at thys present, and hathe bene of late yeares."[13] If usury gave birth to a monster, it was "a many-headed monster, a hydra," incorporating a heterogeneous multiplicity of commercial practices and practitioners.[14] Social and economic historians have linked such observations to the expansion of the credit economy and scarcity of specie during the period, as a result of which usury was not restricted to wealthy male creditors but was widely practiced by anyone and everyone with ready cash.[15] Contemporary treatises complained that usury was "practiced almoste of all."[16]

The usury statute of 1571 is thought to have contributed to the increasingly widespread practice of moneylending by tolerating interest rates of up to 10 percent[17] and thereby to have played a crucial role in the rise of the first purpose-built theaters in London, which were financed with the aid of "many Hundred poundes taken up at interest."[18] When these commercial ventures launched on credit began to generate their own capital, theater entrepreneurs like Shakespeare and Philip Henslowe themselves joined the class of moneylenders.[19] In 1598, around the time Shakespeare wrote *The Merchant of Venice*, his Stratford friend Richard Quiney wrote to him requesting a loan of £30. Shortly after, Richard's son-in-law Abraham Sturley wrote to Richard cautioning, "I will like of [the loan] as I shall heare when wheare & howe" and "if it mai sort to any indifferent condicions," implying in Ernst Honigmann's words that Shakespeare "might drive a hard bargain" in negotiating the terms of the loan.[20] It is no accident that much of what we know about the stage in Shakespeare's time is derived from an account book, Henslowe's so-called diary, which details his pawnbroking and moneylending as well as his theatrical ventures. Keeping track of credit and debt was as crucial to the commercial success of theater people as of shopkeepers, tradespeople, and merchants.[21]

A great deal of critical attention has been paid to the social mobility afforded to merchants and others with access to ready cash in early modern England and the perceived threat this posed to the gentry and aristocracy.[22] Such scholarship has demonstrated the way in which moneyed wealth, when placed in the hands of the lower and middling sort, worked to destabilize the social hierarchy. Yet little attention has been paid to the figure of the female moneylender and how her lending practices may have worked to destabilize the gender hierarchy.[23] This chapter will examine women moneylenders' and creditors' activities in and around the commercial theaters and in the economy more broadly as a hitherto unexplored context within which to read Shakespeare's Sonnets and *The Merchant of Venice*, and other contemporary plays, ballads, sermons, pamphlets, prints, and paintings representing their commercial practices. The advent of the female usurer, as we shall see, invested the standard tropes of usury literature—and in particular those of unnatural reproduction and the creation of wealth ex nihilo—with new significance. The language of counting and accounting in these texts is richly suggestive of the central role played by bookkeeping and formal instruments of credit, such as bonds, in the expanding credit economy that gave rise to the commercial theaters.[24] The analysis that follows centers on the gendered bonds of credit and lexicon of counting and accounting that feature so prominently in the Sonnets and *The Merchant of Venice* in an effort to understand the complex power dynamics between female creditors and male debtors, as these dynamics affected social bonds of friendship, kinship, marriage, and civic community, including the community or fellowship of the all-male playing companies. My more particular focus will be on the ways in which female creditors are figured and themselves figure—or quite literally count, using ciphers or Hindu-Arabic numerals—during a period in which they were financing commercial ventures, including theatrical ventures, by lending money at interest and and on bond and using new techniques of (ac)counting to do so.

In the Sonnets and *The Merchant of Venice*, the trope of the cipher or zero is used to figure the (ac)counting practices deployed by female creditors to create something out of nothing. Exemplifying the cultural poetics of women's work as "never done," the trope of the cipher represents the labor of female financiers as both unceasing and un-done. If the history of women moneylenders' work in and around the theaters—their (ac)counting and lending practices, exercise of financial and legal expertise, and funding of theatrical and other commercial ventures—has hitherto been lost, it is thus in part because these labors were never simply or fully present in early modern culture. Diligently calculating the terms of their bonds behind the scenes of male commercial enterprise, female creditors were nonetheless defined as the antithesis of "honest" laborers. Yet by the end of the sixteenth and beginning of the seventeenth centuries, an emergent ethos of Christian exactitude began to revalue diligence and precision in (ac)counting as virtues, a shift that is registered, I argue, in *The Merchant of Venice* and other cultural texts during this transitional period.

Although scholars have often noted echoes of the usury debate in Shakespeare's Sonnets addressed to the young man, which chide him as a "Profitless usurer" (4.7) for failing to generate reproductive "increase" (1.1), less attention has been paid to the reappearance of the usury trope in Sonnet 134, where a female addressee is taken to task for the opposite offense: she is an all-too-successful "usurer," who "put[s] forth all to use" (l. 10) and thereby profits too much.[25] The poet, who claims he has "mortgaged" himself to this female creditor's "will," offers to "forfeit" himself to redeem the young man, who stands "surety-like" on the poet's behalf under the terms of her "bond" (ll. 2, 3, 7, 8). The offer is refused, however, because the female creditor is "covetous" and insists upon taking all that she can under the "statute of [her] beauty" (ll. 6, 9). She would rather "sue" than release the poet's "friend" (l. 11) from her bond. Sonnets 135 and 136 extend the trope, drawing on a lexicon of (ac)counting or "reckon[ing]" (136.8) to describe the usuress's "overplus" of "Wills" (135.2)—a phrase that suggests her excessive willfulness, sexual desire, and use of legal instruments, as well as her multiple male debtors.[26]

This lexicon and the gendered bonds of credit it describes likewise appear in the roughly contemporaneous *Merchant of Venice* (1596–98), when Portia accuses Bassanio of forfeiting their marital bond—which she likens to an "oath of credit" (5.1.246)—and Antonio stands "surety" for him (l. 254).[27] Yet in spite of Portia's positioning of affective trust/trustworthiness and fiscal credit/creditability at the center of the marriage bond, her provision of capital to pay off her husband's debts, and the exactitude with which she wages law in the trial scene, the critical tradition has largely resisted reading her as a creditor, much less a usurer.[28] That tradition has preferred to view Portia as one who freely and unconditionally gives, rather than one who lends, as a profitless purveyor of capital between men, due in part to its image of the usurer as the "*man* with the moneybags."[29] Recent archival evidence culled from probate inventories, wills, and court records suggests that it is time to revise this image, however, as there is mounting evidence that women were among the most prominent lenders of money at interest in early modern England.[30]

There are several possible explanations for this phenomenon. Because women tended to inherit liquid assets or movables, rather than landed property, their portions were in demand as a source of business capital, whether in the form of dowries or loans.[31] While some women turned to moneylending before marriage to increase the size of their inherited portions, others remained unmarried and were able to live off the interest from loans.[32] Unmarried women and widows, who had fewer claims on their money and who were unconstrained by the law of coverture restricting married women's legal and financial rights, were among the most important providers of credit, often putting large portions of their estates out at interest to friends, neighbors, and kin, as well as tradesmen, merchants, and even local town governments.[33] The growing numbers of women lending money at interest in the late sixteenth century may be linked to legislation easing restrictions on the practice, such as the above-mentioned 1571 Usury Act.[34] In the century following this act, the numbers of single women lending money at interest and of those never marrying both increased significantly, suggesting that some began to view "formal lending as a route to increased autonomy."[35] Women's moneylending may likewise be linked to restrictions on female employment: not all widows were able to carry on their deceased husbands' trades, and crafts- and tradeswomen, as described in the previous chapter, often met with strong opposition from guilds and civic authorities.[36] For such women, moneylending represented an attractive alternative source of income.

While it was formerly thought that women's moneylending was altruistic in nature, taking the form of small-scale, interest-free loans to friends and relatives, we now know that women often loaned large sums and charged interest, not only to members of their families and communities but also to merchants and tradesmen who lived at a considerable distance and who were previously unknown to them.[37] When women did lend money to kin, usually to finance family business ventures, their "assertive, business-like approach . . . contradicts the standard assumption that female lenders treated kin differently," as they used formal bonds and charged interest even with relatives and close friends.[38] Indeed, Amy Froide argues that single women were "in the vanguard" of the transition to written instruments of credit, which "specified a date for repayment as well as a penalty for non-payment." They thereby "ensured that they would be able to recoup their considerable investments in court if need be" and "were not shy" about doing so.[39] Her findings should be viewed against the backdrop of the rising number of women involved in litigation more generally. For as Tim Stretton has shown, more women were traveling long distances to London and staying there for extended periods in order to "wage law."[40]

Widows, like never-married women, were actively involved in the world of credit. Moneylending has been described as the "most prominent economic function of the widow in English rural society between 1500 and 1900"[41] and as a common means of support for widows in towns and cities, including London, as well.[42] Historians describe widow moneylenders as astute investors who diversified their assets in investment portfolios that included secured and unsecured loans at varying rates of interest in order to minimize risk and maximize profit.[43] Widows loaned out substantial portions of their estates, and in several local studies the average size of their loans exceeded those of men.[44] Yet widow moneylenders were not always wealthy. When the widow Joan Snowe died in 1628, she had only nine shillings "in her keeping" but £30 in "Debts upon Specialtye [i.e., on bond]" and twenty-three shillings in "Debts without Specialtye."[45] In his *Discourse Uppon Usurye* of 1572, Thomas Wilson expressed astonishment that usury was being practiced by women of all stripes, describing it as "merveilous straunge and uncharitable." His depiction of female creditors includes "weomen" of small means "in whome a man woulde thinke were no crafte or subtiltie to live," who nonetheless "aske the shillynge pennie for a weeke, which in a yeare amounteth to foure shillynges & foure pence besydes the principall," as well as wealthy women who make "lone[s] of a hundred pounds by the yere" at interest.[46]

The wills of theater people and other documents of stage history reveal that the commercial theaters were not insulated from these dramatic changes in the gendered landscape of urban credit. Women were active within the networks of credit upon which the professional stage relied as they were within the culture at large. Actors turned to female moneylenders, including the wives and widows of theater people, when they were in need of ready cash, borrowing money on bond and at interest. The abstract of the 1620 will of Joan Hovell, widow of actor William Hovell, refers to "£10 and odd money due to her from John Swynnerton and John Edmondes, two players, by obligations [i.e., bonds]."[47] The 1635 will of actor John Shank left the considerable "somme of Threescore and Tenn poundes debt which I doe owe unto her the said mrs Morgan and for which she hath my bond."[48] One playing company (Queen Anne's Men) became indebted to actor Thomas Greene's wife, Susan, when he died in 1612, left her his share in the playing company (worth £80) along with other credits (worth £37) owed to him by the company, and made her executrix of his will.[49] Susan was unrelenting in pursuing these claims and further financial arrangements made with the company, including two additional loans (of £57 10s. and £38), for which the company was to pay her 1s. 8d. for every playing day.[50] At one time, she enlisted the services of a scrivener to draw up "covenants" and "bondes for performing of the said covenants" and eventually filed a suit in the Court of Chancery against the company in 1623 to enforce the payment of their bonds, as a result of which, according to Gurr, the company was forced to break.[51] After the break, three members of the defunct company filed a bill of complaint in Chancery against her, claiming among other things that for the previous eleven years she had charged them "excessive usery" on their debts.[52]

Yet theater people were not always resentful regarding the loans provided them by female creditors: Elizabeth Burbage, wife of Cuthbert Burbage, is mentioned as a creditor in the will of actor Nicholas Tooley (a.k.a. Wilkinson), who left her "the somme of Tenn poundes over and besides such sommes of money as I shall owe unto her att my decease," describing the bequest as "a remembraunce of my love in respect of her motherlie care over me."[53] Based on the evidence of theater people's wills, their attitudes toward the female creditors upon whom they relied ranged from deep gratitude to fierce resentment and indignation. The intensity of such responses arose from the complex "bonds" linking female creditors to male debtors, bonds that were legal and commercial but also affective, and imbued with power relations. Depending on the circumstances, women moneylenders were regarded as indispensable facilitators of, or irritating impediments to, male commercial enterprise and (ad)venture. Among the circumstances that influenced how female creditors were perceived were marital status, "credit" or sexual reputation, and the degree of agency and self-interest (or "will") and expertise (or "skill") they exhibited in their financial and legal dealings. These factors, as we shall see, were crucial in shaping contemporary representations of female creditors in a broad range of cultural texts and provide a compelling context within which to read the gendered bonds of credit in the Sonnets and *The Merchant of Venice*.

Although single-women moneylenders were often depicted as objects of desire, sought-after by men who harbored financial designs on their assets, they were likewise subject to derision and slander by a society prone to view commercially active, unmarried women as prostitutes. An anonymous seventeenth-century broadside ballad entitled *The Mother and Daughter*, for example, casts both the eponymous mother (who is described as a "Meretrix" or bawd) and her unmarried daughter as sexually incontinent. When the mother chides her daughter for her swelling belly, the unwanted sign of a recent sexual tryst, the daughter returns the favor by recounting her mother's myriad sexual escapades (with a Weaver, Tinker, Taylor, etc.). The mother begs her to stop, and the daughter agrees, stipulating, "Upon condition you will give / me all the bondes of your use-money, / To maintain me bravely while I live, / that I may be both blith and bonny." The mother accepts the bargain, promising, "Two fifty pound bonds i'le give into thy handes, / Sweet Nan it is all thy own." The ballad conjures the image of a self-sustaining economy of single female creditors in which fiscal and sexual excesses are passed down from widowed mothers to their unmarried female heirs. It likewise exemplifies the way in which the advent of single women and widows lending money at interest and on bond endowed the commonplaces of usury literature with new, gendered forms. Thus, for example, the common trope of the male usurer with the swollen belly (distended because he "eats the poor") here morphs into the single-woman usuress whose belly is pregnant with bastards as well as coins.[54] The Mother chides Nan that her belly is so large, she appears to be "with-child with two [i.e., with twins]," an image that links Nan's sexual and financial avarice to the excessive fiscal and human capital she generates (recall Autolycus's "usurer's wife [who] was brought to bed of twenty money-bags at a burthen"). The ballad thereby stigmatizes single women's financial independence by linking it to sexual promiscuity. Nan's reply to this charge ("I think that twenty times before, I have been on the very same score") further links unmarried female moneylenders' financial and sexual excesses to their (ac)counting practices by suggesting that in both arenas they are keeping "score."

Another ballad, *The Cloath-Worker Caught in a Trap*, tells of a London cloth worker who is cozened out of forty pounds by a single woman, whom he woos because she makes him believe "she ha[s] mony at use." The cloth worker confesses, "My fingers did itch to be at her coin, / As hoping the mony and she should be mine. / . . . / I followed her closely by day and by night, / The hope of her Mony was all my delight." Perceiving his "greedy intent," the single woman invents a trick to cheat him: she sends an old woman accomplice to tell him that his "Sweet-heart is taking the Lease of a house" but that because "her Money's at use, and out of her hands," she cannot do so unless he lends her forty pounds. If he agrees to the loan, the old woman promises, his sweetheart will become his bride and "make over the house unto [him]" when they are married. The cloth worker gives the old woman forty pounds, but he soon discovers that his wit has been "over-matcht" and that he has "reckon'd [his] Chickens before they were hatcht." The next time he goes to see the young woman, she will "not come neer" him and bids him to go packing. When he asks her to repay the forty pounds, she tells him: "If you were so foolish to give [the old woman] your Coin, / Who came in my name, the fault is not mine." In a repeated refrain, the cloth worker laments, "She made me a promise she would be my Bride. / But I have lost her and my Mony beside." The ballad's mockery is aimed as much at the avaricious cloth worker as it is at the single-woman moneylender: he acknowledges that while he "had mony," it was she who "had the wit" and that he would not have been cozened had his fingers not "itch[ed] to be at her coin." Although the single woman in the ballad merely feigns that she has "mony at use" as a "Plot" to "Cheat Him of His Money," the success of that plot relies on the familiarity of all involved with the phenomenon of single-women moneylenders.

Both ballads play on the cultural visibility of single women who support themselves by lending money at interest. While positing the desirability of such women as marriage prospects, they also acknowledge that certain savvy female moneylenders use their wits to remain single. Both depict single women as conspiring with and relying on one another, echoing historical evidence that unmarried women's social relationships were "significantly female-centered" and that they often opted to live or work with female kin or other, unrelated, single women.[55] Finally, both represent self-propagating female economies that function at the (financial and sexual) expense of "honest" male crafts- and tradesmen. In so doing, both function as cautionary tales, albeit to slightly different ends. While the first warns of the sexual and financial excesses of single-women moneylenders by suggesting that they let their bodies out to "use," just as they do their money, and further links this excess to their implementation of "bonds," the second ballad cautions men who have designs on single women's "use-money" that such women cannot be trusted to hand over their property to their fiancés in marriage, even when they promise to do so, and that they will more likely use their wits to accumulate wealth for themselves in order to remain unmarried.

Other popular literature responded to the advent of the female moneylender not by cautioning male consumers but by offering them a compensatory fantasy of sexual mastery in which female creditors were duped out of their money by male debtors. These narratives often focus on female creditors at the lower end of the social spectrum, such as the figure of the "hostess" of a tavern, inn, or ordinary. (Hostesses were known not only for extending sales credit to their customers but for lending money to those who ate, drank, or lodged with them.) The jest is usually at the female creditor's expense, turning on her failure to be repaid for the credit she has extended. This failure is attributed to her being overly credulous and allowing herself to be gulled and/or seduced. In a ballad entitled *The Kind Beleeving Hostesse*, for example, the hostess is both "pretty" and "witty," but not witty enough to outsmart the balladeer, who is her debtor. His constant refrain is: "I owe my Hostesse money, / shee takes mee for her Debtor: / on the buttery doore / stands my Score, / the further on the better." Her own wit apparently lies in her practice of serving scant measures at full price ("her pots are small") and keeping prostitutes on the side ("She keepes both Besse and Dolly, / Brave wenches stout and jolly"), practices that rationalize the balladeer's reluctance to repay his debt by casting her commercial and sexual "credit" or reputation in an unfavorable light. The balladeer brags that in spite of her wit, "To trust me shee is willing" and that he will therefore "look to her filling"—that is, when she fills his pots with ale, he will sexually fill her "pot" instead of paying her. He concludes with the promise, "With hony words I will screw her, / And many a fine tricke shew her, / I'le keep me away, / When she is to pay, Her Baker and her Brewer. / I owe my Hostesse money, etc." The term "screw" here suggests not only that the balladeer will insinuate himself into the hostess's favor but that he will screw her both sexually and financially by forcing or coercing money from her (see *OED*, "screw, *v.*" 5b, 10b, 13).[56] Although still depicted as desirable, this female creditor is clearly also a dupe. The sexual act between male debtor and female creditor is here construed as a way to avoid repayment rather than as a form of repayment exacted by her, as in Sonnets 134–36.

Shakespeare explores the conpensatory fantasy of the credulous female creditor in several plays. The comedic potential of the hostess-as-creditor is taken up in the Induction scenes of *The Taming of the Shrew*, where the Hostess threatens to have Christopher Sly arrested for failing to pay a debt owed for glasses he has broken (Ind. 1.6–13).[57] When Sly later awakens in the Lord's chamber he apparently believes he is still at the alehouse and asks for "a pot of small ale" (Ind. 2.1). When told he is mistaken and is in fact a great lord, he replies: "Ask Marion Hacket, the fat ale-wife of Wincot, if she know me not. If she say I am not fourteen pence on the score for sheer ale, score me up for the lying'st knave in Christendom" (Ind. 2.21–24). Sly's remark offers a facetious rendition of the contemporary notion (discussed at greater length below) that keeping an accurate reckoning of one's accounts provided a mirror of one's Christian virtue. The play draws an implicit connection, as does *The Kind Beleeving Hostesse*, between the male customer's refusal to pay his debts to the hostess and her refusal to serve "seal'd quarts" (Ind. 2.89) or full measures of ale. When Sly "call[s] out for Cicely Hacket," the "woman's maid of the house" in his sleep (l. 90), we infer that he has filled Cicely's "pot" sexually in lieu of paying the hostess for filling his.

The topos of the overly credulous female creditor likewise appears in the second Henriad, where Falstaff chalks up an ever-mounting score with Hostess Quickly. In *1 Henry IV* he is indebted to her not only for the linen shirts, "diet, and by-drinkings" she has provided but for "money lent" to him in the amount of four and twenty pounds (3.3.71–72).[58] Refusing to pay her "a denier" (l. 77), he accuses her of harboring thieves who have picked his pockets. In *2 Henry IV*, Quickly has become a widow, and Falstaff's debt to her has escalated to "a hundred mark" (2.1.30–31).[59] Like other widow moneylenders of the period, she decides to wage law, entering an "action" of debt against him (l. 1). "A hundred mark is a long one for a poor lone woman to bear," she complains, "I have borne, and borne, and borne, and have been fubbed off [i.e., put off deceitfully; see *OED*, "fob, *v.*"], and fubbed off, and fubbed off, from this day to that day, that it is a shame to be thought on. There is no honesty in such dealing, unless a woman should be made an ass and a beast, to bear every knave's wrong" (ll. 30–37). Although the bawdy language Quickly characteristically uses to describe her forbearance of Falstaff's debts places her squarely within the tradition of the hostess who is financially and sexually "screwed" by her male customers, the pathos of her description of the plight of the "poor lone woman" invites a sympathetic response. When the Lord Chief Justice arrives, she pleads her cause to him directly, describing herself as "a poor widow of Eastcheap" (2.1.68). We might discern a degree of rhetorical strategizing in her plea, insofar as similar complaints were commonly used by women, whether impoverished or not, Tim Stretton has shown, when they sought to defend their financial interests in equity courts.[60] The strategy is an effective one, as the Chief Justice chides Falstaff, "Are you not ashamed to enforce a poor widow to so rough a course to come by her own?" (ll. 80–81). As she continues to prosecute her complaint, however, her credulity once again comes to the fore when she reveals that she was seduced into believing Falstaff would marry her and make her a "lady" (l. 90). In the end, the scene returns to the stereotype of the susceptible, oversexed hostess when Quickly demands, "didst thou not kiss me, and bid me fetch thee thirty shillings?" (ll. 99–100). The Chief Justice determines, "You have, as it appears to me, practised upon the easy-yielding spirit of this woman, and made her serve your uses both in purse and in person" (ll. 112–15), and orders him to pay the debt. After further wrangling and seduction, however, she is once again "fubbed off" and promises to withdraw the action and lend Falstaff an additional ten pounds, even if she has to pawn her gown to raise the sum (l. 156).

A similar scene in Marston's *Histrio-Mastix* (1598–99) does not end so well for the hostess's male debtors, who in this case are a motley troupe of players, Sir Oliver Owlet's Men. Fallen on hard times (the play repeatedly references the dearth and famine of the 1590s), the players are unable to pay their tavern bill.[61] The "Hostesse" enters, chiding, "Post me no posting [i.e., don't try to delay]; pay me the shot [i.e., tavern bill], / Yow live by wit; but we must live by mony." When the players "fub" her off, as Falstaff does Quickly, she calls in the Constable, in response to which they bring in their "hamper" of costumes and offer her a "cloke to pawne." Complaining that the cloak is only worth "fower groats," the Hostesse begrudgingly accepts it as collateral for their debt. Realizing that their credit is "crakt," the players decide that they must "leave playing" and "fal to worke" again, taking up their former trades, even though "worke after playing [is] unpossible." The scene serves as a reminder of the players' precarious finances and reliance on credit to remain solvent, credit relations that might place them under the obligation of lowly hostesses and female shopkeepers, as well as wealthy widows like Susan Greene. Although the play's satire of Owlet's Men serves to distance the threat of insolvency—while also deriding unskilled players in terms used by puritan preachers and civic authorities to attack players in general—it nonetheless demonstrates the high stakes of day-to-day credit transactions through its depiction of the company's break, however humorously conceived. As Henslowe's accounts reflect, the professional players were known to spend both small and large sums not only drinking and dining but also transacting theater business and conducting play readings at inns and taverns.[62] That the sort of predicament faced by Sir Oliver Owlet's Men as portrayed by Marston was not at all far-fetched, particularly during the tough times of the 1590s, is suggested by a letter from Henslowe to Alleyn in September 1593, where he relates that the Earl of Pembroke's Men were forced to pawn their costumes and return home after touring unsuccessfully (and undoubtedly running up inn and tavern bills) in the provinces.[63]

Compensatory fantasies in which male debtors avoid repayment of loans to female creditors by means of their wit or sexual prowess were not surprisingly quite popular during the 1590s and likewise appear in city comedies whose plots centered on the seduction and marriage of wealthy usurers' daughters.[64] In William Haughton's *English-men for My Money: or, A Pleasant Comedy, Called, A Woman Will Have Her Will* (1598), for example, "three English Gentlemen," who have "pawnde . . . their Livings and their Lands" to the "Portingale" usurer Pisaro, marry his daughters and thereby "possesse / Their Patrimonies and their Landes againe," as the daughters' "Dowries redeem th[eir] debt[s]" (ll. 23–24, 26–27). In this wishful solution to the dilemma of the male debtor, the agency or "will" of the usurer's daughters, referred to in the play's subtitle, perfectly mirrors that of their suitors: Pisaro's daughters want nothing more than to hand over their father's wealth, interest free, to his debtors via their dowries when they marry. They even encourage their suitors to "spend at large" and borrow more money in the meantime, since their "mariage day will all [their debts] discharge" (ll. 368–69). "Weele pay the intrest, and the principall," they promise (l. 389). Although purportedly about female willfulness, the play effectively elides the independent wills of the daughters, who function as conduits of interest-free capital between men. In the end, the sexual mastery of the three male debtors compensates in full for their prodigal spending habits: "Weele make you mothers of six goodly Boyes," they promise the daughters, and gloat among themselves, "Weele . . . / . . . cansell all our bondes in their great Bellies" (ll. 1907, 1912). In contrast to the swelling belly of Nan, the usuress's daughter in the ballad of *The Mother and Daughter*, Pisaro's daughters' pregnant bellies represent the cancellation, rather than the escalation, of male indebtedness. *English-men for My Money* depicts a world in which Englishmen use their wits to access "use-money" through their sexual seduction of single women, who appear to have no independent "will" of their own, and thus holds out a promised alternative to the cautionary tale of *The Cloath-Worker Caught in a Trap*.

Pisaro's daughters are further sexualized by their tutor, Anthony, when he is about to be dismissed by Pisaro for delivering the young women love missives from their suitors instead of lessons. Anthony facetiously defends himself by commenting, "Well sir, I taught them not to keepe a Marchants Booke, or cast accompt: yet to a word much like that word Accounte" (ll. 150–52). As Lloyd Kermode glosses this line, "Anthony jokes that he is teaching the daughters something very similar to 'account[ing]': (1) how to settle the accounts of their lovers, now mortgaged to their father, and (2) how to use 'a cunt.'"[65] Anthony's bawdy pun on (ac)count/a cunt also seems to imply that teaching girls "to use 'a cunt'" is in his view less objectionable than teaching them to "cast accompt" (i.e., to sum up or reckon scores, do arithmetic, and "keepe a Marchants Booke"), as Pisaro unquestionably does. Through their marital alliance with the English gentlemen, he intimates, the girls will be purged of the mercantile values and practices associated with their usurer-father. His remark, it is worth noting, suggests that teaching young women "to keepe a Marchants Booke, or cast accompt[s]" was a contested, although by no means unheard of, practice during the period.

The phenomenon of women lending money at interest and on bond, and using new accounting techniques and legal instruments to protect their assets, thus generated a range of responses in popular print culture, as inflected by the marital status, sexual chastity (or lack thereof), and perceived "will," "skill" and "wit" of the female creditor in question. More often than not, cultural representations of female creditors were distinctly ambivalent, carrying both positive and negative valences. Single-women moneylenders were simultaneously objects of desire, seduction, and courtship by men who "itched" to be at their coin and were slandered for their purported sexual incontinence. They were viewed with a mixture of gratitude (for their provision of much-needed business capital) and resentment (for charging interest and exacting penalties for non-payment). The positive and/or negative valence of these representations often turned on the degree to which women moneylenders were perceived as exercising fiscal or legal ability and expertise in their own self-interest. Those who kept track or "score" of their excessive gains and who manifested financial and legal savvy by waging law against their debtors, like the usuress of Sonnets 134–36, were decried as covetous, lustful, and deceitful, while those deemed lacking in agency, resorting to moneylending out of poverty or necessity rather than greed, were by contrast depicted as victims worthy of sympathy and charity.

Within the contemporary theological debate on usury, the female creditor's agency became a subject of explicit controversy. Polemicists who wished to defend lending money at interest seized on the many scriptural references to God as the protector of widows and the "fatherless" in order to characterize single women's and widows' interest-bearing loans as evidence of God's special mercy toward them.[66] In so doing, they tended to portray female moneylenders as lacking in agency and ability, or "will" and "skill." Widows who had "stockes of money" but wanted "skill or power to imploy the same"[67] and whose "inhabilite to manage worldly affaires, & to withstand wrong" left them "no other way to get their living" would "spend their stockes" and be "quite undone" if they were not allowed to lend money at interest.[68] Since God exhorts us "so often in Scripture to provide for the fatherlesse and widowes," it was reasoned, "is it not a safe way by this meanes to allot them a certainty for the use of their moneyes, their principall being still preserved; they maintained by the interest; and the Common-weale to enjoy both the moneyes of them who want skill [i.e., orphans and widows], and the skill of them who want money [i.e., male investors whose business ventures will be funded by their loans]?"[69] By 1641 an anonymous "Well wisher of the Common-wealth" would go so far as to argue against lowering the legal maximum interest rate, claiming that to do so would hurt widows who had "neither Skill nor Will to manage it in Trade of Merchandize" and who consequently put their "money [out] . . . to Interest."[70] By characterizing widows and maids as lacking in will and skill, and as socially vulnerable and victimized, their defenders could construe women's moneylending as an expression of God's mercy rather than as a self-interested, profit-making venture. Ironically, as mentioned above, this rhetorical strategy was adopted by financially savvy single women and widows themselves when they defended their own commercial interests in equity courts.

Opponents of usury refused to accept this interpretation of scripture, arguing that the Bible draws no fine distinctions between "the Merchants Usurie . . . and the Widdowes Usurie."[71] God demonstrates his condemnation of "Widdowes Usurie," they maintained, by immediately following his admonition "Ye shall not trouble any widowe" with the prohibition *against* usury (Exod. 22:22–25).[72] Rather than offering widows a special dispensation to practice usury, the proximity of these two injunctions indicates that widows "of all others" should "not come neere unto that transgression."[73] Far from being a manifestation of God's charity, widows' moneylending actually precludes such charity and expresses a lack of faith in divine providence: "Hath God then so many waies bound himselfe by promise to provide for widowes . . . and shall these by usurie withdraw themselves out of his fatherly providence? Shall these be secured by usurious contracts against the act of God himselfe? Verily God will take it more unkindly at their hands, then at any other."⁷⁴ Opponents of female moneylending likewise drew on gender ideology to cast maids and widows as inappropriate moneylenders: "Shall these two Ages, which of all others ought to be most holie and heavenlie," one treatise asks, "the one for innocencie, and the other for devotion, be stained with usurie?"⁷⁵

In effect, anti-usury polemicists accused their opponents of bad faith, of allowing the general practice of usury to "creep in under the pretence of widowes."⁷⁶ Widows who are truly needy, they claimed, "have no stocke at all" to lend. How, then, shall those widows be provided for who "lacke money to put out?"⁷⁷ In Thomas Wilson's treatise, which takes the form of a dialogue, the Lawyer (who favors widows' moneylending) inadvertently demonstrates the hypocrisy of the "poor widow" defense by citing the example of a purportedly impoverished, helpless widow who is left the considerable sum of £500 by her merchant husband, with an additional £200 to support each of her children. The Preacher responds that such a widow would be quite able to support herself and her children through "buyinge or sellyng" or some other "lawful trade" without entering "into the devils dungeon, and seekyng out these croked corners of wicked ockre and dampnable usurye." Under no circumstances, he argues, should "unlawfull trade . . . be used, to advance welfare," for God "wylleth all . . . to lyve as he hath commaunded by lawful trade."⁷⁸ Ironically, polemicists opposed to female moneylenders thus endowed them with greater agency, financial savvy, and capacity to earn a living through "honest" trades than did their defenders (while failing to acknowledge the restrictions many of these trades placed on female employment).⁷⁹ Such treatises deployed a variety of rhetorical tactics to buttress this argument. The allegorical figure of "impudent ladie Usurie," for example, was invoked to impugn the pride and willfulness of women who loaned money at interest. By depicting usury in the abstract as female, authors made their arguments appear particularly applicable to women moneylenders.⁸⁰

As if to underscore the agency of the widow moneylender, Roger Fenton addresses her directly in his 1611 *Treatise of Usurie*—apparently assuming that such women took an active interest in the contemporary debate and formed part of his readership. "I write unto you widowes," he apostrophizes, admonishing, "during the time of your widowhood, by this trade of Usurie, divers of you have attained unto farre greater wealth then your husbands themselves ever could." "Is it not strange," he asks, "that a sillie woman . . . should thrive better, with greater ease and security, then her husband with the same or better meanes ever could?" His imaginary widow-interlocutor interprets this insult as a compliment and "thanke[s] God for it," claiming "it is his blessing." Fenton scoffs that the widow's good fortune has come not from any "extraordinary blessing of God" but from "the ordinarie trade of Usurie." God, he instructs, ordains widowhood "to bee an estate of humiliation," but she has "made it, by the practise of Usurie, to be an estate of exaltation." Eschewing the risks of "honest and lawful trading" and "lawfull adventures," she instead embraces the security afforded by written instruments of credit. Her "resolute purpose," he maintains, is "to be secured against any act both of God and man."[81]

Religious polemics against female moneylenders were particularly opposed to women's use of formal instruments of credit, such as bonds, whose purpose was to guarantee this ungodly security.[82] Rather than resort to such means, Fenton argues, widows should entrust their estates to men who will employ them in lawful, albeit risky, business ventures: "Why dare you not trust [men] to imploy your money for you by way of partnership; allowing them a proportion of gaine for their skill and care, and bearing answerably part of the losse?"[83] In spite of the financial savvy he imputes to her, Fenton persists in calling his imaginary widow "sillie woman" because her care for her business affairs is not matched by her care for her soul or for the commonwealth.[84] "How doe you silly women know who is oppressed or bitten by such gaine?" he asks, and chides that she does not care so long as they "*pay you your money.*"[85] In a final plea he invokes gender ideology, exhorting the widow to "let the tendernesse of [her] sexe worke unto a remorse" and cautioning her not to believe other treatises that may favor her cause because "it is dangerous to relie upon them, who give most liberty in the matters of deceitfull *mamon.*"[86]

Conduct manuals for women likewise participated in the contemporary debate regarding the propriety of female moneylending, particularly concerning their exercise of independent "will" and "skill." Richard Brathwaite's 1631 treatise *The English Gentlewoman* assumes his female readership's familiarity with the figure of the "Usuresse" and admonishes those who would follow her trade. Such women, he maintains, "are onely for profit" and "become so wedded to the world, as they . . . estrange themselves from offices of Neighbourhood, to improve their revenewes." Female moneylenders are represented as placing self-interest above the interests of community or the common weal. With respect to usury, they are more interested in knowing what is allowed by statute than what is allowed by God. As a cautionary tale, Brathwaite offers the example of "a certaine Usuresse" who is visited by a "Religious Divine" on her deathbed. He tells her that in order to be saved, she must be "contrite in heart," "confesse her sinnes," and "make restitution [to her debtors] according to her meanes." She replies, "Two of those first I will doe willingly: but to doe the last, I shall hold it a difficulty; for should I make restitution, what would remain to raise my children their portion?" When the Divine insists that she must do so if she wishes to save her soul, she asks dubiously, "Yea but . . . Doe our Learned men and Scriptures say so?" He replies, "Yea surely." Refusing to take his word for it, however, she determines, "I will try . . . whether they say true or no, for I will restore nothing."[87] It is not entirely clear whether the phrase "I will try" refers to the widow's resolve, come what may, to bequeath her usurious profits to her children, making an experiment with her soul in order to see what will come of it, or whether she intends to make her own inquiry into this doubtful, doctrinal question by reading the varied opinions of "our Learned men and Scriptures" in order to arrive at her own conclusion. We might recall in this context Fenton's assumption that the widow moneylender who has bought his treatise will attempt to consult the opinions of other learned divines and in so doing may discover that some have written in her favor. Fenton's and Brathwaite's texts are clearly addressed to a female readership interested in the controversies surrounding usury and familiar with the intricacies of statute law concerning formal instruments of credit.

Such an audience might well have admired Portia's exercise of wit, will, and skill in protecting her assets, waging law, and interpreting statutes regarding bonds of credit in the trial scene of *The Merchant of Venice*. Having surveyed the complex roles played by women in early modern England's credit economy and their varied cultural representations, we are better equipped to consider Portia's agency vis-à-vis her portion, a question that has loomed large in previous scholarship on the play. The longstanding interpretation of Portia as one who freely gives and is herself given, rather than as one who lends, follows from the traditional contrast between Belmont, construed as a green world of mercy and aristocratic largesse, and Venice, with its pettifogging, mercantile commercialism.[88] According to this interpretation, Portia's portion is initially circumscribed by the dictates of her dead father's will and bypasses her agency entirely as it is passes to her husband under the law of coverture.[89] This reading assumes that single women's and widows' financial interests in and management of their inherited capital simply evaporated when they married. Yet scholars have known for some time that "there were important ways in which wives were able to circumvent [the] rigidities"[90] of the common law, such as their use of trusts for "sole and separate estate," a practice that began in the 1580s and spread rapidly thereafter.[91] Fathers could establish such trusts on behalf of their daughters to protect their portions or inheritances, as could heiresses whose fathers had predeceased them prior to marriage; they could even be established during coverture by an agent on the wife's behalf. Stipulating (in contradiction of the law of coverture) that the assets in question "shall be for [the wife's] sole and separate use and benefit, independent and exclusive of her husband and without it being anywise subject to his debts, control, interference or engagement,"[92] such trusts were defensible in equity courts, such as the Court of Chancery. Beginning in the 1590s, petitions were increasingly exhibited to Chancery by married women and their agents seeking to enforce the terms of these legal instruments, and a series of favorable rulings led to their more confident use. By such means, fathers were able to protect their daughters' assets and wives and widows their own assets from avaricious, impecunious, or insolvent spouses. More important in the present context, the advent of trusts for separate estate enabled married women to lend money during coverture, even to their own husbands.

Margaret Hunt and Craig Muldrew cite evidence of seventeenth-century wives lending money drawn from their separate assets to their husbands and other male relatives and employing formal instruments of credit to do so.[93] Even when wives had no formal trusts set aside for separate estate, Amy Erickson has demonstrated, they still expected to take out of their marriages what they had brought in, which suggests that women may have thought of their marital portions as de facto loans, rather than gifts, to their spouses.[94] If wives did consider their portions as loans, it would help explain their active interest in the financial management of their assets during marriage. Needless to say, men did not relinquish their claims on their wives' portions easily, particularly when hard-pressed by creditors.[95] Hunt cites numerous cases of husbands resorting to violence when their wives refused to hand over money set aside for their own use: one husband held a dagger to his wife's throat, threatening to "cut her Neck off" unless she would consent to sell some of her separate property to pay off his debts.[96] Such violence reveals that wives' separate property was hardly uncontested terrain in early modern England. Indeed, it was the source of considerable strife within marriages and of ideological conflict within the culture at large. Still, Hunt argues, as the concept of separate estate gained increasing cultural acceptance it "undeniably had the effect of empowering some women," who administered their assets "as part of an ongoing trade or program of investment" that included interest-bearing loans.[97] In the remainder of this chapter, I shall argue that *The Merchant of Venice* registers the tensions within early modern culture surrounding the advent of wives' separate estate and that this cultural context illuminates previously puzzling aspects of the play, in particular Portia's display of wit, will, and skill in the trial scene and the marital strife that unsettles act 5.

Shakespeare and his contemporaries were well aware of the advent of wives' separate property: plays of the period contain numerous references to trusts for separate estate, and the wills of theater people reveal their familiarity with and use of them.[98] The 1634 will of actor William Browne, for example, makes clear that his mother, Susan Greene, had set aside separate property for herself in the form of a trust held by him when she married her third husband, James Baskerville.[99] She was wise to have done so, as several years after her marriage to Baskerville he fled to Ireland when it was discovered that he had a second wife.[100] It was during Susan's marriage to Baskerville that she would be accused by Queen Anne's Men of charging "excessive usury" on their debts to her, as mentioned above. Susan Baskerville and her peers set important precedents in a number of ways: they belonged to the first generation of women to inherit shares and other credits in the all-male, professional playing companies, to protect their assets by setting aside trusts for separate estate during marriage, to pursue such claims in equity courts, and to lend money as a profit-making enterprise using formal instruments of credit to members of their own families (including their own husbands) and others to fund commercial and theatrical ventures.[101] It is with such women in mind that I would like to reconsider Portia's exercise of wit, will, and skill in protecting her marital portion, waging law, and interpreting statutes regarding bonds of credit.[102]

The social tensions surrounding wives' separate property were in all likelihood heightened during the economic crisis of the 1590s when *The Merchant of Venice* was written, when a combination of price inflation, scarcity of hard currency, and sudden reduction in the availability of credit, according to Craig Muldrew, "meant that more households were unable to pay their debts," leading to "a domino effect along chains of credit."[103] Toward the end of the decade, as we have seen, William Haughton's *English-men for My Money* (1598) would depict the interest-free capital of a usurer's daughters as a wishful resolution to the dilemma faced by insolvent male debtors. Although *The Merchant of Venice* likewise plays on the scenario of the wealthy-heiress-as-debt-dissolving-cash-cow in its fashioning of both Portia and Jessica, the play also pushes this scenario past its comfort zone in exploring how issues of trust and credit between wealthy single women and their suitors play out post-nuptially.

Portia's novel solution to the legal strictures that circumscribe her agency or will does not abrogate the law but maneuvers skillfully within it. In so doing, she relies on precisely the sort of ingenuity exhibited by Susan Greene/ Baskerville and her peers in pursuing equitable remedies to the rigidities of the common law of coverture.[104] Read within this context, Portia's vexed evocation of the rhetoric of coverture in her dealings with Bassanio hardly seems to represent a "'taming' of the independent woman" reduced to a will-less gift exchanged between men.[105] Her ambivalence is first signaled by her indecision as to whether (or how) to "teach" Bassanio "to choose right" (3.2.10–11) and by her strikingly equivocal references to the legal fiction of coverture:

> Beshrew your eyes,
> They have o'erlook'd me and divided me,
> One half of me is yours, the other half yours,—
> Mine own I would say: but if mine then yours,
> And so all yours; O these naughty times
> Puts bars between the owners and their rights!
> And so though yours, not yours.
> (ll. 14–20)

We might simply read this speech as expressing a daughter's divided duty to her father and her potential future husband, in which case the "bars" she reproves would be the paternal dictum that prevents Bassanio from claiming what is rightfully his. Portia's recourse to the language of coverture ("if mine then yours, / And so all yours") would then indeed function to elide her will, agency, and inherited estate by suggesting that they are already possessed by Bassanio, who surveys and divides her as an owner would his property. Yet Portia's tone is neither passive nor acquiescent but rather chiding: she "beshrew[s]" her suitor directly, her "naughty" father indirectly, and the law's rigidity more generally. Insofar as it is Portia who apportions or divides her property here and elsewhere in the play, her will and skill would seem merely to be veiled or covered by the rhetoric of coverture rather than simply eviscerated, suggesting that her "Mine own I *would* say" (emphasis added) has a volitional resonance. Read in this way, the legal stricture or "bar" she scorns would refer to the formulaic rehearsal of the (il)logic of coverture, and she herself would be the owner whose rights are denied. Her "though yours, not yours" might then be read as an apt motto of the skillful maneuvering through which women began in the 1590s to circumvent the "bar" of coverture and as suggestive of the control she will herself retain over her inherited portion.[106]

When the rhetoric of coverture reappears later in the scene, Portia rings a change within it that will allow her to retain mastery over what she is so loath to relinquish:

> Myself, and what is mine, to you and yours
> Is now converted. But now I was the lord
> Of this fair mansion, master of my servants,
> Queen o'er myself: and even now, but now,
> This house, these servants, and this same myself
> Are yours, my Lord, I give them with this ring,
> Which when you part from, lose, or give away,
> Let it presage the ruin of your love,
> And be my vantage to exclaim on you. (ll. 166–74)[107]

From the moment it appears, the wedding band is defined by Portia as a contractual bond (the terms "bond" and "band" were used interchangeably during the period)[108] of trust and credit. The gift of herself and her estate are bound to the ring, becoming conditional upon its (and by extension their) protection. Although her husband's, it is yet not his ("though yours, not yours"), since he may "neither sell, nor give" it away (4.1.437–39). The wedding band is thus defined as something a husband must "keep for" his wife (5.1.225) and as such is more loan than gift. When Portia discovers that her groom's financial condition is "worse than nothing" (3.2.259), she apportions him capital to pay off his debts and then follows him to Venice to ensure its safekeeping.[109] In so doing, she skillfully maneuvers within the legal system to protect her portion and hedge against risk. In the end, she will devise a scheme to provide "surety" for her marriage bond as well (5.1.254). The play thereby associates Portia's will and skill with the surety of bonds and contrasts it with the risks of male (ad)venture. Unlike contemporary polemics against female moneylending, however, it does not condemn Portia's safeguarding of her band/bond as an attempt to circumvent divine providence but rather aligns it, I shall argue, with an emergent ethos of virtuous, Christian exactitude.

When Portia bestows her ring on Bassanio with the condition, "when you part from, lose, or give [it] away, / Let it presage the ruin of your love, / And be my vantage to exclaim on you" (ll. 172–74), she echoes Shylock's earlier use of "advantage" as a synonym for the interest paid on a loan, when he says to Antonio: "Me thoughts you said, you neither lend nor borrow / Upon advantage" (1.3.64–65).[110] Yet to say that Portia's language echoes Shylock's is not entirely accurate, for she demonstrates her own familiarity with formal instruments of credit even before Shylock is ever mentioned or appears onstage. In act 1, for example, she jokes that her Scottish suitor "borrowed a box of the ear" of her English suitor "and swore he would pay him again when he was able," adding that her French suitor "became his surety, and seal'd under for another" (1.2.76–79). In the trial scene, it is Shylock's language that replicates Portia's, rather than vice versa, when he describes his pound of flesh as "dearly bought" (4.1.100), recalling her earlier remark to Bassanio, "Since you are dear bought, I will love you dear" (3.2.312), a comment that underscores his debt to her, both in purse and person. Through such parallels, the play invites us to question how Portia's marriage bond differs from, and how it resembles, Shylock's pound of flesh. Critics who read Portia as Shylock's antithesis have difficulty with the lexicon of credit and accounting that characterizes her vocabulary throughout the play, which is replete with references to accounts, full sums, terms in gross, oaths of credit, sureties, and the like (see also 3.2.155, 157–58, 5.1.246, 254).[111] Without discounting Portia's rhetoric of liberality, I would like to suggest that the ideological resonances of her speech and her character pull in two directions: toward the familiar figure of the bountiful heiress who willingly hands over her portion to pay her husband's debts, on the one hand, and, less familiarly, toward the emergent figure of the married female creditor whose use of bonds, new (ac)counting techniques, and skilled navigation of legal systems enables her to exercise her will with respect to her marital property and to extend loans, even to her own husband, on the other.

Portia's vocabulary of counting, ciphering, and reckoning recalls similar language in Sonnets 134–36 addressed to the female usurer, inviting comparison of the two figures.[112] In certain respects they would appear to be diametrically opposed: whereas Portia laments that she "cannot choose one, nor refuse none" (1.2.25–26) because her "will" has been "curb'd by the will of a dead father" (ll. 24–25), the usuress of the Sonnets has "*Will* to boot and *Will* in overplus" (135.2), yet can still "add . . . / One will . . . more" (ll. 11–12), both because she is "covetous" (134.6) and because "In things of great receipt" the "number one is reckon'd none" (136.7–8). In addition to deploying the imagery of female avarice associated with the figure of "impudent Ladie Usurie," Sonnet 136 here draws on the classical notion that one is no number but is rather the principle of number, indivisible in itself, in order to set up a gendered opposition between the male one and the female "nothing" (136.12).[113] This opposition is destabilized, however, by the usuress's surplus of "will[s]"— a term suggestive of her insatiable wants and the spaciousness of the receptacle in which her sexual and monetary "treasure" (l. 5) is stored. So large is her will that her debtors "pass untold" (l. 9) or uncounted, suggesting an inexactitude in her (ac)counting practices born of excess. Although her debtors "[pay] the whole" (134.14) or full sum of their debt, she always demands more—the "overplus" (135.2) of usury. The "whole" or unified "one" they pay disappears into her unfillable hole, consumed by her "nothing," like a drop of rain in the sea (l. 9), and they remain perpetually indebted to her. The usuress is thus figured as a cipher or zero that turns her debtors' all into naught while at the same time increasing her own profit or "great receipt."[114] Her willfulness is thereby coupled with her "surety" and exaltation, and with the perpetual uncertainty, insecurity, and want (both lack *and* desire) of her male debtors. The usuress's "nothing" is likewise suggestive of her "noting," or the notarial practice associated with the bonds that afford her this surety.

Elizabethans in general, and Shakespeare in particular, were fascinated by the figure and mathematical function of the cipher or zero due to its association with Hindu-Arabic numerals, which were only just starting to come into widespread use in England.[115] The term "cipher" referred not only to the symbol for zero but also to Hindu-Arabic numeration generally and its use in arithmetical calculations, or what was then considered the new math. Although of no value in itself, the cipher increased or decreased the value of other figures, depending on its positioning relative to them: placed after a number, it increased the value of that number tenfold; placed before it in decimal fractions, it decreased the number's value in the same proportion. Because many people still used Roman numerals and relied upon counters to do calculations, however, ciphering in general, and the cipher or zero in particular, took on cryptic or occult associations.[116] During a period in which the legally tolerated rate of interest on loans was 10 percent, the cipher also came to be associated with the calculation of interest and indebtedness: its power to increase or decrease by a factor of ten suggested the gains and losses of creditors and debtors, respectively.[117]

Portia evokes the cipher and ciphering when she tells Bassanio, "[T]he full sum of me / Is sum of [nothing]" (3.2.157–58) when they are betrothed. Although editors frequently prefer the Quarto's "full sume of something" to the Folio's "sum of nothing,"[118] Q's reading elides Portia's evocation of the cipher's power to render naught as well as to generate increase (as it does in the preceding lines, where she says she "would be trebled twenty times [her] self" for Bassanio [l. 153] and wishes herself "A thousand times more fair, ten thousand times more rich, / . . . only to stand high in [Bassanio's] account" [ll. 154–55], or when she later tells him to "Pay [Shylock] six thousand, and deface the bond," then to "Double six thousand, and then treble that," and finally

"To pay the petty debt twenty times over" [ll. 298–99, 306]). More troubling to critics than Portia's language of multiplication (suggestive of liberality), however, is her language of division (suggesting divisiveness and economic self-interest), deployed most famously when she bars Shylock from taking "the division of the twentieth part / Of one poor scruple" more than what is stipulated by his bond (4.1.325–26; see also 3.2.15). Although Portia's vocabulary evokes the (ac)counting practices of contemporary female creditors, her exactitude aligns her with an emergent ethos of virtuous, Christian exactitude that sets her apart from the untold or un(ac)countable excess associated with both Shylock and the "Dark Lady" usuress of Sonnets 134–36.

Early English treatises on arithmetic and accounting helped institute this emergent ethos and offer a compelling context within which to understand Portia's use of such terminology, as well as her rhetorical emphasis on exactitude in the trial scene.[119] Such treatises repeatedly stress the "many daungers and discomodities" visited upon those who fail to keep and understand their accounts "exactly," "diligently and perfightly."[120] This ethic of exactitude was grounded in the capacity of Hindu-Arabic numeration or "ciphering" to calculate and record with the precision afforded by decimal arithmetic. Because account books were often used in the absence of, or in addition to, formal instruments of credit as evidence in legal proceedings involving debt, exactitude and precision likewise took on a juridical value: treatises on accounting insist that "there may not be any alteration of Cyphers, [or] blotting" in account books, "otherwise the books are of no credit in Law, or before any Magistrate; whereas otherwise much credit is given to books well and orderly kept, for the deciding and determination of many controversies."[121] These treatises maintained that justice in debt litigation relied upon precision, which was a matter not only of neatness but of mathematical rigor. One popular treatise claimed, "The man, that is ignorant of Arithmetike, is no[t] neither meete to be a Judge. . . . For howe can hee wel understande another mannes cause appertayning to distribution of goods, or other dettes, or of summes of money, if he bee ignorante of Arythmetike?"[122] Portia's arithmetical verdict would doubtless have appealed to those who embraced this ethic of exactitude, including an emergent class of numerate female creditors who kept account books and waged law to protect their portions.[123] An early seventeenth-century English engraving by George Glover depicts the allegorical figure of Lady Arithmetic, one of the seven liberal arts, using her newly acquired skill of ciphering with Hindu-Arabic numerals to produce "goulden summes" or increase her wealth, as reflected in her rich apparel (see Figure 5).

Figure 5. George Glover, *Arithmetica*, c. 1625–35, multiplying using ciphers. Engraving from a series of the seven liberal arts, composed of three-quarter-length women in fashionable attire. The caption reads, "Thy depth *Arithmetick* there's none can knowe, / since from bare one, such Countles numbers growe. / W^ch multiply'de, to Infinites it comes; / making base counters, stand for Goulden summes." © The Trustees of the British Museum.

Critics' discomfort with Portia's reliance on exactitude and precision in the trial scene stems from its apparent discord with the view that the scene represents a contest between the Old Testament law of the flesh and the New Testament law of the spirit and/or between the rigidity of the common law and the flexibility of equity.[124] From this perspective, Portia's verdict disappoints, for it seems to rely on the casuistry of a hyper-technical, legalistic verbal quibble "more literal-minded than Shylock's."[125] From the perspective of contemporary treatises on accounting, however, Portia's exactitude would have been viewed not as a contradiction but as a confirmation of her Christian virtue. Instruction in the newly precise techniques of counting and accounting was intended for "the laude of God and increase of vertue."[126] Keepers of account books were instructed "at the beginninge of their writtingis," before entering their accounts, "to put fyrst the name of God" and "the signe of the crosse."[127] A phrase such as "In the name of God and Profit" is typically found at the beginning of extant business ledgers.[128] Exactitude, construed as a means of conveying one's trustworthiness or creditability, reflected the justice or rectitude of the profits one earned and was therefore opposed to the unjust profits of the usurer.[129] This diligent striving after "perfection" was a way of "approching toward the image of God," described in Pythagorean terms as the "true fountaine of perfect number."[130] Insisting on perfection, while recognizing that absolute exactitude belonged only to the divine, accounting treatises sought to develop virtuous alternatives to the vice of blotting so that "there shalbee no cause to blame or suspecte the [account] boke," such as marking the error with the sign of the cross, "betokening that it was entred by negli-. gence" rather than by fraudulent intent.[131]

Although we tend to associate Shylock with rigor and exactitude and to assume that Portia's verdict merely hoists him with his own petard, there is in fact a great deal of evidence in the play that Shylock is not a convert to the Christian ethic of precision or the new math of ciphering. "I am debating of my present store," he tells Bassanio and Antonio, admitting that he must resort to the "the near guess of [his] memory" to determine whether he can "instantly raise up the gross / Of full three thousand ducats" (1.3.48–50). His "near guess" would have sounded an alarm to merchants versed in the art of double-entry bookkeeping, who were guided by Luca Pacioli's mantra that one "can never be too clear" about the state of one's accounts.[132] Shylock then appears to forget the length or duration of the loan: "I had forgot,—three months,—you told me so" (l. 62). When he begins to calculate the rate of interest, he says: "Three thousand ducats, 'tis a good round sum. / Three months from twelve, then let me see the rate" (ll. 98–99). In describing the sum as "round," Shylock means that it is a large or considerable amount (*OED*, "round, *a.*" 7a). Yet in the context of mathematical calculation, the term "round number" meant one that was "only approximately correct, usually one expressed in tens, hundreds, [thousands,] etc., without precise enumeration of units" (*OED*, "round, *a.*" 7b). A "round reckoning" was one that was "[a]pproximately exact; roughly correct" (*OED*, "round, *a.*" 7c). Shylock seems pleased that the sum does not involve the "precise enumeration" of an irregular amount. Although there is no stage direction to indicate whether he uses a counter table or attempts to "cipher" with pen and ink, the fact that the calculation seems to take him some time (Antonio impatiently interrupts him) might suggest the former, as the new math of ciphering was promoted as a quicker and more efficient method than casting by counters.[133] When Shylock later says to Bassanio, "If every ducat in six thousand ducats / Were in six parts, and every part a ducat, / I would not draw them, I would have my bond!" (4.1.85–87), his mode of reckoning evokes calculation with counters, which was based on the classical concept of number as a plurality of indivisible units.[134] According to this system, when the one or unity was divided, it was "not cut, but . . . Multiplied into [more] Unities."[135] When Shylock breaks the one into parts, he counts each part as a one.

Although this inexactitude may initially be strategic (a method of drawing out his clients' discomfiture and buttressing his claim that the loan is not for gain but for friendship), Shylock's hatred of Antonio leads him to succumb to a passion that privileges vengeance above profit or precision. Over the course of the play, this passion supplants the profit motive entirely. Shylock's rigor is motivated not by monetary gain or meticulous accuracy but by revenge. In consequence, he is not so much exact as he is exacting. Our impression of his exactitude stems not from mathematical accuracy but from his rigid insistence on the "exaction" (1.3.160) of his bond, an insistence conveyed through stubborn repetition: "let him look to his bond! . . . let him look to his bond! . . . let him look to his bond!" (3.1.42–44).

> I'll have my bond . . .
> . . . I will have my bond:
> I'll have my bond. I will not hear thee speak,
> I'll have my bond (3.3.4–5, 12–13)

As he himself avows, his "lodg'd hate" induces him to pursue a "losing suit" (4.1.60, 62) for a pound of flesh, which "Is not so estimable, profitable neither"

(1.3.162). His hatred makes him obdurate and impenetrable to reason (e.g., 3.3.12, 17, 4.1.65). The excess of his passion exceeds account and renders his willfulness or desire for vengeance un(ac)countable: "You'll ask me why I rather choose to have / A weight of carrion flesh, than to receive / Three thousand ducats: I'll not answer that! / . . . there is no firm reason to be rend'red / . . . I can give no reason, nor I will not" (4.1.40–42, 53, 59).[136]

It is Shylock's passion for vengeance at all costs, the play suggests, that clouds his judgment and ability to reckon. His obduracy, impenetrability, and unaccountability are manifestations of the materiality of the Old Law of the flesh and the materiality of the old math, with its reliance on the abacus or counter table.[137] By contrast, Portia's eagerness to learn (cf. 3.2.160–62) is linked not only to the New Law of the spirit and of equity but to the new math of abstract ciphering, new techniques of accounting, and an ethic of Christian exactitude that would slowly come to define early modern England's culture of credit. "Shed thou no blood" (4.1.321), she says to Shylock,

> . . . nor cut thou less nor more
> But just a pound of flesh: if thou tak'st more
> Or less than a just pound, be it so much
> As makes it light or heavy in the substance,
> Or the division of the twentieth part
> Of one poor scruple, nay if the scale do turn
> But in the estimation of a hair,
> Thou diest, and all thy goods are confiscate . . . (ll. 321–28)

Portia affiliates justice with the exactitude of the decimal fraction and the precision of the "just pound," the term "just" here denoting an "[e]xact, as opposed to approximate" unit of measure or calculation (*OED*, "just, *a.*" 9). In so doing, she proves the contention of contemporary mathematical treatises that one who "is ignorant of Arithmetike, is no[t] neither meete to be a Judge." Yet her verdict also evokes the limits of precision, for it is because absolute exactitude belongs only to God on the day of reckoning, when all souls are called to account, that her verdict prevents Shylock from taking his pound of flesh, insofar as perfect accuracy is beyond his mortal capacity.

Through her skillful exactitude and shunning of excess, Portia demonstrates at several crucial junctures that she has learned Nerissa's lesson that "competency [i.e., moderation, sufficiency]" is preferable to "superfluity" or "surfeit" (1.2.9, 8, 5). "O love be moderate," she says when Bassanio chooses the lead casket, "allay thy extasy, / In measure rain thy joy, scant this excess" (3.2.111–12). Portia embraces measure and moderation (associated with justice and rectitude) over excess (associated with willfulness and usury) and in so doing forges a virtuous identity for the wife-as-creditor. Her ciphering and (ac)counting, used so often to stigmatize female creditors' sexual and financial excess, are deployed in the service of virtuous exactitude and just measure. She accomplishes this not only through her verdict in the trial scene but also through her skillful manipulation of the ring, a visual emblem of the cipher and its complex associations with the wedding band, the marital bond, the "nothing" of female sexuality, and the "noting" of the bond-wielding, scorekeeping, female creditor. While investing the ring with these associations, at the end of the play, Portia pointedly dissociates herself from the covetousness and sexual promiscuity they were commonly used to convey. In so doing, she associates the surety of the marital bond and marital chastity with moderation and the balanced scales of just measure: "Let me give light, but let me not be light," she says to Bassanio when he returns to Belmont, "For a light wife doth make a heavy husband" (5.1.129–30). In the end, she deploys the juridical rhetoric of fidelity in accounting practices ("charge us there upon inter'gatories, / And we will answer all things faithfully" [ll. 298–99]) in order to defend her own creditability and thereby the sexual and financial virtue of wives as creditors.[138]

In likening marriage to a bond of credit, Shakespeare draws on the Pauline doctrine of "due benevolence,"[139] which conceived of the sexual bond within marriage as a reciprocal debt between husband and wife, a concept that accords well, at least in theory, with Portia's embrace of just measure. The doctrine was frequently cited in contemporary domestic manuals as a prescription for marital harmony and chastity.[140] In his 1622 work *Of Domesticall Duties*, William Gouge defines "due benevolence" as "one of the best remedies" to prevent adultery and ensure the production of a "legitimate brood." To this end, he instructs, the sexual bond in marriage must be performed "with good will and delight, willingly, readily and cheerfully."[141] Gouge explains the term "due" not only in fiscal terms as that which is "owing or payable, as an enforceable obligation or debt," but also as that which is "adequate, [or] sufficient" in measure (*OED*, "due, *a.* and *adv.*" 1a, 7). Although the sexual bond within marriage "is said to be *due* because it is a debt which the wife oweth to her husband, and he to her," this debt is "warranted & sanctified by God" only to the extent that it is exacted in due or appropriate measure. Yet achieving due or just measure is no simple matter in practice: "There are two extremes contrarie

84 Chapter 2

to this dutie," Gouge warns, "One in the *defect*: another in the *excesse*." Those who deny their sexual duty when it is "justly required . . . denie a due debt." The "punishment inflicted on *Onan* (Gen. 38. 9, 10)," according to Gouge, "sheweth how great a wrong this is." Those who demand "*Excesse* . . . In the measure," as "when husband or wife [is] insatiable," likewise pose a threat to marital chastity.[142] In the Sonnets addressed to the young man, Shakespeare refers to the doctrine of due benevolence when the poet asserts, "That use is not forbidden usury, / Which happies those that pay the willing loan" (6.5–6).[143] In onanistically wasting his seed by "having traffic with [him]self alone" (4.9) and "spend[ing] / Upon [him]self [his] beauty's legacy" (ll. 1–2), the young man fails to pay his due debt to a wife and thereby to produce what Gouge terms a "legitimate brood." The female usurer of the Sonnets is guilty of the other extreme, that of "excesse": her insatiable lust causes her to exact sexual payments from multiple male debtors outside of wedlock. Portia, by contrast, seeks to "allay . . . extasy" and "scant . . . excess!" (3.2.111–12) by embracing the virtues of moderation and just measure.

In spite of the play's evocation of the rhetoric of just measure and due benevolence in its portrayal of the marriage bond, the scales of justice and marital harmony in the final act of *The Merchant of Venice* are not, as many commentators have noted, perfectly in balance. The disharmony that unsettles act 5, I want to suggest, points to a broader cultural shift that destabilized the ideal of marriage as a reciprocal debt. For if this ideal had long been contradicted by the common law of coverture, which tipped the scales of reciprocity in favor of the husband ("if mine then yours, / And so all yours"), the rise of separate estate and the phenomenon of wives lending money, even to their own husbands, threatened to tip the scales in the other direction ("though yours, not yours"). In exercising her wit, will, and skill and deploying the language of (ac)counting or ciphering to protect her "bond," Portia evokes the female creditors who financed male (ad)venture during the period and who extended loans to players and playing companies behind the scenes of theatrical production. The discordant strains that surface in act 5 of the play register the tensions that might arise from such loans, particularly when extended during coverture and when female creditors set conditions and exacted penalties on their bonds. At the end of the play Portia thus conjures, in an effort to ward off, the threat of excess associated with the usuress, restoring her marital bond/band as a symbol of due benevolence only *after* likening it to the pound of flesh (she describes the ring as "riveted" to Bassanio's "flesh" [5.1.169]) and evoking the dangers of cuckoldry ("For by this ring the doctor lay with me" [5.1.259]). The specter of the wife as usuress remains, for in the end, all are indebted to Portia,[144] who continues de facto, if not de jure, to treat her property as her own,[145] while enforcing the terms of her marital bond and demanding "surety" (l. 254). It is an outcome that may have led audience members, including female creditors as well as male debtors, to view her as a skillful lender upon advantage, for better or for worse.

From this perspective, *The Merchant of Venice*, far more than *English-men for My Money*, merits the subtitle *A Woman Will Have Her Will.* The tensions generated by these two aspects of Portia's character, although most acute in act 5 of the play, are present throughout, not only in her lexicon of (ac)counting but also in the stage properties associated with her character: the ring, the caskets, and the scales used in the trial scene. The function of these properties within the play is analogous to Portia's language of ciphering in that they evoke in an effort to revalue the iconography associated with female moneylenders. Jewels, scales, and caskets all feature prominently in contemporary visual renderings of female avarice and women's (ac)counting practices. Paintings and prints of women counting money and weighing gold were particularly popular in the Low Countries in Shakespeare's time, reflecting Netherlandish women's active role in the world of commerce. In the next chapter, I examine how commercially active crafts- and tradeswomen who emigrated to England from the Netherlands influenced the material culture of the professional stage, and how both they and their wares were depicted in dramatic literature and other cultural texts. To preface that discussion, I shall conclude this chapter with a consideration of how the visual iconography of the female moneylender may have influenced Shakespeare's staging of the ring, caskets, and scales in *The Merchant of Venice* and how this iconography was itself influenced by the shifting attitudes toward women's (ac)counting practices described above.

Sixteenth- and seventeenth-century engravings of Lady Avarice or Vanity frequently feature rings and caskets as symbols of her riches while containing cautionary visual cues to remind the viewer of the empty transience of worldly riches and beauty. An early seventeenth-century engraving after the Dutch printer Abraham Bloemaert, for example, depicts the lovely Lady Vanity richly attired, with an open casket of gold at her feet. Jewels adorn her neck and wrists and cascade off the table (see Figure 6). A small box on the table is overflowing with rings, several of which have spilled out. Vanity busily counts coins with one hand while blowing bubbles from a pipe with the other. The coins themselves and her (ac)counting of them are thus visually linked to,

Figure 6. After Abraham Bloemaert, *Allegory of Vanity*, c. 1630. Engraving of a female figure, surrounded by riches on a table and in an open casket (below right). Counting coins with one hand and blowing bubbles (ciphers of her vanity) with the other, she is caught in the midst of discovering she is an "ass." An earlier state of this image was printed in 1609. © The Trustees of the British Museum.

and revealed to be the equivalent of, her production of empty, insubstantial ciphers of wealth, prompting her discovery that she is an "ass."[146]

Netherlandish paintings of male and female moneylenders produced during the commercial supremacy of Antwerp and later Amsterdam draw on a similar iconography, including rings, jewels, coins, and caskets. Yet such paintings also register a gradual shift in attitudes toward female participation in the world and work of accounting, in part through their visual rendering of the tools of the trade. Such tools include the scales moneylenders used to weigh gold coins (which also serve the admonitory function of reminding the viewer of the Last Judgment), lead weights, account books, and so forth. An early sixteenth-century painting by Quentin Matsys entitled *The Moneylender and His Wife* (1514) in the Louvre depicts a moneylender weighing gold coins in a balance as his wife anxiously looks on, turning the pages of a prayer book (perhaps referencing contemporary theological debates over whether moneylenders' wives were culpable for their husbands' sins). The painting contains numerous visual cues of the sin of avarice and the transience of wealth, such as an apple (referencing mankind's fall) and a burnt-out candle (a symbol of mortality). Later versions of the painting, however, such as one by Marinus van Reymerswaele (1539) in the Prado, replace the open prayer book in the wife's hands with an open account book and change her anxious expression to an interested one, suggesting that she is participating in her husband's commercial activities. In other versions, she has a beatific smile, indicating that their (now collaborative) commercial practices were no longer viewed as a threat to their salvation. The candle and apple in the Matsys painting are likewise replaced in later versions with a precise and detailed depiction of the mundane implements of the trade (e.g., account books, pen and ink, counters, lead weights, etc.). The precision with which they are rendered would appear to reflect their status as emblems of virtuous exactitude.[147]

Shifting attitudes toward women's involvement in the world of commerce and credit in the Low Countries are likewise registered in paintings of women weighing gold. An early example by the Flemish painter Jan Sanders van Hemessen (c. 1530) depicts a young girl gazing directly at the viewer, holding scales in one hand as she removes lead weights from a box with the other (see Figure 7). Although at first glance there are no obvious visual cues of her youthful vanity, we soon notice that her scales are out of balance and the box of lead weights and book underneath it—perhaps her account book—are precariously balanced on the edge of the table. The gold chalice that sits atop them—a symbol of worldly riches—is about to cause them to fall, recollecting

Figure 7. Jan Sanders van Hemessen, *Woman Weighing Gold*, c. 1530. Oil on oak. Gemaeldegalerie, Staatliche Museen, Berlin. © Bildarchiv Preussischer Kulturbesitz/Art Resource, N.Y.

Figure 8. Jan Woutersz, *Woman Weighing Gold*, c. 1630. Oil on canvas. By permission of The Samuel Courtauld Trust. The Courtauld Gallery, London.

the fall of mankind as well as the precarious state of the young girl's soul. In a later portrait by the Dutch painter Jan Woutersz (c. 1630), a more mature woman's box of lead weights is placed securely on a table in the foreground along with other implements of her trade, which are now rendered in precise and mundane detail as in the van Reymerswaele painting (see Figure 8). Her scales appear to be perfectly in balance, although her pensive expression simultaneously registers studied concentration and a lingering concern with the outcome of her task—and, we surmise, with the state of her soul—reflecting ongoing cultural ambivalence regarding women's (ac)counting practices.

Still later in the seventeenth century, Vermeer's *Woman Holding a Balance* (c. 1664), formerly titled *Woman Weighing Gold*, features a painting of the Last Judgment directly behind the woman who holds the scales to emphasize the spiritual significance of her activity. As in the Woutersz portrait, the scales are perfectly balanced, although here the woman's expression is tranquil and beatific. None of the mundane implements of commerce featured in previous examples of the genre (e.g., box of weights, account book, etc.) is present, aside from the scales in her hand. Although the painting draws on the iconography of vanity through its depiction of the coins and strands of pearls visible on the table and in an open casket, the pans of the woman's balance are empty of gold or jewels and instead reflect the light from the window. Arthur Wheelock has therefore suggested that the painting should be read as "a positive statement, an expression of the essential tranquility of one who understands the implications of the Last Judgment and who seeks to moderate her life in order to warrant her salvation," conveying the "message that one should lead a life of temperance and balanced judgment."[148] Svetlana Alpers likewise reads the scales as an emblem of justice, not of commerce: "does not her action—testing the accuracy or balance of the scales, not weighing valuables—and the order of the composition suggest that she herself is a just judge? A most common image of justice is, after all, a woman holding scales."[149] This interpretation is certainly more in keeping with the tranquil tone of the painting and its balanced composition. Yet to suggest that the painting's evocation of the well-known iconography of Lady Vanity and of earlier paintings of women moneylenders completely evacuates them of their commercial resonance may be protesting too much; the painting clearly raises the specter of female avarice and excess, if only to assuage it. Its equilibrium is generated by the tension between temperance and excess, a tension that both the woman and the painting hold in the balance.[150]

The Merchant of Venice likewise draws on the iconography of worldly

Figure 9. Johannes Vermeer, *Woman Holding a Balance* (formerly *Woman Weighing Gold*), c. 1664. Oil on canvas. © The Board of Trustees, National Gallery of Art, Washington, D.C. Widener Collection.

versus spiritual accounting through its use of stage properties to generate dramatic tension. The familiar iconography of covetousness associated with Dame Usury—rings, caskets, scales—is deployed only to be revalued as emblematic of "just reckoning." If in Shylock's house caskets function as familiar icons of avarice (and in Jessica and Lorenzo's hands, of prodigality), at Belmont they serve to remind us of the falseness, emptiness, transience, and vanity of worldly wealth: *"All that glisters is not gold, / . . . Gilded tombs do worms infold*" (2.7.65, 69), the gold casket instructs. "*Some there be that shadows kiss, / Such have but a shadow's bliss*" (2.9.66–67), preaches the silver, while Bassanio refuses to be "deceiv'd with ornament" (3.2.74) and "gaudy gold" (l. 101) in choosing "meager lead" (l. 104). Yet the casket full of gold Portia gives to Bassanio to take to Venice (l. 305) reveals that the icon still retains its commercial resonance within the play. Portia and Nerissa's rings are symbols of "due benevolence" while still retaining the threat of excess associated with women's "bonds" and "not(h)ing." In the trial scene, the scales of the moneylender undergo a revaluation that would seem to render them a symbol of justice, right reckoning, temperance, and mercy, in terms similar to those that would later inform Vermeer's painting.[151] Yet the threat of excess reemerges in the trial scene as well, which does not end with Portia's evocation of Christian exactitude. "Thou shalt have justice more than thou desir'st" (4.1.312), she warns, "The law hath yet another hold on you" (l. 343). Portia's "more," her pursuit of the hold the law has over Shylock, both in purse (through the confiscation of his property) and person (as an alien), raises the specter of excess that carries over into act 5. Tensions thus persist in the iconography of female accounting in both *The Merchant of Venice* and *Woman Holding a Balance* in spite of the efforts of both play and painting to align this iconography with an emergent ethos of virtuous exactitude.

Chapter 3

Froes and Rebatos

THE VISIBLE, ACTIVE role played by Netherlandish "froes" in the world of work and commerce was hardly a remote concern in Elizabethan and Jacobean London, which was inundated by religious refugees from the Low Countries and northern France who emigrated there during the Dutch revolt and French wars of religion.[1] English response to the perceived gendered division of labor among Netherlanders was mixed, as reflected in Fynes Moryson's *Itinerary* of 1617:

> By reason of the foresaid industry of the people inhabiting the united Provinces, . . . there is no where greater abundance of all things. . . . One thing not used in any other Countrey, is here most common, that while the Husbands snort idly at home, the Weomen especially of *Holland*, for trafficke sayle to *Hamburg*, and manage most part of the businesse at home . . . . In the shops they sell all, they take all accompts, and it is no reproch to the men to be never inquired after, about these affaires, who taking money of their wives for daily expences, gladly passe their time in idlenesse.[2]

Moryson's admiration for the "industry" of Netherlanders, to which he attributes the Low Countries' commercial success ("there is no where greater abundance of all things"), quickly segues into a satirical account of Netherlandish women's purportedly pivotal role in this success, deploying the familiar topos of the "woman on top."[3] The Low Countries have been brought on high, he suggests, through the topsy-turvy commerce of its women, who "manage" business at home, "trafficke" abroad, "sell all," and "take all accompts," unsupervised by men.[4] Moryson blames the commercial activities of the region's women for effeminizing its men, who "snort idly at home," passively confined within the traditionally feminine domestic sphere, offered only an allowance for their "daily expences."[5]

Yet the industry and commercial activity of Netherlandish women were not always mocked or reproved by contemporary English commentators. Edward Grimeston's *Generall Historie of the Netherlands* (1608), for example, links these qualities to their heroic resistance during the Spanish onslaught:

> The women (being many in regard of the men, who are much consumed by the wars, and at sea) are so industrious, as by their spinning and weaving of Holland cloth . . . they are spoken of throughout all the world: and besides, the women are so politike, diligent, and carefull; as they can buy and sell, keepe accounts, traffique and travell from place to place, as well as their husbands, in their absence, without any touch of lightnesse or dishonestie. The like of them are not to be found in any countrey, being . . . so active, as they are more respected than women in other countries, where[] jealousie, lightnesse, and pride, raigneth, more than simple honestie.[6]

Grimeston's depiction of Netherlandish women's honest, hardy industriousness as manifested in their "spinning and weaving of Holland cloth" and ability to "buy and sell, [and] keepe accounts" grounds his later account of their heroic labors in resisting the Spanish siege: "yea the women laboured with such courage," we are told, "as they respected not the great Ordinance, to the mercy whereof they did expose themselves willingly and without feare."[7] Having established their chastity (they are "without any touch of lightnesse"), honesty, and heroism, he prompts his readers to be all the more outraged by the "execrable ravishing and forcing of wives and maidens" by Spanish soldiers later in his narrative.[8]

The visibility of Netherlandish working women in London's immigrant community, and in the networks of commerce surrounding the commercial theaters, likewise met with a mixed response in contemporary dramatic literature, where they were at times portrayed as promiscuous commercial agents (if not as prostitutes) and, at other times, as paragons of domestic virtue renowned for their thrift, chastity, and industry—or some combination thereof.[9] When the starched linen attires for which they were famous became fashionable in England and began to appear onstage, they similarly took on divergent associations: the stiffness of starched linen came to stand, as it were, for their assertive, masculine conduct in the world of work and commerce, while its whiteness evoked feminine virtues such as chastity, cleanliness, and diligence.[10] In this chapter, I turn to the labors of immigrant sempstresses, laundresses, and starchwomen who manufactured these luxury attires for the London stage, and of the immigrant tirewomen who dressed the boy-actors who wore them. As in the previous chapters, I draw together a wide range of evidence to consider how women's work in the broader economy contributed to theatrical production behind the scenes, and their transformative impact on the material culture of the stage. As we shall see, this impact was often cast as immaterial (insubstantial, impertinent, and unimportant), insofar as it was manifested through the evanescent, fleeting substance of starch. The starched ruff may thus be read as a material cipher of female labors that were by definition never done.

In his analysis of the commodity form, Marx distinguishes between the "stiff and starchy existence" of commodities as physical things and their "sublime objectivity" as values.[11] The language he uses to describe the materiality of the commodity in general derives no doubt from the particular example he chooses to demonstrate its workings, namely, linen. The stiffness of starched linen in his view exemplifies the raw material or *stuff* of commodities as they "come into the world"—their "plain, homely, natural form" before they are worked upon, bought, or sold.[12] Yet in associating starch with the commodity in its raw, pre-cultural, unworked-upon state, Marx oddly effaces the labor of starching that was required to produce linen's stiffness, an effacement that is perhaps less odd in that this labor was traditionally performed by women, whose work has so often been lost to history. When starch was first introduced to England during the late sixteenth century, the work of starching was performed by craftswomen from the Netherlands and northern France who emigrated there to escape religious persecution, bringing sophisticated skills in luxury textile manufacture with them.

The starched, linen neck- and head-attires and other wares manufactured by immigrant craftswomen in early modern England had a profound influence on fashion trends in the late sixteenth and early seventeenth centuries and, consequently, on the material culture of the apparel-driven stage. There is perhaps no icon of fashion more readily associated with the theater in Shakespeare's time than the starched ruff. Yet, like Marx, we tend to forget the female labor that was literally "congealed" (to borrow another of his peculiarly starchy terms) in this most fetishized of commodities.[13] We forget, for example, that the distinctive folds of ruffs had to be painstakingly remade every time they

Figure 10. Michiel van Mierevelt, *Portrait of a Lady*, 1628. Oil on oak. By kind permission of the Trustees of the Wallace Collection, London/Art Resource, N.Y.

were laundered, a process that involved washing, bleaching, and dipping them in starch, molding or setting them over heated metal rods into a variety of scrolling forms, and finally pinning them, all of which took many hours. The labor time congealed in starched ruffs extends from hours into days, weeks, and even months if we include the manufacture of the ruff itself. This involved meticulously pleating up to nineteen yards of gossamer-thin lawn or cambric into as many as six hundred pleats, which were sometimes triply or quadruply layered, as well as the manufacture of cutwork or bonelace with which they were ornamented and the processing of starch itself out of wheat flour, bran, corn, or other grains—a nasty, smelly, and time-consuming business.[14]

Yet sweat, soil, and toil are the very last things called to mind when we gaze at the spectacular form of ruffs in their finished state. Their exquisite delicacy, pristine whiteness, and fragile shape distance the body of the wearer and the mind of the spectator from the messy world of manual work.[15] Worn about the neck and wrists, they effectively precluded those attired in them from engaging in laborious activity. Soil, of course, was to be shunned. But any exposure to the elements, including excessive dampness—which in England meant outdoor activity on most days—might cause them to wilt and necessitate their laundering and starching anew.[16] Devoid of any ostensible use-value, their only apparent function was to signify their wearers' ability to afford servants, avoid bodily exertion or exposure to the elements, and thereby announce their elite or would-be elite social status. From this perspective, ruffs are themselves complicit in our forgetting of the labor necessary to produce them. The layered irony of starched ruffs inheres in the fact that their very labor-obliterating form required the extraordinary and ongoing labor of women to be produced and maintained. As such, they perfectly exemplify the cultural status of women's work as "never done." Unending and ever-present, the work of starching was continually placed under cultural erasure and thereby undone. As an icon of the Shakespearean stage, the starched ruff would further seem to epitomize the way in which the defining attribute of that stage as "all-male" depends upon the erasure or forgetting of female labor that took place offstage or behind the scenes of theatrical production.

Like the fragile glass beads sewn onto costumes by female spanglers, ruffs, cuffs, and bands had the material form of an O or empty cipher, a morphology that was not lost on contemporary moralists, who decried them as lacking in "true" substance and inherent use-value, and dismissed the work necessary to produce them as false and deceitful, if not demonic. The historical recovery of such work, however, poses particular challenges. The labor hidden within the folds and fleeting forms imprinted in ruffs by female starchers, sempstresses, and tirewomen would seem to be especially resistant to archival study, which tends to concern itself with less ephemeral forms of print culture. In what follows, while drawing on sources used throughout this book, including traditional documents of theater history and documents aimed at controlling women's work in the informal sector, I also consider artifacts of material or, rather, (im)material culture—the "stiff and starchy," yet transient and unenduring, *stuff* of the Elizabethan and Jacobean stage. My particular focus is on the costumes and properties manufactured by Netherlandish craftswomen and their staging in plays mounted in the aftermath of the immigrant influx.

My aim here is not simply to recover the diverse forms of immigrant craftswomen's work and its shaping influence on theatrical production in Shakespeare's time but to attend to the ways in which their work was materially recollected (and forgotten) in dramatic texts and textiles. Starch is particularly evocative in this context, insofar as it functions to fix, solidify, or set the worked-upon form of fabrics, only to forget or efface that work when it dampens and returns to its liquefied state. I borrow the term "material memory" from Ann Rosalind Jones and Peter Stallybrass, who use it to describe the way in which clothing remembers or retains the shape or scent of its wearer.[17] Yet to what extent and under what conditions do material objects recollect their makers? Jones and Stallybrass address this question in their work on women's textile-related manufactures, arguing that aristocratic women wove themselves into the social fabric by embroidering symbolic and sometimes even subversive and politically charged meanings into the material "texts" they stitched on samplers, handkerchiefs, clothing, cushions, tapestries, and the like, thereby "materializing a countermemory" for themselves.[18] Yet the embroidery of symbolic or political content derived from scripture or classical mythology by aristocratic women, whose "fine stitchery" was defined as "a hobby rather than a wage-earning necessity," arguably represents an exceptional case in which textile literally becomes text.[19]

What of the working women who spun, wove, stitched, and starched the fabric of early modern culture? Were they recollected in or through the textiles and clothing they produced? Did they, too, have a "counter-memory"? Here, Jones and Stallybrass are more ambiguous, arguing that early modern culture "dematerialized" ordinary women's textile work: female spinners were "trivialized " or confined to "silent anonymity," while weaving "was increasingly becoming a man's craft" and represented as such.[20] Although the distaff and the wheel were sometimes represented as weapons in the hands of harridans or shrews, such monstrous and deeply misogynist depictions constitute an ambiguous "counter-memory" at best.[21] Equally monstrous and misogynist are the late Jacobean and commonwealth satires of yellow starch, produced in the aftermath of Frances Howard's implication in the murder of Sir Thomas Overbury in 1613 (Howard helped popularize the fashion).[22] Although Jones and Stallybrass acknowledge that immigrant women were primarily responsible for the work of starching during the Elizabethan and early Jacobean periods, they do not consider the ways in which their work was represented and/or elided in dramatic literature and other cultural texts. What follows is an examination of this earlier period when starch was first introduced to England, focusing in particular on the transformative impact that immigrant women's imported skills and technologies had on theatrical attires and attiring, and culminating in a consideration of theatrical stagings of starched linen attires that recollect the labor congealed within their folds by pointing to their pre- or offstage histories of manufacture. To what extent and to what ends were theatergoers made aware of the material culture of the stage as "worked upon" (to borrow Marx's formulation) by women?[23] And, beyond a strictly Marxian paradigm, in what ways were these behind-the-scenes dramas of economic production marked by gender, national identity, and the social dynamics of immigration? These are the concerns that inform the present chapter.

Although the immigrant population in early modern London was probably never greater than 12.5 percent of the city's total population, their impact was proportionally greater in the suburbs and liberties where they were most heavily concentrated and where the commercial theaters were located. In these areas immigrants made up as much as half of the total population.[24] The population of aliens was particularly high in the liberties of Blackfriars (home to the Blackfriars theater) and St. Katherine's (near the Red Lion theater), and in the suburban parishes of Southwark (where the Rose, Globe, Hope, and Swan theaters were located), Clerkenwell (location of the Red Bull theater), Cripplegate (location of the Fortune theater), Whitechapel (near the Boar's Head Inn), and Bishopsgate (near The Theatre and the Curtain).[25] Given the high concentration and visibility of alien artisans in the environs of the innyard, private and public theaters, it is not surprising that they—and especially those from the Low Countries, who far outnumbered others[26]—appear frequently in the drama of the period. Nor is it surprising that certain theater people, as we shall see, formed personal ties to the immigrant community or were themselves of immigrant descent.

Many of the refugees, both male and female, were skilled artisans in the textile and clothing trades, and their importation of new skills and technologies had a huge impact on this sector of the economy:[27] they contributed vitally to the development of silk manufacture in England,[28] introducing "new methods for throwing silk, new designs for damasks and other figured patterns, special knowledge of dyeing and finishing cloth, [and] improvements in ribbon-weaving and knitting silk stockings";[29] they are credited with improvements in linen weaving and lace making;[30] and they were largely responsible for the successful manufacture in England of the "New Draperies" (or *nieuwe draperij* in Flemish)—smooth, light cloths such as bays (or baize), says (or serge), mockadoes, "and other outlandish comodityes as hath not been used to be made within this our realm of England."[31] Together, these innovations revitalized the English cloth and clothing market following years of commercial depression in the mid-sixteenth century; yet there has been no study of the ways in which this revolution in textile manufacture influenced theatrical production, in light of the theaters' dependence on the clothing trade, or how it may have shaped contemporary dramatic depictions of aliens.[32]

The response of the native population to the massive influx of skilled, immigrant artisans was divided, as John Strype (himself of Dutch descent) recounts: "The English Nature being somewhat inhospitable to Strangers, jealous of their Industry, and suspecting them to get their Trade away from them, the wiser and better sort were rather for cherishing these Strangers, as well as perceiving what Advantages they brought to the Nation . . . for their Callings and Examples of Thrift and Diligence."[33] Those who looked favorably on or encouraged immigration included government officials and entrepreneurs or "projectors," who wished to import the skills of foreign artisans in order to manufacture expensive imported commodities domestically, as well as religious sympathizers. The "inhospitable" included native artisans and tradesmen to whom "the new arrivals appeared less as an economic stimulus than as a threat to their livelihoods."[34] Contemporary dramatic texts suggest that theater people's attitudes ranged across this spectrum, in part as a result of their own positioning on the cusp of the formal and informal economies. As informal entrepreneurs they had similar interests to those of the projectors; yet many theater people were also guildsmen, who commonly resented alien artisans' infringement of their prerogatives.

Recent scholarship has demonstrated that contemporary dramatic depictions of aliens were neither always nor simply xenophobic but rather shifted in accordance with the complex vicissitudes of Anglo-foreign relations and the dictates of various dramatic genres.[35] Such scholarship has made important contributions to our understanding of the ways in which generic protocols shift in response to social and economic change.[36] Yet the connections hitherto drawn between dramatic texts and the historical context of mass immigration have tended to remain at a macro level of analysis, focusing on generalized social or economic "anxieties" in response to the alien influx and the ways in which they were given form in different dramatic genres. What has been elided by this approach is a microanalysis of the networks of commerce that brought immigrant artisans into contact with theater people and how they may have influenced theatrical production. The "macro" approach has likewise tended to elide the female alien population (which made up roughly 47 percent of the adult immigrant community in London in 1593),[37] insofar as women tend to be more visible in historical records that deal with the "micro." Previous scholarship on alien women in early modern literary texts has tended to focus on their prostitution or intermarriage with English men, rather than on their productive work in various crafts and trades, and has thereby privileged the traffic *in* women over the traffic *of* women. I shall therefore begin by examining the available evidence concerning alien women's work in the networks of commerce that surrounded the commercial theaters as it intersected with theatrical production. I then turn to a diverse array of cultural representations—including prints, pamphlets, poems, as well as plays—that variously depict (and elide) the incessant, yet ephemeral and insubstantial, work of immigrant starchwomen, laundresses, and tirewomen. I conclude with a consideration of plays that stage the ruffs, cuffs, rebatos (flat, fan-shaped, vertically standing collars), and head-attires manufactured by Netherlandish women in such a way as to recollect, to varying degrees and ends, their pre- or offstage histories of manufacture.

The Returns of Aliens for early modern London contain a wealth of information regarding immigrant women's work in the textile and clothing trades. The Returns comprise census data collected at periodic intervals under the supervision of the Lord Mayor of London by the City's aldermen, in part to placate anti-alien sentiment by demonstrating that the immigrant population was smaller than the native population feared. (This motivation may have led to under-recording of the actual numbers of aliens, as might the transient nature of the immigrant population, the difficulty of defining who was an immigrant, the counting only of householders in certain Returns, and the incentive of non-denizen aliens to hide during searches.)[38] The data collected varied but usually included the men, women, and children of each ward, their names, surnames, and occupations, how many lived in each household (in response to complaints of overcrowding), and which church they attended (in response to complaints that many immigrants came for economic rather than religious reasons).[39] The inclusion of alien women's occupations in the Returns may have been in response to complaints by native artisans regarding their commercial activities in areas proscribed to native women. Later Returns also include data about the nationalities of workers employed by both male and female strangers in response to complaints that immigrant artisans were refusing to hire or share trade secrets with the native population. The Returns thus contain valuable information about the occupational identities of immigrant women in London, for which we have no comparable source of evidence about native English women. As we have seen, evidence about native English women's work tends, by contrast, to come from guild ordinances or civic legislation restricting or proscribing their labor or from court records concerning women who were caught working outside or in breach of these regulations.

The Returns are particularly informative about the work of single women and widows, whose occupational identities are easier to discern than are those of married women. Alien widows' occupations in cloth- or clothing-related crafts and trades included some that would have competed with low-status, native women's work, such as spinning, twisting, carding and combing wool, or working as a sempstress, needlewoman, or botcher (mender of old clothes). Other widows, however, were employed in occupations that drew on more sophisticated, imported skills, such as starching, dyeing, embroidery, tapestry making, fine lace making, button making,[40] and millinery, as well as many occupations connected to the manufacture of silk.[41] Still other alien widows worked in trades that in England were male dominated (such as "linen draper," "taylour," or "merchaunt").[42] These more affluent widows may have benefited from the favorable legal provisions for widows in the Low Countries, which entitled them to recover their full marriage portions together with any gifts or personal possessions acquired during their marriages.[43] A significant number of alien widows worked as silk weavers, an occupation considered to be the province of men by the London Weavers' Company.[44] Other alien widows ran successful businesses in starching, linen weaving, and thread dyeing and selling, as well as such non-textile-related businesses as shoemaking and beer brewing.[45]

The occupational identities of married women are more difficult to recover in the Returns than are those of single women, as they are only inconsistently recorded. Often, married women's labor is invisible, as the record will list only the husband's occupation and not indicate whether the wife participated in his trade or had a different trade. Other records list occupations for neither husband nor wife but only which church each attended. The phrasing of some records, however, suggests that immigrant wives worked alongside their husbands in a variety of trades. Thus, for example, the occupations of husband and wife are sometimes listed in the plural, as in "Giles of the Hage, and Elizabeth his wife silkewinders," or in phrases such as "they do lyve by byinge and selling of bayes" (baize being one of the New Draperies) or "their trade is twistinge yarne."[46] Other trades in which husbands and wives, or entire families, are clearly listed as working together include all of the silk-related manufactures mentioned above and the making and retailing of fine lace.[47] Certain records also make clear when the occupations of husband and wife differed. Sometimes it was the husband who did skilled textile work while the wife worked another trade, as in the case of "Audrian Medler and Ellin Medler his wyfe . . . he a silckwever . . . hir profession is a baker,"[48] or the wife of a dyer of kersey who ran a large brewing business that employed more than thirty-three people.[49] Yet in other cases it was the reverse, as with the wife of a brewer who worked as a dyer of kersey, or the wife of a Dutch merchant who worked as a silk weaver.[50] There are also examples of Dutch women who married English men but continued to work in textile-related manufactures, such as "Anne Savage, bonelacemaker, the wife of Jerom Savage, an Englishman."[51]

The Returns list many female occupations relating to the fabrication, adornment, and sale of starched linen attires, such as "starcher," "linen weaver," "linen draper," "seller of lynen cloth," "selleth linen wares," "maker of purled lace," "bonelace maker," "silk lace worker," "parchmentlacemaker," "bewgell [i.e., beaded] lace maker," "sempster," "myllener," "laundresse," and "whitster [i.e., bleacher]." Both the fabrics and the fabrication skills associated with these attires were imported to England during Queen Elizabeth's reign because, according to the 1615 edition of Stow's *Annales*, "there was none in England [who] could tell how to starch" the delicate linen fabrics out of which they were made, which included lawn, imported from Laon in northern France, cambric from Cambray in Flanders, and holland from Holland.[52] Consequently, Elizabeth "made speciall meanes for some Dutchwomanne that could starch," hiring the wife of her Dutch coachman, Gwillam Boonen, to perform this service in 1562.[53] Two years later, Mistress Dinghen van den Plasse, a Protestant refugee from Flanders, capitalized on the growing demand among the "curious wives" of London to learn the skill of starching by opening her own starching school, charging her pupils twenty shillings to learn how to "seeth" or process starch and a further £4–5 to learn how to starch fine linen ruffs.[54] Such attires feature prominently in portraits of Elizabeth, including a 1586/7 portrait miniature by Nicholas Hilliard of the queen wearing a head-attire and starched lace ruff (see Figure 11).[55] As the size of starched ruffs and rebatos grew during the late sixteenth and early seventeenth centuries, they had to be propped up with various kinds of ornamental wire or cardboard supports known as "supportasses" or "underproppers," such as the one in Figure 12 from the Victoria and Albert collection.[56]

Over time, immigrant tirewomen also became known for their manufacture and retail of perukes and periwigs, which required powdered starch to

Figure 11. Nicholas Hilliard, portrait miniature of Queen Elizabeth I, 1586/7. © The Victoria and Albert Museum London. Bequeathed by Mrs. Doris Hershorn.

maintain their shape, and a wide array of other fashion accessories. In George Chapman's *Bussy D'Ambois* (1600–1604), Clermont speaks of a Madam Perigot of Cambray who "live[s] by retailing . . . complexion, poudring of your haire, / Shadowes [i.e., a type of head-tire that shaded the face], Rebatoes, Wires, Tyres, and such trickes."[57] An engraving by Pieter Serwouters found in a Dutch translation of Ovid's *Ars Amatoria* illustrates both the tools and wares of the tirewoman's trade in a section devoted to female ornament (see Figure 13). A deep and elaborately set starched ruff and head-attire sit perched atop a pile of ornate clothing on a pedestal, as though they have taken on a life of their own. On either side hang the tools used to dress women and adorn and prop up their head- and neck-attires, including pins, ribbons, laces, scissors, setting and crimping irons, mirrors, and so forth. The sheer copia of these tools is suggestive of the incessant labors necessary to maintain starched linen attires. Yet the static image is also oddly evacuated of the labor to which it bears silent testimony. The absent-presence of the tirewoman haunts the empty, stiffened attires

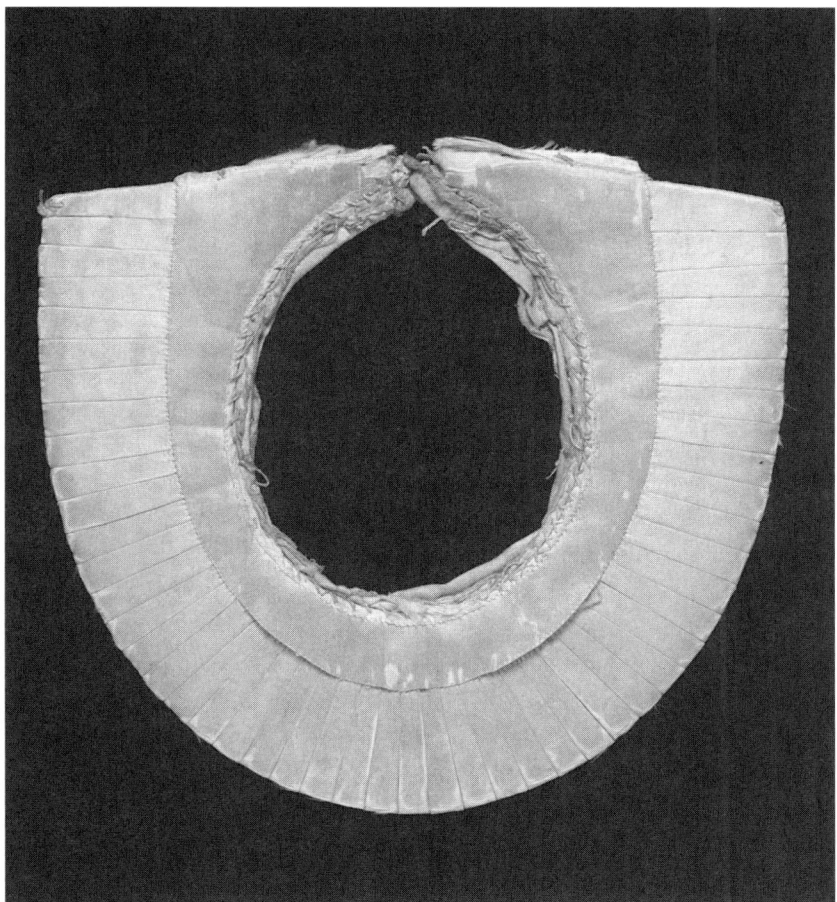

Figure 12. Supportasse or underpropper, England, c. 1600–1625. Cardboard padded with cotton wool and covered with satin, hand sewn with silk and linen thread. © The Victoria and Albert Museum, London. Given by Lady Spickernell.

(and the shadow cast by them), which have replaced her, their illusory substance underscored by the contrasting solidity of the surrounding architecture.

A contemporary account of the activity of head- and neck-attiring, from the perspective of a French Huguenot living in London, appears in a French-English language manual written by Pierre Erondelle for an elite female audience entitled *The French Garden: For English Ladyes and Gentlewomen to Walke In* (1605). The popularity of Erondelle's manuals (a second edition of

Figure 13. Pieter Serwouters, engraving of tools and attires pertaining to the tirewoman's trade, including a starched ruff and head-attire, mirror, dress pins, and setting and crimping irons. In Johan van Heemskerk, *Ovidii Nasonis Minne-Kunst [Ars Amatoria]* (Amsterdam, 1626 [1622]), 105. By permission of The British Library.

The French Garden was published in 1621) may be attributed not only to their pragmatic approach to language instruction but also to their utility as how-to books for elite or middling-sort women who wished to learn the lexicon as well as the latest styles of fashionable, foreign attire.[58] The manual contains thirteen bilingual dialogues, including one between the fictional Lady Ri-Mellaine, who is dressing, and her "Wayting Gentle-woman" named Jolye. The section of the dialogue on head- and neck-attiring offers a fascinating glimpse into the elaborate materials and laborious activities they required:

> *Lady*: Jolye, come dresse my head . . .
> *Jolye*: What doth it please you to weare today Madame? Will it please you to weare your haires onely, or els to have your French whood? . . .
> *Lady*: Set up then my French whood and my Border of Rubies, give me an other head attire [*atour de teste*]: take the key of my closet, and goe fetch my long boxe where I set my Jewels (for to have them out) that I use to weare on my head, what is become of my wyer [*mon mole*]? Where is the haire-cap [*la houppe*]? Have you any ribans to make knots? Where be the laces for to bind my haires [*les chevellieres pour m'entortiller le poil*]? . . .
> *Jolye*: What dooth it please you to have Madame, a ruffe band [*une fraise*] or a Rebato [*un rabat*]?
> *Lady*: Let me see that ruffe. How is it that the supporter [*le porte-fraise*] is so soyled? . . . take it away and give me my Rebato of cut-worke edged [*mon rabat de point-coupé a dentelle*], is not the wyer [*le porte-rabat*] after the same sorte as the other?[59]

The passage points not only to the labor of attiring (e.g., dressing, knotting, lacing, binding, propping, etc.) but to the attendant labor of laundering required to keep ruffs and rebatos suitably clean, white, and starched. Because linen bands and underclothes, however ornate, were worn close to the skin, absorbing sweat and other bodily fluids and protecting outerwear, the labor of laundering served a crucial function. Yet, as we shall see, the character of this labor changed radically with the importation of new textiles and starching techniques from the Netherlands.

By the late sixteenth and early seventeenth centuries, these ornate head- and neck-attires had become must-have fashion accessories for elite and would-be elite English women and came to feature prominently in plays and court masques. Immigrant tirewomen, starchwomen, silkwomen, spanglers, sempstresses, and laundresses, and eventually native women who learned their skills, played a crucial role in fabricating such attires for the stage. Professional tirewomen, as discussed in Chapter 1, specialized in the manufacture, decoration, and retail of neck- and head-attires and other ornaments, and assisted in dressing female performers in court entertainments and boy-actors playing women's parts on the professional stage.[60] All told, the Revels Office accounts during Elizabeth's reign include payments to eleven different tirewomen who manufactured head-attires for plays and masques staged at court, including the four foreigners working in mother-daughter teams dressing the heads of boy-actors.[61] The account books of Sir Philip Sidney's daughter, Elizabeth, Countess of Rutland, include a payment of twelve pounds three shillings to an unnamed "tyre woman" for a head-attire, ruff, and other accessories for a court masque in 1606.[62] In act 2 of George Chapman's *The Gentleman Usher* (c. 1602–4), probably performed by the Children of the Queen's Revels at Blackfriars, an Italian widow named Corteza serves as a tirewoman to boy-actors who "fill up womens places" in a pastoral masque. After arranging their "head-tyres," as well as their "petticotes" and "clokes," she asks: "Looke master Usher, are these wags wel drest? / I have beene so in labour with-um truly."[63] The elaborate attires in which immigrant women specialized appear to have been particularly popular among children's companies who performed at indoor, private theaters (which provided a more felicitous environment for attires stiffened with starch, and catered to more elite audiences). As mentioned in Chapter 1, the Articles of Agreement made in 1607/8 concerning Whitefriars theater includes in its list of theater personnel a "tyrewoman," indicating that tirewomen sometimes worked in the tiring-houses of private theaters as dressers for boy-actors.[64]

Yet the head- and neck-attires in which Nethlandish and other immigrant women specialized also appear in inventories of props and costumes and theatrical records pertaining to adult playing companies who performed in outdoor amphitheaters. A December 1596 entry in Henslowe's accounts records three pounds ten shillings paid for "a headtier & a Rebata & other thinges" for the Admiral's Men, and the inventory of costumes and properties taken by the company two years later includes "vi head-tiers" and "iiii rebatos."[65] In January 1598/9, the company paid three pounds for, among other things, "ii Rebates & j fardengalle"; in April 1599 they paid ten shillings for "A frenche hoode"; in January 1601/2 they paid ten shillings for "ij tiers"; in May of the same year they paid twenty-five shillings for "Rebatous & other things"; in

August they paid forty shillings for "Rebatose & fardingalls"; and in October they paid twenty pounds for "ij hedtyers," among other articles of apparel.[66] An inventory of playing apparel in the hand of Edward Alleyn dated circa 1602 includes "ij hedtirs sett wt stons."[67] Such records reveal that boy-actors in adult companies were wearing head- and neck-attires on the stage by the late 1590s and suggest that the demand for them increased in the early seventeenth century. Moreover, two of the entries from this period reveal that several of the Admiral's Men's head-attires were purchased from a Dutch tirewoman: in December 1601 and February 1601/2 they made two payments of twelve shillings each to a Dutchwoman named "m^{rs} gosen for a head tyer."[68] The many head-attires, rebatos, and farthingales (whalebone hoops for skirts) purchased by the company between January and October 1601/2 may likewise have been purchased from Mistress Gossen. A second tirewoman appears in the accounts in January 1603, when Henslowe loaned John Thare of the Earl of Worcester's Men ten shillings to purchase "ij curenets for hed tyers" from a "m^r calle," who was probably French, for a performance at court.[69]

Given the appearance of immigrant tirewomen and their wares in contemporary playhouse inventories, it hardly seems coincidental that Shakespeare lodged with a family of Huguenot tiremakers named Mountjoy on Silver Street in London from 1602, or perhaps earlier, until at least 1604, around the same time that the Admiral's and Earl of Worcester's Men were purchasing head- and neck-attires from Mistresses Gossen and Calle. Our knowledge of the Mountjoys' association with Shakespeare is derived mostly from legal documents of a suit brought by Stephen Belott (who served an apprenticeship with them and later married their daughter) against Christopher Mountjoy for failing to pay the dowry that Belott claims they had agreed upon. Shakespeare was summoned to London to give a deposition in the case in 1612, both because he had lodged with the family (in a tenement above their shop) and because he had helped negotiate the dowry.[70] Previous scholarship on Shakespeare's connection to the Mountjoys has assumed that the family trade was practiced only by Christopher, with little or no assistance from his female family members. If they participated at all, it has been assumed, it was as "the public face of their business, the customer services department."[71] Yet the manufacture, adornment, arrangement, and sale of women's neck- and head-attires, as we have seen, were predominantly the specialty of tirewomen during the period, and foreign tirewomen in particular. (Although male tiremakers certainly existed, the trade was strongly associated with women, particularly when it involved attiring women, or boy-actors who wore women's attires.) Randle Cotgrave's *Dictionarie of the French and English Tongues* (1611) defines a *Perruquiere* as "A Tyre-maker, or Attire-maker; a woman that makes Perriwigs, or Attires." There is clear evidence that in the Mountjoy family, the trade of tiremaking was practiced by both Christopher's wife and daughter. In his response to Belott's suit, Christopher claimed that although he had not been able to provide a dowry in cash for his daughter, he had "brought her to a good perfection in his sayd trade of Tyermakinge" and had given the couple "things Concerninge their trade . . . to the value of Twenty poundes" when they left his house, including "An ould drawinge table," "one Twistinge wheele of woode, twoe paire of little Scyssers," and "One Bobbine box."[72] Christopher Mountjoy clearly viewed the craft as a valuable property of skill that should be considered part of his daughter's dowry, as it would continue to generate income during her marriage.

Marie Mountjoy, Christopher's wife, appears to have become quite successful in the trade, as the account books of Queen Anne for 1604/5 include payments totaling £59 to "Marie Mountjoy tyrewoman" for "necessaries belonging to Her Highnes Roabes and other ornaments."[73] A portrait of Queen Anne from this period by Marcus Gheeraerts the Younger depicts her in a head-attire and rebato of the kind she might have purchased from Marie (see Figure 14). The famous Droeshout portrait of Shakespeare featured in the First Folio depicts the bard himself sporting a starched rebato supported by an underpropper, a sign, perhaps, of his own rise in status (see Figure 15). Whether or not Shakespeare acquired this particular collar from the Mountjoys, as Charles Nicholl has suggested, the portrait is nonetheless richly suggestive of theater people's reliance on alien craftswomen's skills and wares.[74] The recently attributed Cobbe portrait, dated to around 1610, if it is indeed of Shakespeare, depicts him in an even more elaborate, starched lace rebato. Shakespeare refers to such attires in several plays, such as *The Two Gentlemen of Verona* (c. 1590–98), in which Julia compares herself to Silvia's portrait, saying, "I think / If I had such a tire, this face of mine / Were full as lovely as is this of hers" and facetiously vowing "I'll get me such a color'd periwig" (4.4.184–86, 191). In *The Merry Wives of Windsor* (1597–1602), Falstaff flatters Mistress Ford by telling her she would "make an absolute courtier" and "has the right arch'd beauty of the brow" that would become "any tire of Venetian admittance" (3.3.62, 56–58). And in *Much Ado About Nothing* (1598–1600), Margaret serves as Hero's tirewoman, counseling her: "Troth, I think your other rebato were better" and "I like the new tire within excellently, if the hair were a thought browner" (3.4.6–7, 13–14).[75] Given that Shakespeare lived over a tiremaker's

Figure 14. Marcus Gheeraerts the Younger, portrait of Queen Anne of Denmark, wearing a starched rebato and lace cuffs, and bejeweled head-attire, holding a fan of feathers, c. 1605–10. Woburn Abbey. Reproduced by kind permission of His Grace the Duke of Bedford and the Trustees of the Bedford Estates.

Figure 15. Martin Droeshout, engraved portrait of William Shakespeare wearing a starched rebato in First Folio, 1623. By permission of The Folger Shakespeare Library.

shop from 1602 (or earlier) to 1604, it seems likely that when the company was in need of ruffs, rebatos, head-attires, or periwigs for plays performed during this period (one of which, *The London Prodigall*, will be discussed later in this chapter), they would have purchased them from the Mountjoy shop.

A number of other dramatists lived nearby and may have had connections to the Mountjoy shop, including Ben Jonson, who mentions the tiremakers of Silver Street in *Epicoene* of 1609, when Master Otter says of his wife: "her hair [was made] in Silver Street. . . . She takes herself asunder still when she goes to bed, into some twenty boxes" (4.2.85–86). *Epicoene* is littered with references to tirewomen and their wares, evoked in its satirical indictment of women's "pieced beauty" (1.1.81). Truewit asks, "Is it for us to see [women's] perukes put on, their false teeth, their complexion, their eyebrows, their nails?" (1.1.112–14), and later lists the retinue of retainers women employ to maintain their artificial allure, including "embroiderers, jewelers, tirewomen, sempsters, feathermen, [and] perfumers" (2.2.105–6). The play's climax famously turns on the removal of Epicoene's "peruke" (5.4.188), revealing that s/he is a boy acting a woman's part. The provision, arrangement, and dressing of the perukes and head-attires worn by the Children of the Queen's Revels when the play was performed at Whitefriars in 1609 would have been the job of a tirewoman, such as the one employed there the previous year by the King's Revels.

Jonson's *Poetaster*, performed by the Queen's Revels in 1601, likewise contains numerous references to head- and neck-attires, as well as to the laundresses who starched them. At the beginning of act 4, Chloe enters, enquiring of Cytheris, "But, sweet lady, say, am I well enough attired for the court . . . ?" (4.1.1–2). Cytheris replies, "you are as well jeweled as any of them [i.e., court ladies], your ruff and linen about you is much more pure than theirs . . . you shall see 'em flock about you with their puff wings, and ask you where you bought your lawn, and what you paid for it, who starches you, and entreat you to help 'em to some pure laundresses out of the city" (ll. 6–8, 16–20). The "pure laundresses out of the city" is probably a reference to the Protestant refugee laundresses and starchwomen from the Low Countries who plied their trade in the suburbs (due to City restrictions on unlicensed trade and the foul smell of seething starch) and were renowned for their expertise in cleaning, bleaching, and starching fine linen attires like the ruff of "pure" (or fine, pristine) lawn worn by Chloe in this scene. The Alien Returns reveal several Dutch and Flemish laundresses running highly successful starching businesses during the period (and hiring English women whom they trained in their craft), such as Widow Stedon of Maastricht, who employed eight English women, and Dionis Welfes of Antwerp, who employed nine.[76] Cytheris's comment reveals Jonson's familiarity with the "laundresses out of the city," and hints that the attires worn by the boy-actor playing Chloe may themselves have been laundered by immigrant starchwomen (whose religious and sexual "purity" was often mocked or called into question).

Although paid laundresses had existed in London since the Middle Ages, prior to the introduction of imported starching technologies in the 1560s their work had been done in their homes or at public conduits.[77] Mistress Dinghen van den Plasse, as we have seen, was credited with transforming the industry from a low-status, service occupation for impoverished women into a lucrative, skilled profession, by "profess[ing] herselfe a starcher wherein shee excelled." Howes, in his edition of Stow's *Annales*, emphasizes that although she was a religious refugee from Flanders, Mistress Dinghen was the daughter of a "worshipfull Knight," and that her customers "payed her very liberally, for her worke." Although at first her business was patronized only by women of "her owne Nation," gradually the "best and most curious wives" of London, "observing the neatenesse, and delicacy of the dutch for whitenesse, & fine wearing of Linnen," sent their own ruffs made of imported cambric and lawn to her and eventually "began to send their Daughters, and neatest kinsewomenne, to Mistris Dinghen, to learne how to starch."[78] (It should be noted that although the majority of refugees were Flemings and Walloons from the Spanish Netherlands, the term "Dutch" was loosely employed during the period to refer to anyone from the Low Countries or regions directly adjacent.)

One might imagine that Dutch starchwomen's transmission of skills to English women would have worked to placate native resentment of alien artisans for refusing to share trade secrets, but the gendered division of labor in early modern England precluded such a favorable reception. London guildsmen, who wished to maintain their prerogative over all skilled textile work, frowned upon any informal exchange of expertise in an unsupervised setting.[79] The perceived threat posed by immigrant women's unregulated dissemination of skills was further exacerbated by the fact that they often lived together in small or large groups (termed "spinster clusters" by historians),[80] sometimes all working together in the same occupation.[81] Widows who were "howsholdrisse[s]" frequently let rooms to immigrant textile workers, including other widows.[82] Some of these houses were extremely overcrowded, including that of a Southwark widow, which housed nineteen Flemish and Walloon immigrants, or that of a widow living in Shoreditch, which housed twenty-three strangers.[83] These all-female households and starch-houses, and widow-run boarding-houses, in the environs of the commercial theaters may have given rise to the association of "Dutch widows" with prostitutes, an association that appears frequently in dramatic literature.[84] This sexualization of Dutch working women is not surprising, given the general tendency to sexualize female labor during the period.[85] Yet it is precisely because of this tendency that we should not assume the veracity of the Dutch courtesan stereotype.[86] Given the economic challenges that immigrant women faced, some undoubtedly did turn to sex work to earn a living. Yet the Alien Returns reveal that many made a living in a variety of other ways, and some of them a very good one judging by the numbers of workers they employed.[87] There are numerous examples of Dutch widows, such as Widow Stedon and Dionis Welfes, running successful businesses that employed large numbers of alien and/or English workers.[88] The purported sexual promiscuity of Dutch widows should therefore be read within the context of their participation in a broader network of unregulated commerce, which included but was certainly not limited to sexual commerce.

Demand for the services of immigrant laundresses and starchwomen (and the native women they trained) grew during the late sixteenth century with the popularity of their starched attires, which themselves grew in size and sophistication. By the 1590s the English middling sort were increasingly sending their fine linens out to be professionally cleaned, bleached, and starched, a practice that appears in *The Merry Wives of Windsor*, where Mistress Ford instructs her servants to carry her basket of dirty linens to be "bucked" or bleached by the "whitsters" and "laundress" in Datchet Mead (3.3.12–13, 121–22, 141).[89] Unlike contemporary satires or puritan polemics decrying native English women's appetite for immigrant women's wares and services, however, Shakespeare's play suggests that English wives may appropriate the domestic virtues of Dutch women, while purging their households of their vices, which are in turn displaced onto Falstaff. Hidden in the buck-basket, Falstaff is "stopped in like a strong distillation with stinking clothes that fretted in their own grease.... half stewed in grease, like a Dutch dish ... thrown into the Thames, and cooled, glowing hot, in that surge ... hissing hot" (3.5.104–5, 109–12). Falstaff is directly linked to the popular stereotype of the Dutch as "butter-boxes," and indirectly to that of Dutch laundresses as steeped in the "strong distillation" of starch or bleach, "hissing hot" (or sexually promiscuous). In so doing, the passage functions to deflect these attributes away from "pure," native wives who send their linens to professional laundresses. Falstaff is likewise made a spokesman for the wares of foreign tirewomen in the play—"the ship-tire, the tire-valiant, or any tire of Venetian admittance" and later a "semi-circled farthingale" (3.3.48–52, 58)—which he deploys as tools of seduction.

By contrast, the play bestows the positive attributes for which Dutch women were renowned on its English wives. They are commercially active—Mistress Ford "has all the rule of her husband's purse" (1.3.49–50) and Mistress Page "do[es] what she will, say[s] what she will, take[s] all, pay[s] all" (2.2.111–12) and "bears the purse too" (1.3.65)—yet emphatically chaste, clean, and industrious. Spurning "lust and luxury" (5.5.94), Mistress Ford refuses the outlandish head-attires Falstaff dangles before her, professing, "A plain kerchief, Sir John: my brows become nothing else, nor that well neither" (3.3.53–54). Her own laundry basket is filled with serviceable linens rather than fine attires ("foul shirts and smocks, socks, foul stockings, greasy napkins" [3.5.83]). By sending the dissolute knight out to be "washed" in the buck-basket, they cleanse the domestic sphere of the threat of sexual incontinence, proving that "Wives may be merry, and yet honest too" (4.2.100).[90] Ford's fear that his wife's rule of his purse and commercial activity outside the home will inevitably lead to cuckoldry is assuaged. The play thereby suggests that English women may emulate their commercially active Dutch sisters while retaining their own, native purity.

The wives demonstrate this distinction again in act 4, when they play the role of tirewomen to Falstaff, dressing him as the fat woman of Brainford and providing "linen for [his] head" (4.2.77; see also ll. 79, 95–96). In contrast to the exotic, ornate head-attires Falstaff offers them, theirs are suggestive of simple, homespun modesty: a humble "thrumm'd hat and . . . muffler" (ll. 74–75). In act 4, the wives again serve as tirewomen, this time to the performers in the masque of the "Fairy Queen" (4.6.20): they dress the masquers ("Nan Page my daughter, and my little son, / And three or four more of their growth, we'll dress / Like urchins, oafs, and fairies . . . / With rounds of waxen tapers on their heads / . . . / My Nan shall be queen of all the fairies, / Finely attired in a robe of white" [4.4.47–50, 70–71]) and design their head-attires (Mistress Page "hath intended" we are told, that Ann "shall be loose enrobed, / With ribbons pendant flaring 'bout her head" [4.6.37, 39–41]). Yet the design of the masque associates these attires with chaste industry, rather than foreign luxury, as the fairies perform a symbolic scouring of Windsor Castle ("Our radiant Queen hates sluts and sluttery / . . . look you scour" [5.5.46, 61]). The buck-basket in *Merry Wives* thus appropriates for English wives Dutch women's renown as paragons of domestic virtue, exemplified by their pure, white linens, while cleansing the wives' native household of the negative connotations of their commercial activity (e.g., lust and luxury). Ironically, the basket used to convey the dirty laundry (along with Falstaff) offstage was in all likelihood the hamper used by the Chamberlain's Men to store costumes and convey their own foul linens and attires to laundresses like Widow Stedon and Dionis Welfes for washing and starching.

Linen underclothes served the important function of protecting expensive costumes from the sweat of the actor's body and would have needed laundering on a regular basis. Given the proliferation of professional Dutch and Flemish laundresses, whitsters, and starchwomen in the environs of the commercial theaters, it seems likely that the players relied on such women (or on native women whom they had trained) not only for the provision of ruffs, cuffs, rebatos, supportasses, head-attires, handkerchiefs, and other linen attires but for their laundering and starching as well. Before turning to examples of plays that acknowledge or recollect the labor of immigrant starch and tire-women in the commercial networks surrounding the professional theaters, let us consider the varied ways in which their labor was represented (and absented) within the culture at large.

Satirical or moralistic indictments of middling-sort women for consuming or aping such foreign fashions appear frequently in plays, pamphlets, and prints of the period and have been the subject of a great deal of critical commentary.[91] Less attention has been paid, however, to representations of the immigrant women who produced these attires, whose labor was decried as the "devil's work," an attribution that functioned simultaneously to highlight *and* elide it. In his *Pleasant Quippes for Upstart Newfangled Gentle-Women* (1595), for example, subtitled a *Pleasant Invective Against the Fantastical Foreigne Toyes, Daylie Used in Womens Apparell*, the anti-theatrical polemicist and clergyman Stephan Gosson attacks "These fashions fonde of countrey strange, / Which English heads so much delight," including "wyers," "glittering caules," "perriwigges," "ruffes," "pinnes," "spangles, chaines, and laces," "startch," "rebating proppes [i.e., underproppers for rebatos]," and "All this new pelfe, now solde in shoppes." Claiming that "(Don Sathan) Lord of fained lies, / All these new fangles did devise" and that they are the "devils ginnes [i.e., contrivances]," Gosson effaces the labor and ingenuity of the craftswomen "of countrey strange" who produced them by attributing their skills and technological sophistication to "Don Sathan." Although himself of Dutch descent (though of no known relation to the Mistress Gossen employed by the Admiral's Men to fabricate head-attires), Gosson dismisses Netherlandish women's starched attires as engines of pride and vanity, akin to peacocks' feathers.[92]

Gosson's description of newfangled attires as the "devils ginnes" may have been influenced by contemporary visual culture, as there are numerous late sixteenth- and early seventeenth-century prints depicting the devil (or death, demons, fools, and even animated feces) plying the tirewoman's trade—starching ruffs, arranging head-attires, and dressing customers.[93] A French engraving by Jacques Callot entitled *Superbia* (c. 1618–25), for example, shows a woman preening before a mirror, with a peacock standing behind her (an emblem of her pride), admiring her starched rebato as a demon arranges her head-attire

Figure 16. Jacques Callot, *Superbia* or Pride, c. 1618–25. Engraving depicting a female figure wearing a starched rebato, gazing into a mirror as a demon arranges her head-attire. © The Trustees of the British Museum.

Figure 17. Hieronymous Nützel, *Satire of French Fashion*, c. 1590. Engraving depicting a tirewoman (above left), demons, and a fool starching ruffs. © Bildarchiv Preussischer Kulturbesitz/Art Resource, N.Y.

(see Figure 16). Like Gosson's pamphlet, the print simultaneously highlights and elides the labor of the tirewoman by transforming her into a devil. Such prints frequently feature starched ruffs or rebatos as literal renderings of prideful stiff-neckedness. In some instances, the devil (or death, figured as a skull or skeleton) himself wears a ruff, while in others, empty ruffs take on a life of their own, as in the Serwouters engraving above (Figure 13). A German engraving by Hieronymous Nützel (c. 1590) satirizing French fashion depicts a tirewoman in her shop assisted by a fool and various demonic figures, one of which has a head shaped like a turd (see Figure 17).

In this print, the tirewoman's labor is evident, albeit still depicted as the "devil's work": she is busily starching a ruff, assisted by a demon who hands her setting irons, and the devil himself, who farts flames as he stokes the fire that heats the irons with his huge bellows—thereby enflaming the desires of the shop's customers for outlandish fashions. A finished ruff sits on the table next to the tirewoman with a large pile of *Scheiß* or feces at its center (signified by the large "S" emblazoned on it), revealing the dirty truth behind its gleaming, white purity. The turd-headed demon wears spectacles, the better to see his workmanship, and holds a mirror up to a couple who patronize the wares produced in the tirewoman's devilish workshop, while a fool stands behind them making a horned gesture to signify their sexual incontinence (further demonstrated by the male customer's hand, which gropes the woman's clothing).[94]

A Dutch engraving attributed to Maarten de Vos satirizing the vanity of women (c. 1600) likewise represents, in order to lambast, the labor of tirewomen, who adorn their customers in a shop (*boutiquel*) with masks, ruffs, and padded hip bustles, known colloquially in England as "bumrolls," while the print's captions suggest they are emissaries of the devil and those who patronize their shop will go to hell (see Figure 18). A male and female tiremaking couple stand at the rear of the shop behind their work table. He cuts out masks with scissors as she fabricates a bumroll; both are themselves wearing masks, emblematizing their false wares. Two tirewomen assist their female customers with dressing themselves in their newfangled attires, including large starched ruffs, false hair, and head-attires. The one at left is being fitted for a mask and clutches several more masks and a fan in one hand as she primps her ruff with the other. The second tirewoman at right kneels in front of her customer, attaching her bumroll as the woman obligingly and immodestly lifts her skirt. The captions in French and Dutch chastise their vanity, while suggesting their

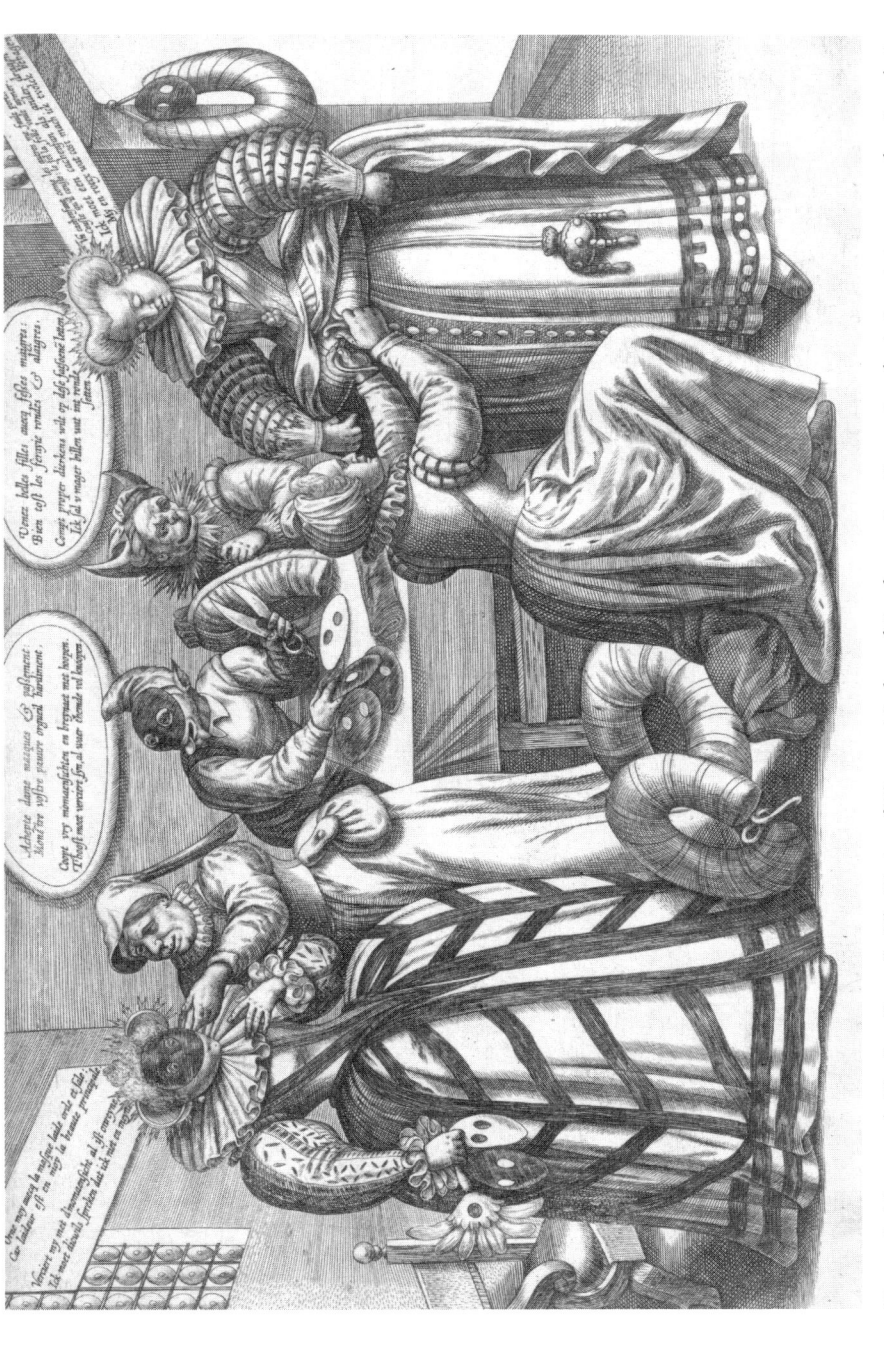

Figure 18. Maarten de Vos (attributed), *The Vanity of Women: Masks and Bustles*, c. 1600. Engraving depicting tirewomen adorning their customers with masks, ruffs, and padded hip rolls, known colloquially in England as "bumrolls." © The Metropolitan Museum of Art/Art Resource, N.Y.

sexual incontinence. The male tiremaker says, "Buy, women, masks and lacing [for your bumrolls], / show your monstrous, pathetic pride," while the female tiremaker promises to make her customers' thin buttocks round and plump (her horned mask suggesting her own sexual incontinence). The female customer at left asks to be decorated "with an ugly, filthy, dirty mask," while the woman at right confesses to needing the bumroll as a "*cachenfant*" to hide her pregnancy, whatever the cost. The inscriptions beneath warn that the women are full of pride, and defile their souls as they adorn their bodies, a sure path to "*gehenne*" or hell.

Another influential account of the devil-as-tiremaker appears in the second edition of Phillip Stubbes's *Anatomie of Abuses* (1584), as well as subsequent editions, under the title: "The devil found setting of great Ruffes." The anecdote concerns a purportedly true event that had occurred two years before to "a very rich Merchauntemannes daughter" of Antwerp, the news of which, according to Stubbes, has "blowne through all the worlde." Having been invited to a wedding, the woman in question makes "great preparation, for the pluming of her selfe in gorgeous arraie." She sends for "a couple of Laundresses," who do the best they can to "set her Ruffes, and Neckerechers to her minde." Because she is "so curious and daintie," however, the woman is dissatisfied with the way the ruffs are set and begins to "sweare, and teare, to cursse and banne, casting the Ruffes under feete, & wishing that the Devill might take her." At this moment, the devil obligingly appears disguised as a suitor and begins "setting of her Ruffes," which he performs "to her great contentation." The woman falls in love with the devil, kisses him, and has her neck broken by him. At her funeral, the coffin proves too heavy to lift, and when opened reveals "the body to be taken away, and a blacke Catte very leane & deformed sitting in the Coffin, setting of great ruffes, and frizzling of haire, to the great feare and wonder of all the beholders." Stubbes claims to have offered this "woefull spectacle" to his female readers, in which the skilled labor of Netherlandish laundresses is literally displaced by that of the devil himself, so that "by looking into it, in stead of their other looking Glasses they might see their owne filthinesse, & avoyd the like offence."[95]

The theatrical potential of the "spectacle" Stubbes presents as a speculum of female pride was apparently recognized by contemporary playwrights John Day and William Haughton, writing for the Admiral's Men, who were paid "in fulle" for a "playe called the prowd womon of an[t]warpe" in November 1601, now lost but thought to have drawn on Stubbes's anecdote.[96] Indeed, the *Proud Woman of Antwerp* is in all likelihood the play for which the company patronized the wares (and possibly the services) of the Dutch tirewoman Mistress Gossen in December 1601. On January 21, 1602, the company paid "harey cheattell for mendinge of the Boocke called the prowde womon the some of xs," a payment that is sandwiched in the accounts between two payments for attires, one to an unnamed tiremaker on the very same day ("the 21 of Janeway . . . pd for ij tiers xs") and the second "to m^{rs} goossen for a headtyer the 17 of febrary 1601[/2] the some of xij^s."[97] If the play did contain a scene of the devil "setting of great ruffes, and frizzling of haire" based on Stubbes's account, then Mistress Gossen may have provided not only the starched attires for the "prowde womon" but also her expertise in dressing, "setting," and "frizzling" the boy-actor who wore them. The staging of her attires and reenactment of her behind-the-scenes work by male actors onstage (e.g., playing the laundresses, devil and "blacke Catte") provide apt instances of both the reliance on and elision of women's offstage labors on the professional stage.

Satirical and moralistic attacks on women's newfangled and outlandish fashions do not simply or invariably ellide the female labors that were necessary to produce them; indeed, they often depict the tirewoman's occupation as exceptionally laborious or, in a well-worn pun, as "tire-some." Barnabe Rich, in his *Newes both from Heaven and Hell* of 1593, for example, describes a proud tirewoman who is on her way to hell with a "fardle" of foreign fashions under her arm, the contents of which include:

> Perewigs of the newe curle, Roules [of hair], and other attyres for
> the heade of the new fashion, Ruffes of the newe sette, newe Cuttes,
> newe Stitches, newe gardes, newe imbroyders, newe devysed French
> Verdingales, newe French bodyes [i.e., bodices, or quilted corsets stayed
> with whalebone], newe bumbasting [i.e., cotton-wool padding], newe
> bolstering [i.e., padding used around the buttocks and hips], newe
> underlayings [i.e., linings for shoes], and twentie newe devyses more
> than I have nowe spoken of.[98]

Rich's tirewoman takes manifest pride not only in the novelty and variety of her wares but in the skilled labor required to produce them, boasting of her "perewigs, curled and frisled by art," her "roules of hayre perfumed an platted by proportion," and her "ruffes" that take "one whole day to wash and starch, and an other daies labour but to pinne them in the fashion." The work of attiring, according to Rich, is never done precisely because it is propelled by the ever-changing, "newe devyses" of the tirewoman. The labor time required to produce, maintain, and arrange this ever-expanding list of commodities is inversely proportional, his account implies, to their lack of "true" substance: starch, bombast, whalebones, and false hair are all used to prop up women's pride and false, artificial beauty.

The tiring labor of attiring spurred by the constant demand for sartorial novelty appears onstage in Marston's *Histrio-Mastix* (1598–99) when a "Tyrewoman" named Mistresse Pinckanie enters in act 3, scene 1 with a "Jeweller" and "Taylour" to attire three fashionable ladies (Perpetuana, Fillisella, and Bellula).[99] Fillisella asks, "Mistresse Pinckanie is my new ruffe done?" to which the tirewoman replies, "Beleeve me Madam tis but new begun." Bellula next inquires when the fan she has ordered will be ready, to which Pinckanie replies, "Maddam not this weeke doe what I can." As the tirewoman exits, she promises in exasperation to work hard to fill their orders, "Well Ladies, though with worke I am opprest, / Workewomen alwaies live by doing, best." Here, the constant "doing" with which "Workewomen" (a colloquial term for women who embroidered and adorned luxury attires) are "opprest" is linked to the perpetual demand of fashionable ladies for their attires and to the constantly changing fashion trends—"The newest fashion (still) must be your guide," Pride announces earlier in the scene—while also hinting at the purported sexual "doings" of women who worked in the trade.[100]

A seventeenth-century epigram by Robert Hayman entitled "Womens Tyers" likewise emphasizes the incessant labor required to produce, as well as consume, head-attires: "Womens head-laces and high towring wyres, / Significantly, rightly are cald tyres; / They tyre them and their Maides in putting on, / Tyre Tyremakers, with variation. / I thinke to pay for them, doth tyre some men; / I hope they'll tyre the Devill that invents them."[101] The demand for novelty gives rise to multiple echelons or tiers of labor in Hayman's account: the Devil "invents them," "Tyremakers" fabricate them, and women and their maids labor "in putting [them] on." (The nouns "tire" and "tier" both derive from the Old French *tire*, meaning a "suite, sequence, range, rank, order," suggesting the layers or rows of both head-attires and ruffs and the division of labor their fabrication entails.)

Richard Brathwaite's *The English Gentlewoman* (1631) deploys the same pun, maintaining that "Commerce with forraine Nations" has "tyred our women with tyres," and that those who are the "compleatest Fashionmongers . . . tyre themselves with their attiring." Brathwaite further instructs that in spite of the tirewoman's tireless industry, hers is not a "proper vocation." Whereas in ancient times, artisans wore a "badge" to signify the discrete and legitimate "Trade[s] whereby [they] lived," the "new-found Artists" who produce "new-minted fashions" —such as the "Periwig, Gregorian-maker [i.e., wig maker], or Tyre-woman"—are "uselesse loyterers" who should "rather [be] derided than approved, geered than applauded." Those who tire themselves with the labor of attiring are like actors who spend "so much time in the Tyring house" that they forget "what part [they are] to play on the Stage."[102] That gentlemen and women have come to rely on the labors of the tirewoman, in Brathwaite's view, has rendered all the world a stage. Yet Brathwaite does not condemn the *theatrum mundi* topos; rather, he deploys it as an exemplum of sprezzatura, valorizing the performance of elite identity on the stage of life while devaluing the labors that produce that identity behind the scenes.

A visual rendering of the incessant and varied labors required to produce starched linen attires appears in a satirical engraving from the 1560s by Pieter van der Borcht (see Figure 19). Female monkeys are depicted fueling the latest fashion in starched ruffs, both as consumers and producers: they "ape" not only the fashion of ruffs but also their fashion*ing* by learning through imitation the requisite skills associated with their manufacture.[103] The print illustrates each stage of the starching process. Customers bring in dirty ruffs to be laundered (above left). The ruffs are then washed (above center), dried on the line (above right), carefully smeared with starch (lower left), dried by the fire (lower right), and molded into sets with a hot iron (lower center). By taking the tools and skills of manufacture into their own hands, these female "apes" posed a symbolic threat to male crafts- and tradesmen, a threat that was frequently cast in sexual terms that centered on the phallic goffering irons or setting sticks—known colloquially as "poking sticks"—that were used by female starchers to set ruffs into their classic figure-eight patterns. Thus, for example, in act 3, scene 1 of Edward Sharpham's *Cupids Whirligig* (performed by the Children of the King's Revels at Whitefriars in 1607/8 while a "Tyre-woman" was employed there), Slack asks, "why doe your Semsters spend their time in pricking, and your Ladies in poking of ruffes; but onely to shew they doe as they would be don unto?"[104]

Slack's satirical jibe aims to disarm these female producers by turning the tools of their trade against them and stigmatizing them as sexually promiscuous: women who wield poking sticks, he implies, are merely demonstrating their desire to be sexually "poked" or "pricked."[105] He may also be intimating that the sempstresses, laundresses, starchwomen, and tirewomen, who inhabit all-female workspaces, use their poking sticks for direct sexual gratification in the absence of men. According to Philip Stubbes, poking sticks were

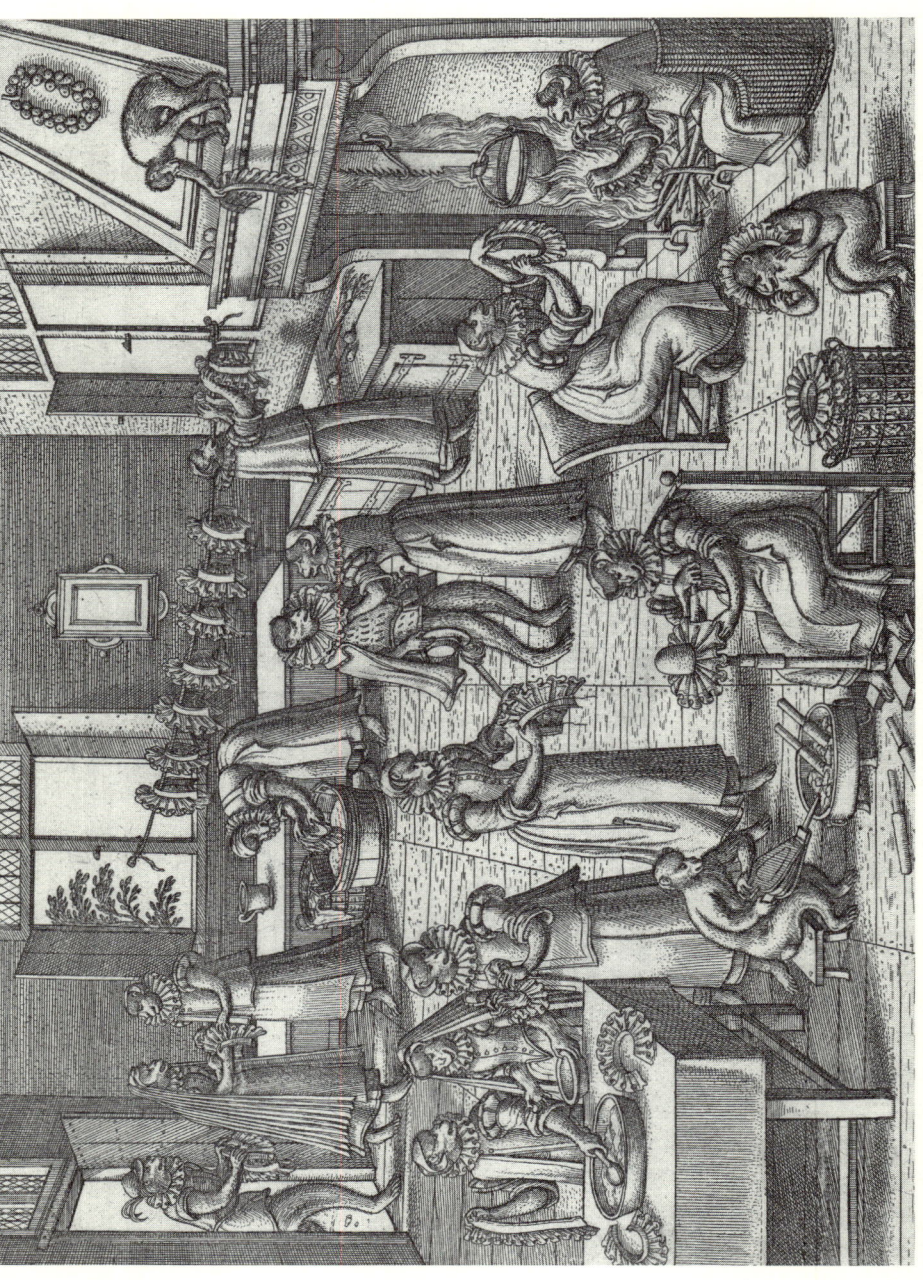

Figure 19. Pieter van der Borcht, *The Laundry*, c. 1562. Engraving of female monkeys aping the latest fashion: starching and setting linen ruffs using poking sticks. © The Trustees of the British Museum.

sometimes fashioned in the manner of "a squirt, or a squibe," which allowed them to "squirt out water withal," closely resembling the contemporary dildos "nourisht with whott water" described by Thomas Nashe in "The Choise of Valentines."[106] The punishment tirewomen will receive in hell for their unnatural sexual proclivities is suggested by an engraving attributed to de Vos in the same series as that in Figure 18, which depicts the devil heating up poking sticks over a flame as he warns, "With this iron that you see warming I'll make you howl in Hell."[107] In the Nützel print (Figure 17), the turd-headed demon stands astride the flame that heats the irons, and that has clearly inflamed him as well: his erect phallus points directly at the female customer who, we surmise, will be "poked" by him as punishment for her pride.

The female workspace of the laundry or starch-house, with its hot, moist environment, constant activity of rubbing and poking, and the two primary tools of the trade—hot poking sticks and the congealed liquid of starch, with its resemblance to bodily fluids and stiffening properties—clearly unsettled the minds of early modern moralists. Beneath the van der Borcht engraving is a motto in Latin, French, and Dutch that roughly translates as: "We'll wash, dry, iron, curl and beautify your ruff, / We're just as good as men—for you can't do enough!"[108] The monkeys perform the labor of starching, the motto suggests, because humans can't "do enough" to satisfy the demand for them. Yet their boast clearly refers to the monkeys' gender, as well as their species. The female starchers run their business as efficiently as men, satisfying and profiting from this demand, while also using their poking sticks to satisfy their own bestial desires because men can't "do enough" to gratify them sexually.

Yet male anxiety surrounding the "poking sticks" brought to England by immigrant tirewomen, sempsters, and laundresses cannot be reduced to their phallic morphology alone; it likewise centered on alien craftswomen's sophisticated skills and technologies and the new forms of desire and consumption to which they gave rise. Stubbes places great emphasis on the technological sophistication required to starch ruffs ("they cannot set them artificially inough," he says, without "their tooles and instruments for the purpose") and goes into great detail describing them.[109] As we have seen, such techniques and technologies transformed the low-status labor of laundering, which had always been and would remain women's work, into a highly skilled and (when it entailed washing and starching fine linen attires) highly paid occupation.[110] A visual rendering of this newly stratified and diversified occupation appears in a watercolor in the friendship album of Adriaen van de Venne depicting professional Dutch laundresses (see Figure 20). On the ground are ordinary

Figure 20. Adriaen van de Venne, c. 1620–26. Dutch laundresses setting out linen ruffs, handkerchiefs, smocks, aprons, sheets, and bolts of fabric to dry and bleach in the sun. At rear is the laundry house. Watercolor and bodycolor, over black chalk, heightened with silver and gold. © The Trustees of the British Museum.

bed linens, smocks, and petticoats, together with higher-status ruffs, bands, and handkerchiefs. The two head laundresses in the foreground are distinguished by their starched neck- and head-attires, suggesting that they delegate the sweaty work of laundering and starching to the five female and two male employees depicted behind them. The three female workers to their left, who wear more modest head-attires, are stretching bolts of linen fabric, indicating that the business served professional linen drapers as well as private customers, a testament to the industriousness of the head laundresses. The bending posture of three of the female laundresses, two of whom present their backsides to the viewer, however, serves as a visual reminder of the bawdy connotations of their trade. At the rear of the painting is the smoke-belching starch- or laundry house, to which men and women carry baskets of clothing to be blued and starched.[111]

These sophisticated starching and laundering techniques would eventually be codified in conduct, receipt, and how-to books for women, such as Hannah Woolley's *The Compleat Servant-Maid; or, The Young Maidens Tutor* (1677). Woolley's manual reveals the stratification of the trade within the households of the elite, where the everyday laundering and mending of household linens was the job of the "laundry-maid," while the laundering and starching of finer fabrics was delegated to the "chamber-maid." Woolley instructs the latter in a diverse array of sophisticated laundering techniques needed for an equally diverse array of fabrics and attires. Young women who would ready themselves "to serve a Gentle woman" and who desire "a good salary, and a great deal of respect," she advises, must "learn how to dress, wash and starch very well, all manner of Tiffanies [i.e., a transparent silk used for veils and other attires], Lawns, Points and Laces" and "learn to work all sorts of Needle work and plain work, [and] to wash black and white sarsenets [i.e., a very fine, soft silk used for undergarments and linings]." The manual obligingly contains instructions for cleaning and starching these fabrics (as well as "Coloured Silk," "Silk Stockings," "Sattin," "Taffety," and "Gold and Silver Lace") and for the removal of ink, fruit, and grease stains.[112]

The low status of laundresses in England prior to the transformation of the trade by immigrant starchwomen in the late sixteenth century may be glimpsed in John Heywood's Tudor interlude *The Playe of the Weather* (1533), where the laundress is cast as "raylyng hore," who curses gentlewomen who "would banishe the sunne" to keep their "face[s] fayre," warning they would then also keep their "smocke[s] beshitten" as laundering requires sun to dry clothes. Although the "dayly toyle and labour" of the laundress was situated at the bottom of the hierarchy of labor in Heywood's time due to its status as unskilled women's work, he does not depict her in entirely negative terms. Rather, we begin to see in this early interlude an emergent ambivalence toward the laundress as an emblem of *both* bodily and moral filth or sexual incontinence *and* cleanliness, chaste industry and spiritual devotion: in spite of her bawdy raillery, the laundress boasts that she is able to provide for herself and avoid idleness through the sweat of her own brow.[113]

One hundred years later, it is not the low status but the social "advancement" and consequent hauteur of laundresses that are satirized in Richard Brathwaite's *Whimzies; or, A New Cast of Characters* of 1631:

> She now scornes to be so meanly imployed in her owne person, as she ha's formerly beene; she ha's got her therefore a brace of Under-Laundresses to supply her place, performe her charge, and goe through-stitch with her trade. The sweate is theirs; but the sweete is hers. These must be accomptants weekely of their comings on; and returne a just particular of all such vailes, profits, or emoluments as usually or accidentally have any way accrued. Shee now stands upon her pantofles forsooth; and will not wet her hand, lest shee spoyle the graine of her skinne: Mistris Joan ha's quite forgot that shee was once Jugge:[114]

The sexual innuendo of Brathwaite's description suggests that the upwardly mobile laundress is more bawd than prostitute: she rules over a "brace of Under-Laundresses," who "sweate" in her place for their "comings on." Her social advancement is a product of her industry (she runs a business with hired employees, keeps accounts, accrues profits, and so forth), yet her industriousness is tainted with the stain of sexual incontinence.

Brathwaite's depiction of the laundress was no doubt influenced by John Taylor's mock encomium, *In Praise of Cleane Linnen, With the Commendable Use of the Laundresse* (first published in 1624 and later reprinted in his complete *Workes* of 1630), which is perhaps the most extensive contemporary account we have of the elevation and transformation of the laundress's trade in the aftermath of the alien influx and textile revolution of the late sixteenth century, as well as of the conflicting attitudes provoked by this transformation.[115] As Taylor's title announces, his "Use of the Laundresse" is from beginning to end a paradox of praise—"for the Anagram of Launder," he notes, "is Slawnder [slander]" (164–65). Playfully drawing on Protestant figurations of God as a laundress or bleacher of the soul,[116] he dedicates his treatise to "the Most Purifying, and Repurifying, Cleanser, Clearer, and Reformer of deformed and polluted Linnen, Martha Legge Esquiresse, transparent, unspotted, Snow Lilly-white Laundresse." The dedicatory epistle begins by christening the laundress with a new name that will better reflect her elevated status and the diversification of her trade:

> [M]y most laborious and purifying Patronesse, your glory shall no longer be Ecclipsed, to be termed a bare Lawndres, or a dresser of Lawne, but a Hollandresse, Tiffanie-dresse, Lawndresse, Lockrumdresse, Dowlesdresse, Callicute and Canvas-dresse, which in the totall is a Linnendresse, as you are the onely Linnen Armouresse, Cap a pea from the declination of the smocke, to the exaltation of the Nightcap, and from the loftie Quoyfe [i.e., coif, a type of head-attire], to the lowly and welbeloved Smockeskirt. (165)

Taylor acknowledges that the contemporary laundress (a term he endows with the false etymology *lawn* + *dress*) should more properly be known as a "Linnendresse," on account of the increasingly diverse types of linen fabric (e.g., holland, tiffany, lawn, lockram, dowlas, calico, canvas, etc.) and attires in which she now specializes. To have "clean linen" is no longer a matter of simple hygiene but of "pleasure, profit, and ornament" (166). Yet, in naming the diverse attires that have become her stock-in-trade, Taylor implies that her social "exaltation" may be as illusory as the starch upon which it is built, for she still washes soiled, "lowly" underclothes.

At the start of his poem, Taylor claims that he was inspired to write it while "in Bed alone, / Where (cares except) Bed fellow had I none. / My drowsy Muse awak'd, and straight she meets / This wel-beloved subject, 'twixt the sheets." The invocation of his muse continues the tension between exhaltation and "Slawnder," as it hints at the laundress's proverbial sexual/bodily/moral incontinence (a commonplace arising in part from her proximity to, and familiarity with, bed linens and undergarments). In keeping with the generic protocols of the mock encomium, the poem maintains a balance throughout between high/low, cleanliness/filth, and chastity/venery, as in the following passage:

> Now of the lovely Laundresse, whose cleane trade,
> Is th'onely cause that Linnen's cleanly made:

> Her living is on two extremes relying,
> She's ever wetting, or shee's ever drying.
> As all men dye to live, and live to dye,
> So doth she dry to wash, and wash to drye.
> She runnes like Luna in her circled spheare,
> In a perpetuall motion shee doth steare.
> Her course in compasse round and endlesse still,
> Much like a horse that labours in a mill:
> To shew more plaine how shee her worke doth frame . . .
> She wrings, she folds, she pleits, she smoothes, she starches,
> She stiffens, poakes, and sets and dryes againe,
> And foldes: thus end of paine begins her paine.
> Round like a whirligigge or lenten Top . . .
> Like a Commaundresse, using martiall Lawes,
> She strikes, she poakes and thrusts, she hangs and drawes,
> She stiffens stiffly, she both opes and shuts,
> She sets, and out she pulles, and in she puts.
> Not caring much if wind blow low or hye,
> Whilst drunkards thirst for drink, she thirsts to dry.
> Thus having shew'd the Laundresse praise and paine,
> How end of worke begins her worke againe:
> I hope amongst them they will all conclude,
> Not to requite me with ingratitude:
> But as an Act they'l friendly have decreed,
> I ne'r shall want Cleane Linnen at my need. (169)

The laundress's trade, which now encompasses the skilled labor of starching, is rendered as a *coincidentia oppositorum* ("Her living is on two extremes relying"), conjoining the activities of wetting/drying, opening/shutting, pulling/poking, and so forth in an endless cycle of labor. Taylor draws on a series of images to depict this cycle as without end or never done. The "circled spheare" of the moon joins day and night, and high and low, and suggests female fickleness and sexual promiscuity (she "works" through the night), as well as chaste industry and devotion (Cynthia or Luna being one of Elizabeth's emblems). The images of the "horse that labours in a mill" and of the "whirligigge or lenten Top," while suggestive of the "perpetuall motion" of virtuous industry, debase that industry as mere drudgery or idle play, respectively (169). These circular images in turn echo the imagery describing ruffs that runs through the poem, figuring them as empty, insubstantial nothings that "pride doth puffe" (167) or as ciphers of female sexuality that have "grow[n] great" (167) and given birth to other, equally empty fashions ("Ruffes are to Cuffes, as 'twere the breeding mothers" [168]), which in turn grow great and repeat the cycle ("Cuffe 'tis prettily encreac'd, / . . . / At first 'twas but a girdle for the wrist, / Or a small circle to enclose the fist, / Which hath by little and by little crept, / And from the wrist unto the elboe leap't" [168]). Like the self-propagating cipher of the usuress discussed in Chapter 2, the empty O of the ruff-producing laundress/starcher is depicted as inflating and re-producing itself within an all-female economy: Taylor insists that "Men there [i.e., in the laundry or starch-house] have nought to doe, they may goe walke" (169). The poking stick is again figured as a phallic implement or weapon with which the laundress pleasures herself sexually in a "perpetuall motion" ("She stiffens stiffly, she both opes and shuts, / She sets, and out she pulles, and in she puts") that takes place in the absence of men.

Having surveyed a wide array of cultural representations that variously sexualize, demonize, appropriate, or simply elide the work of immigrant starchwomen, laundresses, and tirewomen, let us now consider two plays that stage starched, linen attires as products of their labor, albeit to very different ends. In act 3, scene 2 of Thomas Dekker, Henry Chettle, and William Haughton's *The Pleasant Comodie of Patient Grissil* (1600), Gwenthyan, the shrewish wife of Welsh knight Sir Owen ap Meredith, is approached by their servant Rice, who informs her: "Tannekin the Froe hath brought your Rebato, it comes to three pound" (3.2.243–44).[117] The play text is quite specific in identifying the attire in question and the immigrant starchwoman from whom it is obtained: the term "froe" was a common and "Tannekin" a proper name associated with Dutch women during the period. Although the rebato stands at the center of the scene's ensuing action—as we shall see, Sir Owen and Gwenthyan nearly come to blows over it—Tannekin is only briefly mentioned and never appears onstage. Why, then, do the playwrights insist on introducing her lexically into the scene as the manufacturer of the rebato? The passing reference would seem to function as a kind of metonymic index, pointing to or standing in for the larger population of immigrant starch- and tirewomen living in the environs of the commercial theaters. Recall that it was around this time that the Admiral's Men, who performed *Patient Grissil*, purchased similar attires from a

Dutch froe named Mistress Gossen. Indeed, it is precisely because Mistress Gossen and her peers were such a visible presence in London during the period that this moniker can so readily assume its referential function without any further explication and Tannekin herself remain invisible as an offstage persona.

A Welsh couple living in Italy, Sir Owen and Gwenthyan repeatedly refer to themselves as British or "Pritish," evoking Welsh lineage to the ancient Britons, and are thereby employed in the play as a vehicle through which English vice and domestic disorder are indirectly satirized. Gwenthyan functions as a comic foil for patient Grissil (or Griselda) throughout the play, setting off the latter's temperance, patience, modesty, and thrift through her own intemperance, impatience, pride, and prodigality. It is only in the last scene that we discover that Gwenthyan has been testing her husband's patience and virtue, just "as her cozen [Gwalter] has tried Grissill['s]" (5.2.262). Part of this test involves her exorbitant spending on fashionable attire, which is where the rebato figures in. The significance of the rebato in the scene is complicated by the Welsh couple's broken English, which renders their linguistic and cultural competency suspect. When Sir Owen espies Rice delivering the rebato to Gwenthyan, he demands, "What a pestilence is this for Gwenthyan?" (3.2.245). She responds, "For her neg [i.e., neck], is cald repatoes, Gwenthian weare it heere, ist not prave [i.e., brave]?" (l. 246–47). The exchange highlights the rebato's status as a high-fashion, luxury attire, identifiable only to those "in-the-know" who have both sufficient means to afford and cultural competency to recognize the latest trends in starched neckwear. Sir Owen himself seems not to know (or at least not to see) what the rebato is, so that Gwenthyan must cue him—and those in the audience not in-the-know—as to its proper name, form, and function. Yet Gwenthyan's response suggests that her own cultural savvy, like her grasp of the English language, may be recent and tenuous acquisitions, insofar as her "is cald repatoes" may imply "—or so I am told."

Sir Owen, stricken by his wife's prodigality, shouts, "Prave? Yes is prave, tis repatoes I warrant her: I patoes money out a crie" (ll. 248–49). Turning the plural noun into an invented verb ("patoes"), Owen suggests that rebatos are synonymous with extravagant spending and demands to know the price of the rebato, crying, "Rees the preece? Rees the preece?" (l. 249). Under instruction from Gwenthyan, Rice inflates the price of the rebato (to further "test" Owen's patience), claiming, "The Froe sir saies five pound" (l. 250). Rice's reiteration of the term "Froe" in connection with the rebato casts that connection as one of extortionate pricing and would therefore seem to play into xenophobic fears of parasitical aliens emptying the purses of native consumers. Insofar as we know that it is *not* the froe but rather Gwenthyan herself who has raised the price of the rebato, however, the reference may play on rather than into such fears by demonstrating that they are blown out of proportion in the minds of "native" consumers. Sir Owen begins to hyperventilate or giggle nervously ("Ha ha ha, pound") and begs Gwenthyan "pray doe not pye it" (l. 251). Gwenthyan insists "her [i.e., I] shall pye it" and "weare it pye and pye" (ll. 252, 254–55), at which point Sir Owen grabs the rebato and rips it, chiding, "so tag [i.e., take] it now, weare it now powte her neg [i.e., your neck], shall pridle sir Owen ha?" (ll. 258–59). It is worth noting that Gwenthyan and Owen both habitually substitute "her" for all other personal pronouns, a (mis)usage that not only confounds the referentiality of their speech but also has the effect of effeminizing Owen, when "he" is referred to as "her," thereby reinforcing his emasculation by Gwenthyan (Gwalter says of Owen, "I doubt his wife will proove the better man" [4.3.172]). The contest between Sir Owen and Gwenthyan over the rebato in *Patient Grissil* is cast in gendered terms as a contest over who will "bridle" whom, a metaphor that is reinforced by the fact that rebatos, like bridles, were worn about the neck. Yet unlike bridles, rebatos were quite delicate, which is why they had to be starched or stiffened by Dutch froes. The scene indirectly depicts Dutch women's skill at starching, which literally stiffens the necks of English wives, as a threat to Sir Owen's "Pritish" manhood.

The association between shrews and (masculine) stiffness or inflexibility—and conversely, between modest wives and (feminine) pliability—is further reinforced by the play's main plot, which visually associates Grissil with her family's trade: basket weaving. When we first see Grissil, she is weaving baskets with her father and his servant onstage, as her father sings, "Worke apace, apace, apace, apace: / Honest labour beares a lovely face" (1.2.101–2). Throughout the play, Grissil's chaste industry and "thrid-bare russets" (1.2.48) are contrasted with Gwenthyan's wasteful expenditure on luxury attire: Grissil's natural beauty and rosy complexion are enhanced by her "honest labour," while Gwenthyan's are produced through the purchase of expensive cosmetics and extravagant attires. This contrast is further linked to that of pliability versus stiffness, when we learn that basket making relies on the pliability of "osiers" (the reeds out of which baskets are woven) when they are young and green (like Grissil), before they are stiffened with age (like Gwenthyan). Thus, when Sir Owen asks Grissil's husband Gwalter to teach him how to tame or "bridle" Gwenthyan, Gwalter instructs him to cut three osiers and to keep them "safe laide up" (3.2.153) to dry, meanwhile taking three himself to preserve, braiding them together. Although Owen (and later Gwenthyan) assumes that the hardened osiers will be used to whip the shrew into compliance, Gwalter has a different lesson in mind: he instructs Owen to braid his stiff, dried osiers together, whereupon the latter discovers that they are "stubberne like Gwenthians" and break into "snip snap peeces" (5.2.235–36). Gwalter boasts that his osiers "did gently bowe" because they were woven together when green; so too "I tride my Grissils patience when twas greene, / Like a young Osier" (ll. 237–39). When Owen seeks to wrest control of the rebato from Gwenthyan in hopes of rendering her more pliant, he thus only succeeds in tearing it into "snip snap peeces," for his widow is herself stiffened with age and will not relent.

As stage properties, Grissil's basket and Gwenthyan's rebato thus metonymically point to the contrast between pliable, young wives and inflexible, recalcitrant widows. The stiffening of baskets is represented as a natural process in contrast to the stiffening of rebatos, which depends on artificially made "froes past[e]" or starch.[118] Baskets are produced within and contribute to the household economy through their pragmatic function, whereas rebatos have no discernable use-value other than to stiffen the necks of wayward widows by inflaming their appetite for foreign fashions purchased outside the home. Like the buck-basket in *The Merry Wives of Windsor*, the basket in *Patient Grissil* thus functions as an emblem of chaste wives' honest industry, homespun values, and rejection of insubstantial, outlandish attires. By contrast, the substance and solidity of Gwenthyan's starched rebato is merely illusory and must be continually reproduced by the incessant labor of Dutch starch- and tire-women, thereby draining domestic resources on useless frivolities.[119] Sir Owen ends the scene by regretting his marriage ("were petter be hang'd and quarter," he says, "then marry widowes") and by warning "awl prittish Shentlemans" against making the same mistake (3.2.273–74, 276). In *Patient Grissil*, the presence of Dutch froes in the environs of commercial theaters is thus recollected in order to satirize the shrewish behavior of "pritish" wives and widows who consume their starched linen attires but do not have the skills necessary to fabricate them.[120] In so doing, however, the play nonetheless reminds its audience of the provenance of the starched attires worn onstage, and of the offstage labors of immigrant women that were necessary to (re)produce them.

A contrasting portrayal of Dutch women's starched linen attires as emblematic of their domestic virtue, chastity, and thrift appears in *The London*

Prodigall (1603–5), a play famously attributed to Shakespeare on the title page of the 1605 Quarto but more recently suggested to be the work of Thomas Dekker.[121] If Dekker did write, or have a hand in writing, this play, as he did in *Patient Grissil*, it might help explain the reference to Dutch froes in both plays, as Dekker is thought to have been "of Dutch parentage himself, though born in London."[122] If Shakespeare suggested the plot, as some have speculated, it might also help explain the play's prominent staging of the skills associated with the tirewoman's trade, as it was written toward the end of or just after his stay with the Mountjoys on Silver Street. The Dutch woman in this play is not a character but rather a disguise assumed by an English character named Luce (the Griselda-like daughter of Sir Lancelot Spurcock) after her marriage to Matthew Flowerdale, the as yet unreformed prodigal of the play's title. Just after they are wedded, Matthew is arrested for his debts and his impecuniousness revealed to Sir Lancelot. When Luce insists upon remaining with her husband in spite of his prodigality she is renounced by her father and summarily rejected by Matthew himself, who cruelly suggests she "turne whore" (3.3.294).[123] At the suggestion of Matthew's father, Flowerdale Sr., who is disguised as his son's servant Christopher, Luce takes up the disguise of a "Dutch Froe" (5.1.165), again named Tanikin, and is employed as a servant by her sister Frances and Frances's husband, Civet. Frances is herself cast as a prodigal throughout the play (she marries Civet, a wealthy moneylender's heir, because he is able maintain her in the style to which she is accustomed).

Through her employment in their household, Luce manifests her ingenuity and chaste industry by demonstrating her skills as a tirewoman. When Luce first appears in her Tanikin disguise speaking with a Dutch accent, she is widely praised by her employers: "I thank thee for my maide," Civet tells Christopher, "I like her very well" (4.3.2–3). Frances also likes her "very well, excellent well" (ll. 5–6), not only because she "speakes so prettily" (l. 5) in her faux Dutch accent but because of the skills she has imported into their household: "O Tanikin," she exclaims, "you are excellent for dressing ones head a newe fashion" (ll. 10–12). At this point in the play, Frances has only just been introduced to Tanikin, who is still standing in front of their house and has not yet entered it, so Frances's knowledge of Tanikin's tiremaking skills can only be derived from the renown of Dutch women as manufacturers of such attires or from her admiration of the head-attire Tanikin is herself wearing. The stage direction tells us that Luce enters disguised "like a Dutch Frow" (4.3.s.d.), and it seems likely that the ethnically distinguishing feature of her costume would have been starched linen head- and neck-attires. When Luce's second sister, Delia, later enters and recognizes Luce through her disguise, Delia whispers, "Sister Luce, tis not your broken language / Nor this same habit, can disguise your face / From I that know you" (5.1.75–78), indicating that Luce's "habit" or costume primarily disguises her head and face.

The play mines the comedic potential of Dutch froes' starched linen attires when Frances voices her desire for an "outlandish" head-attire of her own.[124] In response to Frances's observation that her maid is "excellent for dressing ones head a newe fashion," Luce/Tanikin replies proudly, "Me sall doe every ting about da head" (4.3.13). Thrilled by this discovery, Frances asks Luce to provide her with "cheekes and eares" (ll. 16, 20), a type of head-attire described by the *Dictionary of English Costume* as a linen coif with "sides made to curve forward over the ears."[125] Contemporary visual depictions of such attires, as in Rembrandt's 1634 portrait of Aechje Claesdr., suggest why they came to have this moniker, as the starched, curved fabric indeed resembled ears, in relation to which the side cloth might be described as cheeks (see Figure 21).

Frances's request is mocked by Flowerdale Sr./Christopher, who asks, "Cheekes and eares, why mistresse Frances, want you cheekes and eares? Me thinkes you have very faire ones" (4.3.22–24). His comment evokes contemporary satires and puritan polemics deriding women's desire to improve on nature through their use of cosmetics and consumption of foreign fashions.[126] Implicit in Christopher's comment is the absurdity of Frances's desire to purchase prosthetic cheeks and ears when she is already provided with those God and nature have given her. The play persistently contrasts Frances's prodigality and sexual appetite with Luce/Tanikin's thrift and chastity. The role of the Dutch froe in *The London Prodigall* is thus directly opposed to her function in *Patient Grissil*. Luce's Griselda-like obedience is identified with the chaste industry and domestic virtue of Dutch women and is contrasted with Frances's Gwenthyan-like prodigality. Her Tanikin disguise serves to reinforce the industry and ingenuity that set her apart from her sister.

The London Prodigall thus deploys the figure of the Dutch froe as a foil to deride native English women's vices. By the time *The London Prodigall* was written, immigration had diminished considerably due to the slackening of the Spanish offensive in the Netherlands and the temporary peace accord established by the Edict of Nantes. The early seventeenth century has been described as a period of steady integration, during which the alien community remained relatively stable in the absence of a constant influx of new immigrants.[127] In disguising herself as a Dutch froe and working to restore order to

Figure 21. Rembrandt, *Portrait of Aechje Claesdr.*, 1634. The subject was the widow of Rotterdam brewer Jan Dammaszyn. Pesser. Here she wears a ruff and a head-attire known in England as "cheeks and ears." Oil on oak. © The National Gallery, London.

an English household, Luce appears to confirm that the perceived threat posed by immigrant starch- and tirewomen's imported skills and technologies was diminishing. Yet she also draws attention to the hybridity of English subjects themselves in the aftermath of the alien influx, when there was no longer a dichotomous split between a native English culture and a monolithic stranger community. During its early phase, complaints against the alien population often cited their maintenance of a separate culture.[128] By the early seventeenth century, however, immigrants were intermarrying and having children who were by law English subjects, hiring English workers or working for English masters and mistresses, and forming commercial ties within their host communities.[129] Yet they were also maintaining business connections with their home countries, worshiping in stranger churches, and retaining to a certain degree the cuisine and attire of their native cultures. In this sense, they were "keep[ing] a foot in both worlds," if not "leading [a] double life."[130] In *The London Prodigall*, it is an English character who assumes an alien persona, effectively inverting the structure of assimilation.[131] By assuming an alien persona and manufacturing foreign wares within a native household, Luce enacts the trope of alien infiltration in a manner that renders it unthreatening. Luce appropriates the imported skills of Dutch starch- and tirewomen just as her compatriots had begun to do by the time the play was written.

As the demand for starched linen attires grew in the early seventeenth century, it could no longer be satisfied by immigrant women alone, although the latter retained their status as the most highly skilled and sought-after starchers and tiremakers. The ruff's preeminence began to give way to a new trend in simple, unfluted "bands," which required less skill to produce, making the fashion in linen neckware more affordable to the middling sort.[132] The changing fashion in starched linen attires and shifting demography of women working in the trade by the second decade of the seventeenth century is reflected in a short skit, entitled *A Merrie Dialogue Betweene Band, Cuffe, and Ruffe*, performed at Trinity College Cambridge in 1614–15. As in *Patient Grissil* and *The London Prodigall*, the dialogue foregrounds the labor of starching as women's work, although here that labor is no longer identified with immigrant craftswomen in particular. Some fifty years after starched attires were first introduced into England, the fashion showed no signs of waning and is the sole subject of this "shew." No longer mere props, Band, Cuffe, and Ruffe here take center stage as full-fledged parts personified by three actors, each of whom is no doubt wearing the attire for which he is named. The dialogue takes the form of a "dissention" between Ruffe and Band as to which is currently the more fashionable, while Cuffe serves as mediator between them. The humor of the skit mostly turns on bad puns: Cuffe is ever "at hand" and warns "we shall have a fray presently"; Band taunts Ruffe, "I thought thou haddest beene worne out of date by this time"; Ruffe threatens to match Band's "Choller" (punning on collar) by making "cut-worke [i.e., a type of lace]" of him, or worse, tearing him "into rags" for "the Paper mills."[133] The stubborn pride of each is figured as stiffness throughout.

The skit is remarkable for its persistent recollection, and no less obstinate forgetfulness, of the female labor congealed in starched linen attires. Cuffe attempts to mediate the "fray" between Band and Ruffe by reminding them (and the audience) of their common debt to the labor of the laundress and sempstress. He chides Ruffe that "his Landresse will beare him witnesse" that he has been "presst oft" into service.[134] When Band and Ruffe continue to ignore Cuffe, he persists: "remember your selves and Misteris Stichwell, one to whom you have beene both beholding in your dayes." The obstinate Ruffe swears "by all the Gumme and Blew-starch in Christendome" that he has never heard of her. Cuffe insists: "I thought so, why its the Semster, one that both [of] you had beene undone had it not beene for her . . . I say Misteris Stichwell the Semster was the very maker of you both, yet thus little doe you regard her, but it is the common custome of you all, when you come to bee so great as you are, you forget from what house you come."[135] Cuffe literally takes the starch out of Ruffe and Band by reminding them whence their "stiff and starchy" stature derives, undoing their forgetting of the female labors that produced their present condition by recollecting their pre- or offstage histories of manufacture. Although Ruffe and Band continue in their obstinate disavowal—Ruffe claims not to care "a pinne" for Mistress Stichwell, and Band adds "nor a button"—their oaths belie them, for they swear by the tools of the starchwoman's and sempstress's trades (gum, blue starch, pins, and buttons). Moreover, it is Cuffe who has the last word, advising, "Well Band and Ruffe, you were best both of you take heede of her" and warning that Mistress Stichwell will punish them for their forgetfulness by "set[ting]" them both "in the Stocks" or worse, "hang[ing]" them with "strings," referring to the wooden stand on which starchwomen set ruffs and the lines on which they hung them to dry.[136] Cuffe ends the controversy by pointing to the latest fashion of wearing *both* a band *and* a ruff, and offers them "a Band [or bond] of your friendship," which he hopes the Gentlemen present will "seale with their hands" by clapping.[137] The dialogue's pun on "band" and "bond" (the terms, as noted in Chapter 2, were used interchangeably during the period) underscores the material economy that links cloth bands and paper bonds or books, for as Ruffe reminds us, "Bands, make rags; Rags make Paper; Paper makes Past-board, and Past-board makes Collar."[138] Although the dialogue is clearly mocking university students who are more interested in following the latest fashion in bands, ruffs, and cuffs than in studying paper bonds or books, it also emphasizes the unstable boundary between them, a conceit that becomes even more prominent in the text's second edition.[139]

Band, Ruffe, and Cuffe was evidently quite popular, for it was republished later the same year in an expanded edition, entitled *Exchange Ware at the Second Hand Viz. Band, Ruffe, and Cuffe, Lately Out, and Now Newly Dearned Up*.[140] As its title makes clear, the second edition continues the punning of the first but with the particular aim of drawing analogies between printers of bands, cuffs, and ruffs and printers of bonds or books. The second edition is compared to—or rather, we are reminded, literally *is*—secondhand linenware (paper made of linen rags) that has been "newly dearned up" or made new by being stitched together with new, paratextual material. The new material takes the form of prefatory verses voiced by a female "Jurie of Seamsters" (including Mistress Stichwell) who offer "their verdi[c]t upon Band, Ruffe, and Cuffe."[141] The jury finds that "the Printer" of the first edition "did Ruffe, Cuffe, Band wrong" because "He spoiled them with his Inke."[142] The women promise to rectify this fault through their own labor by washing them clean: "What though the Printer Ruffe, Cuffe, Band hath stayn'd?" they say, "[We'll] get it forth, or else let [us] be blam'd. / For all his black foule fingers never feare, / But that the Landresse . . . can make them cleare."[143] Here, the work of the female laundress threatens to undo that of the male printer, rather than vice versa. *Band, Ruffe, and Cuffe* and its sequel blur the boundary between (female) printers of starched linen and (male) printers of linen paper: both desire that "they still should stand in print."[144]

Puns are repeatedly deployed to call attention to the many tools and terms the two trades have in common: the phrase "stand in print" or "set in print," for example, meant both to set type and to "arrange the pleats of (a ruff etc.) in a neat or precise fashion" (*OED*, "print, *n.* and *adj.*" 7c). The terms "press," "stitch," and "set" were likewise common to both trades. In the hands of the starcher, setting sticks were poking sticks used to set pleats in ruffs, but in the hands of the compositor, they were composing sticks, used to set type. The glutinous paste known as "size" applied to paper to stiffen it and prepare its surface for printing was very similar to the gum and starch used to stiffen ruffs, cuffs, and bands; indeed, the two terms were sometimes used interchangeably.[145]

Rather than contrasting the ephemeral prints left by female starchers to the permanence of those left by printers, *Exchange Ware at the Second Hand* insists on the ephemeral character of both: books are worn out and go out of style, and must be printed anew. If the prior edition is the "worse for wearing," it advertises, "now new washt and starcht, 'tis thus much more."[146] After the jury of female sempsters deliberates, Mistress Stichwell offers their punning verdict: "My sentence is," she says, "The Booke shall be represt," meaning not that it will be censored but that it will be re-pressed or reprinted, because the desire to see starched linen "in print" (in both senses of the term) continues unabated, fueling both industries.[147] In materially recollecting the labor of printing performed by starchers and sempsters, and its status as "never done," *Band, Ruffe, and Cuffe* and *Exchange Ware at the Second Hand* position that labor as exemplary of the impermanence and reiterative character of print culture more generally.

The rebato in *Patient Grissil*, the starched head-attire in *The London Prodigall*, and the band, ruff, and cuff of the Cambridge skit, to differing degrees and ends work to highlight the material culture of the "all-male" stage in Shakespeare's time as worked upon by women. The staging of starched linen accessories in these plays thereby functions to undo the forgetting of the female labor that was literally congealed in these fetishized commodities by recollecting their pre- or offstage histories of production. Although such moments in early modern dramatic literature are often as fleeting as the ephemeral forms imprinted in ruffs, they nonetheless give us a glimpse into the tireless work of attiring that took place behind the scenes of theatrical production. As we shall see in the following two chapters, the professional players' and playwrights' relation to such work shifted with their own rise in status, which motivated them to distinguish their labors from those of the "rude mechanicals," devilish tirewomen, rapacious usuresses, and boisterous vendors who toiled offstage to produce dramatic spectacle and support theatrical commerce. In order to define their occupation as a legitimate, "workmanly" calling, players and playwrights stigmatized the offstage labors of working women in and around the professional theaters as trivial, amateurish, unskilled, uncouth, or, quite literally, obscene. Having examined the ciphering practices of female financiers and the material ciphers produced by starch- and tirewomen, I shall turn next to a different kind of cipher used both to evoke and elide women's offstage work, namely, the cries of female hawkers of fruit, nuts, ale, and a variety of other commodities in and around the commercial theaters. At once linguistic and non-linguistic, signifiers and pure sound, staged cries conveyed the ghostly presence of women's offstage work by echoing their hauntingly hollow, yet resoundingly full, vocal idiom.

Chapter 4

Cries and Oysterwives

> The ghost . . . cried so misera[b]ly at the Theator, like an oisterwife, *Hamlet, revenge.*
> —Thomas Lodge, *Wits Miserie, and the Worlds Madnesse* (1596)

> Speak the speech, I pray you, as I pronounced it to you—trippingly on the tongue. But if you mouth it as many of our players do, I had as lief the town-crier spoke my lines.
> —William Shakespeare, *Hamlet* (1600–1601)

IN HIS *Wits Miserie, and the Worlds Madnesse* of 1596, Thomas Lodge famously ridicules the ghost in *Hamlet* by likening his miserable cries to those of a common oysterwife.¹ The *Hamlet* here in question is most likely not Shakespeare's but rather the so-called *Ur-Hamlet*, possibly penned by Thomas Kyd and first performed (as Henslowe records) in 1594 by the Admiral's and Chamberlain's Men together at Newington Butts and later by the Chamberlain's Men alone at The Theatre as witnessed by Lodge.² Whether the *Ur-Hamlet* represents a source text for Shakespeare's version or an earlier draft of his play, the mockery to which the *Ur-Hamlet*'s ghost was subject may help explain what was motivating the later *Hamlet*'s advice to the players. For among the working women who plied their wares in and around the commercial theaters of early modern London there was perhaps no figure more reviled than that of the oysterwife, whose cacophonous cries provided much fodder for comic ridicule. It is Lodge's derisive merging of the voice of the male actor onstage with the proximate, intruding voice of the female crier offstage, I shall argue, that Hamlet's metatheatrical intervention seeks to counter. The stakes of this intervention were heightened during the contemporary War of the Theaters

(c. 1599–1602), which represented a particularly tense moment in the players' ongoing quest for professional legitimacy. It was during this period that the pressure of competition between adult and children's companies spurred players and playwrights increasingly to define their own "workmanship" over and against the "unworkmanly," effeminized labors of theater personnel who worked offstage, as well as of amateur players who performed in the streets. The female crier epitomized both: her raucous advertisements to theater audiences characterized her as both a low-status performer and a low-status worker, whose proximity to the stage rendered her a ready-to-hand foil against which the professional players might contrast their own skilled eloquence and newly elevated status.

A cry is by definition both a loud and an inarticulate utterance (*OED*, "cry, *n.*" I.1.a). In early modern dramatic texts, actors' cries were often signaled by an "O," a cipher of sound, at once empty or hollow and full of emotive resonance. The "O" prompted actors to "tak[e] away . . . all of the tongue"—the vocal instrument of articulation—and "turning the lippes rounde as a ring," to "thrust[] forth . . . a sounding breath."[3] Within the walls of the outdoor amphitheaters—which Shakespeare famously likens to "wooden O"s—the sound of the cry would have had a visceral resonance. The public theaters, as Bruce Smith has argued, functioned as acoustic "instruments for producing, shaping, and propagating sound." The stage "acted as a gigantic sounding board: made of reverberative material," producing "a harmonically rich amplification of the voices of actors," while the polygonal walls served to augment sound further by reflecting it off of multiple surfaces.[4] Yet this "harmonically rich amplification" of actors' voices was continually challenged by the cries of female hawkers in the pit and galleries, which were likewise amplified, albeit less harmonically, by the amphitheaters' wooden O.

Construed as sonic ciphers, at once present to the ear and absent to sight, the cries of female hawkers aptly figure the absent-presence of women's offstage work in the "all-male" theaters.[5] To decipher the echoes of working women's cries in dramatic literature, we must therefore attend to what Smith calls the "acoustic world" of the theaters and their environs, and the ways in which play texts and players engaged with the sounds of working life that surrounded them. My aim in this chapter is not, however, to conjure the gendered soundscape of the commercial theaters and their environs by making the sounds of female street-criers present to modern ears (a quixotic project, as we shall see, initiated by folklorists and antiquarians). Rather, it is to examine the forms of cultural mediation through which working women's cries were represented and absented in early modern culture, focusing in particular on those staged in theaters by the voices of male actors.

The War of the Theaters was waged, I shall argue, not only through play texts but also through performance styles, in particular through the actor's voice and the register of sound. Competition from the children's companies, which satirized the adult players and their audiences as unrefined, prompted the adult companies to develop their own performance style and argue for its refinement. The boy-companies had a powerful weapon in this competition: their trained singing voices, together with the musical sophistication of their songs and the acoustic ambience of the indoor theaters, combined to produce a distinctive performance idiom defined largely through the medium of sound. The adult companies were thereby forced to define and defend a distinctive vocal register of their own. It was during this period that the vocalizations of street-criers, and of female criers in particular, became a convenient rhetorical weapon deployed in the *poetomachia* to stigmatize the productions of rival players or playwrights as vulgar, "unworkmanly," and amateurish. Having done so, however, the players also at times self-consciously appropriated the crier's vocal idiom, to both low-comic and high-tragic ends.

It has long been known that apples, nuts, ale, and tobacco were "carried around" and vended to audiences before, during, and after performances in the public amphitheaters and in the intervals between performances in the private theaters.[6] Archaeological excavations of the Rose and Globe theater sites have unearthed material remains of such commerce and revealed that "a much wider range" of comestibles was consumed in theaters than previously imagined. Residues of foodstuffs found at the Rose include not only the predictable pippins, pears, hazelnuts, and walnuts but also more exotic and imported fare, including berries, cherries, peaches, plums, almonds, pumpkin seeds, dried fruits, such as raisins, prunes, and figs, and many varieties of shellfish, including cockles, mussels, and a large quantity of common oysters.[7] It would thus seem that Londoners who attended the commercial theaters were lured there not only by the foreign fashions flaunted onstage, explored in the previous chapter, but also by the tasty, imported delicacies on offer as snacks. Other evidence examined below suggests that the work of vending such foodstuffs in London, in particular fish, shellfish, and fruits, was predominantly performed by market women.[8] Yet theater historians have had relatively little to say about such commerce in the theaters and the influence it may have had on theatrical production or dramatic literature.

How, we might wonder, did the professional players and their audiences view this boisterous, largely female, sideshow?

Andrew Gurr argues, plausibly, that hawking in theaters would have been viewed as "a distraction from the play," citing contemporary commentators who complain of the noise caused by cracking nuts and the possibility of players confusing the hissing caused by bottle opening with that of disapproving audience members.[9] In treating the presence of criers in theaters as an annoying distraction, Gurr echoes the complaints of seventeenth-century satirists like Henry Fitz-Geoffrey, who tells of being "made *Adder*-deafe with *Pippin-crye*" at the Blackfriars playhouse, or John Tatham, who speaks of "*Apple-wives*" at the Fortune theater, "Whose shrill confused Ecchoes loud doe cry."[10] Yet to conclude that the female vendors who sold wares in and around the playhouses were invariably viewed as mere nuisance or noise is to ignore the performative dimension of crying wares, which the professional players themselves recognized and at times self-consciously appropriated, even as they sought to elevate their own performance idiom above it. As we shall see, the cries of female hawkers, who flouted codes of feminine decorum encouraging women to remain mute or speak with "small" voices, spurred the imaginations, as well as the opprobrium, of contemporary male players and playwrights.

Any attempt to grasp the significance of the cries staged in plays and their relation to those of female vendors in and around the commercial theaters must confront the problem of evidence. In the case of street-cries this problem is oddly one of abundance rather than dearth, albeit abundance of a peculiar and particularly problematic kind. For despite the ephemerality of early modern street-cries in their own time, they have enjoyed a remarkably durable presence in a wide array of cultural forms—including ballads, prints, and plays, among many others—whose large-scale dissemination began in the sixteenth century and extends in a seemingly unbroken oral tradition into the present. Antiquarians and folklorists of the nineteenth and early twentieth centuries had no small part to play in creating this canon—commonly called the "Cries of London"—and in perpetuating the impression of its *longue durée* through their prodigious cataloguing of the myriad types of cries and criers and of the cultural forms in which they were reproduced. Indeed, were it not for the antiquarian collectors, many of the ephemeral forms in which street-cries appear would undoubtedly not have survived.[11] Our access to early modern street-cries and criers has thus in no small measure been shaped by the antiquarian endeavor to catalogue what were viewed as unmediated voicings of a bygone, pre-industrial past. Works such as Charles Hindley's *History of the Cries of London (Ancient & Modern)* of 1884 reflect an investment in what Adam Fox calls "the idea of a pure oral tradition of the folk which had perpetuated itself since time immemorial, untainted by the influence of the written word."[12] Hindley catalogues literally hundreds of examples of street-cries with virtually no contextualizing framework within which to situate or comprehend them. Yet this is precisely the antiquarian point: their collections purport to be transmissions of a popular, oral tradition that is allowed to speak for itself. No distinction is drawn between the disparate historical contexts or cultural forms within which cries were reproduced.

The rich "archive" of cries preserved by antiquarian scholars presents an intriguing yet problematic source of evidence for scholars interested in the social and economic history of working women. What are we to make of this treasure trove of images, texts, and songs depicting the voices, gestures, attitudes, wares, and marketing techniques of female vendors who worked in London's informal economy? Precisely what sort of "evidence" does the canon of street-cries constitute regarding early modern women's work? To answer this question, we will have to decipher these cultural representations in relation to other kinds of evidence, such as contemporary legislation aimed at curbing or controlling the unruly commerce of female hawkers, which pose problems of a different sort. Such commerce appears to have increased dramatically in the late sixteenth century, when increasing numbers of impoverished workers migrated to the city's suburbs and took up occupations outside guild control, "eking out an existence on the margins of economic life."[13] London's expanding population—which, by some estimates, nearly trebled during the second half of the sixteenth century[14]—put increasing pressure on the city's traditional markets, which "spilled over in time and space from their accustomed limits."[15] The growing numbers of hawkers and hucksters who peddled wares in the streets beyond or on the fringes of the traditional markets fulfilled a vital, if contested, distributive function and were the subject of numerous legislative initiatives, particularly during the economic "crisis" of the 1590s, when their practice of "regrating" (or reselling wares bought at established markets elsewhere for a profit) was blamed for rising prices.[16]

One such initiative was a proposal for reforming market offenses presented to the Lord Mayor by Hugh Alley, a freeman of the Plasterers' Company, in 1598. Alley's proposal targets the "*Haglers, Hawkers, Huxters,* and *wanderers,*" who roamed "uppe and downe the streetes . . . buyenge into their owne handes, to rayse the prices, for their own luker, and pryvate gayne, all kinde of provisions, and *victuals* . . . and presently sellinge the same agayne."[17]

Committees of the Court of Aldermen considered Alley's proposals in February and July 1599, and in September appointed him overseer of the markets, charging him with preventing hawkers and hucksters from buying up wares for resale. By February 1600, the Court of Common Council extended this provision, appointing four additional overseers and again targeting "hucksters hawkers haglers and wanderers up and downe the streetes."[18] The frequency of such legislative initiatives, together with their repeated assertions that the number of such hawkers was "greate & excessive" and growing, rather than abating, suggests that the efforts to rein in the rising tide of informal commerce during the period met with little success. Yet it is important to recognize that the terms in which this economic "threat" was cast were determined by civic officials, who sought to stigmatize the labor of those who worked in the informal sector and frequently scapegoated them for problems the source of which lay elsewhere.

The Repertories of the Court of Aldermen and the Journals of the Court of Common Council for the City of London are filled with attempts at controlling such trade, attempts that were often targeted specifically at women.[19] An Act of Common Council of 1602, for example, specified that the "Huxters, Pedlers and Haglers" who "walke upp and downe the streetes hawkinge with wares and offeringe the same to be soulde openlie to all sortes of people . . . be for the most parte women."[20] Similar orders regarding the criers who sold "oysters ffishe fruites . . . and other victuals" in the streets describe that population as made up predominantly of "wives, widdowes weomen" and "maides."[21] A mayoral order of 1590 claimed the numbers of such women "are of late yeres . . . wonderfully encreased."[22] Five years later, a similar order complained of "an exceeding great number of lewd and wicked women called fishwives, which swarm about in all parts of this city liberties and suburbs," accusing them of "such vile behavior and condition as is not fit any longer to be suffered" and of "greatly enhanc[ing] the prices," and calling for the immediate "reformation of their intolerable abuses."[23] Such legislation, which was aimed at controlling women who worked outside sanctioned forms of trade, may well have augmented their numbers to suit political purposes. Female hawkers served as convenient scapegoats for economic anxieties surrounding the "decay of trades" and were frequently blamed for economic problems that were certainly not of their making, such as unemployment and inflation; they were also accused of diminishing the crown's revenues by "weakeninge the cittizens in suche sorte as they shall not be hable to yelde their aide in bearinge scott and lott [i.e., municipal taxation]."[24] Market women were thus perceived to be a direct threat to the prerogatives of guildsmen and their apprentices, who on several occasions during the 1590s attacked female hawkers during apprentice riots.[25] As a result, it was female hawkers who were most often apprehended and fined by civic authorities. The Book of Fines includes numerous examples of market women or "huxsters" who were fined and whose wares were confiscated for infringing market regulations (e.g., "certein heringe whiche were forstalled and ingroced by dyvers women," "halfe a pake of small nuttes taken from a huxster for forstallinge and regratinge the same," and "two baskettes cheryes engroced by an huxster").[26]

It is certainly no coincidence that English broadsheet engravings and woodcuts of street-criers and their cries became extremely popular during the very period in which their numbers increased dramatically and their labor became the focus of so much juridical attention. Although these prints do not constitute straightforward "evidence" concerning women's working lives, they do have something to tell us about how their commerce was perceived. Although only eight prints dating from this period survive, their present scarcity should not be taken as an indication of their popularity in their own day. Indeed, Tessa Watt estimates the survival rate of such broadsheets at about one in ten thousand.[27] Already popular on the Continent, printed cries first began to be produced in England in the 1590s, initially by visiting engravers and then by native craftsmen who imitated them.[28] More expensive than halfpenny or penny ballads, broadsheet cries cost in the range of sixpence and were consumed by "the middling sort and those a little less prosperous . . . , which explains why [so] few have survived."[29] Along with ballads and other popular print forms, they served as inexpensive wall decorations, papering the walls of taverns, where they were also bought and sold.[30]

The static arcade structure of all of the surviving prints from this period appears to be aimed at controlling and classifying the population of street hawkers, sequestering each within a safely contained space with their cries blazoned beneath them, as in Figure 22[31] and Figure 23,[32] both of which date from the 1590s.[33] Recalling the architecture of markets like the Royal Exchange, this structural containment belies the tense relationship hawkers and regraters had to the regulated markets.[34] Yet there are subtle hints even within the rigid architecture of these early printed cries that this population was not so easily contained. The engraving in Figure 23 depicts twenty-two female criers and only fifteen male, according each a sense of movement that impinges upon the print's static framework.[35] Although each stands as if frozen in time and space, their varied stances give some sense of the individualized, theatrical gestures that characterized the

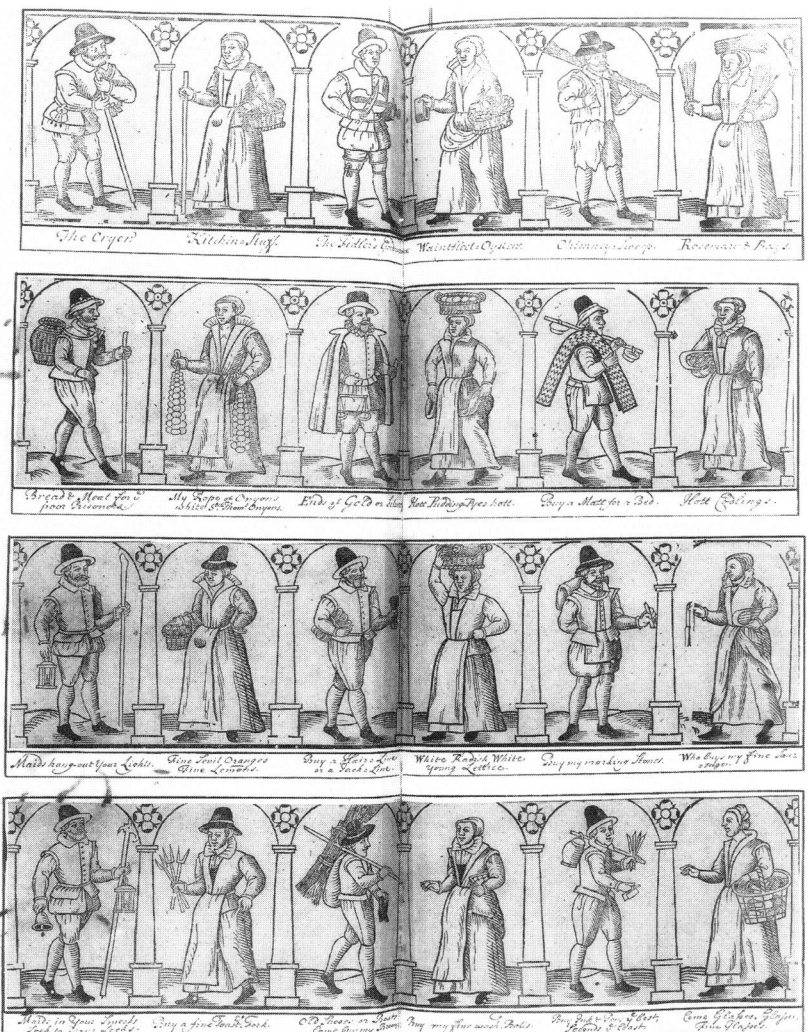

Figure 22. *Cries of London*, with town crier at upper left and women crying oysters, fruit, and other foodstuffs sold in theaters. Late sixteenth-century woodcut. By permission of the Pepys Library, Magdalene College, Cambridge.

FIGURE 23. *Cries of London*, with bellman at center. Late sixteenth-century engraving. By permission of Jonathan Gestetner, Marlborough

solicitations of itinerant tradespeople and perhaps linked them in the minds of their customers or spectators to other popular entertainers. The criers on the far right of the print—three of them female and one male—who cry from top to bottom "new spro[u]ts," "new cod," "reasons [i.e., raisins]," and "glasses to mend" are each depicted with a quite different stance and gesture. Of the twenty-two female criers in this print, seven are crying various types of fish (e.g., "Buy any shrimps," "Buy any maydes [i.e., young skate]," "Buy any whyting maps [i.e., whiting mops, young whiting]," "New Hadog [i.e., haddock]," "New sprots new [i.e., sprats or smelt]," "Buy a dish a flownders," "New Cod new") and four fresh and dried fruits (e.g., "Buy some figs," "Buy any prunes," "Buy any reasons," "Rype damsons") of precisely the kind sold in the commercial theaters. Two other female criers in the print are also selling foodstuffs that might have been sold in theaters ("Good sasages," "Hote mutton pays [i.e., pies]"). Of the remaining nine female criers, eight are crying wares that might have contributed to theatrical production, including articles of used clothing ("Buy a purs," "Buy a paire a shoos") and wares relating to textile manufacture ("Buy any tape [i.e., ribbon]," "Yards and ells [used to measure fabric]," "Buy any bottens") or laundering ("Buy a whyt [i.e., bleach] pot," "Buy a washingbale," "Buy any blew starch").[36] In Figure 22 all of the foodstuffs are likewise sold by women.

The architectural sequestration and segregation of the street-criers depicted in these prints belie the flexibility and fluidity that characterized their commerce. Whereas the prints identify each crier with a single cry, Donald Lupton's *London and the Countrey Carbonadoed and Quartered into Severall Characters* (1632) emphasizes the variability that defined their trade: "These Crying, Wandring, and Travailing Creatures carry their shops on their heads.... They are free in all places, and pay nothing for shop-rent.... They change every day almost, for Shee that was this day for Fish, may bee to morrow for Fruit; next day for Hearbs, another for Roots: so that you must heare them cry before you know what they are furnisht withal."[37] The cries of itinerant vendors functioned as advertisements that alerted potential customers to the particular wares on offer, in contrast to the common cry of stationary shopkeepers, which simply asked, "What is it you lack? What is it you buy?" The labor of itinerant female vendors (their travel and travail) was characterized not only by spatial mobility ("Wandring, and Travailing"), Lupton suggests, but by the flexibility of their work identities ("this day for Fish, ... to morrow for Fruit; next day for Hearbs," etc.). Within the formal economy, the laborer's identity was clear and fixed, at least in theory: one belonged to a livery company, such as the Carpenters, Grocers, or Plasterers, which accorded one the privileges of citizenship, civic identity, and membership in a community defined by one's skill in a particular trade. For these privileges one paid the price of quarterage to the company and obedience to its regulations. By contrast, female hawkers had none of the privileges of citizenship or of the civic identity that went along with it. Yet they also had none of its obligations ("They are free in all places, and pay nothing for shop-rent"). Nor was their identity tied to the production or retail of a single product ("They change every day almost"). As such, like the ciphering usuresses discussed in Chapter 2 and the tireless tirewomen and laundresses in Chapter 3, they were viewed as a threat to and the antithesis of legitimate trade and the virtuous, civic identity it conferred. Unlike the commerce of usuresses or skilled tire- and starchwomen, who earned ungodly profits and economic security by practicing the devil's work, however, the trade of female street vendors was defined by its economic insecurity and by the travel and travail that characterized their advertising, imploring cries. Lupton's assertion that "you must heare them cry before you know what they are furnisht withal" suggests that the presence of street-criers was perceived first and foremost by the ear rather than by the eye. Given the narrowness of London's streets and alleys and the city's overpopulation, it seems likely that pedestrians often heard criers before they were able to catch a glimpse of them. Although printed cries do not neglect the acoustic register of the crier's trade, the textual cries that appear in broadsheet prints function as indexical tags rather than attempts to convey the aural dimension of cries as vocal performances. Before turning to plays that deployed the voice to this effect, let us therefore consider how the vocal register of the cry was appropriated in popular musical forms.

Contemporary balladeers recognized and drew on the performative idiom of street-cries and criers, as players and playwrights did. Although ballads circulated orally as well as in manuscript and print form, it would be false to conclude that they are merely transparent vehicles that convey unmediated voices from the past.[38] Rather, ballads, like broadsheet prints and plays, appropriated street-cries in order to refashion them to particular ideological ends. To decipher the cultural work that street-cries performed, it is therefore crucial that we attend to the specific contexts within which they were reproduced. The Stationer's Register lists a number of entries for late sixteenth-century ballads, now lost, that contained street-cries, including one entitled "The Common Crie[s] of London" of 1580/1.[39] An extant manuscript of a street-cry ballad (probably copied from a broadsheet in 1589 or 1590) entitled "A sounge of the guise of London" suggests that female cries were a popular element of this emerging genre, as it contains versions of the cries of fish- and oysterwives, apple-wives, "kitchen stuffe" [i.e., lard or grease] women, and herb-wives.[40] Yet the ballad also registers the ambivalence prompted by these commercially active women when the fishwife cries, "Come buy all my fishe, and send me awaye." By the early seventeenth century, this ambivalence edges toward outright hostility in a ballad entitled "The Common Cries of London Town, / Some go up street, some go down," or "Turners Dish of Lenten Stuff," which first appeared in print in 1612. Although the ballad acknowledges the entertainment value of street-cries, promising to "please" its audience by telling it "what they cry, / in London all the yeare"[41] and features the cries of female hawkers, including the fishwife who begins the ballad by crying, "[a]nye Musckles lylly white: / Hearings, Sprats, or Pleace, / or Cockles for delight," it simultaneously appropriates and stigmatizes the performance idiom of the female crier in an effort to position its own entertainment as superior. The ballad thus pointedly contrasts its own melodic rendering of a diverse array of street-cries with the harsh, guttural, inarticulate voice of the fishwife: "She had need to ha[v]e her tongue be grease[d]," we are told, "for she rattles in the throat."

Turner's ballad goes on to stigmatize the fishwife's commercial practices as well: "to tell you out of doubt," we are told, "Her measure is to[o] little, / go beate the bottom out. / Halfe a Pecke for two pence, / I doubt it is a bodge." The ballad here plays on several meanings of "bodge," which was a unit of measure roughly corresponding to half a peck (*OED*, "bodge, *n.*²") but was also related to the verbs "badge," meaning to "regrate" or "buy up (provisions) for resale elsewhere" and "hawk for sale" (*OED*, "badge, *v.*²"), and "botch," which originally referred to the patching of old garments but by the sixteenth century had come to refer to shoddy workmanship generally (*OED*, "botch, *v.*¹" and "bodge, *v.* and *n.*¹")—an apt etymological illustration of the stigmatization of those who, like botchers and badgers, worked in the informal sector. The term links the fishwife's vocal assault on her passersby—her "badgering" cries—with her shifty and shady marketing practices (she charges too much and measures too little). The ballad goes on to assert that such practices are rampant in London: "Thus all the city over, / the people they do dodge." The verb "dodge," meaning to move around so as to "elude a pursuer" and also to "change about deceitfully," "haggle," or "avoid discovery" (*OED*, "dodge, *v.*" 1a, 1c, 2a, 2b), similarly stigmatizes the mobility, flexibility, and ingenuity that characterized the informal commerce of female hawkers. The shady dealings of the itinerant fishwife are taken to exemplify the commercial practices of female hawkers generally, which threaten the livelihoods and trade of honest citizens. Not only do they engage in such "tricks" as jacking up prices and using false weights and measures, but the wares they sell are subpar: attractive to the eye and vaunted as high quality, they turn out to be shoddy, flimsy, or even rotten (a subject explored in greater depth in Chapter 5).

The ballad appropriates the entertainment value of street-cries while at the same time disparaging them, and those of the oysterwife in particular. Yet not all of the female criers in Turner's ballad "rattle in the throat." As an apparent foil to the fishwife, the balladeer describes the idealized figure of the blushing milkmaid:

> Will you buy any Milke,
>   I heare a wench to cry,
> With a paile of fresh Cheese and creame,
>   Another after hies.
> Oh the wench went neately,
>   M[e] thought it did me good:
> To see her che[r]ry cheekes,
>   So dimpled ore with blood,
> Her wastecoate washed white:
>   As any lilly flower,
> Would I had time to talke with her
>   The space of halfe an houre.

Unlike the oysterwife, whose inarticulacy is suggested by a tongue that needs greasing, the balladeer suggests that the milkmaid merits extended discourse, while implying, of course, that it is not mere talk that he is after. Although the milkmaid is clearly painted in a more positive light than the fishwife, her commercial activity is not so much denigrated as negated entirely. The description works to commodify the maid herself, insofar as it is her own whiteness and purity that the ballad advertises rather than those attributes of her product.

The pure, yet eroticized, figure of the creamy, blushing milkmaid reappears as the dominant figure in another street-cry ballad of the same year, entitled "I Have Fresh Cheese and Cream."[42] Here, the chaste, fair purity of the milkmaid's voice and appearance is explicitly contrasted with the salty, sexual stench and cacophonous cries of the oysterwife, while positioning the milkmaid as an obscure object of desire. The balladeer describes his walk "along the streetes" of London and the multitude of female criers he encounters there:

Many a pretty Wench I saw,
Along the streetes to cry:
But none so sweete,
Which I there could meete,
As there was a handsome Wench,
That sang in Colman streete,
    I have fresh Cheese and Creame,
    I have fresh Cheese and Creame.

Upon her backe she wore
A Fustian wastcoate white,
Her Bodyes and her Stomacher,
Were fastned very tite.
Her Neckenger of Holland sure,
Her voice was shrill and very pure:
Her Ware she opened straight
To any that would buy.
    I have fresh Cheese and Creame,
    I have fresh Cheese and Creame.

She pleased me full well,
In singing of her noate;
She sung not like an Oyster whore,
That ratleth in the throat:
Which made me to admier,
And askt her name, but with the same,
She cryed then more higher.
    I have fresh Cheese and Creame,
    I have, &c..

The ballad's ambivalence toward the female street-crier, exemplified by the contrast it establishes between the milkmaid and the "Oyster whore," is also expressed within the figure of the milkmaid herself, whose advertising of "fresh Cheese and Creame" renders her at once sexually attractive (she is "sweet," "handsome," and "pleas[ing]" and fastens her bodice and stomacher "very tite"), available (she opens her wares "To any that would buy"), and yet nevertheless unattainable and chaste ("very pure"). Although the purity of her voice, in contrast with the rattling of the "Oyster whore," pleases the balladeer, its "shrill," piercing quality also hints at the negative connotations of female volubility. Her wayward wandering and incessant cry simultaneously solicit the balladeer's attention, arouse his desire, and frustrate both by remaining unfixed and unfixable: she refuses to stay put long enough for him to satisfy his desire. While enumerating the many other cries that fill the city streets (which by contrast are all disembodied, unattached to descriptions of the criers themselves), the ballad continually circles back to the refrain, "I have fresh Cheese and Creame / I have fresh Cheese and Creame," as if to echo the balladeer's own obsession with the milkmaid. In spite of the ballad's repeated refrain, however, the balladeer never manages to grasp his object of desire, for the ballad concludes:

> By no meanes can I get,
> To know her dwelling place:
> She was so deckt with comlines,
> And bodyed with such grace.
> I would not care a rush,
> So [I] might have my wish,
> To have her stay all night with me,
> Which were a better dish,
>   Then her fresh Cheese and Creame,
>   Then her fresh Cheese and Creame.

The female crier here appears to win out over the balladeer in the arena of performance as well as commerce. Her cry positions him as her audience. When he attempts to trade places she refuses to listen and instead cries "higher," overwhelming his voice with her own. Refusing to satisfy his desire to consume her as a "dish" of eroticized "cream"—which is sweeter, he implies, than the dairy products she sells—she insists upon maintaining the place of subject, rather than object, of commerce.

By contrast, Turner's ballad seeks to situate its own brand of entertainment not only above that of the female street-crier but above the entertainment on offer in the public theaters as well. After surveying the "common cries of London town," Turner turns his attention to the "players of the Banke side, / the round Globe and the Swan," comparing the "idle tricks" performed by the players to those practiced by itinerant hawkers: "You Pedlers give good measure, / when as your wares you sell: / though your yard be short your thum[b] wil slip, / your trickes I know full wel, / And you that sel your wares by waight, / and live upon the trade: / Some beames be false, / som[e] waits to[o] light / such tri[c]kes there have been plaid." Like street peddlers, the ballad suggests, players make their living "idly" by playing tricks rather than by working in honest trades. Here, female hawkers are situated on a continuum with the "players on the Banckeside," while the balladeer who reveals their "idle tricks" positions himself as superior to both.

Around the same time that the cries of female hawkers appeared in English broadside ballads, they began to appear in plays. A Tudor interlude entitled *The Three Ladies of London,* attributed to Robert Wilson, depicts the female street-crier and her vocal idiom quite sympathetically as exemplifying the virtues of honest work. Wilson was an actor-playwright and famed antic who wrote the play in the early 1580s, when he was one of the principal actors of the Earl of Leicester's Men, although it is not known whether it was performed while they were on tour or at The Theatre in London. In this hybrid morality play, Lady Conscience has fallen on hard times at the hands of Lucre and Usury, who are in ascendancy in London. Refusing to practice any of the tricks of dishonest tradespeople—which are enumerated in great detail, including the "unsavorie thinne drinke" of the Brewer, the "light bread" of the Baker, the "deceitfull weights, [and] false measures" of the Chandler, and so forth—she decides to "learne to sell brome" to "get [her] living, / Using that as a quiet meane to keepe [her] selfe from begging" (ll. 1192–93).[43] Driven to make "a vertue of necessitie" (l. 1301), Lady Conscience exemplifies honesty, chastity, and, true to her name, a clean conscience. Her cry is not shrill but rather depicted as a "quiet" means of earning a living, and the song she sings emphasizes the purity of her wares to the "maydens" to whom she sells: "New broomes, greene broomes, will you buy any: / Come Maydens, come quickly, let me take a peny. / My broomes are not steeped, / but very well bound / My broomes are not crooked, / but smooth cut and round" (ll. 1289–94). The Prologue of the interlude, like Turner's ballad, draws an analogy between players and criers, although here it is the honesty, good conscience, and substantial, well-made wares of both, rather than their dishonest "tricks," that are emphasized. Announcing the play, the Prologue cries: "young and olde come and behold our wares, and buy them all. / Then if our wares shall seeme to you, well woven, good and fine, / We hope we shall your customse have, againe an other time" (Prologue, ll. 16–18). Wilson clearly does not perceive or depict the female street-crier as threatening or antithetical to his own status as player. Indeed, he appropriates the crier's idiom into his own arsenal of popular performance practices. Situating criers and players within the same nexus of urban commerce, he defends the commercial practices of both. His interlude situates both playing and street peddling as "honest" vocations, dealing in "well woven, good and fine" wares. If the play was indeed performed while the company was touring, the analogy would have been especially apt in defending the itinerant commerce of both players and peddlers, and challenging the claims of vagabond legislation that both were "idle" rogues.

Will Kempe, another famed antic who was celebrated for his performances of post-play jigs for the Chamberlain's Men, appropriated the street-crier's idiom in several jigs performed for the company before 1595, including one called "master Kempes *Newe Jigge of the kitchen stuffe woman.*"[44] (Female criers of "Kitchen-stuffe" collected the kitchen grease used in the manufacture of soap or candles.) Yet by the early seventeenth century, the Chamberlain's Men had begun to view such jigs contemptuously as an inferior, "lewd," or amateur form of entertainment—as Hamlet does when he says of Polonius, "he's for a jig, or a tale of bawdry, or he sleeps" (2.2.438). When Kempe left the Chamberlain's Men in 1599, the company appears to have given up performing jigs altogether.[45] It was around this time that the War of the Theaters prompted the company to assert the refinement of their performance style as part of a broader quest for professional legitimacy, a project that was executed in part by contrasting their own skilled eloquence with the cacophonous voices of criers, as Hamlet does in his advice to the players.

Let us return, then, to Hamlet's famed speech, which has long been a fulcrum for scholarly meditation on the professionalization of playing in Shakespeare's time. Muriel Bradbrook regarded the speech as the apotheosis of the "rise of the common player" and of the concomitant emergence of playing as both a profession and "a recognized art."[46] Bradbrook famously linked this development to the 1572 "Acte for the Punishment of Vagabondes," which required itinerant players to be licensed by a nobleman or two justices of the peace. Although the act aimed "to stop poor strollers from pestering the country," its unintended effect, she maintains, "was to define the actors' status, restrict the number of licensed troupes, and . . . foster the growth of professionalism" through the construction of purpose-built theaters.[47] The stability and fixity of the public playhouses in London provided the conditions under which the drama of the period could thrive: "there would have been no Elizabethan drama," she argues, "if players had remained strollers."[48] From Bradbrook's perspective, Hamlet's advice to the players marks the emergence of "dramatic art as an independent skill" from the "cocoon" of mere "playing," defined as the gallimaufry of merriment, games, festivities, tumbling, songs, and jigs that characterized the repertoire of the itinerant players.[49] His speech self-reflexively comments upon the players' rise in status by detailing the performance practices and aesthetic criteria that differentiate those who have mastered the mystery of playing from those who strut and bellow on the stage like mere "journeymen" (3.2.32–33).

Robert Weimann has more recently offered a less teleological and more dialectical account of the relationship between the performative repertoire of the professional players and those who preceded them.[50] The "exclusion from Elizabethan stages of the clown, the jig," and other heterogeneous modes of performance, he argues, was "a long drawn-out affair, a by no means linear process."[51] In his view, the "theoretical dimension" of Hamlet's advice to the players, far from representing the achieved disavowal of mere playing, "cannot control and does not discipline the practical side of what the staging of *Hamlet* actually involves."[52] Weimann focuses on Hamlet's "antic disposition" (1.5.170) and its appropriation of the legacy of clowns like Dick Tarlton, Robert Wilson, and Will Kempe to new effect.[53] Because "the crisis in the courtly and humanistic world of the play cannot be adequately dealt with in the language of courtesy and rhetorical eloquence," he claims, "the play reaches out and taps another repertoire of articulations."[54] The forceful intrusion and "shattering impact of the 'antic disposition' upon high Renaissance ideals" of courtesy and eloquence are for Weimann "what is most enigmatic, but for all that highly effective, in the characterization of Hamlet."[55]

What neither Bradbrook nor Weimann considers, however, is the way in which the "repertoire of articulations" and popular performance practices from which the professional players sought to distinguish themselves (according to Bradbrook) and upon which they simultaneously drew (according to Weimann) was inflected by gender. We have known for some time that female performers, who were excluded from the professional playing companies, engaged in a variety of theatrical activities, such as tumbling, juggling, and rope-dancing, as itinerant entertainers in the provinces.[56] The *Records of Early English Drama* include many examples of such women, such as "a young maide a Tumbeller" in Gloucestershire in 1521, a "dansyng wyff" of Plymouth in 1528, "rare feates of Activity with Dancing on the Ropes performed by a woman" in Norwich in 1616, and a "Vagrant woman a ffidler" in southeast Somerset in 1637.[57] Scholarship on this "hidden tradition" of female performance, as discussed in Chapter 1, has helped broaden the purview of theater history beyond the bounds of London's professional stage, thereby expanding our knowledge of the repertoire of early modern performance practices and venues considerably. The 1572 vagabond act, which describes the diverse population of migrant workers and entertainers to which the players were then thought to belong, emphasized that this population was made up of both men and women. It reads: "all and everye persone and persones beynge whole and mightye in Body and able to labour, havinge not Land or Maister, nor using any lawfull Marchaundize Crafte or Mysterye whereby hee or shee might get his or her Lyvinge, and can gyve no reckninge howe hee or shee doth lawfully get his or her Lyvynge," including "Fencers Bearewardes Comon Players in Enterludes & Minstrels . . . [and] all Juglers Pedlars Tynkers and Petye Chapmen . . . [who] shall wander abroad . . . shalbee taken adjudged and deemed Roges Vacaboundes and Sturdy Beggers, intended of by this present Act."[58] The legislation notably draws no distinction between itinerant entertainers (such as fencers, bearwards, common players in interludes, minstrels, and jugglers) and other migrant workers, such as street hawkers and peddlers, and emphasizes that this population was made up of both men and women.

Among this diverse population, street criers, represent a hitherto unacknowledged source of the repertoire of articulations and performance practices upon which *Hamlet* and other plays of the period drew, while at the same time providing a foil against which the professional players sought to distinguish themselves. Hamlet's advice to the players not only describes this distinction but enacts it: he demonstratively and exaggeratedly saws the air with his hand "thus," and vocally contrasts the graceful eloquence of the skilled player, instanced by the articulate alliteration of *s*peak/*s*peech/*s*poke, *p*ray/*p*ronounced/*p*layers, *t*rippingly/*t*ongue/*t*own, with the disgraceful bellowing of the crier, echoed in the ungainly, recurring diphthong of pro-n*ou*nced/m*ou*th/t*ow*n. Following Weimann's lead, we can see that Hamlet is here doing the very thing he decries: he "is telling the players what not to do, but . . . does so by doing it himself"[59]—in this case, by pron*ou*ncing the s*ou*nds m*ou*thed by the t*ow*n crier. This is not, moreover, the only instance in the play in which Hamlet mouths off: "'Swounds, show me what thou'lt do. / Woul't weep? Woul't fight? Woul't fast? Woul't tear thyself?, / Woul't drink up easel," he demands of the grieving Laertes, "Nay, an thou'lt mouth, / I'll rant as well as thou" (5.1.263–65, 272–73). Faced with being "outface[d]" (l. 267) by Laertes' leap into Ophelia's grave, Hamlet vows to strut, bellow, rant, and rave to prove his love, out-Heroding Herod, if not out-crying the crier, in the process.

Shakespeare's substitution of the figure of the town crier for that of the oysterwife subtly works to bolster the player's status by comparing him to a civic official, rather than subjecting him, as in Lodge's slur, to inordinate ridicule. Yet the broadsheet prints discussed above suggest that Hamlet's evocation of the town crier would nonetheless have called to the minds of early modern theatergoers the broader population of street-criers, some of the most visible and vocal of whom were women. All of the surviving prints follow a remarkably similar format, in which the figure of the town crier (or the related figures of the bellman or nightwatch) either leads the diverse series of criers depicted, as in Figure 22, or is placed at their center, as in Figure 23.[60] The town crier was thus viewed as at once a part of and apart from the broader population of street-criers. As civic officials, the town crier, bellman, and nightwatch were representatives of order and authority. Indeed, in Figure 22, they appear to wield their authority over the female criers depicted. The first, third, and fourth columns are led by the town crier, the nightwatch, and the bellman, respectively, each of whom confronts a female crier who faces in the opposite direction (as do all of the female criers in the series), heightening the sense of conflict.[61] The cries of the nightwatch and bellman appear to address the women directly, advising respectively, "Maids hang-out Your Lights" and "Maids in Your Smocks / Look to your Locks," as if seeking to contain the unruly commerce of female street hawkers by ushering them back into the domestic sphere.[62] Hamlet's mention of the town crier serves a similar function, in that it simultaneously evokes and elides Lodge's oysterwife and her peers, who vended their wares in and around the theaters. Yet, as we shall see, the unruly vocal register associated with street-criers, and with female street-criers in particular, nonetheless haunts the play's soundscape.

In the early modern period, Gina Bloom has powerfully argued, vocal self-restraint was understood to be a defining trait of dominant masculinity.[63] Whereas the "disorderly flow of voice from women's bodies served as an analogous symptom of the female body's extraordinarily porous boundaries," men's ability to control their own voices through rhetorical training, and the voices of their subordinates through the exercise of authority, served as a signifier of manliness.[64] Because the voice was understood in physiological terms to be "inherently unstable" and resistant to training, however, the masculinity thereby constituted was often depicted as imperiled, while the unruly, female, or effeminate voice was portrayed as destabilizing to or subversive of gender hierarchies.[65] Early modern plays performed by the all-male playing companies in particular, Bloom argues, "repeatedly stage the efforts of male characters to reassert control over the fugitive, unpredictable voice," while depicting "female characters who embrace, instead of attempting to overcome, their unpredictable vocal flows" as "able to elude patriarchal regulation" and to exercise "vocal agency."[66] Read within this context, Hamlet's advice to the players, which attempts to refine or assert mastery over the voice of the professional actor, stands in stark contrast to his own vocal outpourings of "unmanly grief" (1.2.94) elsewhere in the play and to Ophelia's unruly vocalizations of madness—even if the latter can in no simple way be read as an instance of female vocal agency.

In attempting to grasp the larger stakes of Lodge's satirical barb and Shakespeare's response to it, we must remember that by the late 1590s it had become something of a vogue to lampoon the ghosts of neo-Senecan revenge tragedies, whose theatrical stock had fallen considerably by then. Thus, in the Induction to *A Warning for Fair Women* (1596–1600), performed by Shakespeare's company just a few years before *Hamlet*, after Ladie Tragedie tries to banish Comedie and Hystorie from the stage, scolding them for the "filthie sound" made by Hystorie's drum and the "filthie fiddling trickes" of Comedie, which she disdains as "poison [to] any noble wit," Comedie replies by lampooning Tragedie's "filthie whining ghost" who "Comes screaming like a pigge halfe stickt, / And cries *Vindicta*, revenge, revenge." Ladie Tragedie argues in rebuttal that while Comedie may "tickle shallow injudiciall eares," her own job is to penetrate the organs of sense more deeply: "I must have passions that must move the soule, / Make the heart heavie, and throb within the bosome, / Extorting tears out of the strictest eyes, / Untill I rap the sences from their course, / This is my office."[67] Although *A Warning* acknowledges that the cries of neo-Senecan revenge tragedy had become a source of comic ridicule, it also seeks to define a new "office" for the tragedies performed by the adult playing companies, one able to "rap the sences from their course" without sounding like a "pigge halfe stickt."

Ladie Tragedie's reply to Comedie counters the burlesque of Senecan bombast that would become a staple feature of the satirical plays staged by the children's companies during the War of the Theaters.[68] Jonson's *Poetaster* (1601), for example, derides players who indulge in such bombast as "two penny tear-mouth[s]" who "cry 'Murder!' " and "*Vindicta!*" (3.4.130–31, 233, 241). The cries and rants of Senecan ghosts and revengers in these plays are frequently lampooned through parodic enactment, as in Marston's *Antonio and Mellida* (1599–1600), where Antonio casts himself on the ground no fewer than four times "To pule and weep, exclaim, to curse and rail, / To fret and ban the fates, to strike the earth" (3.2.209–10). At other times, they are met with such withering lines as "What rattling thunderclap breaks from his lips?" (*Antonio and Mellida*, Ind. 91–92) or are preempted, as in *Antonio's Revenge* (1599–1601) by lines like "I will not swell like a tragedian / In forced passion of affected strains" (2.2.105–6). To suggest that the cries of neo-Senecan revenge tragedy had exhausted their performative potential as high tragic utterance by the late 1590s, however, would fail to recognize that the hyperbole of the tragic cry and its potential to descend into parodic excess were already characteristic of the revenge tragedies of the 1580s, and indeed, of Senecan drama itself, whose extravagant, cataclysmic cries were themselves belated avatars of those found in Aeschylus, Sophocles, and Euripides. Inherent in such cries is what T. S. Eliot terms a "monotony of forcefulness."[69] Because the cries of revenge tragedy are defined by their very forcefulness or excess, their rehearsal always has the potential to transform pathos into bathos. The solution to this dilemma, however, was resolved quite differently in different tragic texts and performative contexts. In Kyd's *The Spanish Tragedy* (c. 1582–92), the name given to this excessive forcefulness is *outrage*, as when Hieronymo's wife, Isabella, mourns the death of her son, crying: "O, gush out, tears, fountains and floods of tears; / Blow, sighs, and raise an everlasting storm: / For outrage fits our cursed wretchedness" (2.5.43–45), or when her maid tries to curtail the excess of her cries, pleading, "Good madam, affright not thus yourself / With outrage for your son Horatio" (3.8.7–8). The term "outrage" comes from the Anglo-Norman *utrage*, meaning excess, extremity, beyond bounds or measure. By the early modern period, however, the false etymology *out* + *rage* had influenced the development of the word such that it signified not only pure excess in word or deed but more particularly a "violent clamor" or "outcry" in response to an injury or injustice (*OED*, "outrage, *n.*" 1b and etymology).

During the War of the Theaters the children's companies, when they were not simply mocking tragic outrage, resolved the dilemma posed by its performance through song. The boys' musical talents were deployed to excite "passions that must move the soule" and in an effort to trump the more experienced actors of the adult companies. This solution is suggested by the terms in which Antonio asks his page to sing in *Antonio and Mellida*: "I prithee sing," he pleads, and "Let each note breathe the heart of passion, / The sad extracture of extremest grief" (4.1.138–40). The use of song by the children's companies to render a refined tragic pathos—or what in *Antonio's Revenge* is facetiously termed the "pathetical and unvulgar" (3.2.38)—allowed Marston and Jonson (and later Dekker and Shakespeare) in their *poetomachia* to deploy the figure of the crier as a tool through which to satirize the cries of neo-Senecan revenge tragedy as bathetic and vulgar. The crier became a convenient foil against which to define the professional playwright and/or player and a vehicle used to stigmatize rival playwrights or playing companies. In act 2, scene 1 of Marston's *Histrio-Mastix* (1598–99), when Sir Oliver Owlet's Men (the owl being known for its screeching cry), a troupe of traveling players who are lampooned throughout the play, comes to town, they cry their play at the market cross, as the stage direction indicates: "*One of them steppes on the Crosse, and cryes a Play.*" The players' cry reveals their ineptitude and lowly social status: "All they that can sing and say, / Come to the Town-house and see a Play, / At three a clocke it shall beginne, / The finest play that e're was seene. / Yet there is one thing more in my minde, / Take heed you leave not your purses behinde." We have clearly come a long way from Robert Wilson's Prologue in *The Three Ladies*, which proudly cries the play to come and embraces the player's likeness to the crier, a likeness that would later become a source of derision. Chrisoganus (Marston's Jonson surrogate) taunts the screeching players: "Write on, crie on, yawle to the common sort / Of thickskin'd auditours."[70]

As Gina Bloom's analysis of the early modern opposition between male vocal self-restraint and female vocal outpouring might lead us to suspect, the cries of unskilled or "unworkmanly" players were frequently lampooned in gendered terms. In Dekker's *Satiromastix* (1601), Tucca describes Horace (his Jonson surrogate) as "a poore Jorneyman Player" who played "mad Jeronimos part, to get service among the Mimickes" (4.1.128–34), chiding: "th'ast a good rouncivall voice to cry Lanthorne and Candle-light" (4.3.154–55).[71] Although Dekker likens Horace's cries to those of the bellman (who, like the town crier, was a male civic official), he nonetheless characterizes them as a boisterous, vulgar, female outpouring of sound. The gendered term "rouncivall" draws on a similar register to that used by Lodge to lampoon the *Ur-Hamlet*'s ghost, for it referred to "a woman of large build and boisterous or loose manners" (*OED*, "rouncival," 3), as epitomized by her "rouncing" or "roaring, noisy" voice (*OED*, "rouncing, *adj.*"). Edmund Gayton similarly speaks of the "reaking, sweaty Rouncifolds of Py-corner" whose cries resemble those of screeching owls. Gayton is referring to the pig-women who, like Jonson's Ursula, dressed and cried their pigs at Pie-Corner in West Smithfield during Bartholomew Fair.[72] Rouncivals were also frequently likened to whores; the *OED* cites Nashe, in *Saffron Walden* (1596), who refers to "a fat Bonarobe [i.e. prostitute] and terrible Rouncevall," and Heywood's *Golden Age* (1611): "I am not yet of that giant size but I may pass for a bona roba, a rouncevall, a virago, or a good manly lass."

How, then, does Shakespeare's *Hamlet* address the dilemma posed by the performance of tragic outrage in the aftermath of this gendered controversy? Rosencrantz obliquely references the vocal abilities of the children's companies in general and of the Children of the Queen's Revels (who began to play at Blackfriars in 1600) in particular when he refers to them as "an eyrie of children, little eyases, that cry out on the top of question" (ll. 3–4). Yet Hamlet, as Bruce Smith and Gina Bloom argue, underscores the mutability of and consequent limitation inherent in the boy-companies' most valuable asset, the boy-chorister's singing voice, which is liable to crack at any moment, when he asks: "Will they pursue the quality no longer than they can sing?" (ll. 10–11). He does so again when he addresses the boy-actor in the company of traveling players: "Pray God your voice, like a piece of uncurrent gold, be not cracked within the ring" (2.2.365–66). As Bruce Smith glosses this line, "'Ring' offers a pun on the shape of the coin, the shape of the windpipe, the shape of the theater, and the 'shape' of the boy's sound."[73] Gina Bloom adds that the line registers anxiety regarding "the actor's windpipe, a round organ that cracks as it expands during puberty, changing the boy's vocal range."[74] I would add that the gendered associations of "crack" and "ring"—both of which were cant terms for the female genitals (while clearly playing as well on the eroticized "crack" of the boy-actor's buttocks)—suggest that the unpredictable and uncontrollable moment at which the boy-actor's voice deepens effeminizes him rather than marking his entrance into manhood.[75] Although Shakespeare's *Hamlet* does not eschew the satire of Senecan bombast (as when Hamlet taunts the Player Lucianus, "the croaking raven doth bellow for revenge" [3.2.247]) or the use of a boy-actor's vocal abilities (as in Ophelia's songs), neither does it reject the vocal register of the cry, defined as an unruly, unmanly, outpouring of sound, which it knowingly reclaims as its preferred vehicle for performing passions that move the soul by violently rapping or piercing the ears of its auditors.

No longer mere "common players" pestering the countryside in league with itinerant peddlers and street-criers, the professional players had become servants of the nobility whose diction, Hamlet advises, should reflect this social distinction. His advice to the players seeks to align the professional player's vocal self-restraint with the "civile conversation" advanced by contemporary rhetorical and conduct manuals marketed to the elite and would-be elite, which cautioned their readers to moderate the voice so as to sound "neither shrill nor loud like a crier."[76] This reference to the uncivil voice of the crier appears in George Pettie's 1581 translation of Stephano

Guazzo's *Civile Conversation* in a discussion of *actio*, or vocal and gestural delivery (the part of rhetoric most pertinent to actors),[77] which he deems to be a key indicator of social status: "like as wee knowe the goodnesse or naughtinesse of mony, by the sounde of it: so by the sounde of woordes, we gather the inwarde qualities and conditions of the man. And for that wee are so much the more esteemed of, by howe muche our Civilitie differeth from the nature and fashions of the vulgar sorte, it is requisite that wee inforce our tongue to make manifest that difference."[78] Hamlet's advice to the players clearly draws on Guazzo's treatise, which encourages the refined orator to "measure its [the voice's] forces . . . in suche sort, that though it straine it selfe somewhat, yet it offend not the eares by a rawe and harshe sownde" or by "opening [the] mouth too muche, fill[ing] it with winde, and mak[ing] the woordes resown[d]e within . . . like a crier."[79] Excessive "libertie of . . . jestures" is likewise to be avoided so that there is "agreement . . . betweene the words and the countenance, and the countenance and the wordes."[80] Whereas Guazzo further associates such crude and exaggerated gestures with a "playerlike kinde of lightnesse," however, Hamlet appropriates Guazzo's oratorical lesson in an effort to elevate the players' status by refining their speech and gestures, instructing them to refrain from "saw[ing] the air too much" with their hands (3.2.4) and to "use all gently" (l. 5) by "Suit[ing] the action to the word, the word to the action" (ll. 16–17).

Yet there is a tension that runs throughout both Guazzo's advice regarding vocal and gestural delivery and Hamlet's appropriation of it. Guazzo's insistence on moderation in oratory is difficult to accord with the importance he places on *moving* the listener: "our chief labour must bee to move the heartes of the hearers," he maintains, but to do so "without offence to the eares."[81] This is no easy feat, for in order to move auditors, he argues, the orator must himself be, or appear to be, moved: "it can not be that you shoulde bee sorowfull for my mishap, if while I recount it unto you, you perceive not me to be sorowfull. . . . You see then, that the inwarde action ought to goe before the outwarde, so that the sounde of the wordes, and the motions of the body, bee thrust forwarde by the affections of the heart."[82] Too much moderation in vocal and gestural delivery will fail to convey the forward thrust of emotion or "inwarde action": if the voice is too "fainte" or gestures "too ceremonious" or restrained, they will not "have force to stirre up mens mindes" or "move the heartes of the hearers."[83] A similar dilemma surfaces in Hamlet's advice to the players when he warns them not to "split the ears of the groundlings," but not to be "too tame, neither" (3.2.15). The speech encourages moderation and self-restraint while at the same time acknowledging that *actio*, particularly when it is deployed in tragedy, depends upon the forceful expression of strong emotion: "in the very torrent, tempest, and, as I may say, the whirlwind of your passion, you must acquire and beget a temperance that may give it smoothness" (3.2.5–8). The dilemma posed by Hamlet's speech, as David Bevington describes it, is that while "strong passions call for vivid acting . . . the violence of such gestures would appear to invite the kind of overacting that Hamlet mistrusts." How, then, he asks, are "Shakespeare and his actors to depict strong emotion . . . without tearing a passion to tatters?"[84]

This tension runs throughout the play, which stages the cry as its preferred mode of tragic utterance. The ear-splitting, soul-harrowing, body-shattering voice of the dead or unjustly murdered is articulated throughout the play through cries.[85] Yet the politics of courtly decorum and indirection impede such violent and direct modes of expression by defining them as rude, common, vulgar, and unmanly. When Hamlet wails and rails, breaching the bounds of courtly decorum like a crier, he is depicted as doing violence to the ears of his auditors, as if to mimic the violence done to King Hamlet himself: "What have I done that thou dar'st wag thy tonge / In noise so rude against me?" (3.4.40–41), Gertrude demands, defining Hamlet's cries as "daggers" that "enter in [her] ears" (l.87).[86] Read from this perspective, the cry with which Hamlet ends his life in the Folio after announcing "the rest is silence" (5.2.342)—"O, o, o, o"—seems entirely appropriate. Although editors often cut this final utterance, arguing that it "is the addition, doubtless, of some actor," this effort to distance Hamlet from the "ranting" of common players elides the acoustic dimension of the cries that resound throughout the play in knowing defiance of the taunts of the "little eyases."[87] The interpolated stage direction with which G. R. Hibbard interprets the excised line—"*He gives a long sigh and dies*" (5.2.311, s.d.)—likewise functions to silence this aspect of the play's soundscape. If we read Hamlet's dying utterance as a cry or howl akin to that of the ghost, or to that of Lear ("Howl, howl, howl! O!" [5.3.256]), when he enters with Cordelia dead in his arms, its efficacy would lie not in silence but in its ability to harrow the souls and freeze the blood of its auditors.[88]

Taken within the context of the play as a whole, Hamlet's advice to the players thus cannot be read as a simple foreclosure or preemptive ridicule of the figure of the crier. For although his advice encourages the actors to be temperate, such temperance fails him in his own efforts to answer his father's cries for vengeance. At these moments, Hamlet himself seems compelled not merely to cry but to cry out like a common player: "What would he do, / Had he the motive and the cue for passion / That I have? He would drown the stage with tears / . . . cleave the general ear with horrid speech / . . . and amaze indeed / The very faculties of eyes and ears" (2.2.495–98, 500–501). Crucially, it is the cry of a player here that moves Hamlet to cry out in a whirlwind of passion. More precisely, it is the player's evocation of an unruly, female outpouring of sound, that of Hecuba upon witnessing the murder of her husband, which brings "Tears in his eyes" (l. 490): "The instant burst of clamor that she made," the impassioned player recounts, "(Unless things mortal move them not at all) / Would have made milch the burning eyes of heaven / And passion in the gods" (ll. 453–56). Hecuba's cry or "burst of clamor" serves as an effective conduit of grief that overwhelms the senses. It moves the player to tears (not to mention the "eyes of heaven"), which in turn brings Hamlet to cry out for vengeance.

Yet these cries are not all of a kind: the clamorous cry of Hecuba is contrasted with the more passive weeping and paleness of the actor. It was in the sixteenth century that the verb "to cry" first evolved from its vociferous sense into its more modern, muted form (i.e., "To weep, shed tears; used even where no sound is uttered" [*OED*, "cry, *v.*" 10]). These two modes of crying have quite different gendered associations within the play. Whereas silent weeping is associated with male effeminacy, as when Laertes weeps and remarks of his tears, "When these are gone, the woman will be out" (4.7.186–87), the clamorous cry is associated with the rouncing voice of a virago or "manly lass." Thus, when Hamlet cries out in a "burst of clamor" like Hecuba, he likens himself to a "whore," "a very drab" (2.2.520–21), and in the Folio text, to a "Scullion" or kitchen wench.[89]

Hamlet's haunting by a vocal register associated with female vociferation in general and female street-criers in particular invites us to consider how it may have influenced the staging of Ophelia's cries following her descent into madness. Like the ghost, the mad Ophelia becomes a wayward wanderer, entering and exiting the stage, to borrow Hamlet's apt phrase, as her "business and desire" direct her (1.5.129). Her attitude toward her interlocutors is one of advertisement, in that she "call[s] the attention of others" in "admonition, warning, precept, [and] instruction" (*OED*, "advertisement" 2): "pray you, mark," she repeatedly insists (4.5.27, 35), echoing the ghost's "List, . . . O list!" Ophelia's evocation of this vocal register is further suggested by her comparison of herself to an owl ("They say the owl was a baker's daughter" [4.5.42–43]), for the term was an onomatopoeia deriving from the Latin *ulula* meaning to howl or ululate (*OED*, "owl, *n.*" etymology). The owl, on account of its doleful, nocturnal cry, was widely perceived to be a harbinger of death and misfortune, and was thus frequently associated not only with the nocturnal world of ghosts and spirits but with the vocal idiom of street-criers, as when Sir Oliver Owlet's Men cry their play at the market cross, or when the owl-like screech of Gayton's rouncival is likened to the pig-women of Bartholomew Fair.

Shakespeare elsewhere associates owls, as birds of prey, with predatory women, and more specifically with predatory female lust.[90] Ophelia's lunacy likewise renders her a menacing, if not sexually predacious, figure. There are suggestions in the text that her voicings of madness may at times have resonated on the stage as cacophonous cries rather than sweetly lyrical singing. Her second entrance, for example, is heralded by Laertes, "How now? What noise is that?" (4.5.152). Yet in Laertes' view, Ophelia's cries stir emotion in a way that eloquence pronounced trippingly on the tongue cannot: "Hadst thou thy wits, and didst persuade revenge," he says, "It could not move thus" (4.5.163–64). The staging of Ophelia's madness represents a novel solution to the dilemma posed by the performance of tragic outrage in the aftermath of the War of the Theaters, insofar as it weaves the tragic pathos of the boy-actor's lyrical voice together with the auditory register of the female crier. If Ophelia's wayward wandering and singing of old lauds are evocative of a crier of ballads, her importunate solicitations are reminiscent of the ubiquitous figure of the herb-wife. Such women, who were known to advertise the medicinal and symbolic properties of their herbs and flowers, as Ophelia does, were so common on the streets of early modern London that an Act of Common Council singles them out from the population of female criers, citing "Herbe wives" as among the "divers unruly people . . . inhabiting in or neere the city," who wander about, crying their wares, and practicing "sundry abuses . . . [in] the common Markets, and streets of the City of London."[91]

If the soundscape of Shakespeare's *Hamlet* and in particular its staging of tragic outrage and female lunacy are indeed haunted, as I have suggested, by the unruly vocalizations of female criers in and around the theaters, later adult-company plays influenced by Ophelia's mad scenes make their appropriation of the female crier's vocal idiom far more explicit. In the Bedlam scene that concludes Dekker and Middleton's *The Honest Whore, Part One* (1604), performed by Prince Henry's Men, for example, Bellafront, the former "whore" of the play's title and present occupant of Bedlam, sings snatches of old ballads and addresses her former customers who have come to view the spectacle of her madness by mimicking the rattling voice of a fishwife, crying:

"[W]ill you buy any gudgeons!" (5.2.312–13).[92] Henry Chettle's revenge play, *The Tragedy of Hoffman* (1602), performed by the Admiral's Men, likewise aims to capitalize on the success of Shakespeare's Ophelia by imitating her performance idiom, which in Chettle's play is explicitly likened not only to that of a ballad singer but to that of a female hawker of old clothes. When Lucibella enters "distract of sense" (l. 1427), she says that she is "going to the rivers side / To fetch white lilies, and blew daffadils" (ll. 1433–34) to mourn her dead husband and father.[93] When she enters for the second time, she carries "*rich clothes*" (l. 1930, s.d.) to attire their corpses and not only sings snatches of bawdy ballads ("Downe, downe a downe, hey downe, downe. / I sung that song, while *Lodowicke* slept with me" [ll. 1976–77]) but addresses the onlookers by imitating the vocal advertisement of a female fripper of secondhand clothes: "[I'm] a poor mayden, mistris, ha's a suite to you, / And 'tis a good suite, very good apparel," Lucibella cries, "How doe you Lady, well I thanke God, will you buy a barga[ine] pray, it's fine apparrell" (ll. 2048–49, 2053–54). Although the appropriation of the vocal repertoire of female street-criers in stagings of female lunacy is perhaps no less demeaning of their status than outright satire, the popularity of Ophelia's performance of madness—attested to by its many subsequent imitations—suggests that the entertainment value of the female crier's vocal idiom continued to be recognized and appropriated by the adult companies in the aftermath of the War of the Theaters, even as they sought to elevate their own skilled performance idiom above it.

Children's company plays continued to manifest a more caustic attitude toward the cacophonous cries of the street, and those of the female crier in particular, as in Ben Jonson's city comedy *Epicoene; or, The Silent Woman* (1609), performed by the Children of the Queen's Revels at Whitefriars. Morose, a gentleman who "can endure no noise" (1.1.142), resides in "a street . . . so narrow at both ends that it will receive no coaches nor carts nor any of these common noises" of the city, in a "room with double walls and treble ceilings, the windows close shut and caulked" (1.1.161–63, 178–80).[94] Staged for an elite audience in the privileged enclave of a private theater, Morose's inner sanctum is represented as under continual assault by the commercial outcry of street vendors and other popular entertainers, including "broom-men," "costardmonger[s]," the "waits of the city," and a "bearward" who "cried his games under Master Morose's window till he was sent crying away with his head made a most bleeding spectacle to the multitude" (1.1.148–49, 156–57, 167–71). First and foremost among the list of offending noise makers, however, are the "fishwives and orange-women," with whom Morose "has been upon divers treaties . . . and articles propounded between them" to keep them silent (ll. 144–46). As the play's subtitle suggests, the sound of the clamorous, unruly female voice is a prominent subject of satire in this play. Yet Jonson continued to borrow from the vocal repertoire of female hawkers in his adult-company plays, as he does in staging the cries of the "Bartholomew-birds" (Ind. 12) in *Bartholomew Fair* (1614), performed by Lady Elizabeth's Men, including the cries of Joan Trash ("Buy any gingerbread, gilt gingerbread!" [2.2.32]) and those of Ursula the pig-woman of Pie-Corner, purveyors of the purportedly false wares considered in the next chapter.

The female "Cries of London" represented in ballads, prints, and plays, far from being unmediated voicings of England's bygone, pre-industrial past as their antiquarian collectors would have it, were shaped by contemporary attitudes toward those who worked outside or on the fringes of the formal economy during a period of economic change and uncertainty. Scapegoated for economic problems like unemployment, inflation, and the perceived decay of "legitimate" trades, female street-criers epitomized all that was antithetical to "honest" work. Their cries sounded through the streets of the city as harbingers of the decline of guild control, the breakdown of market regulation, and the new forms of unlicensed commercial activity that mushroomed in the suburbs and liberties of the city. With the rise of the professional stage, they likewise came to represent the antithesis of the skilled players' "workmanship." Yet their visible presence in and around the theaters served as a constant reminder to the professional players of the itinerant forms of popular entertainment from which their own repertoire had emerged. Representations of female street-cries and criers thus performed their own cultural and ideological work as complex negotiations of the gendered division of theatrical labor. The visible and vocal presence of female criers in and around the commercial theaters suggests that we need to revise our understanding of the "all-male" Shakespearean stage, for a diverse array of working women and popular, female performance practices cry to be heard, echoing within and without the walls of the theaters. As we shall see in the chapter that follows, by the second decade of the seventeenth century, the professional players began to define their skilled workmanship in opposition to not only the inarticulate voices of market women but the purportedly inferior, "unworkmanly" wares they produced and sold as well.

Chapter 5

False Wares

> As there is no woman made without a flaw, your purest lawns have frays, and cambricks bracks.
> —Thomas Middleton, *A Chaste Maid in Cheapside* (1613)

> [W]ell-joyning, cementing, and coagmentation of words, . . . [is] like a Table, upon which you may runne your finger without rubs, and your nayle cannot find a joynt.
> —Ben Jonson, *Discoveries* (pub. 1641)

WITHIN THE CIVIC imaginary of early modern London, vice was often located in the feminized "skirts" or suburbs of the city. It was in these extramural precincts that laborers who were excluded from citizenship sought to earn a living beyond the reach of guild and civic authorities. Yet the boundary between formal and informal commerce was far more unstable and permeable than its conflation with the walls of the city might suggest. This boundary was in constant flux, varying with the shifting parameters of "legitimate" trade, and was subject to continual contestation, particularly during periods of perceived economic crisis or change. In this chapter, I explore the policing of this boundary through the staged destruction or confiscation of the purportedly "false" wares produced and sold by market women in Thomas Middleton's *Chaste Maid in Cheapside* (1613) and Ben Jonson's *Bartholomew Fair* (1614). Both plays, as we shall see, were performed during a particularly tense period of conflict surrounding the boundaries of legitimate commerce, and surrounding the legitimacy of playing as a profession. At stake in the policing of these boundaries was an ideal of virtuous, civic masculinity to which the professional players aspired but from which they had long been excluded.

Although we tend to think of virtue and vice as attributes of subjects, rather than objects, in the context of early modern market regulation it was often *things* that were deemed virtuous or branded—and punished—as vicious. Market regulation was viewed not simply as an economic but as a moral imperative. The term "virtue," from the Latin *virtus* (manliness, valor, worth) and *vir* (man), was associated with the masculine vigor and worth of "honest" work. When applied to objects, it conveyed the superiority, excellence, and potency of goods produced by such work (*OED*, "virtue, *n.*" II and etymology and "virtuous, *a.*" II). "Vice," from the Latin *vitium* (fault, defect, failing), was conversely associated with unmanliness, imperfection, and impotency. Vicious wares were impaired or spoiled by some fault, flaw, blemish, defect, or impurity ("vice, *n.*¹" 4, 5; "vicious, *a.*" 6). The term "evil" was likewise used in the regulation of markets to stigmatize commodities produced by unguilded or non-citizen laborers (e.g., foreigners, aliens, and women). Evil commodities were purportedly unwholesome, inferior in quality, and generally unsatisfactory and defective. Used as an adverb, "evil" meant not only wickedly but also badly, defectively, imperfectly, or unskillfully, as in the phrase "evil made" ("evil, *a.* and *n.*" A, 8; "evil, *adv.*" 5, 8c). Goods produced outside the masculine fellowship of the urban guilds by foreigners, aliens, and women were thus by definition not good in both a moral and an economic sense, and were variously branded as evil, "unworkmanly," unwholesome, false, and deceitful.[1] They were also, as we shall see, frequently associated with the faults of womankind.

When the vicious wares manufactured by women and other unguilded or non-citizen laborers were discovered in workshops or for sale in London's markets, they were destroyed with a degree of ceremonial display worthy of critical scrutiny. The ritual destruction of false wares was a routine aspect of civic and guild regulation of economic production and trade within the city. The "powers of search," as they were called, were carried out at regular intervals throughout the year by civic authorities and livery company wardens, dressed in official regalia and carrying official insignia, who inspected workshops, warehouses, fairs, and markets. A variety of sanctions were exacted against offenders, including the levying of fines and various forms of punishment (public shaming, stocking, and imprisonment), but also the seizure and destruction of goods that were deemed "false" on account of their unlawful manufacture.[2] This "ritualized public destruction of faulty products," according to Michael Berlin, sometimes took the form of "quasi-judicial proceedings in which prosecution and punishment were as much directed at the inanimate object as at the person." After being "condemned by a 'jury,'" the offending goods were ceremonially destroyed, either by being burnt on a pyre or smashed with a hammer.³ In another common form of punishment, the producer was made to wear the offending object around his or her neck as a form of public humiliation. Thus, for example, bakers accused of using "evill and unholsome paste" or of using short measures were bound and drawn on a hurdle from the Guildhall to their own houses through the streets with the vicious loaves hung around their necks.⁴ Sometimes these processions through streets and markets resorted to more elaborate forms of pageantry and "rough music": one baker accused of eking out his flour with sand was born to the pillory "with one of the obnoxious loaves carried behind him on the point of a lance," while another whose bread was short of weight was carried through the streets on a hurdle while a minstrel played on a tabor behind him.⁵

Borrowing elements of public shaming rituals such as charivari and Skimmington, used to humiliate cuckolded or wife-beaten husbands and adulterous or scolding wives, the punishment of unguilded workers and ritual destruction of their wares likewise took on gendered overtones. Male artisans and tradesmen accused of producing or selling wares that were "adulterated" (and therefore not fully "potent"), "short of measure," or otherwise faulty were punished for their lack of masculine virtue in the practice of their crafts and trades in the same manner as men who were married to emasculating scolds, shrews, or adulteresses. The form of their punishment implied that their masculinity was itself faulty, adulterated, or short of measure. Wife-beaten husbands, for example, were made to wear their wives' clothes (and cuckolds, animals' horns) and were beaten with kitchen utensils or pelted with filth and dung while being "ridden" through town, accompanied by the "rough music" of pots and pans, and finally dumped in a river to be "washed."⁶ In the case of market regulation, the association of masculine virtue with "just measure" was further reinforced by the "Sylver yard[s]" carried by the wardens of clothworkers' guilds who were responsible for searching out false wares: a "yard" was not only a unit of measure, a symbol of authority, and an instrument of punishment, but also a phallus (*OED*, "yard, *n.*²" 3, 4, 7, 11). An account of searches conducted by the Drapers' Company of the Southwark and St. Bartholomew fairs in 1587 describes how the master wardens and clerk deployed the "Sylver yard":

> And so, as in tymes past it hath ben accustomed, they went and measured all the yards in the faire, . . . and the said Masters, havinge taken divers yards unmerked amongst the same from one Nicholas

Costyn nere the white horse in Southwark a yard to shorte, and also from Mary Richardson the wife of Richard Richardson, then standing by half a yarde to short . . . and gave them sharpe warninge of their ill measures, contrary to the lawes of this Realme used.⁷

If masculine virtue was at stake when male artisans and tradesmen were accused of having short "yards," adulterating wares, or failing to serve the seven-year apprenticeship that entitled them to practice their trades as freemen, female virtue was likewise at stake when crafts- and tradeswomen like Mary Richardson were accused of market abuses. Yet the implications of women taking up the yard, or other trade tools (as seen in the case of the poking sticks used to starch ruffs, discussed in Chapter 3), carried a very different set of cultural associations and entailed different forms of gendered punishment.

Because female virtue was strongly associated with chastity or sexual purity (*OED*, "virtue, *n.*" 2c; "virtuous, *a.*" 2b), women accused of manufacturing impure, adulterated, or defective wares were stigmatized as sexually unchaste or impure (or as aggressive usurpers of male authority) and were disciplined with the same forms of punishment used for prostitutes, adulteresses, and scolds. Records dating back to the thirteenth century specify an apparatus called the "thew" as the punishment set aside for women who committed market abuses.⁸ The term appears to have been used loosely to refer to a variety of apparatuses, including the bridle or *collistrigium* (an iron collar or cage that enclosed the head and neck, sometimes with a spiked tongue depressor to prevent speech, also used to punish scolds and shrews), the cart (used to punish prostitutes and adulteresses), and the ducking or cucking stool (a chair or close stool used to dunk disorderly women in a pond or river). The term derived from the Old English *théaw*, a term that denoted "virtue," both in the sense of a "good quality or habit" and of the "bodily powers or forces of a man" (*OED*, "thew, *n.*¹" 2b, 3b, and etymology). To be "thewful" was to be "characterized by good qualities; good, virtuous, moral," while to be "thewless" was to be "vicious, immoral" (*OED*, "thewful, *a.*" and "thewless, *a.*"). The Worshipful Company of Bakers punished women in the thew, while confiscating or destroying their wares, for offenses such as selling a penny bun under weight, counterfeiting the trademarks of City bakers, and passing off bread made "of evill and unholsome paste."⁹ The thew not only doled out corporal punishment for women's informal manufacturing and marketing activities but defined such women as thewless or lacking the masculine virtue associated with "honest" work; it symbolically linked market women's informal commerce to female sexual, verbal, and moral incontinence. The cucking stool further reinforced this link, insofar as the term "cuck," in addition to its association with the call of the cuckoo and with cuckoldry (from the cuckoo's habit of laying its eggs in other birds' nests), also meant to void excrement (*OED*, "cuck, *v.*¹"). This link was materialized by the close stool or privy used in the manufacture of cucking stools, on which women who vended false wares were made to sit. The association of market women with incontinence was likewise used to brand the wares they sold as excremental, as in the case of alewives who, like Elinor Rumming, were accused of adulterating their ale with urine and other unwholesome ingredients.[10]

We might pause here to ponder the cultural significance of the ritualized punishment not only of working women who produced evil wares but of the offending objects themselves. The aim of removing such wares from the marketplace to protect consumers from unwholesome or defective goods does not fully explain the necessity of their ritualized—and often quite dramatic—destruction. Although such rituals might seem to have the effect of obliterating the "material memory"[11] of women's work, this explanation evades a crucial aspect of their enactment, namely, the way in which the destruction of false wares was publicly *staged*. For it is on account of such public stagings, and in the accounts through which they were memorialized for posterity in civic and livery company records, that the obliteration of material memory in a crucial sense fails. Staging the eradication of market women's evil wares was as, if not *more*, important than their annihilation itself, I would suggest, because the "evil" character of the things destroyed was more the effect than the cause of their ritualized destruction. Because the boundary between legitimate and illegitimate trade was in constant flux, it was in need of continual redefinition for the producing and consuming public. When these boundaries became particularly murky or contested, their redrawing through the public punishment of offenders became all the more important. In this sense, the staged ritual through which false wares were destroyed functioned to re-produce the status of the wares in question as always already un-done (i.e., improperly made from the start and therefore unworthy of existence). Although the purported lack of substance inherent in false wares ostensibly rendered their ritualized destruction nothing more than a consequence or confirmation of their status as "false" (e.g., unwholesome, adulterated, insubstantial, or imperfectly manufactured), this classification had to be continually reasserted, and in consequence, the ritual of destruction was itself "never done." The necessity of such public rituals and of their repetition further underscores the temporary and provisional nature of the meaning and indeed the very being of material objects whose cultural value, significance, and legitimacy must be continually, and sometimes violently, staged.

The ritual destruction or confiscation of false wares was part of an ongoing contest over the meaning and value of London's expanding market of consumer goods and who was entitled to produce and profit from them. As discussed in the previous chapter, the exponential population growth of London during late sixteenth and early seventeenth centuries made civic and guild control of informal commerce increasingly difficult, if not impossible. The growing numbers of migrants who took up occupations outside the guild system were accused not only of manufacturing false wares but also of illegitimate trafficking in true wares through market abuses such as forestalling, engrossing, or regrating.[12] The effective enforcement of market regulations against such offenses was hampered by the absence of a professional police force, which left the discovery of market abuses to civic and livery company officials and to an unpaid and overworked constabulary, whose numbers were unequal to the task.

City and guild officials were forced to rely on private informers called "promoters" to search out offenders.[13] Economic offenses were "zealously pursued" by promoters because they were the most lucrative: the informer was entitled to a share (usually half) of the fine, which was set in proportion to the value of the property confiscated. During the period when promoters were most active, from 1550 to 1624, they functioned as the "chief instrument for the enforcement of economic legislation."[14] Yet the legions of promoters who sought to earn a living or to supplement their incomes by informing on market abuses failed to establish a clear or fixed boundary between legitimate and illegitimate commerce, as they were themselves prone to "chickanery."[15] The expense of going to trial led most defendants, whether guilty or not, to negotiate out-of-court settlements or "compositions" (in cash or goods) with promoters, which amounted to a kind of informal tax and at times to outright blackmail.[16] Promoters thus benefited from the continuance, rather than the cessation, of illicit trade. The corruption of promoters consequently became a frequent subject of complaint and satire during the period leading up to the legislative reforms of 1624, which greatly reduced the numbers of private informers.[17] Accusations of marketing offenses brought by promoters rose by 80 percent between 1609 and 1613, reaching their peak in 1616, when serious reforms began.[18] It was during this period, when the activity of private informers reached its apex and effective governmental reforms had yet to be enacted, that Middleton and Jonson would bring the drama of contestation over the parameters of legitimate trade and the policing of false wares onto the stage.

Yet this drama had quite different implications when performed by professional players in London's commercial theaters than by civic officials in its streets, markets, and fairs. For in the eyes of City authorities and puritan preachers, playing was itself the very antithesis of a legitimate calling and had no claim to true workmanship.[19] The ideological link between playing and effeminacy, discussed in Chapter 1, was frequently grounded in the status of playing as an "idle occupation."[20] According to Stephen Gosson, "Most of the Players have bene . . . men of occupations, which they have forsaken to lyve by playing . . . & have now no other way to gete theire livinge."[21] Like other occupations in the informal sector, playing was relegated to the status of mere idleness, the "Mother of vice," rendering the players effeminate and "unfit for manly discipline."[22] Playing in turn made spectators idle and effeminate by luring them away from "honest" vocations.[23] City authorities repeatedly complained to the Privy Council that the players and playhouses "maintaine idlenes in such persons as have no vocation & draw apprentices and other servantes from theire ordinary workes . . . to the great hinderance of traides."[24]

For their own part, the players defended the status of their craft as a legitimate calling. Professional playing, in the words of actor Nathan Field, was a trade just like that of "the mercer, draper, goldsmith, or a hundred trades and mysteries that at this day are lawful."[25] John Stephens's *Essayes and Characters* (1615) describes the "common Player" as "politick . . . to perceive the common-wealth doubts of his license, and therefore in spight of Parliaments or Statutes hee incorporates himselfe by the title of a brotherhood."[26] His implication is that the professional playing companies strategically modeled themselves on the guilds, by virtue of their incorporation as "brotherhoods," in order to gain legitimacy. Because Stephens's purpose is satirical, however, he derides the illegitimacy of the playing companies as *pseudo*-guilds,[27] describing the common player as "A daily Counterfeit . . . there is no truth in him: for his best action is but an imitation of truth . . . he is but a shifting companion; for hee lives effectually by putting on, and putting off. If his profession were single, hee would think himselfe a simple fellow, as hee doth all professions besides his owne."[28] The players were deemed counterfeits not only because they appropriated the "title of a brotherhood" but also because they performed "all professions besides [their] own" on the stage; they figured the flexibility of those who labored in the informal sector by serially "putting on, and putting off" trades to which they were not entitled.

The charge that players counterfeited legitimate trades often centered on their own trafficking in false or evil wares. Stage properties were viewed by anti-theatrical writers as inherently false both because of their fictive status and because they were often actual counterfeits. From this perspective, theaters exemplified the vices of the marketplace, for they traded in wares that were not what they appeared to be. The players could rarely afford the "real" thing in the manufacture of props, costumes, and scenic elements and therefore relied on the same techniques (such as gilding, the use of cheap or defective materials, and so forth) used by deceitful crafts- and tradesmen and -women. Playwright Thomas Heywood describes the "thin leaves of gold foile" that "guilde the wood" in "gorgeous Theater[s]," making their "collumes seeme all massie gold" (ll. 346–48), likening them to the "golden ensigns" (l. 345) of women's head attires upon which theatrical spectacle had grown increasingly reliant. Heywood, as an apologist for the professional stage, is here praising the artistry of the theater (and of tirewomen) for the spectacular effects they create.[29] Anti-theatrical polemicists, by contrast, inveighed against the falseness of the theaters' glittering props, costumes, and spectacles. Stephen Gosson, for example, derides the "waste of expences in these spectacles that scarce last like shooes of browne paper, the pulling on."[30] Gosson is referring to the players' practice of making properties out of brown paper and paste, and likens their insubstantial wares to those of a cobbler who produces flimsy or defective shoes. He further describes theaters as "markets of bawdry, where choise without shame hath bene as free as it is for your money in the royall exchaung to take a short stocke, or a longe, a falling band, or a french ruffe," cataloguing the expensive, yet insubstantial wares sold by tirewomen and flaunted in theaters to suggest that the "soule of . . . playes is . . . meere trifles."[31] The players' use of copper lace instead of gold to adorn costumes was likewise cited as evidence of their status as counterfeits: Henry Crosse, in his *Vertues Common-Wealth* of 1603, derides players as "copper-lace gentlemen" who "growe rich" and "purchase lands by adulterous Playes."[32] Although Crosse is undoubtedly referring to the adulterous plots of many plays, his reference to copper lace also suggests that the players grew rich by attracting crowds with their display of falsely gilded and adulterated costumes and properties. In response to such attacks on the legitimacy of playing as a profession, the anonymous author (possibly John Webster) of the character of "An

Excellent Actor," written in response to that of the "common Player" cited above, claims, "I valew a worthy Actor by the corruption of some few of the quality, as I would doe gold in the oare; I should not mind the drosse, but the purity of the metall."[33] While it may be true, he acknowledges, that the "common" player is mere dross, the value of a "worthy Actor" is pure gold; playing is indeed a "quality" or legitimate calling, he insists, involving skills that must be perfected as in any other trade. The status of this occupation as a vigorous, virtuous, and manly (not idle) calling is further emphasized by his choice of the term "Actor" rather than "Player" to designate it.

Against this backdrop, the staging of false wares in the commercial playhouses clearly had implications that bore on the legitimacy of playing itself as a profession. For in order to bolster their own virtuous, civic masculinity the players had to distinguish their occupation from other types of informal commerce that were branded as idle and effeminate. In so doing, they likewise sought to distinguish themselves from hypocritical promoters and puritan preachers who purported to discover market abuses while profiting from such abuses themselves. In what follows, we shall see how this rather complex agenda is negotiated in two city comedies whose ostensible aim was the satirical discovery of market abuses. Both were written at the height of the controversy surrounding the boundaries of legitimate trade but also at a particularly tense moment in the ongoing debate over the legitimacy of playing as a profession: Thomas Middleton's *A Chaste Maid in Cheapside* (1613) and Ben Jonson's *Bartholomew Fair* (1614) appeared just after the publication of Thomas Heywood's *Apology for Actors* (1612), which sought to defend the "ancient Dignity" of the profession, and just before the publication of I. G.'s response to Heywood, *A Refutation of the Apology for Actors* (1615). The latter treatise reasserted the argument that players are "Idle, for they . . . know not how to worke, nor in any lawfull calling to get their living" but rather "avoid labour and worke" by taking money from "every one that comes to see them loyter and play. Hence it is that they are Vicious; for idlenesse is the mother of vice."[34] Of particular interest in the present context is the staging in both plays of the destruction or confiscation of market women's wares.

Recent scholarship on city comedy has contributed a great deal to our understanding of the genre's participation in the cultural definition of new forms of urban masculinity attendant upon London's growth as a commercial center. As Jean Howard demonstrates, city comedies staged "complex narratives about the pressures on masculinity in the urban context and the struggle between old and new ways of achieving and displaying masculine privilege."[35] One such pressure, I have suggested, arose from the rapid expansion of informal commerce in London and its growing population of non-citizen laborers, including market women, who threatened the ideal of civic masculinity fostered by the urban guilds. If city comedies represented the growing metropolis as a crucible where gender identities were constantly being renegotiated, these identities were materially crafted through the staging of virtuous and vicious objects as well as subjects. In staging the contestation over the manufacture and sale of false wares, Jonson and Middleton sought to forge a new definition of civic masculinity to which the professional players and playwrights themselves might lay claim. They did so in part, I argue, by contrasting the workmanship of their own productions with the false wares or "trash" produced and sold by market women.

Although first performed in the suburbs of London at the Swan theater on the bankside by the Lady Elizabeth's Men just after Lent in 1613, *A Chaste Maid in Cheapside* takes as its subject and location the walled city's commercial center: the Cheapside market district located in "the heart of the city of London" (1.1.92–93).[36] In so doing, the play reveals that the effeminizing vices of the marketplace are not confined to the "skirts" of the city where the public theaters were located but run rampant at its core in what purports to be a bastion of manly, civic virtue and honest trade. Middleton no doubt chose Cheapside from among the city's many official markets for its purported exemplarity: Stow describes Goldsmith's Row at its center as harboring "the most beautiful frame of fayre houses and shoppes, that bee within the Walles of London."[37] Cheapside's eastern half was home to the largest official marketplace in the city, held on weekday mornings until noon. As a thoroughfare, Cheapside was perhaps the widest open space in a city of dark, narrow alleyways. From this perspective, Vanessa Harding has argued, Cheapside exemplified the virtues of the marketplace (e.g., light, openness, and honesty) and became an ideal setting for city pageants celebrating these virtues.[38] Yet the peculiar architecture of Cheapside was from another perspective perfectly suited to Middleton's purpose of revealing that all that glitters is not gold. The street was delimited by three conduits or public water sources: the Little, or "Pissing" Conduit at its western end, the Standard (also a monument where public punishments were performed) at its center, and the Great Conduit at its eastern end. In Middleton's play, these conduits figure Cheapside's commercial incontinence (its inability to contain or regulate market abuses), which is in turn associated with female incontinence.

Although in other respects the geography of Cheapside suggested an orderly, bounded structure, with side streets named after discrete trades such as Milk Street, Bread Street, Ironmonger Lane, and Goldsmiths' Row, by the late sixteenth century this structure had begun to give way to a disorderly influx of immigrant and itinerant vendors. In Harding's words, market supervision, which had always been "troublesome for City government . . . now became something of a nightmare."[39] In 1588 the City attempted to improve the market's organization by assigning itinerant female vendors to discrete locations within the market, but with little success.[40] City aldermen likewise tried to restrict the number of baskets female vendors were allowed to carry to three · and stipulated that they were not allowed to set up tables or stalls. Such orders reveal that the commerce of informal market women had grown to "fill the whole street," so that in 1592 it was objected that Goldsmiths' Row and Cheapside's west end were "so pestered with herbwives, fruiterers," and other vendors that passersby could not get through, and that these vendors were not obeying market hours but were selling from morning until night, even on the Sabbath.[41] By the second decade of the seventeenth century Goldsmiths' Row (the pride of Cheapside) was in decay, signaling the Goldsmiths' Company's "loss of control over the sale of jewels, gold and silver plate within the city due to competition from strangers."[42]

It was in response to the growing disorder of the city's markets that a promoter named Hugh Alley, mentioned in Chapter 4, submitted his proposal for reform to the Lord Mayor in 1598, titled "A Caveatt for the Citty of London, OR a forewarninge of offences against penal Lawes."[43] The text of the proposal makes clear that for Alley market reform was a moral as well as an economic imperative. His avowed purpose is that "godes glorie maie bee advanced" and "Vice and Idlenes utterlie overwhelmed and brought to nothing." Alley informs the mayor that he has spent time "observinge and lookinge, into every markett" and has "founde manye things, of greate moment, cleane out of course and order." He recommends stricter surveillance by "Carefull lookers" into market abuses. Part of Alley's own work of market surveillance are the illustrations of the "true plott of everie Markett," which he attaches to his proposal, depicting the reforms he wishes to institute.[44] In his illustration of Cheapside market, Alley includes not only existing architectural elements, such as the Standard and the Great Conduit, but also new architectural features, including six pillars around which the foreign vendors who had overrun the market would (according to his proposal) in the future congregate (see Figure 24). Each pillar is labeled in orderly fashion with the home county

Figure 24. Hugh Alley, "A Caveatt for the City of London," 1598. Watercolor of Cheapside Market. Folger MS. V.a.318, fol. 15. By permission of the Folger Shakespeare Library.

from which the respective vendors have come. Other illustrations include pillars labeled with particular market abuses, such as "Regraters," underneath which market offenders were to be punished (see Figure 25). As we have seen, and as Alley's own illustrations make clear, many of the "Haglers, Hawkers, Huxsters" and regraters against whom he inveighs were women.

A Chaste Maid in Cheapside opens in a shop on Goldsmiths' Row, where the abuses sought out by promoters such as Alley are readily apparent. Maudlin, the wife of Yellowhammer the goldsmith, is chastising their daughter Moll for her shortcomings in terms that might have been borrowed from the Goldsmiths' Company's ordinances concerning false wares. Boasting that she herself was "lightsome, and quick, two years before [she] was married" (1.1.8–9), she reproves Moll for being "dull" and "drossy spirited" (l. 10). Although ostensibly bragging about her lighthearted, cheerful, and animated disposition in her youth, Maudlin's revelation that she was "lightsome" and "quick" well before she married further intimates that she was sexually active (*OED*, "light, *adj.*¹" 14b), if not actually pregnant (*OED*, "quick, *adj.*, *n.*¹, and *adv.*" 5b), prior to her espousal. Insofar as the terms "lightsome" and "quick" were also used to describe the dazzling radiance of gold (*OED*, "lightsome, *adj.*²" 1 and "quick, *adj.*" 15b), Maudlin's betrayal of her sexual lightness reminds the audience that the luminosity of gold is never a guarantee of its purity. The Goldsmiths' Company's ordinances are replete with references to deceptive practices used to counterfeit the luminosity of gold and brilliance of gems. The "Oath of the New Men" of the company dictated, "you shall work and cause to be worked good and true gold and silver without any deceit; and you shall not set glass or counterfeit stones in gold." Another ordinance stipulated, "no member of the Company shall set a deceptive color upon gilt wares, such as layting up in helle." The phrase "layting [i.e., lighting] up in helle" (from the Middle High German *hellen*, to make bright) referred to a method of gilding wares to make them appear brighter, while also suggesting the infernal destination of those who engaged in such practices.[45] Although a citizen's wife, Maudlin betrays that she is herself "lit up in hell," that she is not what she seems, so that when she describes her daughter as "drossy" we suspect the justness of her appraisal. Her use of the term "drossy" betrays her familiarity with deceitful market practices, for gold that was "drossy" was mixed with impure, worthless matter (*OED*, "drossy, *adj.*" 1). Although in Maudlin's estimation, lightness is better than heaviness, market justice dictated otherwise: "light" gold was gold that, due to adulteration, was below the standard or legal weight (*OED*, "light, *adj.*¹" 1b).

When Yellowhammer enters, the implications of Maudlin's commercial

Figure 25. Hugh Alley, "A Caveatt for the City of London," 1598. Watercolor of New Fishstreet Market. At left, a pillar to be used for the public punishment of regrators, with market woman and fishwives below. Folger MS. V.a.318, fol. 10. By permission of the Folger Shakespeare Library.

lexicon, and her likening of women to "light" wares, are soon made explicit. Maudlin tells her husband that she has been informing their daughter "of her errors" (l. 22), to which he replies:

> 'Errors,' nay the city cannot hold you wife, but you must needs fetch your words from Westminster; I ha' done i' faith. Has no attorney's clerk been here alate and changed his half-crown-piece his mother sent him, or rather cozened you with a gilded twopence, to bring the word in fashion for her faults or cracks in duty and obedience, term 'em e'en so, sweet wife? As there is no woman made without a flaw, your purest lawns have frays, and cambricks bracks. (ll. 23–30)

Yellowhammer's assertion that "there is no woman made without a flaw" renders explicit the equation of women with false wares, while diverting attention from the "faults or cracks" of goldsmiths' wares to those of clothworkers. (The eastern end of Cheapside was dominated by textile dealers and home to the Mercers' Company.)[46] His speech simultaneously acknowledges the ubiquity of "light" wares and coins in the city, and deflects criticism from these "cracks" in the formal economy by insisting that even the "purest" wares (and women) have flaws. Priding himself on being "of the freedom" (ll. 126–27), that is, on his status as a citizen tradesman, Yellowhammer chides his wife for her linguistic, commercial, and, we surmise, sexual incontinence, linking her use of the latinate term "errors" instead of "plain, sufficient subsidy words" (ll. 128–29), such as "frays" and "bracks," to the permeable boundaries of the city's walls and wives. Maudlin's response once again associates evil wares with the fault of female sexuality: "But 'tis a husband solders up all cracks" (l. 31), she teases, implying that her own cracked chastity has been soldered up by her marriage to him.

It is soon revealed that Yellowhammer and his wife's concern with their daughter's faults arises from their own desire to capitalize on her assets in the marriage market, for Moll's sexual purity renders her a valuable and sought-after commodity and sets her apart from the deceptive women and wares of Cheapside. Touchwood Junior, the suitor Moll favors, boasts that the diamond he plans to set in their wedding ring is "a pure one" because "So is the mistress" (1.1.181–82). The Yellowhammers, however, plan to trade their commodity more advantageously—or so they think—to Sir Walter Whorehound. When Yellowhammer breaks in on the clandestine nuptials of Moll and Touchwood, he thus threatens to lock her up "As carefully as my gold" in a "close room" to "keep her from the light" (3.1.51–52). While acknowledging the value of Moll's purity, the Yellowhammers repeatedly betray their suspicious familiarity with the deceitful practices of their trade. Yellowhammer's reference to a darkened "close room" in his house in which wares are hidden would have sounded a warning to any honest goldsmith, for the Goldsmiths' Company's ordinances restricted its members from "keep[ing] chambers in secret places" where they might hide deceitful wares and methods of manufacture.[47] When Maudlin calls her daughter a "counterfeit" jewel (4.2.62) after Moll escapes for the second time, her slurs likewise compromise her own credibility, rather than her daughter's. Yet there are counterfeits aplenty in this play, such as the Welsh prostitute whom Sir Walter hopes to betroth to the Yellowhammers' son Tim. "I bring thee up [to London] to turn thee into gold wench, and make thy fortune shine like your bright trade," he informs her, noting, "A goldsmith's shop sets out a city maid. . . . Here you must pass for a pure virgin" (1.1.99–101, 104). Sir Walter suggests that a goldsmith's shop is an appropriate place for a prostitute's "bright trade" because both the wares and women on display there are liable to be false, gilded wares. His prediction proves accurate, as the prostitute is revealed to be no more incontinent than the wives of Cheapside.

The sexual/bodily incontinence of Cheapside's cracked wives is compared throughout the play to the defects of the wares on offer in its shops. Simply put, they are, to borrow Gail Kern Paster's apt phrase, "leaky vessels."[48] Female incontinence within the play comes to figure the porous boundaries of the formal economy and the false wares or leaky vessels that breach these boundaries. The faults or cracks of Cheapside's wives are revealed at the christening of the bastard child of Allwit, whose wife is pregnant by Sir Walter Whorehound. The scene's satire of female incontinence is aimed in particular at the counterfeit virtue of the puritan wives, who commend the event for being "Without idolatry or superstition" (3.2.5), while proceeding to gorge themselves gluttonously on comfits and wine until they hiccup and wet themselves. Female sexual/bodily incontinence becomes a subject of conversation as one of the gossips tells another that she cannot find a husband for her nineteen-year-old daughter because she has "a secret fault . . . she's too free . . . she cannot lie dry in her bed" (3.2.107, 111, 113). The scene ends when the wives all run off to see a show performed "by the Pissing-conduit" (l. 205), and Allwit discovers puddles of liquid under their stools and surmises they have "drunk so hard" (l. 201) that they could not contain their urine. The vulgarity evidenced in their conduct at the christening is likewise reflected in their lowly theatrical tastes: Allwit gets them to leave his house by telling them that "two brave drums and a standard bearer" (l. 206) are playing "yonder," to which they eagerly cry "Where? Where sir? . . . O brave" as they rush out the door (ll. 204, 207).

In spite of his name, Allwit is hardly a paragon of wit, or for that matter of virtuous, civic masculinity. Rather, he epitomizes the effeminizing vice of idleness so abhorred by city and guild officials. He professes himself to live in the "happiest state that ever man was born to" (1.2.22), namely, that of a wittol, or a willing, complacent cuckold. The term was apparently modeled after "cuckold" but with the substitution of the prefix "wit-," suggesting the wittol's knowing complicity in his own cuckoldry, and evolved to mean the very opposite of all-knowingness, a fool or simpleton (*OED*, "wittol, *n.*"). Allwit gladly hands over his wife to Sir Walter because the latter is willing to pay all his family's expenses, allowing him to eschew any and all productive work: "the knight / Hath took that labour all out of my hands; / I may sit still and play . . . / . . . I live at ease; / He has both the cost and torment; when the strings / Of his heart frets, I feed, laugh, or sing, / *La dildo, dildo la dildo, la dildo dildo de dildo*" (1.2.51–57). Although a common refrain used in ballads, the term "dildo" also referred to a substitute or counterfeit phallus, and thus to a particular type of false wares (*OED*, "dildo, *n.*¹"). The suggestion here is that Allwit's failure to produce legitimate wares or children causes his wife to resort to a substitute phallus and thereby to produce illegitimate or adulterated offspring. When one of his servants enters to find Allwit singing this refrain, the servant comments: "Now's out of work he falls to making dildoes" (1.2.59). Allwit makes dildos, he intimates, because he shuns honest work. When used to describe a man, the term "dildo" suggested effeminacy, cowardice, and a lack of manly virtue, as in the phrase "a milke liverd Dildo."[49] When Allwit's servant refers to Sir Walter as his master, Allwit asks, "Pray am not I your master?" to which another of his servants replies, "O you are but our mistress's husband" (1.2.64–65). Allwit's idleness, his production of dildos, rather than honest wares or offspring, is represented as a threat to honest trade and male authority. The dildo stands as an apt emblem of the sex/gender trouble associated in the play with Cheapside's incontinent, unruly marketplace, for it simultaneously suggests male inadequacy, female usurpation of masculine tools and prerogatives, and the counterfeit or adulterated goods that result from such disorder.

Throughout the play, Allwit brags of his blissful state of unconstrained idleness, boasting, "That's all the work I'll do, nor need I stir, / But that it is my pleasure . . . / . . . I am tied to nothing / . . . what I do is merely recreation, / Not constraint" (2.2.2–6). Yet it is clear that his lifestyle is not being condoned, for it is subject to ridicule by all. Even Sir Walter disdains him as a living example of what happens when the "fat of ease o'er-throws the eyes of shame" (2.2.41). The only work Allwit is willing to perform is aimed at trying to maintain his state of idleness by ensuring that Sir Walter never marries (1.2.115). In an effort to prevent Sir Walter's marriage to Moll, Allwit disguises himself as a distant relative of Yellowhammer's and reveals to the latter the lascivious knight's fornication with his wife, boasting of his own wittolry: "'tis his living; / As other trades thrive, butchers by selling flesh, / Poulters by venting conies, or the like" (4.1.239–41). Although ostensibly arguing for the legitimacy of his own "idle occupation" by comparing it to the honest trades of the city, Allwit suggests that all city trades, including his own, are vice-ridden through his choice of examples: "selling flesh" (i.e., prostitution) and "venting conies" (i.e., trading in cunts). Allwit's plan backfires, however, because Yellowhammer himself lacks virtue and is not dissuaded from marrying his daughter to Sir Walter, even though the latter is a "whorehound": "Pray what serves marriage, but to call him back," he reasons, admitting, "I have kept a whore myself, and had a bastard" (4.1.271–72).

A Chaste Maid foregrounds the rampant reproduction, rather than destruction, of illegitimate wares, which is associated with the unconstrained reproduction of illegitimate children. Cheapside is replete with bastards (the products of its many adulterous liaisons), who are likened to its false, hastily manufactured wares, insomuch as they, too, are "things / Put to making in minutes" (2.3.38–39). The play veritably teems with them: we see four onstage, but many more are referred to. Touchwood Sr. alone admits to having gotten no fewer than seven illegitimate children (2.1.62). When one of the wenches he has impregnated confronts him, she demands, "Do you see your workmanship?" (2.1.65), implying that it is faulty indeed. His apology does not refute her analogy: "Do but in courtesy faith wench excuse me / Of this half yard of flesh, in which I think it wants / A nail or two" (2.1.82–84). His analogy references tradespeople who sell by short measure (a nail was a measure of length, equal to one-sixteenth of a yard, or of weight, equal to roughly seven or eight pounds; see *OED*, "nail, *n.*" 8, 9), as well as the offspring of syphilitics, who were sometimes born without fingernails. It thus builds on the play's continual conflation of illicit sexual and commercial (re)production, as does Touchwood Sr.'s offer of money to the wench, which equates his illegitimate offspring to faulty shopwares that must be sold as quickly as they were "put to making": "Here's all I have, i'faith, take purse and all, / And would I were rid of all the ware i' the shop so" (2.1.98–99).

Touchwood Sr.'s reference to his bastard child as a "half yard of flesh" further conflates illicit sex and commerce. Set during Lent, *A Chaste Maid* foregrounds market regulation, and the vice it breeds rather than prevents, by centering it around the "flesh" trade—evoking both the trade in contraband meat (prohibited during Lent) and in human flesh (prostitution). When the wench accepts Touchwood Sr.'s offer of cash and exits with his purse, he wonders, "What shift she'll make now with this piece of flesh / In this strict time of Lent . . . / Flesh dare not peep abroad now" (2.1.106–8). The play's conflation of illicit sex and commerce comes to a head in a scene that brings to light what Allwit refers to disparagingly as the "corruption of promoters, / And other poisonous officers that infect / And with a venomous breath taint every goodness" (2.1.115–17), revealing that those charged with policing the market are as corrupt as its deceitful tradespeople. Shortly after Touchwood Sr.'s encounter with the wench, two promoters enter searching for infractions of the prohibition against eating or selling flesh during Lent. Allwit, who espies them, brings to light their corruption, revealing that they are involved in the "flesh" trade in more ways than one: "This Lent will fat the whoresons up with sweetbreads / And lard their whores with lamb-stones; what their golls / Can clutch goes presently to their Molls and Dolls. / The bawds will be so fat with what they earn / Their chins will hang like udders by Easter eve" (2.2.68–72). The promoters, he claims, take compositions in kind, confiscating the flesh of those against whom they inform to eat themselves or to fatten the prostitutes they keep on the side. Allwit decides to play a trick on them, posing as a customer in search of contraband meat who has been directed to a street harboring black-market butchers who "kill and sell close in some upper room . . . apple loft" or "coal house" (2.2.95–96). The promoters reveal that they are indeed corrupt in an aside, claiming, "This butcher shall kiss Newgate, 'less he turn up the / Bottom of the pocket of his apron" (2.2.99–100). At this point Allwit turns on them, taunting that he will seek out the butcher "Where you shall not find him; / I'll buy, walk by your noses with my flesh, / Sheep-biting mongrels, hand basket freebooters! / . . . a foutra for promoters!" (ll. 101–4).

The satire of promoters continues as we witness their corruption in action when a man enters with a basket of contraband meat. Discovering and confiscating the meat, they regret that it is "all veal," as they had promised "a fat quarter of lamb to a kind gentlewoman in Turnbull street that longs" (ll. 123–26)—Turnbull street being a notorious prostitution district. City commerce in Middleton's play is represented as a vicious, endless cycle of trade in tainted "flesh": the wares of unlicensed butchers are confiscated by promoters, who fatten pregnant prostitutes, who in turn produce bastards, populating the city with non-citizens, who grow up to be illicit butchers, and so on. The promoters' corrupt practices continue when a second man enters with a basket containing a "rack of mutton . . . and half a lamb" (2.2.134) and one of the promoters confronts him, while the other realizes that he is "Mr Beggarland's man, the wealthy merchant / That is in fee with us. / . . . / You know he purchased the whole Lent together, / Gave us ten groats apiece on Ash-Wednesday" (ll.140–41, 143–44). In the end, the corrupt promoters get their comeuppance when the final patron of the illicit flesh market whom they apprehend turns out to be Touchwood Sr.'s wench with her bastard child secreted in a basket "*under a loin of mutton*" (2.2.145, s.d.). Seeing them, she confides in an aside, "Women had need of wit, if they'll shift here, / And she that hath wit may shift anywhere" (2.2.148–49). She uses her wit to bait the promoters with the mutton, which she leaves uncovered in her basket. When they threaten to confiscate it, she pretends to be the servant of a wealthy but ill gentlewoman whose doctor has prescribed mutton as physic. They insist that she leave her basket with them, and she makes them swear to keep it until she returns with her master. Searching through the basket, they wager as to whether it conceals "a quarter of lamb" or a "shoulder of mutton," and as they grope, the promoter who wagered on lamb is gleeful when he feels what he takes to be "a lamb's head" (ll. 180–81, 187). Eventually he discovers that the head belongs to the foundling infant and curses, "Life had she none to gull but poor promoters / That watch hard for a living?" (ll. 198–99). They resolve to "go to the Checker [Inn] at Queen-hive and roast the loin of mutton, till young flood; then send the child to Branford" to be brought up in a bawdy house (2.2.213–15). And so the cycle of illicit commerce continues.

Although Middleton's city comedy satirically lays bare the "shifts" of wit used by those who earn their living in London's informal economy, *A Chaste Maid* can hardly be said to contain a moral lesson, as the vices of the market go unpunished. Indeed, the wench who figures the migrant women who bring their wares in baskets to sell in Cheapside market gets the better of the corrupt promoters. While the flexibility and ingenuity of women's informal commerce are referenced by her motto ("she that hath wit may shift anywhere"), her work is simultaneously effaced, insofar as she trades in bastards instead of beef. The play's emphasis is on the unending reproduction of illegitimate children and wares. Cheapside's informal commerce is characterized by a hyper-productivity and fertility that cannot be staved, and from which all seek to profit. In the end, all are invited by Yellowhammer to dine at Goldsmiths' Hall, suggesting that Cheapside will continue to accommodate the incontinent commercial practices the play has revealed. Although Middleton distinguishes the workmanship of his play from the false wares it uncovers, this distinction remains implicit in the distinction between the lowly entertainment enjoyed by the incontinent women of Cheapside (two brave drums and a standard-bearer at the Pissing Conduit) and that offered by his own play's satirical discovery of the incontinent vices of the city. This implicit distinction raises a number of questions that lie at the center of the controversy surrounding the legitimacy of the commercial stage: Is the "purpose of playing" the discovery and correction of vice? Is this discovery in and of itself a virtuous, manly activity and legitimate way to earn a living? Or do those who earn their living in this way, whether they be promoters or professional players, participate in and profit from the very vices and false wares they purport to put down? If such questions remain implicit in *A Chaste Maid in Cheapside*, they take center stage in *Bartholomew Fair*.

First performed a year after *A Chaste Maid* by the same playing company at the newly built Hope theater on the bankside, and soon after at court, Jonson's *Bartholomew Fair* likewise takes as its subject the discovery of market abuses in one of London's renowned market fairs, which took place in and around suburban Smithfield for three days every August. Yet Jonson's play explores in far greater depth the status of play-making in relation to the "idle occupations" of the city and its suburbs, highlighting the similarities as well as the differences between the false wares of the theater and those of the fair. Like Middleton, Jonson foregrounds the corruption and hypocrisy of those charged with reforming market abuses. Yet Jonson is engaged in his own project of reform vis-à-vis the theater: he aims to reform the reformers themselves, to enlighten them as to the higher purpose of playing, and thereby to define and defend the "workmanship" of his craft. Consequently, Jonson's Justice Overdo, unlike Middleton's promoters, undergoes his own reformation within the play. Whereas Middleton's promoters clearly intend to continue their corrupt practices after the play's end, having learned nothing from the trick played on them by the wench, Justice Overdo ultimately recognizes that correcting the vices of the market (and of the theater) is not best accomplished through outright destruction—that it is better to build up or edify than to tear down: "*ad correctionem, non ad destructionem; ad aedificandum, non ad diruendum*" (5.6.107–8).[50]

As Jonas Barish famously argued in "Jonson and the Loathèd Stage," Jonson's attitude toward the false wares of theatrical spectacle is *not* simply one of loathing.[51] Certainly, Barish acknowledges, Jonson professes a "deeply rooted antitheatricalism." Yet his comedies, and *Bartholomew Fair* in particular, manifest an undeniably virtuosic showmanship that places his own "declared doctrine" in tension with the spectacular performative effects his plays enact. It is precisely the "uneasy synthesis between a formal antitheatricalism, which condemns the arts of show," and an exploration of the power these same arts hold over audiences, Barish argues, "that lends to Jonson's comic masterpieces much of their unique high tension and precarious equilibrium."[52] In *Bartholomew Fair* this tension manifests itself in Jonson's staging of the spectacle as well as the attempted destruction of the false wares of the fair, and in particular those manufactured and sold by market women, which are set up as a foil to the true "workmanship" of the professional playwright and player. In so doing, Jonson seeks to demonstrate that although stagecraft or embodied theater relies on such wares, the "soule of plays" is not, pace Gosson, mere "trifles."

Jonson's play brings to the fore the problematic status of stage properties as false wares through its lavish staging of the trumpery on offer at the fair. His reproduction of the fair's market stalls and merchandise onstage highlights the status of the commercial theaters as showplaces of eye-catching costumes and properties, drawing customers in through their display of insubstantial, yet nonetheless dazzling, wares.[53] By staging his drama at a seasonal fair, rather than one of London's permanent markets, Jonson underscores the ephemeral aspect of stage spectacle while at the same time distinguishing the temporary standings of the fair from the new permanence of London's purpose-built theaters, thereby implicitly conferring a legitimacy on the professional players that is lacking in the informal and itinerant tradespeople they portray. This distancing of actor and role does not, however, prevent Jonson from staging the paraphernalia of the fair to full dramatic effect, deploying a wide range of stage properties to re-create the fair's wonder-inducing merchandise. Among the many small properties used to counterfeit the ephemeral and insubstantial wares on offer at the fair are Leatherhead's "Rattles, drums, halberts, horses, babies [i.e., dolls] . . . Fiddles" (2.2.29), "Jew's trumps [i.e., harps]" (3.4.69), and other musical instruments, toys in the shape of lions, bulls, bears, dogs, cats, and "birds for ladies" (2.4.4–5, 3.2.31–34, 3.4.4), haberdashery wares, such as "Fine purses, pouches, pin-cases, pipes" (3.4.15–16), a costard-monger's pears, Joan Trash's gingerbread, Ursula's roast pig, ale, and tobacco pipes, and Nightengale's broadside ballads.

The play's large properties include not only the fair's canvas booths but painted signs advertising the (dubious) quality of the merchandise on sale: the sign of the "*Pig's Head with a large writing under it*" at Ursula's stall boasts "she does roast 'em [i.e., her pigs] as well as ever she did" (3.2.52, s.d., 62–63). The motto damns through faint praise, as Ursula earlier reveals the unsavory ingredients of her adulterated wares: she admits, for example, to mixing "a quarter of a pound of coltsfoot" with each "half-pound of tobacco" she sells (2.2.87–88). Her booth is a site of both sexual and commercial adulteration. Like Middleton, Jonson sexualizes market women who trade in "flesh": "Here you may ha' your punk [i.e., whore] and your pig in state, sir, both piping hot" (2.5.38–39), Ursula advertises. Several of the wives who visit her booth come close to adulterating themselves when they become inebriated and are nearly prostituted. Unlike Middleton's city wives, however, the independent, unmarried market women of *Bartholomew Fair* reproduce false wares *instead of* children: Ursula is described as the "mother o' the pigs" (2.5.68; see also 2.3.2) and Joan Trash's wares are called her "gingerbread-progeny" (2.2.3–4). Ursula's booth is depicted as a veritable incubator of market abuses. She instructs her tapster Mooncalf in the arts of selling by short measure, misreckoning accounts, and conniving to increase profits:

> Froth your cans well i' the filling at length, rogue, and jog your bottles o' the buttock, sirrah; then skink out the first glass, ever, and drink with all companies, though you be sure to be drunk; you'll misreckon the better, and be less ashamed on't. But your true trick, rascal, must be to be ever busy, and mis-take away the bottles and cans in haste before they be half drunk off, and never hear anybody call, if they should chance to mark you, till you ha' brought fresh, and be able to forswear 'em. (2.2.92–100)

The work of producing and vending false wares, Ursula's instruction demonstrates, is "never done," in that it is incessant (she is "ever busy") but produces nothing of substance. The insubstantial wares of market women are exemplified by the froth and smoke of the ale and tobacco on sale at Ursula's booth and by Knockem's humorous use of the term "vapours" as an all-purpose catchphrase or motto for the fair and its wares. Like the airy bubbles and vaporous smoke produced by Lady Vanity in the Bloemaert engraving discussed in Chapter 2 (see Figure 6), they are mere ciphers conveying a false illusion of substance.

Jonson's suburban fair is depicted as a site of disorderly commercial activity conducted primarily by non-citizen foreigners and unruly market women. The foreigners are distinguished by their dialects, such as the Irish bawd Whit, who speaks with a brogue, Northern, a north-country clothier, and Puppy, a wrestler from Cornwall. The play draws attention to their faulty trade practices, as when Northern gets drunk at Ursula's booth and says he can drink no more, and Puppy teases him about the defects of northern cloth, which was notorious for shrinking: "Do my northern cloth zhrink i' the wetting, ha?" (4.4.13). Jonson's suburban market women are not "daughters of the freedom" like Middleton's city wives but independent commercial agents who seek to earn their living beyond the purview of guild and city control. The strong female presence at the fair includes not only the memorable Joan Trash and monumental Ursula the pig-woman but an offstage population signaled by passing references to market women who populate the suburbs, such as the "blue-starch-woman" (1.3.129) or the "Catherine-pear-woman" (1.5.109). This presence is likewise foregrounded by the striking embodiment of the play's female vendors, whose market abuses are literally made flesh: Joan Trash's body is as "crooked" (2.2.23) as her commercial practices, while Ursula's "enormities"—Justice Overdo's term for market infractions—are materialized in her corpulence. Ursula's gargantuan proportions come to figure Bartholomew Fair itself, whose dimensions continued to grow throughout the seventeenth century so that by 1641 it was described as "of so vast an extent, that it is contained in no lesse then four several parishes."[54] Ursula is called the "Body o' the Fair" (2.5.67) because she not only practices but herself embodies its myriad vices: Justice Overdo describes her booth as "the very womb and bed of enormity, gross as herself!" (2.2.102–3). Ursula's incontinence, like that of Middleton's city dames, figures that of the city's markets. Knockem thus refrains from vexing her in "this hot weather, for fear of foundering [her] i' the body, and melting down a pillar of the Fair" (2.3.48–50).

The analogy Jonson draws between Joan and Ursula's malformed, misproportioned bodies and wares may have been inspired by the opening lines of Horace's *Ars Poetica*, twice translated by Jonson, which asks, "If to a Womans head a Painter would / Set a Horse-neck, and divers feathers fold / On every limbe, ta'en from a severall creature, / Presenting upwards, a faire female feature, / Which in some swarthie fish uncomely ends: / Admitted to the sight, although his friends, / Could you contain your laughter?" (ll. 1–7).[55] In

Bartholomew Fair, Jonson's appropriation of Horace's image of a monstrous female body as metaphor for faulty (poetic) workmanship further associates that image with market women's poorly crafted wares. In his *Discoveries,* Jonson defines the poet-playwright as a skilled craftsman or "Maker . . . From the [Greek] word *poiein* which signifies to make,"[56] adopting the term Sir Philip Sidney uses to defend the manly virtue of poetry as "an Art . . . not of effeminatenes, but of notable stirring of courage."[57] He compares a well-wrought poem or play to an expertly crafted piece of furniture, characterized by a "well-joyning, cementing, and coagmentation of words . . . like a Table, upon which you may runne your finger without rubs, and your nayle cannot find a joynt."[58]

To achieve such poetic skill, Jonson claims in "To My Old Faithfull Servant," the playwright like the craftsman must serve "A Prentise-ship," which, he chides, "few doe now a dayes." In the present age, he complains, "Both learned, and unlearned, all write Playes. / It was not so of old: Men tooke up trades / That knew the Crafts they had bin bred in, right / . . . / The Cobler kept him to his nall; but now / Hee'll be a Pilot, scarce can guide a Plough."[59] In this poem, dedicated to his own former "apprentice," actor/playwright Richard Brome, Jonson appropriates the language of honest craftsmanship used by guilds and civic authorities to delegitimize the "idle occupation" of playing in order to validate the virtue of his profession as a "Fellowship" akin to other (guilded) crafts, as an "Art" that may be "justly gained" by learning its "Lawes" from a "Master" like Jonson himself.[60] By contrast, he compares unskilled poets or playwrights to makers of false, poorly made or insubstantial wares, in that both cobble or botch together "dis-joyn'd" works that are mere "fripperie[s] of wit."[61] This distinction between well- and poorly crafted poetry allows Jonson to refute the anti-theatrical claim that "the soule of . . . playes is . . . meere trifles." Rather, he argues, the master playwright creates the "Soule" of a play through the skilled "Poeticall worke" of his craft.[62] Yet, instructed by Horace's *Ars Poetica,* Jonson nonetheless recognizes that stage spectacle has an undeniable power: "ever, things that run / In at the eare, doe stirre the mind more slow / Then those the faithfull eyes take in by show" (ll. 256–58).[63] Elsewhere, in his prefatory lines to the masque *Hymenai* (1606), he similarly acknowledges that "bodies oft-times have the ill luck to be sensually preferr'd," even if the senses should seek to "lay hold on more remov'd mysteries."[64]

In *Bartholomew Fair,* Jonson mines market women's commercial activities and wares for their theatrical potential as spectacle while at the same time seeking to distinguish the "soul" of his play from their faulty, insubstantial products. Joan's surname, "Trash," reinforces the devaluation of market women's wares as defective, adulterated junk. In Jonson's day, the term "trash" not only meant "worthless stuff; rubbish" (*OED*, "trash, *n.*" 3a), but more specifically referred to material that was discarded in the manufacturing process, such as the dross removed from pure gold or the chaff removed from wheat (*OED*, ibid., 1a). Both Joan Trash and Ursula are mercilessly taunted for the purportedly inferior quality of their merchandise. Quarlous teases Ursula that she should be publicly punished or thewed for her market abuses: "Do you think there may be a fine new cucking-stool i' the Fair to be purchased? One large enough, I mean. I know there is a pond of capacity for her" (2.5.106–8). Leatherhead, the hobby-horse seller, likewise threatens Joan Trash: "Do you hear, Sister Trash, Lady o' the Basket? Sit farther with your gingerbread-progeny there, and hinder not the prospect of my shop, or I'll ha' it proclaimed i' the Fair what stuff they are made on" (2.2.2–5). Leatherhead condescends to Joan because she is an itinerant vendor who sells out of a basket rather than from a stall, and asserts that her gingerbread is made from cheap and unwholesome ingredients. Joan does not allow his aspersion of her wares to go uncontested, however, replying, "Why, what stuff are they made on, Brother Leatherhead? Nothing but what's wholesome, I assure you" (ll. 6–7). Leatherhead persists, making his accusation explicit, "Yes, stale bread, rotten eggs, musty ginger, and dead honey, you know" (ll. 8–9), and threatening, "I shall mar your market, old Joan" (l. 11). Joan responds in kind, calling Leatherhead a "too-proud pedlar" and taunting, "Are you puffed up with the pride of your wares? Your arsedine?" (ll. 12, 17–18). In claiming that Leatherhead's wares are gilded with "arsedine" or orsedue, an alloy made of copper and zinc used "in imitation of gold leaf" (*OED*, "orsedue, *n.*"), Joan insinuates that his wares are false or counterfeit.

The exchange concludes with each threatening to inform against the other in the Court of Pie-Powders for committing market abuses. Derived from the Anglo-Norman *pié poudrous*, or "dusty-footed," used to describe the itinerant dealers who traded at fairs, the term "piepowder" came to refer to the courts set up in fairs to administer justice (*OED*, "piepowder, *n.*" 1, 2, and etymology). Because verdicts had to be determined during the time of the fair, they came to be known for their hasty and often cursory judgments—precisely the sort that we witness Justice Overdo making throughout the play.[65] Importantly, Jonson reveals that such accusations were often motivated by commercial competition. Leatherhead casts aspersions on Joan's wares and threatens to destroy or "mar" them because she poses a threat to his trade. She responds in kind in order to diminish the commercial advantage afforded by his permanent stall. The scene thus functions to satirize the opportunism that characterized accusations regarding market abuses in the ongoing dispute over trade prerogatives. Such opportunism is further reflected in the fact that the Court of Pie-Powders was set up to deal with accusations of slander ("if one slander any with Trades, and Merchandises in the Market, in any thing which concerns his trade"), as well as accusations of evil making.[66] The cry with which Joan advertises her wares suggests that her slurs against Leatherhead's use of "arsedine" are indeed opportunistic, for it reveals that she, too, gilds her wares: "Buy any gingerbread, gilt gingerbread!" (2.2.32).

The reference to "arsedine" underscores the status of the false wares staged in *Bartholomew Fair* as stage properties, and vice versa, for orsedue was commonly used to gild the props used in plays, pageants, and masques.[67] At the end of the play, the status of Leatherhead's false wares as stage properties is actualized when Bartholomew Cokes learns that Leatherhead sidelines as a puppet master and all-around theatrical impresario. Cokes ends the competitive quarreling between Leatherhead and Joan by offering to buy the entire contents of his stall and her basket. At this point, the two end their competition and begin to collude together to increase their profits. Joan advertises Leatherhead's "qualities" as a theatrical jack-of-all-trades, known for his puppet shows, trials of wit, parodies of contemporary players, and mock bear-baiting contests (3.4.114–19). Thrilled at the prospect of such spectacles, Cokes asks whether Leatherhead can "set out a masque," to which Joan replies, "O Lord, master! Sought to, far and near, for his inventions" (ll. 124–25). Their gambit pays off, as the delighted Cokes orders Leatherhead to "shut up shop," promising that his wares "shall furnish out the masque" (l. 133) for Cokes's own wedding, and that Joan's gingerbread will provide the wedding banquet, as well as gilt gingerbread "wedding gloves" and "delicate brooches for the bridemen and all" (ll. 145–50), rendering Joan a sort of gingerbread tirewoman. Far from denying the status of stage properties as false wares, Jonson thus highlights it; yet he does so, as we shall see, in service to his project of theatrical reform.

Certainly, Cokes's belief that such lowly spectacles performed at his wedding will bring him "credit" (3.4.135) is being mocked. Throughout the play, he stands as an emblem of mindless consumerism, sacrificing all he has for toys and trifles, and of mindless spectatorship, gawking at the spectacles of fair and puppet show like the uncouth "stare-abouts" who frequent plays only to have their purses pilfered (3.5.121). Cokes gains nothing through his vulgar consumption of false wares. Indeed, he loses himself and everything he owns at the fair: "I ha' lost myself, and my cloak and my hat, and my fine sword, and my sister, and Numps, and Mistress Grace . . . and a cut-work handkerchief she ga' me, and two purses, today. And my bargain o' hobby-horses and gingerbread, which grieves me worst of all" (4.2.77–82). Yet Jonson does not simply renounce the theater's reliance upon false wares through his satire of Cokes, for he equally derides those who would destroy the false wares of the theater through his satire of Zeal-of-the-Land Busy, the puritan preacher. Drunk on Ursula's ale, Busy focuses his wrath with greatest venom on Joan Trash's wares, crying, "Hence with thy basket of popery, thy nest of images, and whole legend of ginger-work" (3.6.68–69). Decrying her "idolatrous grove of images" (l. 90), he "*Overthrows the gingerbread [basket]*" (l. 91, s.d.), destroying her merchandise. Leatherhead threatens him with arrest "for disturbing the Fair" (3.6.71). Jonson thereby reverses the typical outcome of market justice: here, the puritan preacher (Busy) and civic magistrate (Overdo) who police the market destroying wares they deem false are arrested and thrown in the stocks rather than the vendors of such wares.

Jonson does not simply abjure the dependency of dramatic illusion on false wares or "trash." Rather, he draws our attention to this dependency from the start, before the play proper even begins. The play is famously introduced to the theater audience by the Stage-Keeper, who is busy sweeping up the "trash" left on the stage—presumably including Joan's broken gingerbread—from the previous day's performance. When the Book-Holder or prompter enters, he chides the Stage-Keeper for offering his uncouth judgment of the play to the audience: "Your judgement, rascal? For what? Sweeping the stage? Or gathering up the broken apples for the bears within? Away, rogue, it's come to a fine degree in these spectacles when such a youth as you pretend to a judgement" (Ind., 49–52). Among the detritus that litters the stage and the pit, he observes, are the remnants of apples sold by fruit-wives during the performance of plays.[68] The Stage-Keeper thus sets the stage for the destruction of market women's wares within the play by sweeping the remnants of such "trash" from the stage. In so doing, however, he does not simply erase the material memory of market women's wares but rather calls attention to the "stuff" of the stage as an integral aspect of the performance to follow.

By dividing the initial action of the play between the Stage-Keeper and Book-Keeper, Jonson personifies the distinction between the play-as-spectacle and the play-as-text. The Stage-Keeper's focus is entirely on the often faulty and patched-together stuff of theatrical staging. He informs us that the actor playing Littlewit has "a stitch new fallen in his black silk stocking"

(Ind., 3–4), which is being mended backstage, and complains that the play does not contain enough "fine sights" (l. 19) for his liking. He attributes the latter fault to the playwright, who is uninformed, he claims, about the spectacles of Bartholomew Fair. "[T]hese master-poets . . . will be informed of nothing" (ll. 25–26), he complains, taking Jonson to task for "not [having] conversed with the Bartholomew-birds" (l. 12) and learned their idiom. (Although the term "bird" may refers to any of the vendors who might serve as informants regarding the activities of the fair [see *OED*, "bird, *n.*" 4.a], the phrase has gendered overtones, insofar as it is modeled on the popular term "Bridewell-birds," used for the female inhabitants of Bridewell prison, who were incarcerated and set to work there for failing to practice honest trades; the term suggests that the "birds" of Bartholomew Fair are of the same ilk.) The Book-Keeper takes the opposite view, faulting the play for containing too many "spectacles" (Ind., 51) and the playwright for having thereby catered to the Stage-Keeper's "meridian" (l. 54). As we have seen, Jonson does stage many of the "fine sights" and sounds of the fair, including the cries and wares of its "birds o' the booths" (2.2.35), drunken brawls, bawdy ballads, and a puppet show. Yet in setting up the play's re-presentation of the spectacles of the fair and re-production of its wares as a subject of explicit controversy, he also opens to critical scrutiny the anti-theatrical claim that the commercial theaters were merely purveyors of unwholesome, light, or counterfeit "trifles."

Jonson's counterattack against this claim is predicted by the Scrivener, the third character of the Induction, whose interest is neither in the play as spectacle nor in the play as text per se but rather in the business of playing— the theater as a commercial enterprise. He famously draws up "Articles of Agreement" between author and audience (ll. 62–65), which position the audience as customers who may judge the playwright's wares only to the extent of the fee each has paid to see the play. Yet he warns that none should expect "better ware than a Fair will afford" (l. 111). To the extent that the audience comes to inspect and judge the "wares" of *Bartholomew Fair*, they are positioned as surveyors of the market the play re-presents, who stand ready to decry its abuses. The Scrivener warns, however, that the playwright likewise stands ready to inform against any corrupt or hypocritical promoters in the audience. The author, he advises, "prays you to believe his ware is still the same, else you will make him justly suspect that he that is so loth to look on a baby or an hobby-horse here, would be glad to take up a commodity of them, at any laughter or loss, in another place" (ll. 155–59). It is the hypocrisy of those who profit from or take pleasure in the false wares they decry, whether they be promoters or puritans, playgoers or playwrights, that the ensuing play will discover.

This discovery perhaps most memorably targets puritan diatribes against the professional players as idle, effeminate drones who eschew virtuous, manly crafts and trades that produce wholesome products in order to purvey vicious, evil wares onstage.[69] Jonson's counterattack cleverly redeploys the term "hypocrite"—the Greek word for both a stage actor and a dissembler—commonly used in puritan attacks against the players, using it instead to describe puritans who indulge in the vices they decry, such as those of Bartholomew Fair.[70] Littlewit thus says of his puritan mother-in-law, Dame Purecraft: "Our mother is a most elect hypocrite, and has maintained us all this seven year with it, like gentlefolks" (1.5.149–50). At the end of the play, Purecraft makes clear precisely how she has profited from her hypocrisy. Boasting that she is worth six thousand pounds, she reveals how she came by her wealth:

> I'll tell you all, and the truth, since you hate the hypocrisy of the parti-coloured brotherhood. These seven years, I have been a wilful holy widow only to draw feasts and gifts from my entangled suitors. I am also, by office, an assisting sister of the deacons, and a devourer, instead of a distributor, of the alms. I am a special maker of marriages for our decayed brethren with our rich widows, for a third part of their wealth, when they are married, for the relief of the poor elect; as also our poor handsome young virgins' [marriages] with our wealthy bachelors or widowers, to make them steal from their husbands, when I have confirmed them in the faith, and got all put into their custodies. (5.2.49–60)

Jonson's description of the incessant industry through which Purecraft accrues her wealth casts the financial and legal savvy of widows (discussed in Chapter 2) as "pure craft" or deceit—the very opposite of a legitimate craft or trade. Dame Purecraft further reveals the hypocrisy of her puritan elder, Zeal-of-the-Land Busy, whom she describes as "the capital knave of the land, making himself rich by being made feoffee in trust to deceased brethren, and cozening their heirs by swearing the absolute gift of their inheritance" (5.2.64–67). Formerly a baker, Busy leaves his trade for the more profitable business of "cooking" wills and swindling heirs, using his zeal to win men's confidence and then defraud them.

The hypocrisy of the play's puritans is perhaps most evident in their attitude toward the false wares on offer at Bartholomew Fair. Busy amplifies to the point of absurdity the contemporary moral imperative against evil merchandise produced and sold outside London's official markets, describing such wares with hyperbolic redundancy as "the wares of devils," "hooks and baits, very baits, that are hung out on every side to catch you," "apocryphal wares," and "the merchandise of Babylon"; and the fair itself a "shop of relics!" or "the shop of Satan," fitter to "be called a foul than a Fair" (3.2.37–39, 3.6.51, 80–81, 84, 88). "Thou art the seat of the Beast, O Smithfield," Busy apostrophizes, "Idolatry peepeth out on every side of thee" (3.6.42–43). The insubstantial wares sold at the fair, he claims, breed other vices in those who consume them: "bottle-ale is a drink of Satan's, a diet-drink of Satan's, devised to puff us up, and make us swell in this latter age of vanity, as the smoke of tobacco to keep us in mist and error" (3.6.29–31). The puritans' diatribe against evil wares is compromised, of course, by their avid consumption of the very merchandise they decry. After associating the "fleshly motion of pig" with the "Tempter" (1.6.13–14), Dame Purecraft nonetheless determines that its profane, unclean flesh may be consumed, as long as "it be eaten with a reformed mouth" (1.6.68). She invokes Busy's religious authority to authorize her daughter Win to gaze at the merchandise on display: "so you hate 'em, as our brother Zeal does, you may look on 'em" (3.6.61–62). Busy and Purecraft both prove themselves to be "right hypocrites, [and] good gluttons" (3.2.107–8) at Ursula's pig-booth. After gorging on pigs and ale, Busy begins another sermon, prompting Knockem to chide, "An excellent right hypocrite! Now his belly is full, he falls a-railing and kicking . . . two and a half [pigs] he ate to his share. And he has drunk a pailful" (3.6.44–47).

The hypocrisy of city magistrates who police market abuses, while ignoring their own faults, likewise comes under attack in the play. The continuity of the play's loose plot structure is held together by Justice Overdo, who decides, "in Justice' name, and the King's, and for the Commonwealth!" (2.1.1–2), to search out the "enormities" or vices of the fair "in the habit of a fool" (ll. 8–9) or wandering Bedlamite named Mad Arthur of Bradley. As a disguised magistrate, Overdo harkens back to the Duke of *Measure for Measure*, who likewise disguises himself to discover the vice and corruption of his realm. Yet Overdo's likening of himself to Junius Brutus (l. 45), who sentenced his own sons to death, and to Horace's "Epidaurian serpent" (l. 5), who looks with an eagle-eye into the failings of his friends while remaining blind to his own, suggests his resemblance to the hypocritical Angelo as well. Overdo's zealous overdoing, signaled both by his name and disguise as a fool, is further revealed in his plan to emulate "a capital member of this city" who was known to disguise himself

> now [in] the habit of a porter, now of a carman, now of the dog-killer in this month of August, and in the winter of a seller of tinder-boxes. And what would he do in all these shapes? Marry, go you into every alehouse, and down into every cellar; measure the length of puddings, take the gauge of black pots [i.e., beer mugs] and cans, ay, and custards, with a stick; and their circumference, with a thread; weigh loaves of bread on his middle finger. Then would he send for 'em home; give the puddings to the poor, the bread to the hungry, the custards to his children; break the pots, and burn the cans, himself; he would not trust his corrupt officers; he would do't himself. Would all men in authority would follow this worthy precedent! For alas, as we are public persons, what do we know? Nay, what can we know? We hear with other men's ears; we see with other men's eyes; a foolish constable or a sleepy watchman is all our information. He slanders a gentleman, by the virtue of his place, as he calls it, and we, by the vice of ours, must believe him; . . . all our intelligence is idle, and most of our intelligencers knaves; and by your leave, ourselves thought little better, if not arrant fools, for believing 'em. I, Adam Overdo, am resolved therefore to spare spy-money hereafter, and make mine own discoveries. Many are the yearly enormities of this Fair, in whose courts of Pie-powders I have had the honour, during the three days sometimes, to sit as judge. But this is the special day for detection of those foresaid enormities. Here is my black book for the purpose. (2.1.14–32, 35–44)

Setting out to rectify the abuses of both market vendors and idle officers and promoters, Overdo ends up revealing his own faults as an informant. The absurd lengths to which the above-mentioned citizen goes and the questionable methods he adopts in his pursuit of false wares and short measures—measuring the "length of puddings" and confiscating custards for his own children—point to an excess of zeal and dubious ethical standards that call Overdo's own reliability and justice into question. Overdo spends most of the play observing firsthand the vices of the market and writing them down in his "black book" (e.g., 2.2.68–69), a practice suggestive of Jonson-the-playwright jotting down his "discoveries," including his observations of the "Bartholmew birds," for future use. Through his satire of Overdo, Jonson thus brings to the fore the playwright's own problematic status as an informer or promoter. Overdo likewise turns his flawed mirror of magistracy on the audience itself, as most of his lines are spoken as asides directly to the audience. He therefore acts as a kind of interpreter of the play's action and, in so doing, brings the audience face-to-face with its split affinities: on the one hand, we are invited to ally ourselves with him, noting the enormities of the fair as they are being committed, while on the other, we are drawn into and admire these enormously entertaining spectacles, just as the magistrate himself is, and does.

Overdo's contention that his own officers and spies are idle fools and knaves is borne out by the network of informants upon whom he relies, including his watchmen, Haggis and Bristle, and their spy, the Irish bawd Whit. The watchmen are revealed to be so enraptured by the fair's spectacles that they fail to do their jobs. Bristle scolds Haggis: "You said, 'Let's go to Ursla's,' indeed; but then you met the man with the monsters, and I could not get you from him. An old fool, not leave seeing yet?" (3.1.10–13). Whit scolds both watchmen for not knowing the time of day (l. 21)—crucial to the prosecution of market abuses that took place outside official market hours. He also makes clear that all three make their living by exacting bribes from those whose crimes they detect (ll. 4–5). Although Overdo is thus justified in his desire to circumvent the information they provide and discover the fair's enormities firsthand, he soon reveals himself to be a highly unreliable informer who believes everything he sees and hears and fails to exercise his critical faculties. He constantly misapprehends what he observes, mistaking the identity of Edgworth the cutpurse, for example, because Mooncalf (ironically) calls him a "civil young gentleman" who "has ever money in his purse" (2.4.22–24). Over the course of the play, Overdo reveals that he shares his subordinates' faults when he becomes implicated in the enormities he detects. Rather than adopting a critical (not hypocritical) distance by watching the fair from afar, he tries to "wind out wonders of enormity" (2.2.10–11) by participating in its activities. As a result of this participation, he is himself accused of being a cutpurse or "lewd and pernicious enormity" (3.5.203–4) and is publicly punished for his abuses in the stocks, becoming in the end the very thing he seeks to discover: "Mine own words turned upon me, like swords" (l. 205).

The pernicious effects of Overdo's overzealous brand of market justice are exemplified by Trouble-all, a former officer of his, who has literally been driven mad by it and now wanders the fair asking all and sundry if they have a license or "warrant" from Justice Overdo for anything they wish to do. When Overdo says of Trouble-all, "What should he be, that doth so esteem and advance my warrant? He seems a sober and discreet person!" (4.1.24–25), he reveals once again his vanity and misapprehension of what he observes. Bristle reveals the true cause of Trouble-all's behavior: "He was an officer in the court of Pie-powders here last year, and put out on his place by Justice Overdo. . . . Upon which he took an idle conceit, and's run mad upon't. So that, ever since, he will do nothing but by Justice Overdo's warrant: he will not eat a crust, nor drink a little, nor make him in his apparel ready. His wife, sir-reverence, cannot get him make his water, or shift his shirt, without his warrant" (4.1.48–49, 51–56). Haggis and Bristle further comment on Overdo's excessive brand of justice, describing him as "a very parantory [i.e., peremptory] person" and "a severe justicer," who "when he is angry, be it right or wrong . . . has the law on's side ever" (4.1.64–65, 74–75). Fearing that Overdo will turn his peremptory wrath on them unless they have his express warrant to put Mad Arthur (Overdo himself in disguise) in the stocks, Haggis and Bristle decide to bring him before Overdo first. Yet Overdo cannot be found; he is absent in his role as Justice all day, so that the Court of Pie-Powders must be delayed, ironically delaying the justice he seeks to promote (4.6.61–64). As the repercussions of the disguise-plot escalate, enormities are committed in Justice Overdo's own name: since Trouble-all will do nothing without his warrant, Knockem forges Overdo's signature on a "warrant" allowing him to drink at Ursula's booth (4.6.11).

When the action of the play moves from fair to puppet show, the opposition between the two extremes of mindless consumerism and overzealous, hypocritical market justice is seamlessly aligned with that between mindless theatrical spectatorship and overzealous, hypocritical anti-theatricalism. Cokes epitomizes the ignorant theatrical spectator mocked in Dekker's *Gull's Hornbook*, when he insists on paying twelve pence instead of the two required to enter the puppet show in order to prove that he is a gallant (after the signifiers of his status, his hat and cloak, have been stolen).[71] Littlewit describes Cokes as "a favourer of the quality" (5.3.60) or profession of acting. Overdo, now in disguise as a porter and observing Cokes's conduct, makes clear that he views the "favouring of this licentious quality" as "a pernicious enormity" (ll. 61–63). Jonson signals his own engagement with the contemporary debate over the status of play-making from the start by referring to himself as the play's "Maker" in his Prologue to the King's Majesty when the play was performed at court, adopting Sidney's term for the poet-playwright's virtuous workmanship. Jonson's satirical version of the debate culminates during the puppet show staged by Leatherhead, which is performed by the very toys and trifles found in his "shop of relics" (3.6.88). The puppet show thus functions as an arena in which the theater's staging of false wares may be brought center stage, and the arguments for and against it rehearsed. Yet the puppet show not only serves as a metaphor for the theater but allows Jonson to distinguish between its staging of false wares and the greater aspirations of the play proper.

Wasp, Cokes's tutor, likens the puppet show to the other vulgar spectacles of the fair, such as "the Bull with the five legs and two pizzles [i.e., penises] . . . the Dogs that dance the morris, and the Hare o' the tabor" (5.4.78–80). The puppet show effectively reduces the "art" of theater to its false wares, or the bodily "stuff" of theatrical spectacle, for the puppets are themselves false wares brought onstage in a basket reminiscent of the one from which Joan sold her "trash." Littlewit compares the puppets to Joan's gingerbread men, joking that one might "eat 'em all, too, an they were in cake-bread" (5.3.71). When Cokes exclaims, "What, do they live in baskets?" Leatherhead replies, "They do lie in a basket, sir, they are o' the small players" (5.3.64–65). The description of the puppets as "small players," or "players minors" (l. 66) sets up an analogy to the professional players, while signaling that the puppets' minor form of entertainment, its reduction of the "soul" of theater to its material or bodily stuff/fripperies, is quite different from the larger ambitions of the "players major." Yet neither Cokes, Overdo, nor Busy is able to comprehend this distinction. Cokes treats the puppets as though they were professional players; indeed, he seems to prefer the former to the latter, claiming, "They offer not to fleer, nor jeer, nor break jests, as the great players do" (5.3.83–84). Overdo similarly reveals his lack of discrimination when he praises Nightengale's ballad as the best "piece of poetry" he has heard in "a good while" (3.5.111). When Busy interrupts the puppet show, decrying the puppets as "heathenish idol[s]" (5.5.4), he likens them indiscriminately to "stage-players, rhymers, and morris dancers, who have walked hand in hand, in contempt of the brethren, and the cause" (5.5.9–11).

Identifying himself as a rabid opponent of the theater, Busy seeks nothing less than the outright destruction of stage spectacle. He warns Leatherhead: "I have long opened my mouth wide, and gaped . . . after thy destruction, but cannot compass it by suit, or dispute; so that I look for a bickering, ere long, and then a battle" (5.5.19–22). In response to Busy's challenge to "end [the matter] by disputation" (l. 28), Edgworth asks Leatherhead, "Hast thou nothing to say for thyself, in defence of thy quality?" (ll. 28–29). The latter professes himself "not well studied in these controversies between the hypocrites and us" (ll. 30–31) but says that the Puppet Dionysius will defend the "quality" of playing. Grace Wellborn, Justice Overdo's ward, suggests that both sides of the controversy—the uncritical defense versus the outright destruction of all theater without distinction—are equally worthy of ridicule: "I know no fitter match than a puppet to commit with an hypocrite!" (ll. 43–44). Addressing the Puppet Dionysius as though he were a player, Busy's first line of attack is to rehearse the familiar charge that playing is not an honest trade or legitimate occupation: "thou hast no calling . . . I mean no vocation, idol, no present lawful calling. . . . I say, his calling, his profession is profane; it is profane, idol" (ll. 45, 49, 58–60). He further argues that theater is "the waiting-woman of Vanity" (l. 73), suggesting that the players' rejection of legitimate trades for the trumpery of the stage and the insubstantial trifles of tirewomen effeminizes them and puffs them up with pride. The puppet derides the hypocrisy of this line of attack, pointing out that among the puritans themselves are renowned "tire-women" (l. 74) who manufacture "perukes . . . puffs [i.e., soft protuberant masses of fabric on a dress] . . . fans . . . [and] huffs [i.e., paddings used to raise the shoulders of a dress]" (ll. 77–78). The puppet thereby reveals that religious purists (including the Netherlandish and Huguenot refugees discussed in Chapter 3) are themselves famed manufacturers of false wares designed to puff up with pride and deceive the eye with false show. "Is a bugle [i.e., bead]-maker a lawful calling? . . . —Or your French fashioner [i.e., costumier]?" (ll. 81–83), he chides. Jonson's association of the false wares of the theater with the fripperies of tirewomen genders the distinction between the feminized "body" and workmanly "soul" of theater, while mapping it onto the gendered division of theatrical labor: he elevates the skill of the male playwright, who crafts the "soul" or true substance of the play, above the bodily spectacle pieced together by tirewomen backstage. The tirewoman's fashions (e.g., perukes, fans, bugles, puffs, huffs, cuffs, ruffs, etc.) here epitomize the false, effeminate trifles and insubstantial, adulterated "trash" upon which theater relies but which Jonson seeks to relegate to its properly subordinated place.

When Busy eventually confesses defeat ("I am confuted, the cause hath failed me. . . . Let [the show] go on. For I am changed, and will become a beholder with you!" [5.5.103, 105–6]), Justice Overdo reveals himself and forbids the continuance of the puppet show, claiming, "It is time to take enormity by the forehead, and brand it; for I have discovered enough" (ll. 114–15). Throughout the play, Overdo expresses his contempt for theater and poetry, which he regards as threats to the commonwealth. Suspecting Edgworth, whom he takes to be a "proper young man" (3.5.2), of "a terrible taint, poetry!" (3.5.6), he concludes that there is therefore "no hope of him in a state-course" or career of public service, or as "a common-wealth's-man" or good citizen (3.5.7–8). Having discovered himself to the fair-goers, Overdo reveals that he is still blind to his own faults, proclaiming: "Look upon me, O London! And see me, O Smithfield! The example of Justice, and Mirrour of Magistrates; the true top of formality, and scourge of enormity" (5.6.31–34). Reprimanding both Busy and Leatherhead for representing two extremes of enormity, the former a "superlunatical hypocrite" and the latter a "profane professor of puppetry, little better than poetry" (ll. 38–40), Overdo nonetheless betrays his own faults by describing puppetry as "better" than poetry, by his praise of Edgworth as an "honest young man" (l. 42), and by mistaking Mistress Littlewit and his own wife for masked prostitutes.

Yet there are inklings throughout the play that cracks are beginning to form in Justice Overdo's self-regard as the "Mirrour of Magistrates" and that through these cracks he is beginning to glimpse the error of his ways. When he sees that he has driven Trouble-all mad, he resolves to make amends to him. His recompense takes the form of a blank check or "warrant," which he gives to Quarlous (disguised as Trouble-all) to ease his own conscience, believing that the madman will not take advantage of his generosity (5.2.121–24). When the inebriated Mistress Overdo reveals herself by suddenly waking up and vomiting in a basin, however, Overdo is humiliated into silence. Quarlous then takes over his project of discovery, revealing to Overdo the enormities he has himself committed (5.6.71–79). Telling Overdo, "get your wife out o' the air," he counsels, "remember you are but Adam, flesh and blood! You have your frailty. Forget your other name of Overdo, and invite us all to supper. There you and I will compare our 'discoveries,' and drown the memory of all enormity in your biggest bowl at home" (ll. 92–97). Overdo consents, avowing, "I will have none fear to go along, for my intents are *ad correctionem, non ad destructionem; ad aedificandum, non ad diruendum* [To correct, not destroy; to build up, not to tear down]" (ll. 106–8). Cokes agrees and invites the "actors" to perform "the rest o' the play at home" (ll. 110–11).

Unlike Middleton, who allows the distinction between market women's false wares and the playwright's true craftsmanship to remain implicit, Jonson seeks to "edify" his audience with regard to the higher purpose of playing and its legitimacy as a profession. This purpose rejects the mindless consumerism and spectatorship of Cokes, the reduction of playing to the stuff of spectacle, while at the same time rejecting the hypocritical disavowal or outright destruction of such false wares by puritan reformers and overzealous magistrates. In foregrounding the theater's reliance on the insubstantial "trash" of market women and false fripperies of tirewomen, Jonson instructs that such wares are necessary to theatrical spectacle but are insufficient to convey the "Soule" of a play, crafted through the skilled "Poeticall worke" of professional male players and playwrights. Although this paradigm reinscribes the gendered division of theatrical labor by subordinating, and literally sweeping away, the devalued wares associated with the offstage labors of women—the wires, tires, pins, laces, bugles, beads, nuts, pears, pumpkin seeds, oyster shells, and so forth, found centuries later by archaeologists—to make way for the virtuous, civic masculinity of the professional players, it nonetheless acknowledges the theater's dependency on such wares, which littered the stage and lay scattered in the pit after every performance. Bearing silent testimony to their own staged destruction, they serve as material mementos of women's tireless work behind the scenes of the "all male" stage, and are thereby recollected from oblivion.

Epilogue

THIS BOOK BEGAN with a simple question: what roles, if any, did women play in the "all-male theater" of Shakespeare's time? Having stumbled across women's activity in the credit networks surrounding the professional stage while researching an entirely different topic, I set out to investigate other forms of commercial activity in which women were involved and how these may have contributed to theatrical production. Some of these contributions were hiding in plain sight because they had long ago been discovered by theater historians but were generally dismissed as exceptional or insignificant. Others emerged only after many years of research. It soon became clear that to make sense of the scattered references to working women that appeared in theatrical records, and of the gendered division of theatrical labor more broadly, I would have to have a firmer grasp on the kinds of work performed by women within the economy at large. Here, I confronted a seemingly implacable obstacle, as historical records concerning the working lives of women in late sixteenth- and early seventeenth-century England are notoriously scarce. It had long been known that female labor in guilded crafts and trades was increasingly proscribed during this period, yet there was at that time little scholarship on the many unguilded forms of women's work in Elizabethan and Jacobean England. I therefore intentionally and of necessity cast a very wide net in my research, one that led me far afield of typical documents of theater history. Time spent in various archives revealed the importance of the expanding informal economy of unlicensed crafts and trades located in London's suburbs and liberties, where women's work was largely concentrated and where the commercial theaters were located. How, I wondered, might the activities of these two constituencies have dovetailed? Previous scholarship on early modern London's labor economy had focused largely on its livery companies. When the expanding informal sector and women's work within it were mentioned, the significance of such work was often minimized through descriptive terms such as "unskilled, of low status, poorly paid, casual, seasonal, and irregular" or "secondary."[1] Yet my own research on women moneylenders and luxury textile workers revealed that female labor in the informal sector was not always carried out by lower-status women, was not invariably poorly paid or casual/seasonal, and that its status as "unskilled" was deeply ideological. Indeed, it had become clear that the language used to define and describe women's informal work, in the early modern period as in our own, would be a central aspect of what the book would have to decipher.

While the elision, devaluation, stigmatization, moral condemnation, trivialization, and sexualization of women's work are certainly prominent features of the revisionist history this book has sought to recount, I have also found other, competing narratives that portrayed women's commercial activities in more positive, albeit no less ideological, terms. The emergent ethos of virtuous exactitude that accompanied the introduction of new (ac)counting techniques in England, for example, made way for a more positive image of female creditors. England's emulation of the commercial practices and religious devotion of Netherlanders allowed immigrant craftswomen's textile work at times to be viewed as a virtuous product of their chaste industry. The wares sold by female hawkers and the cries that advertised them were sometimes portrayed with pride in London's ascendency as a center of conspicuous consumption. Such positive images of laboring women were often tinged with ambivalence regarding their encroachment on the prerogatives, tools, and skills of male guildsmen or their activities in new unguilded industries like the commercial theaters. The hybrid economic structure of professional theater companies, which emulated the guilds in certain respects and joint-stock ventures in others, rendered them relatively unique, as did their attempt to redefine "play" as a legitimate form of work. The split affinities of the theater as a commercial institution, and of many of its individual practitioners, who straddled the boundary between formal and informal commerce, likewise produced ambivalent portrayals of women's offstage work.

To capture the complexity of working women's contributions to and shaping influence on the theater in Shakespeare's time, I have focused on several exemplary theatrical tropes or ciphers that best captured the elusive presence of women's work in and around the "all-male stage." This heuristic has allowed for attention not only to dramatic form but also to the varied aspects of the theater as a commercial institution and to the material culture of the stage. It has likewise enabled simultaneous attention to women's absence from the stage and their presence in various aspects of theatrical production and commerce situated in and around the playhouses. On the stage, and in the culture more broadly, the absent-presence of women's work in the informal economy was variously figured as the creation of something out of nothing (as in the case of the ex nihilo profits of the usuress) or the creation of a nothing that deceptively appeared to be something (as in the case of the insubstantial fripperies and false or adulterated wares manufactured and sold by starchwomen, tirewomen, and market women). Yet these activities, although discounted as legitimate work, were nonetheless represented as requiring incessant (if not infernal) labor and thus as "never done." The ever-changing fashions and ever-accumulating profits they fueled were ever-present, and yet placed under cultural erasure and, thereby, un-done.

The very characteristics used to censure women's work in the informal sector were likewise used by anti-theatrical writers and civic officials to censure the profession of playing, which was attacked for creating something out of nothing or a nothing disguised as something. The wares produced by theater people were decried as false, deceptive, adulterated, and insubstantial and their profits depicted as illegitimate because generated from idleness or play rather than "honest" work. In seeking to defend the legitimacy of playing as a profession, theater people thus modeled their fellowships on the guilds, laying claim to a skilled "workmanship" of their own, training apprentices, and relying on the work of women even as they relegated it, as guildsmen did, behind the scenes of production. Claiming their own brand of virtuous, civic masculinity, players and playwrights would increasingly deflect the criticism leveled at them onto theater personnel who worked offstage or in the purely commercial side of the business. Paradoxically, as professional players and playwrights grew more reliant on stage spectacle, emulating court fashions and entertainments and relying on the wares and expertise of tirewomen and other stage personnel to do so, they increasingly derided such wares as false female fripperies that merely adorned the "bodies" of plays, in contrast to their own skilled craftsmanship, which produced the "soul" or "truth" of drama. This paradox reaches its apex, perhaps, in the character of "Venus, a deaf tirewoman" (l. 88) in Ben Jonson's *Christmas, His Masque*, performed at court in 1616, who embodies the trappings of stage spectacle but is literally deaf to the masque's textual soul.[2] (She may also represent an effeminized avatar of Inigo Jones, the architect of Jonson's masques, whom he would later decry as a "Tyre-man" concerned with "Showes! Showes! Mighty Showes!" rather than the "Soule of Masque.")[3] Yet like all of Jonson's masques, this one nonetheless relies heavily on the tirewoman's work and wares: Christmas, for example, "is attired in round hose, long stockings . . . little ruffs . . . scarfs and garters" (ll. 1–3).

The gendered division of theatrical labor would change radically with the Restoration, which saw the advent of the professional actress, yet there are also interesting continuities with the pre-Restoration theater that are worthy of mention and further study. Perhaps the most radical break was itself grounded in a continuity: the division of labor in the theaters continued to mirror that of the broader economy, insofar as both the playing companies and the livery companies began admitting women. As we have seen, the economic expansion of the sixteenth century resulted in women "pushing into new areas, inside, beside, and underneath the guild system."[4] Although the guilds initially responded by attempting to tighten their reins, punishing or fining unguilded female artisans who breached their restrictions, by the late seventeenth century, in the aftermath of labor shortages caused by plague and the Great Fire, they tried a new tactic, enrolling increasing numbers of female apprentices starting in the 1660s and admitting female members in an effort to formalize (and profit from) their work.[5] The textile guilds in particular used this tactic to exert control over female labor in the new cloth and clothing industries.[6] During the same period, Charles II issued a royal proclamation allowing women to act on the professional stage. Although these two momentous shifts had quite different etiologies, they may have served to reinforce one another.

The advent of the professional actress had profound implications for, and in certain cases may have arisen out of, women's offstage work in theatrical production. Female performers on the Restoration and eighteenth-century stage required both tirewomen (to arrange their increasingly elaborate head-attires and perukes) and female dressers. A "tirewoman" appears in the theatrical records of the King's Company at the Bridges Street playhouse as early as 1666.[7] The gendered division of labor glimpsed at Whitefriars, which employed both a tirewoman and tireman in the early seventeenth century, carried over and became standard practice in the Restoration theater, which hired female dressers and wardrobe mistresses for the actresses and male dressers and wardrobe masters for the actors.[8] The greater number of female roles, however, required far greater numbers of tirewomen, wigmakers, dressers, and wardrobe mistresses, resulting in a stratification of the trade: a Mrs. Carter, for example, served as head female dresser at Lincoln's Inn Fields with several female under-dressers in her employ,[9] while a dresser at the same theater named Elizabeth Bubb appears to have eventually worked her way up to become a costume supplier.[10] Grace Gould worked at Covent Garden as a tirewoman (supplying feathers, scarves, hoods, and other attires) and sempstress, eventually advancing to wardrobe keeper.[11]

The presence of female vendors in theaters likewise carried over from the pre-Restoration stage and became a more organized and stratified industry under licensed female concessionaires. Martha Brandon was in charge of the fruit concession at Covent Garden Theatre for many years, where she also sold playbooks and copies of songs. She payed the theater for "fruit rent" and was herself paid an annuity when she retired.[12] A widow named Mary Megg, known as "Orange Moll," became the concessionaire for the King's Company in early 1663, paying £100 for "full, free & sole liberty, license, power, & authority to vend, utter, & sell oranges, Lemons, fruit, sweetmeats, & all manner of fruiterers & Confectioners wares & commodities" in their new Bridges Street playhouse. Her license ran for thirty-nine years and stipulated that she was to hire no more than three wandering vendors at a time, two in the pit and one in the boxes and lower galleries.[13] One of Megg's employees appears to have been the young Eleanor or "Nell" Gwyn. Contemporary literary references claim that Gwyn vended oranges and other "lovely fruit" to "th'wondring Pit" and that she may also have worked as a fishwife, "with open throat / . . . cry[ing] fresh herrings e'en at ten a groat," or an "oyster wench."[14] Such references echo the satires of fruit- and fishwives discussed in Chapter 4 and cannot be taken at face value, for they are clearly intended to suggest the sexual availability of the actress, implying that Gwyn was selling her own "lovely fruit" from a young age, and mocking her "open" sexual/vocal organs. Yet the link they suggest in the popular imagination between the women who had worked in the pits and galleries of the commercial theaters since their inception and those who first trod the boards may nonetheless have been grounded in stage practice, particularly during the early years of the Restoration, when actresses appear to have been recruited from theater families and personnel. At Drury Lane Theatre, for example, a child actress named Ann Heath was the daughter of the theater's wardrobe master and mistress (who lived in the theater), and a dancer named Elizabeth Bride was the daughter of a married couple who worked as female dresser and scene-shifter there.[15]

The incidence of familial ties among theater personnel in the Restoration theater is quite striking. Other notable examples include Lucy Gwinn, a silk dyer and launderer, wardrobe keeper, and "Engenier" (e.g., inventor or designer) at Lincoln's Inn Fields, who was married to the theater's doorkeeper and boxkeeper,[16] and the widow of actor Theophilus Keene, who supplied feathers and worked as a dresser at both Lincoln's Inn Fields and Covent

Garden, while running a business of her own letting out "Masquerade Habits."[17] Anne Knapton was a dresser at Drury Lane; one of her sisters was married to the theater's co-manager and the other (herself a wardrobe mistress) to an actor.[18] Mrs. Stede, who was a dresser at the Queen's Theatre, was married to the theater's prompter.[19] Elizabeth Taswell, wife of actor James Taswell, was a dresser and property woman at Covent Garden Theatre.[20] The frequency of such familial ties raises the question of whether similar patterns were prevalent among theater people in the Elizabethan and Jacobean period.[21] The "deaf tirewoman" in Jonson's *Christmas, His Masque* is depicted as the mother of a "playboy" or boy-actor, whom Burbage and Hemminges of the King's Men have been trying to hire from her "by the week" (ll. 118–21). More research needs to be done on the lives of theater women and families to determine whether such family ties between actors and female offstage personnel were as common in Shakespeare's time as they were in the Restoration theater.

Rather than taking a case-study approach to individual women involved in theatrical production, this book has sought to provide a broad overview of the varied forms of theatrical labor in which women were involved while providing an in-depth study of several categories of female labor and commerce in and around the theaters as they were depicted in dramatic texts, on the stage, and in the culture at large. It is my hope that the gendered division of theatrical labor studied in this book will provide a point of departure for future research, as there are many avenues that remain to be explored. A more detailed study of women's roles as theatrical investors, for example, building on the analysis of women moneylenders in Chapter 2 of the present study and on Susan Cerasano's study of female shareholders in theaters, would help illuminate women's roles as theatrical stakeholders, as enabled by emergent financial and legal instruments.[22] Such roles may have set a precedent for later female investors in and managers of playing companies, such as Lady Mary Davenant, who took control of the Duke's Company following her husband's death in 1668. She is described as "a shrewd and sensible businesswoman . . . [who] took a particular interest in the company's accounts" and oversaw the completion of the Dorset Gardens Theatre, which opened in 1671, three years after William Davenant's death. As Gilli Bush-Bailey has shown, Lady Davenant "held the purse-strings" of the company and patronized the work of one of the first professional female playwrights, Aphra Behn. When the control of the company passed to her sons, she "insisted on her rights to the fruit concession" at the theater.[23] The role of sex work in the networks of commerce surrounding the theaters is another area that merits further study, as surprisingly little archival research has been done on the commercial ties between the playhouses and the bawdy houses, many of which were owned or managed by women.[24]

Although there have been several studies of cosmetics in early modern literature and culture, more work needs to be done on the role of women in the cosmetics trade and its contribution to theatrical production.[25] Recent scholarship on women's work in the manufacture and sale of cosmetics and other beautification products and techniques suggests a similar pattern to that found in other occupations undergoing professionalization: a gendered political struggle in which male physicians and surgeons laid claim to practices that had been the purview of female practitioners (in this case, of "physic"), pushing the latter into the expanding informal economy. As many as three hundred informal female practitioners are estimated to have earned an economic livelihood through beautifying "physic" in London between 1550 and 1640. They advertised such wares and services as "masks and forehead pieces, red pomatum for the lips, paste to whiten the hands, cosmetics to anoint the face after smallpox, preventatives for baldness, tooth powder, hair remover and coloring, and the ability to pluck eyebrows."[26] Our knowledge of women's roles in fabricating the material culture of the Shakespearean stage is likewise evolving with archaeological excavations of the sites of early modern theaters, including most recently that of the first successful, purpose-built London playhouse, The Theatre in Shoreditch, which is concluding as I write this epilogue. These are only a few of the avenues of research that might be pursued to illuminate the varied contributions of working women to the rise of the professional stage. The many unexplored paths that remain serve as an important reminder that such work is never done.

Notes

PROLOGUE

1. Bowsher and Miller, *The Rose and the Globe*, 144.
2. The earliest appearance of this proverb, in the second, augmented edition of Thomas Tusser's enormously popular compendium of domestic wisdom, *A Hundreth Good Pointes of Husbandrie*, retitled *A Hundreth Good Pointes of Husbandry, Lately Maried Unto a Hundreth Good Poynts of Huswifery* (1570), had a slightly different form. Introducing the newly appended section on huswifery is the following bit of domestic doggerel: "Some respite to husbands the weather doth send, / but huswives affaires have never none ende." Insofar as work is defined as effortful action "directed to a definite end, especially as a means of gaining one's livelihood" (*OED*, "work, *n.*" 4), female labor, particularly when it takes place within the domestic sphere, remains unrecognizable as work because it is without respite and remains un- or under-remunerated. In Tusser's terms: "huswiferie labours seme equall in paynes" but nonetheless fail to "bring in the gaines." Tusser, *A Hundreth Good Pointes of Husbandry*, fol. 26r. See also Tilley, *Dictionary of the Proverbs in England*, 329.
3. *A Womans Work Is Never Done*, 1 sheet.
4. Stevens, *A History of International Women's Day*, 46–51.
5. Bennett, "History That Stands Still,'" 278.
6. Ibid., 280, 271. Bennett's point echoes a research proposal outlined by Maurice Godelier in "Work and Its Representations," 164.
7. Hafter, "Introduction," x, xiv.
8. Alice Clark, *Working Life of Women*. More recent studies that complicate Clark's thesis include Bardsley, "Women's Work Reconsidered"; Barron, "The 'Golden Age' of Women in Medieval London"; Bennett, "History That Stands Still"; Bennett, *Ale, Beer, and Brewsters in England*; Erickson, *Women and Property in Early Modern England*; Froide, *Never Married*; Honeyman and Goodman, "Women's Work, Gender Conflict, and Labor Markets in Europe"; McIntosh, *Working Women in English Society*; Ogilvie, *A Bitter Living*; M. Roberts, "Women and Work in Sixteenth Century English Towns"; Wiesner, *Working Women in Renaissance Germany*; and Wiesner, "Spinning out Capital."
9. McIntosh, *Working Women in English Society*, 4.
10. T. Rutter, *Work and Play*, 7.
11. Ibid., 7–9.

12. McManus, *Women on the Renaissance Stage*; Tomlinson, *Women on Stage in Stuart Drama*; Findlay, Hodgson-Wright, and Williams, *Women and Dramatic Production*; Brown and Parolin, *Women Players in England*.

13. See also Karen Newman's comparative study, *Cultural Capitals*, which examines the city as a site of early modernity and consumerism in a wide range of literary genres but does not attend to the role of working women in shaping London's consumer culture.

14. In this respect, *Labors Lost* follows the lead of John Archer's *Citizen Shakespeare*, which analyzes the language of urban citizenship through a range of genres in Shakespeare's dramatic canon, although the present study's focus on women foregrounds working subjects who were excluded from citizenship and includes non-Shakespearean drama as well.

15. See, e.g., Orlin, *Material London*; Jones and Stallybrass, *Renaissance Clothing*; Richardson, *Clothing Culture*; McDonald and Hurcombe, *Gender and Material Culture in Historical Perspective*.

16. Castiglione, *The Book of the Courtier*, 43.

17. In Tom Rutter's words, "men and women of early modern England went to the theater seeking something different from their everyday lives; indeed, the very word 'play' implies that to speakers of English, there is something about drama that is fundamentally at odds with the workaday world" (*Work and Play*, 1–2).

18. Ibid., 2–3.

19. Ellinghausen, *Labor and Writing*, 1.

20. Ibid., 92. Ellinghausen elaborates, "When applied to authorship, the courtly notion of *sprezzatura* represents a fantasy that the composition of poetry, like the ideal courtly self, needs no process. In these terms, the opposite of *sprezzatura* would be art that *calls attention to* this process" (69).

21. Mendelson and Crawford, *Women in Early Modern England*, 3.

22. McIntosh, *Working Women in English Society*, 36.

23. Ibid.

CHAPTER 1

1. Callaghan, *Shakespeare Without Women*, 7.

2. Ibid., 31, 18.

3. Ibid., 7.

4. Thus, Callaghan argues, "The exception does not mitigate the patriarchal rule. We must keep looking at exceptions, but it is equally urgent that we keep in mind that they were just that" (ibid., 13). She more recently, in her introduction to *The Impact of Feminism in English Renaissance Studies*, describes "two divergent perspectives" that have produced an "impasse" in feminist early modern studies. The first, which emphasizes female presence and participation in culture, she terms "revisionism," while the second, which emphasizes female absence and subjugation, she terms "exclusionism." Her current embrace of a "post-revisionist" approach that analyzes "women's simultaneous participation in *and* exclusion from early modern culture" is akin to the argument elaborated in this chapter (5, 7, 13).

5. Rackin, *Shakespeare and Women*, 25.

6. Ibid., 46. Andrew Gurr's *Playgoing in Shakespeare's London*, the first study to gather and examine the evidence for female spectatorship in the public and private theaters in London throughout the period from 1567 to 1642, posits a "high proportion" or "plentiful supply" of "women from every section of society" but concludes that "few assertions, beyond the bare fact that women were present, can be trusted entirely" (65, 67). Richard Levin examines the evidence provided by prologues, epilogues, prefaces, and commendatory verses of printed plays in an effort to discern whether women "were regarded by the playwrights and acting companies as a constituency whose interests and feelings should be considered," concluding that women's "interests and feelings seem to have been taken into account by at least some of the playwrights of the period" ("Women in the Renaissance Theater Audience," 165, 174). Alan H. Nelson uncovers evidence of female spectators at university plays, asserting that their presence "increase[d] the pressure for plays in English," but says little about how their presence may have affected content beyond the observation that "women characters in Cambridge plays were often presented sympathetically" ("Women in the Audience of Cambridge Plays," 335). Other scholars have ascribed greater cultural significance to female theatrical spectatorship, asserting that it had a profound and shaping influence on the drama of the period. Michael Neill suggests that female spectatorship was "an important factor in shaping Caroline taste" with regard to plays staged in the private theaters ("'Wit's Most Accomplished Senate,'" 343). More recently, Jean E. Howard has argued that anti-theatrical writers' preoccupation with female spectatorship is a manifestation of male anxiety in response to certain forms of autonomy the theaters afforded female spectators, such as licensing them to look actively, thereby positioning them as subjects, rather than objects, of the gaze and even to make "themselves into spectacles" (*The Stage and Social Struggle in Early Modern England*, 79). See also Cook, *The Privileged Playgoers of Shakespeare's London*; Osborne, "Staging the Female Playgoer."

7. Callaghan, *Shakespeare Without Women*, 15.

8. Ibid., 165.

9. R. Levin, "Women in the Renaissance Theater Audience," 174; McLuskie, "The Patriarchal Bard," 92.

10. Those emphasizing female absence view the genre of closet drama as having little to do with plays written for production and as yet another example of women's exclusion from the professional stage, secondary social status, and confinement to the domestic sphere. Those emphasizing female presence contend, by contrast, that "lack of evidence does not preclude the possibility that plays by women were produced at the time of their composition, or were intended for performance" (Findlay, Hodgson-Wright, and Williams, *Women and Dramatic Production*, 2). See also Cotton, *Women Playwrights in England*; Cerasano and Wynne-Davies, *Renaissance Drama by Women*; Cerasano and Wynne-Davies, *Readings in Renaissance Women's Drama*; Acheson, "'Outrage Your Face'"; Raber, *Dramatic Difference*; Straznicky, "Closet Drama"; and Straznicky, *Privacy, Playreading and Women's Closet Drama*. Phyllis Rackin goes one step further in arguing that lack of evidence should not preclude the speculation that women may have written for the professional stage as well: "it would not be surprising to discover that some of these many anonymous plays—as well as

some of the plays sold to the players as the work of men whose names are now associated with them—may actually have been written in whole or in part by women." When it comes to women's social history, she reasons, absence of evidence does not necessarily constitute evidence of absence. Rackin, *Shakespeare and Women*, 45.

11. Bergeron, "Women as Patrons of English Renaissance Drama."

12. Cole, *The Portable Queen*; Barroll, *Anna of Denmark*.

13. See Westfall, *Patrons and Performance*; Erler, "'Chaste Sports'"; Westfall, "'A Commonty a Christmas Gambold or a Tumbling Trick'"; Findlay, Hodgson-Wright, and Williams, *Women and Dramatic Production*; Mueller, "Domestic Work in Progress Entertainments."

14. Klausner, *Records of Early English Drama*, 34, 189–93. Other scholarship on Jefferies includes Tittler, "Money-Lending in the West Midlands"; Tittler, *Townspeople and Nation*, 177–200; and Tittler, "Joyce Jefferies."

15. Kathman, "Alice Layston and the Cross Keys." On women rentiers and innkeepers, see McIntosh, *Working Women in English Society*, 114–16, 202–9.

16. General surveys of female performance practices in early modern England include: Graves, "Women on the Pre-Restoration Stage"; Thompson, "Women/'Women' and the Stage"; Cerasano and Wynne-Davies, *Renaissance Drama by Women*; Orgel, *Impersonations*, 3–9; Findlay, Hodgson-Wright, and Williams, *Women and Dramatic Production*; and Brown and Parolin, "Introduction."

17. Clubb, *Italian Drama in Shakespeare's Time*; P. Brown, "The Counterfeit Innnamorata"; Barasch, "Italian Actresses in Shakespeare's World: Flaminia and Vincenza"; Barasch, "Italian Actresses in Shakespeare's World: Vittoria and Isabella"; Parolin, "'A Strange Fury Entered My House'"; Campbell, "'Merry, Nimble, Stirring Spirit[s]'"; Gough, "Courtly *Comediantes*"; Katritzky, "Reading the Actress in Commedia Imagery"; Poulson, "Women Performing Homoerotic Desire in English and Italian Comedy."

18. Tomlinson, "'She That Plays the King'"; Wynne-Davies, "The Queen's Masque"; Gossett, "'Man-Maid, Begone'"; Barroll, *Anna of Denmark*; McManus, *Women on the Renaissance Stage*; Gough, "'Not as Myself'"; Tomlinson, "Theatrical Vibrancy on the Caroline Court Stage"; Gough, "Courtly *Comediantes*"; Tomlinson, *Women on Stage in Stuart Drama*.

19. Erler, "'Chaste Sports'"; Stokes, "Women and Mimesis in Medieval and Renaissance Somerset (and Beyond)"; Sale, "Slanderous Aesthetics and the Woman Writer"; Stokes, "Women and Performance"; Williams, Findlay, and Hodgson-Wright, "Payments, Permits and Punishments."

20. Rollins, "The Black-Letter Broadside Ballad," 307–10; Graves, "Women on the Pre-Restoration Stage"; Thompson, "Women/'Women' and the Stage," 104–6; S. Clark, "The Broadside Ballad and the Woman's Voice"; Mirabella, "'Quacking Delilahs.'"

21. Levin, "'We Princes, I Tell You, Are Set on Stages'"; P. Brown, *Better a Shrew than a Sheep*.

22. Dowling, "A Note on Moll Cutpurse"; Eccles, "Mary Frith"; Orgel, *Impersonations*, 8–9, 139–53; Ungerer, "Mary Frith"; Korda, "The Case of Moll Frith."

23. Thompson, "Women/'Women' and the Stage"; Orgel, *Impersonations*, 8–9.

24. Callaghan, *Shakespeare Without Women*, 8.
25. Orgel, *Impersonations*, 35.
26. Ibid.
27. Shapiro, "The Introduction of Actresses," 187.
28. Ibid., 178.
29. Ibid., 185.
30. Ibid. Shapiro likewise argues that women would have been "liabilities for itinerant acting troupes" without citing evidence to support this claim and in spite of the fact that continental touring companies included women, as did troupes of itinerant entertainers of other sorts in England (189). On women in itinerant troupes, see Graves, "Women on the Pre-Restoration Stage"; Thompson, "Women/'Women' and the Stage."
31. Erickson, "Introduction," vii–viii.
32. Ibid., xv–xxxii. See also Bennett, *Ale, Beer, and Brewsters in England*, esp. chap. 8.
33. Cited in Rappaport, *Worlds Within Worlds*, 38.
34. Cited in ibid. (emphasis added). The Weavers' Company records offer additional evidence of this dynamic. In spite of several oft-cited company ordinances restricting women's work in 1555, 1577, and 1596, it is clear that women continued to be employed both as weavers and in subsidiary activities, as many freemen were fined for employing women. Cited in Consitt, *London Weavers' Company*, 230, 92, 320; Plummer, *London Weavers' Company*, 61–62.
35. Rappaport, *Worlds Within Worlds*, 41.
36. Consitt, *London Weavers' Company*, 320.
37. Alice Clark, *Working Life of Women*, 156. On wives' involvement in the financial end of their husbands' businesses, see Shepard, *Meanings of Manhood in Early Modern England*, 198–99.
38. Kowaleski, "Singlewomen in Medieval and Early Modern Europe," 53; Froide, "Marital Status as a Category of Difference," 237.
39. Rappaport, *Worlds Within Worlds*, 38.
40. P. Earle, "The Female Labor Market in London," 337–38, 342 (emphasis added). Sheilagh Ogilvie's study of women's work in early modern Germany similarly finds that 90 percent of guilded labor was performed by men, whereas 90 percent of unguilded or informal labor was performed by women. Ogilvie, *A Bitter Living*, 322n8.
41. Lemire, *Dress, Culture and Commerce*, 120.
42. Castells and Portes, "World Underneath," 12.
43. Portes, Castells, and Benton, conclusion, 298; Castells and Portes, "World Underneath," 26. See also Hoyman, "Female Participation in the Informal Economy."
44. Castells and Portes, "World Underneath," 15; Gaughan and Ferman, "Toward an Understanding of the Informal Economy," 15. See also Henry, "The Political Economy of Informal Economies."
45. Castells and Portes, "World Underneath," 11–12. See also Gaughan and Ferman, "Toward an Understanding of the Informal Economy," 23; B. Roberts, *Perspectives on the Informal Economy*.
46. Ferman, Henry, and Hoyman, "Preface: The Informal Economy," 13.

47. Stallybrass, "Worn Worlds."
48. Shugg, "Prostitution in Shakespeare's London"; Griffiths, "The Structure of Prostitution in Elizabethan England"; Dawson and Yachnin, *The Culture of Playgoing in Shakespeare's England*; Varholy, "Representing Prostitution in Tudor and Stuart England"; Ungerer, "Prostitution in Late Elizabethan London."
49. Walker, "Women, Theft and the World of Stolen Goods"; Ungerer, "Mary Frith."
50. Gaughan and Ferman, "Toward an Understanding of the Informal Economy," 20.
51. The population grew from 70,000 in 1550 to 400,000 in 1650. Finlay, *Population and Metropolis*, 51.
52. Kellet, "The Breakdown of Guild and Corporation Control"; I. Archer, *The Pursuit of Stability*, 52–55, 61–63, 202–3, 242–45; Archer, Barron, and Harding, "Introduction," 11; Muldrew, *The Economy of Obligation*, 48.
53. Unwin, *The Gilds and Companies of London*, 245–46, 51; Kellet, "The Breakdown of Guild and Corporation Control," 381–82; D. Johnson, *Southwark and the City*, 87–92, 313–15; I. Archer, *The Pursuit of Stability*, 225–26, 234.
54. Cited in, respectively, Archer, Barron, and Harding, "Hugh Alley," 15, and Luders et al., *Statutes of the Realm*, 1038.
55. A 1603–4 statute, for example, held that informal brokers "are growen of late to many Hundreds within the Citie of London, and other places next adjoining to the Citie and Liberties of the same, and are like to increase to farre greater multitudes." Luders et al., *Statutes of the Realm*, 1039.
56. Hoyman, "Female Participation in the Informal Economy," 69.
57. Ogilvie, *A Bitter Living*, 329.
58. Hoyman argues that women's contributions to the informal sector have historically been "so dramatic—although invisible—that if ever recorded, it would usher in a new chapter in the book of women in the work force" ("Female Participation in the Informal Economy," 82).
59. Rappaport, *Worlds Within Worlds*, 53.
60. A. Johnson, *History of the Drapers*, 2:163, 174. See also Kellet, "The Breakdown of Guild and Corporation Control"; Fisher, "Some Experiments in Company Organization"; Kramer, *The English Craft Gilds and the Government*, 138.
61. Tawney and Power, *Tudor Economic Documents*, 1:379. On this custom, see also Unwin, *The Gilds and Companies of London*, 262–64; D. Johnson, *Southwark and the City*, 314; and Kellet, "The Breakdown of Guild and Corporation Control," 314.
62. I. Archer, *History of the Haberdashers' Company*, 62.
63. A. Johnson, *History of the Drapers*, 2:174.
64. Ibid., 2:165.
65. Thrupp, *A Short History*, 64; I. Archer, *History of the Haberdashers' Company*, 62. Although the degree of control they were able to exercise over the crafts and trades was weakening, the livery companies nonetheless retained their status and privileges within the municipal life of the walled City as a result of their wealth and landed property, control over entrance to the freedom and citizenship, and election to government offices. A. Johnson, *History of the Drapers*, 2:175–76, 240.

66. Wither, *A Collection of Emblemes, Ancient and Moderne*, 148. It would be a mistake, however, to read Wither's analogy as a wholesale condemnation of the stage. He goes on to defend those who make their living by plying the craft of poetry (or playing), including himself: "I my selfe (you'l say) have medlings made, / In things, that are improper to my Trade." (Wither was himself trained in the Inns of Court.) He replies: "No; for, the Muses are in all things free; / Fit subject of their Verse, all Creatures be; / And, there is nothing nam'd so meane, or great, / Whereof they have no Liberty to treat. / Both Earth and Heav'n, are open unto these; / And (when to take more libertie they please) / They Worlds, and things, create, which never were; / And, when they list, they play, and meddle, there" (ibid.). Wither thus reserves for writers a special "Poeticall Libertie" to "play" and "meddle" as their craft requires. His condemnation is of those who are "imperfect" in their art, or in the case of players, whose parts are "evill-acted." Players who are well trained, his emblem implies, are as necessary to the commonwealth as "honest" craftsmen.

67. Lawrence, "Elizabethan Players as Tradesfolk"; O'Neill, "Elizabethan Players as Tradesmen"; Baldwin, *The Organization and Personnel of the Shakespearean Company*, 37n; Forse, *Art Imitates Business*, 8–9; Kathman, "Grocers, Goldsmiths, and Drapers."

68. Bristol, *Big-Time Shakespeare*, 38–39.

69. See Agnew, *Worlds Apart*, 54.

70. Orgel, *Impersonations*, 65; Kathman, "Grocers, Goldsmiths, and Drapers."

71. Streitberger, "Personnel and Professionalization," 347.

72. Orgel, *Impersonations*, 65.

73. See Bristol, *Big-Time Shakespeare*, 31–40.

74. Cited in Wallace, *The First London Theatre*, 141. My argument here is indebted to S. Howard, "In Praise of Margaret Brayne."

75. It was not unheard of for women to work as carpenters or joiners during this period. Alice Clark, *Working Life of Women*, 172–78; Snell, *Annals of the Laboring Poor*, 286.

76. Honigmann and Brock, *Playhouse Wills*, 192–93.

77. Foakes ed., *Henslowe's Diary*, fol. 28v; see also fols. 28r, 38v, 42v, 124r.

78. According to Ned Alleyn, Henslowe's son-in-law, Henslowe at the start of his career was "of small means or abillitie" and through his marriage to Agnes "gained all or the most parte of her estate to a greate value." Public Record Office, STAC 8/168/18, cited in Cerasano, "Henslowe's Biography," 71.

79. Ogilvie, *A Bitter Living*, 328.

80. Foakes ed., *Henslowe's Diary*, fol. 123r. A second entry on fol. 41v lists the amount paid to Griggs for Mary's apprenticeship as £3 instead of £5.

81. Thirsk, *Economic Policy and Projects*, 113.

82. Dated January 10, 1586/7, it states: "the saide Phyllipe . . . shall . . . wth as muche expedicon as may be ereckte fynishe and sett upp or cause to be erected finished and sett upe by John Gryggs Carpenter his servants or assignes the saide playhouse wth all furniture therunto belonginge." Foakes ed., *Henslowe's Diary*, appendix 1, muniment no. 16, 305.

83. Foakes ed., *Henslowe's Diary*, appendix 1, articles 10, 11, 14 on 275–76, 281.

84. Rebecca Perry was apprenticed to William Addington "to learne the Art of a Sempstress of his wife" and another girl "to Anne Joyse sempstress & sole merchant without

Thomas Joyse her husband." Of twenty-one girls apprenticed to the Carpenters' Company in the mid-seventeenth century nine were apprenticed to Richard Hill and his wife "to learn the trade of a sempstress." Clark also cites several examples of girls apprenticed to the wives of carpenters to learn the trade of millinery. Alice Clark, *Working Life of Women*, 174–76.

85. The loan agreement with Henslowe was made in 1592, the same year that he worked as a carpenter on the Rose. See Foakes ed., *Henslowe's Diary*, fol. 12r.

86. Essex County Record Office, D/Dp 226, cited in Arnold, Tiramani, and Levey, *Patterns of Fashion 4*, 9.

87. In *Twelfth Night*, Duke Orsino mentions the "maids that weave their thread with bones" (2.4.45). William Shakespeare, *Twelfth Night*, ed. J. M. Lothian and T. W. Craik, The Arden Shakespeare (London: Routledge, 1988). On bonelace as women's work, see McNeill, "Free and Bound Maids," 101–3.

88. Foakes ed., *Henslowe's Diary*, fol. 124r.

89. There is also evidence that the yeoman of the Revels Office was in the habit of renting out masque costumes to players and others to make money on the sly. A complaint lodged in 1572 by Thomas Giles, a haberdasher whose services were sometimes used by the Revels Office, notifies the queen that "the yeman of the queens Magestyes revelles doth usuallye lett to hyer her sayde hyghnes maskes to the grett hurt spoylle & dyscredyt of the same to all sort of parsons that wyll hyer the same, by reson of wyche commen usage the glosse & bewtye of the same garments ys lost." Giles, it turns out, was himself in the practice of renting out costumes and felt himself to be "grettlye hynderyde of hys lyvynge" by the yeoman because he could not rent out his own "so cheplye . . . as hyr hyghnes maskes be lett." Feuillerat, *Office of Revels, Queen Elizabeth*, 409.

90. Chambers, *The Elizabethan Stage*, 1:184–90.

91. Donne, "Satire IV," cited in Cerasano, "'Borrowed Robes,'" 55.

92. Platter, *Thomas Platter's Travels in England*, 167. See also Jones and Stallybrass, *Renaissance Clothing*, 189.

93. For example, an entry describing payments to artisans who worked on several masques performed during Christmas 1552/3 reads: "Maskes. one of covetus men with longe noses with a maske for babions faces of tinsel blak & tawny one other maske of pollenders with a mask of soldiours to their torchberers & one maske of women of Diana hunting with a mask of matrons to their torchberers for which was Bought and provided of the Mearser sarcenet of divers colours for attier of hedpecis . . . Draper red & white cottons for lynings of garmentes . . . Silke woman frenges & flours of silk & other garnitures . . . Myllener ribben gloves & other necessaries for maskes . . . ffethermaker plumes of phesauntes & capons tailes . . . Skynner savage heads and caps for maskes . . . Glover gloves for handes & feete like cattes fete & paws . . . Grocer colours gum Arabek & other painters stuffe . . . Carver swordes & bottons of wood for maskes . . . Turner ii head blockes to trym hattes & garnish hedpeces . . . propertie maker one mask of satires & ii doz. counterfet aglettes" (Feuillerat, *Revels at Court, King Edward VI and Queen Mary*, 116). One might argue that the payment to the "Silke woman" should be taken as an indication that women artisans were so unusual that their gender was remarked upon and that we should therefore assume that all of the

artisans whose gender is not specified were male. The term "silkwoman," however, was the standard term used to refer to women who worked in the silk industry in the period (see discussion of silkwomen below), whereas most occupational names were gender neutral. Moreover, entries that do specify gender in the Revels accounts offer examples of female mercers, drapers, and milliners, so we should not assume that ungendered artisans listed were invariably male. The turner referred to in the entry above, for example, may have been a woman, since an earlier record for the same year lists "Alys perkyns for turnnge of iii headblockes to fasshion and Trymme hattes upon" (Feuillerat, *Revels at Court, King Edward VI and Queen Mary*, 108).

94. Feuillerat, *Office of Revels, Queen Elizabeth*, 197; see also 60, 227, 306. An ambiguous entry, which may be evidence of women's work in the fabrication of stage props for a masque performed for Elizabeth at Whitehall in 1559, reads: "Wages of taylours karvars propertie makers wemen and other woorking and attendinge theron" (110).

95. Feuillerat, *Office of Revels, Queen Elizabeth*, 180. William Elderton was Master of the Children of Eton and of Westminster.

96. Feuillerat, *Office of Revels, Queen Elizabeth*, 196.

97. Ibid., 134, 173, 196, 207, 215, 233.

98. Ibid., 180, 196, 206.

99. Ibid., 180. Other examples of single women or "maids" (or possibly married women working as *femes soles*) who were hired to work in the Revels Office for wages include Anne Prynne and Alice Tayler, who worked alongside Mistresses Pilkington, Moorer, and Morgan. Feuillerat, *Office of Revels, Queen Elizabeth*, 196.

100. Ibid., 194.

101. The Revels accounts mention a similar workforce of garland weavers: "214 woorkfolkes the most of them being women" were hired to gather, sort, and string "1560 ffadam [i.e., fathoms]" of flower garlands to adorn the banqueting house at Whitehall for entertainments on the occasion of the Duc de Montmorency's visit in 1572. Feuillerat, *Office of Revels, Queen Elizabeth*, 164.

102. See Snell, *Annals of the Laboring Poor*, 292–93. On women milliners, see Alice Clark, *Working Life of Women*, 176, 234, 293.

103. Stubbes, *The Anatomie of Abuses*, sig. E8r.

104. Ibid., 39–42; see also 42–43 for a description of women's ruffs.

105. Elizabeth's tirewomen included Lady Cobham, Lady Carewe, Dorothy Abington, Mary Ratcliffe, and Blanche Parry, who manufactured and arranged "hoodes," "mufflers," "Cawles," and "Crippens [i.e., nets for the hair] and habilliaments [i.e., hair ornaments]." On one occasion, Parry received "one yerde half quarter of satten of sundrye coulours . . . to be used aboute the attyre of our [i.e., the queen's] hedde." Arnold, *Queen Elizabeth's Wardrobe Unlock'd*, 202.

106. Ibid., 203–4.

107. Ibid., 206.

108. Feuillerat, *Office of Revels, Queen Elizabeth*, 156.

109. Ibid., 219.

110. Ibid.

111. Ibid., 24r.

112. Foakes ed., *Henslowe's Diary*, fols. 95v, 104r, 118v.

113. Ibid., fol., 22v; see also fols. 44r, 54v, 106r, 106v, 108r, 115r.

114. Cited in Greenstreet, "The Whitefriars Theatre in the Time of Shakespeare," 275–76.

115. Feuillerat, *Office of Revels, Queen Elizabeth*, 272.

116. Sharpham, *Cupids Whirligig*, sig. K4v.

117. Lewis Machin and Gervase Markham, *The Dumb Knight, A Historicall Comedy, Acted Sundry Times by the Children of His Majesties Revels* (London, 1608), sig. B1v.

118. On the homoerotic puns of the Children of the King's Revels plays, see Bly, *Queer Virgins and Virgin Queans on the Early Modern Stage*.

119. Jonson, *Complete Plays*, 2:1–117.

120. In Middleton, *Thomas Middleton*.

121. She elaborates: "A narrow-eared wire sets out a cheek so fat and so full, and if you be ruled by me, you shall wear your hair still like a mock-face behind; 'tis such an Italian world, many men know not before from behind" (ll. 8–9, 17–21). The innuendo of her remark suggests that she is instructing her client in sexual as well as sartorial fashions and homoerotically gestures at the fat and full cheeks of the boy-actor "behind" the "c(o)untry" wench/courtesan. The tirewoman's parting fashion advice continues the coupling of sartorial and sexual modes when she warns: "I pray, have an especial care, howsoever you stand or lie, that nothing fall upon your hair to batter your wire" (ll. 70–72).

122. Arnold, *Queen Elizabeth's Wardrobe Unlock'd*, 218.

123. Tomkis, *Lingua*, sigs. I2r–I2v.

124. Bowsher and Miller, *The Rose and the Globe*, 141–44, 200–203.

125. Feuillerat, *Office of Revels, Queen Elizabeth*, 134.

126. Ibid., 172.

127. The word "frolic," derived from the Dutch adjective *vrolick* and the Flemish verb *froliken*, was imported into the English language during the mass immigration of Protestant refugees during the late sixteenth century. The Revels Office also hired several Dutch men as scene painters, including "Hans Eottes" (probably Hans Eworth), "Hans Bonner," and a number of other immigrant artisans from the Low Countries. Feuillerat, *Office of Revels, Queen Elizabeth*, 160, 181, 195, 207–8. On Netherlandish women painters, see Chapter 3, note 55.

128. Dale, "The London Silkwomen of the Fifteenth Century," 331–33. See also Alice Clark, *Working Life of Women*, 138–42; Kowaleski and Bennett, "Crafts, Guilds, and Women in the Middle Ages"; Sutton, *The Mercery of London*, 4–5, 9, 12, 30, 202–9, 443–46; Lacey, "'Narrow Ware'"; Arnold, *Queen Elizabeth's Wardrobe Unlock'd*, 219–27; and Stern, "The Trade, Art or History of Silk Flowers." On silkwomen elsewhere in Europe, see Brown and Goodman, "Women and Industry in Florence"; Wiesner, *Working Women in Renaissance Germany*, 183–84; and Vicente, "Images and Realities of Work," 133–35.

129. Consitt, *London Weavers' Company*, 230.

130. Ibid., 292.

131. Over the course of the seventeenth century, many freemen were fined for

employing women, including Richard Sampson for having six looms "and two maidens at work in two of the looms" and John Hogg for keeping a "wench at work for a whole year contrary to the Ordinances." Another weaver was ordered to discharge "four wenches who were working in his looms." Company members came up with a variety of prevarications to explain the presence of women in their workshops, such as passing young women off as the master weaver's daughter or claiming they were not put to work in the looms but only to "wind silk and [do] other household business" (Plummer, *London Weavers' Company*, 61). When ordered to dismiss a female employee, one Richard Ainton simply called the Court officers "a Company of fools," while another named George Chiefe, who had employed two women, became "very refractory and quarrelsome . . . and damn'd the Court" (61–62).

132. Plummer, *London Weavers' Company*, 62.

133. Consitt, *London Weavers' Company*, 320.

134. Luu, *Immigrants and the Industries of London*, 186–93.

135. The growth of the nascent broad-silk industry during this period is reflected in the annual imports of raw silk, which rose from 11,000 lbs. (worth £8,004) in 1565 to 52,000 lbs. (worth £40,000) in 1592. Luu, *Immigrants and the Industries of London*, 181.

136. Ibid., 184.

137. Ibid., 204–7; I. Archer, *The Pursuit of Stability*, 7; Goose, "'Xenophobia' in Elizabethan and Early Stuart England," 119.

138. Consitt, *London Weavers' Company*, 313–14.

139. Plummer, *London Weavers' Company*, 149. The London Weavers' Company in the early seventeenth century (1622) "accused the strangers of employing women illegally. . . . In their complaint, the native weavers claimed that the immigrants employed women to sell their goods from door to door rather than in common marketplaces, which was a violation of London's customs . . . the newcomers were willing to employ their women in a way that undermined the ability of freemen to support their own. This clash of economic interests was therefore cast as a clash between two systems of gender relations" (Ward, *Metropolitan Communities*, 128). The Book of Fines contains many references to strangers hawking silk products in the streets of London in the 1590s. Luu, *Immigrants and the Industries of London*, 184.

140. In her appendix of London silkwomen active during the fourteenth and fifteenth centuries, Kay Lacey lists one named Margaret as apparently Flemish, while the names of several others suggest they may have been immigrants as well. "'Narrow War,'" appendix A, 200–204.

141. Feuillerat, *Office of Revels, Queen Elizabeth*, 90, 93, 110, 116–17, 156, 161, 209. See also Feuillerat, *Revels at Court, King Edward VI and Queen Mary*, 85, 19, 70, 116.

142. Bowll provided "Cop*per* Sylver ffrenge Twist and bone Lace," "Golde ffrenge," and "Cop*per* silver & silk Buttons and loopes," while Wyett provided "carna*ci*on and sylver Lawne," "Sylver Tyncell," and "Ribbon of Silver & golde." Feuillerat, *Office of Revels, Queen Elizabeth*, 156, 161.

143. The jacket is displayed in the British Galleries, room 56e, case 9 (Museum number T. 106:1 to 4–2003). According to the object history note, "The alterations and addition of more spangles and beads may have been done to adapt the jacket for use as a masque costume." See http://collections.vam.ac.uk/item/O86509/jacket/.

144. W. Ingram, *The Business of Playing*, 68.

145. For example, "a longe black vellvet clock*e* layd wth sylke lace," "A payer of hosse of clothe of gowld layd thick wth blacke sylk lace," and "A blacke vellvet gercken layd thicke wth black sylke lace & A payer of Rownd hosse of paynes of sylke layd wth sylver lace." Foakes ed., *Henslowe's Diary*, fols. 50v, 52r, 53r.

146. Such as 'A scarlett cloke wth ij brode gould Laces: w^t gould buttens," "A scarlett cloke Layd downe w^t silver Lace and silver buttens," and "A damask cloke . . . garded w^t vellvet." Ibid., appendix 1, article 30, 291.

147. Bowsher and Miller, *The Rose and the Globe*, 140.

148. Ibid., 142–44.

149. Such as a velvet cloak "embroydered w^t gould and gould spangles," a "blak bugell cloke," "A vellvet dublett cut di*a*mond lact w^t gould lace and spang[les]," a "blak tafata [doublet] cut on blak velvett lacte w^t bugell[s]," and "frenchose" embellished with "black bugell[s]" and "spangled." Foakes ed., *Henslowe's Diary*, appendix 1, article 30, 291, 293–94.

150. On women's work as frippers or secondhand clothing dealers (also known as upholders or upholsters) and pawnbrokers in the economy at large, see Holderness, "Widows in Pre-Industrial Society," 439; G. Walker, "Women, Theft and the World of Stolen Goods," 91–93; and McIntosh, *Working Women in English Society*, 230–31. Kay Lacey cites evidence of women working as informal pawnbrokers and secondhand clothing dealers in London as early as the fourteenth century. Lacey, "Women and Work," 52–53.

151. Cerasano, "'Borrowed Robes,'" 51.

152. Jones and Stallybrass, *Renaissance Clothing*, 184–86.

153. On the gendered division of labor among tailors and sempstresses, see McIntosh, *Working Women in English Society*, 229.

154. The bulk of these records may be found in Foakes ed., *Henslowe's Diary*, fols. 55r–61r, 73r–81r, 133r–136r. There are other references to actors pawning their costumes with Henslowe scattered throughout Henslowe's accounts, some dated well after 1596 (see fols. 19v, 28v, 37r, 41v) and one as late as 1602. For a more extended discussion of Henslowe's pawnbroking records, see Korda, "Household Property/Stage Property." See also Jones and Stallybrass, *Renaissance Clothing*, chaps. 1, 7.

155. Greg, *Henslowe's Diary*, 1:xxi.

156. Of the total number of loans, 55 percent were to women, 15 percent to men, and 30 percent to anonymous debtors. Jones and Stallybrass calculate that there were fifty-nine different named women (not including his female agents, discussed below) and thirty-five named men among Henslowe's pawnbroking debtors. Jones and Stallybrass, *Renaissance Clothing*, 31, 285n91.

157. Her first entry in the accounts is in June 1594, when she pawns a bundle containing "A manes gowne & A blacke Clocke tied in A clothe" for 40 shillings. It was not until three months later, on September 17, that she appears to have become a paid agent of Henslowe's. On that day she pawned no fewer than five bundles containing a diverse range of men's and women's apparel and other goods for over £5 10s. Several of these entries contain the curious phrase "the Intreste of goody watsones" or "goody watsones Intreste." It seems unlikely that the term "interest" here refers to interest that Henslowe was charging

Goody Watson, since the term he ordinarily uses for this is "use," or a simple numerical calculation in the margins of his accounts. Rather, it is more likely that he is referring to a more common definition of the term "interest" in the period, namely, "having a right or title to, a claim upon, or a share in . . . [a] property, or to some of the uses or benefits pertaining to [that] property" (see *OED*, "interest, *n.*" I,1a, c, e). The designation would seem to suggest, in other words, that the bundles of goods that Goody Watson began pawning with Henslowe on a regular basis in September 1594 were bundles in which she herself had a financial interest. Foakes ed., *Henslowe's Diary*, fols. 78v, 79v.

158. Foakes ed., *Henslowe's Diary*, fols. 133v–136r.

159. On female intermediaries in the pawnbroking trade, see Korda, "Labors Lost," 212–13.

160. That Henslowe appropriated and resold unredeemed pledges at least on occasion is clear from an entry of March 1595, which reads: "d[elivere]d unto goody watsone . . . severalle garmentes of my owne to be sowld as foloweth." The entry then describes the articles and indicates the prices at which she will sell them. These six garments were in fact unredeemed pledges that Goody Watson had herself delivered to Henslowe three to five months earlier. Henslowe made a healthy profit on the transaction, charging between one-quarter and two-thirds more for the items than he had originally loaned on them. The entries suggest that Goody Watson was not only involved in the pawnbroking trade but had expertise as a secondhand clothes dealer as well. Foakes ed., *Henslowe's Diary*, fols. 19v, 80r–80v.

161. It is often assumed that early modern pawnbrokers could appropriate unredeemed pledges only after they had kept them for a full year and a day, but this rule became law only in 1872 with the passage of the Pawnbroker's Act (35 & 36 Vict. c. 93). "Every pledge is redeemable within twelve months from the day of pawning, exclusive of that day, . . . if not redeemed within the year and days of grace, [the pledge] becomes, at the end of the days of grace, the absolute property of the pawnbroker." Hardinge, *The Laws of England*, 251.

162. McIntosh, *Working Women in English Society*, 107.

163. Boulton, *Neighborhood and Society*, 88. Similar cases appear in the Middlesex Sessions Rolls, Justices of the Peace, Quarter Sessions, *Middlesex County Records*, Calendar of Sessions Rolls 485–9 for the year 1610, 4:109, 10:136.

164. McIntosh, *Working Women in English Society*, 110–11.

165. For examples of unredeemed female gowns in the pawn accounts, see Foakes ed., *Henslowe's Diary*, fols. 55r, 57r, 57v, 58v, 59r, 79r, 80r, 134v.

166. Thomas Platter, cited in Thaler, "Playwrights' Benefits and 'Interior Gathering' in the Elizabethan Theatre," 92.

167. Ibid., 195. See also Gurr, *Playgoing in Shakespeare's London*, 74.

168. Chambers, *The Elizabethan Stage*, 2:389; Berry, *The First Public Playhouse*, 36.

169. Eccles, "Elizabethan Actors II: E–J," 456.

170. Gurr, *Playgoing in Shakespeare's London*, 234, 240.

171. Greg, *Henslowe Papers*, 63. See also Chambers, *The Elizabethan Stage*, 1:356, 2:187.

172. Bentley, *The Jacobean and Caroline Stage*, 2:616.

173. Bowsher and Miller, *The Rose and the Globe*, 133–34.

174. Greg, *Henslowe Papers*, 85.

175. Ibid., 63.

176. Ibid., 3.

177. Chambers, *The Elizabethan Stage*, 2:389–91; Bentley, *The Jacobean and Caroline Stage*, 6:128.

178. See Lawrence, *Those Nut-Cracking Elizabethans*, 45–46.

179. Greg, *Henslowe Papers*, 137. Greg surmises that the "Stephen" who appeared with other "mutes" as "Beggars" in Dekker and Chettle's *Troilus and Cressida* (also performed by the Admiral's Men c. 1599), as indicated in the plot of that play, was Stephen Magett, the company's tireman (142, 44, 50).

180. Jonson, *Bartholomew Fair*.

181. Platter, *Thomas Platter's Travels in England*, 166. See also Gurr, *Playgoing in Shakespeare's London*, 43, 272–73, 286, 299–300.

182. Overbury caricatures the "Puny Clarke" who "eats ginger-bread at a play-house." Cited in Chambers, *The Elizabethan Stage*, 2:548.

183. A verse by Alexander Gill of 1632 on Jonson's *Magnetic Lady* refers to the "apell-wyfes" at the Fortune theater. Cited in Bentley, *The Jacobean and Caroline Stage*, 1:268.

184. For numerous references to nuts, vended and cracked, in theaters, see Lawrence, *Those Nut-Cracking Elizabethans*, 1–7.

185. Cited in Chambers, *The Elizabethan Stage*, 2:549.

186. Cited in Greenstreet, "The Whitefriars Theatre in the Time of Shakespeare," 275.

187. Sisson, "Mr. and Mrs. Browne," 100.

188. On women's continued involvement at the lower end of the drink trades, see McIntosh, *Working Women in English Society*, 160–63. For examples of women tobacco sellers, see Le Hardy, *County of Middlesex*, 1:202–3, 215, 451.

189. Korda, "Gender at Work in the Cries of London."

190. See Pollard, *Shakespeare's Theater*, 101, 73–74.

191. Gosson, *Plays Confuted in Five Actions*, sig. B3r.

192. See, e.g., Thrupp, *A Short History*, 62.

193. See Pollard, *Shakespeare's Theater*, 81, 117, 193. "Is it not . . . strange," asked Samuel Cox, secretary to Sir Christopher Hatton, in 1590, "in these days that (professing Christ as we do) we should suffer men to make professions and occupations of plays all the year long, whereby to enrich idle loiterers with plenty, while many of our poor brethren lie pitifully gasping in the streets, ready to starve and die of penury?" Cited in Wickham, Berry, and Ingram, *English Professional Theatre*, 168.

194. T. Rutter, *Work and Play*, 33–44.

195. Ibid., 35–36, citing complaints lodged by the Lord Mayor to Lord Burghley and the Privy Council in 1580 and 1597, respectively.

196. Ibid., 37.

197. Gosson, *The Schoole of Abuse*. See also Rankins, *A Mirrour of Monsters*, sig. B1v.

198. Luders et al., *Statutes of the Realm*, 1038–39.

199. Gosson, *Plays Confuted in Five Actions*, sig. G6v.

200. Black, *Guilds and Civil Society*, 15.

201. Dod and Cleaver, *A Godly Forme*, sig. D7r (emphasis added).

202. See, e.g., ibid., sigs. D7r–D7v, and the "Homilie Against Idlenesse," in Jewel, *The Second Tome of Homilies*, 249–55.

203. Dod and Cleaver, *A Godly Forme*, sig. D7r.

204. Perkins, *A Treatise of the Vocations*, 4. Perkins inveighs against those who, not content with their estates, aspire to better their occupations: "when we begin to mislike the wise disposition of God, and to thinke other mens callings better for us then our owne, then followes confusion and disorder in every societie" (29).

205. Gouge, *Of Domesticall Duties*, 536.

206. Ibid., 537; Dod and Cleaver, *A Godly Forme*, sig. D9v.

207. Gosson, *Plays Confuted in Five Actions*, sig. G6v.

208. Ibid., sig. E2r.

209. Beard, *The Theater of Gods Judgements*, 374.

210. Northbrooke, *A Treatise*, 19 (emphasis added).

211. Ibid., 71.

212. Rankins, *A Mirrour of Monsters*, sig. D1r.

213. Nathan Field to Revd. Mr. Sutton of 1616, Pollard, *Shakespeare's Theater*, 277.

214. Sidney, *An Apologie for Poetrie*, sigs. G4r, I2r.

215. Heywood, *Apology for Actors*, sig. C3r.

216. Ibid., sig. F4r.

217. "In upholding the idea of time off for employees," Rutter argues, "Dekker was insisting on the right of a significant proportion of his audience actually to be in the theater at all" (*Work and Play*, 94).

CHAPTER 2

1. Aristotle, *Aristotle's Politics*, 46 (book 1, chap. 10, 1258b3–10). See also Le Goff, *Your Money or Your Life*, 18.

2. The usurer was thought to be "an especially scandalous idler, for the diabolic labor of money that he initiated was but the inverse of his own odious sloth." In this respect usurers were viewed as akin to prostitutes and actors. Le Goff, *Your Money or Your Life*, 42; see also 30–31, 50–51.

3. T. Wilson, *A Discourse Uppon Usurye*, 184–85. On usury contributing to the "decay of trades," see Culpeper, *A Tract against Usurie*, 1–2, 4; *Usurie Araigned and Condemned*, 14.

4. T. Wilson, *A Discourse Uppon Usurye*, 184.

5. Ibid., 183–84. See also Fenton, *A Treatise of Usurie*, 102.

6. Muscul[us], *Lawful and Unlawful Usurie*, sig. A5v; Caesar, *Damnable Sect of Usurers*, fol. 5v.

7. Fenton, *A Treatise of Usurie*, 67; H. Smith, *Examination of Usury*, 15.

8. Sander, *A Briefe Treatise of Usurie*, 52.

9. Fenton, *A Treatise of Usurie*, 15, 67. In the words of Thomas Pie, "the Usurer maketh that breed, gender, and increase, which by nature is barren and unapt to increase: for in usurie money genders, gets, or bringes foorth money; whereupon . . . the Usurer maketh

something of nothing" (*Usuries Spright Conjured*, 19). See also Muscul[us], *Lawful and Unlawful Usurie*, sig. A5v; Sander, *A Briefe Treatise of Usurie*, 52.

10. Shakespeare, *The Winter's Tale*. The excess of usury's unnatural generation is similarly evoked by Thomas Pie: "Other creature[s] have a time to bring foorth perfect yongue: but the usurers money is borne to day, and to day begins to bring foorth. Other creatures the sooner they ingender, the sooner they leave of ingendring: but the usurers money ingendreth quickly, and never leaveth off" (*Usuries Spright Conjured*, 35–36).

11. Henry Smith argues, "When God had finished his creation, he said unto man . . . *Increase and multiplie*, but he never said unto money, increase and multiplie, because it is a dead thing which hath no seede, and therefore is not fit to ingender. Therefore he which saith to his money, increase & multiply, begetteth a monstrous birth. . . . When God set Adam his worke, he sayd, *In the sweate of thy browes shalt thou live*: not in the sweate of his browes, but in the sweate of thy browes; but the Usurer liveth in the sweat of his browes, & her browes: that is, by the paines and cares, and labours of another, for he taketh no paines himselfe, but onely expecteth the time when his interest will come in, like the belly which doth no worke, & yet eateth all the meate" (*Examination of Usury*, 15). Francis Bacon in "Of Usury" says usury "breaketh the first law that was made for mankind after the fall, which was, *in sudore vultus tui comedes panem tuum*, not *in sudore vultus alieni*; not in the sweat of another's face" (*The Essays*, 183). There were, of course, explicit references to usury in scripture (e.g., Exod. 22:25, Lev. 25:35–37, Deut. 23:19–20, Prov. 28:8, Psalms 15, Ezek. 18:13–17, Luke 6:30–36); the interpretation of these passages was hotly debated within the pamphlet controversy on usury as discussed below.

12. Caesar claims usury has "growen to suche a perfecte ripenes in Englande, as almoste there is no man, but, if he have spare money, out it muste" (*Damnable Sect of Usurers*, sig. A6). Culpeper likewise notes: "Neyther are they rich trades-men onely that give over trading . . . but landed-men, Farmers, and men of profession that grow lazie in their professions, and become Usurers" (*A Tract against Usurie*, 2). There was, in fact, little consensus within the controversy about what constituted usury. The considerable divergences of opinion did not merely distinguish pro and contra positions, for those who argued against usury differed as to what defined the practice, just as those who argued for the legalization of certain practices associated with usury failed to agree about which ones were acceptable. Nor can one always take a commentator's self-description as pro or contra at face value, as most of the so-called liberalizers, such as Calvin, Bucer, Beza, and Bullinger, claimed to be against usury and merely categorized the commercial practices they found acceptable as non-usurious. See Tawney, "Introduction," 114–15.

13. T. Wilson, *A Discourse Uppon Usurye*, sig. C4.

14. Le Goff, *Your Money or Your Life*, 17. Early modern commentators invoke a variety of images to describe this heterogeneity: Fenton describes usury as "woven and twisted into every trade and commerce, one moving another, by this engine, like wheeles in a clocke, that it seemeth the very frame and course of traffick must needes be altered before this can be reformed," while Powel calls the myriad types of usury "an endlesse maze" or "labirinth out of which Theseus himselfe" could not be extricated (Fenton, *A Treatise of Usurie*, 2; Powel, *Theologicall and Scholasticall Positions Concerning Usurie*, sig. A4). Henry

Smith facetiously calls usury a "mystery," not because it is an honest trade but because of its mysterious, shifting forms: "As other crafts are called Mysteries, so I may fitly call it, the Mysterie of Usurie, for they have devised mo sorts of Usurie, than there be tricks at cardes, I cannot recken halfe, and I am afrayde to shew you all, least I should teach you to be Usurers" (*Examination of Usury*, 17).

15. Tawney, "Introduction," 105; Clarkson, *Pre-Industrial Economy in England*, 146–48; Stone, *Crisis of the Aristocracy*, 506; Froide, *Never Married*, 132.

16. Caesar, *Damnable Sect of Usurers*, sig. A4r. Fenton likewise notes "the generall practise of it, even amongst them of good note and reputation" (*A Treatise of Usurie*, 110).

17. Muldrew, *Economy of Obligation*, 114. See also Tawney, "Introduction," 134, 155, 165.

18. According to Cuthbert Burbage, son of Richard Burbage, "The Theater hee [Richard] built with many Hundred poundes taken up at interest," and the Globe was built "with more summes of money taken up at interest, which lay heavy on us many yeeres." Reproduced in Chambers, *William Shakespeare*, 2:65–66. See also W. Ingram, "The Economics of Playing," 316.

19. On the moneylending activities of Shakespeare and his father, John, see Chambers, *William Shakespeare*, 2:102–3; Schoenbaum, *William Shakespeare: A Documentary Life*, 179–81; Thomas and Evans, "John Shakespeare in the Exchequer."

20. Schoenbaum, *William Shakespeare: A Documentary Life*, 180–81; and Honigmann, "Shakespeare's Life," 7.

21. Foakes ed., *Henslowe's Diary*.

22. Stone, *Crisis of the Aristocracy*, esp. chap. 9. See also Agnew, *Worlds Apart*.

23. In her recent biography of Ann Hathaway, *Shakespeare's Wife*, Germaine Greer speculates that Ann may have been involved in Shakespeare's moneylending and other business activities in Stratford (220–21). Although Greer cites no firm evidence to support this claim, she mentions Henry Smith's sermons on usury published in 1591, which chide usurers who "give leave to their wives" to lend money at interest, charging "every month a penny for a shilling" (*Examination of Usury*, 49, cited in Greer, *Shakespeare's Wife*, 220).

24. Although indebted to Mary Poovey's account of the epistemological shift toward a cultural valorization of exactitude in accounting and of truth claims grounded in quantification in late sixteenth- and seventeenth-century England, my analysis departs from her contention that this shift was grounded in a wholesale exclusion of women. Poovey argues that the mercantile credibility established by double-entry bookkeeping could only be defended "by opposing such rule-governed writing to the unruly writing associated with women" and that the new techniques of accounting "could be represented as 'perfitte'" only by excluding female imperfection, excess, and risk. Poovey's account is almost entirely grounded in prescriptive literature, however, which often bears little relation to material practice; archival evidence suggests that women's role in early modern England's credit economy was considerably more complex, both in practice and in theory, than this narrative of exclusion suggests. Poovey, *History of the Modern Fact*, 62–63. See also Poovey, "Accommodating Merchants."

25. All references to the Sonnets are to William Shakespeare, *Shakespeare's Sonnets*, ed. Duncan-Jones. On the trope of usury in the Sonnets addressed to the young man, see

Mischo, "'That Use Is Not Forbidden Usury'"; Herman, "What's the Use?"; and Dolan, "Shylock in Love." David Hawkes's analysis of sodomy and usury in the Sonnets culminates in a reading of Sonnet 134; yet Hawkes downplays the agency and significance of the figure of the female creditor by suggesting that she is not so much a lender as a "borrower" (of the young man) who profits from the poet's "usurious transaction" (his lending of the young man to her) and is thus only "in effect though not in law or intention, a 'usurer'" ("Sodomy, Usury, and the Narrative of Shakespeare's Sonnets," 360).

26. The figure of the predatory usuress likewise appears in Shakespeare's *Venus and Adonis*, where Venus's embrace is figured as a "band" (ll. 225, 363) or bond that fetters Adonis, her unwilling object of desire. She promises that "one sweet kiss shall pay his comptless debt" (l. 84) but continues to up the ante, soon claiming that he owes her not one but a "thousand kisses" (l. 517) with the condition, "Say for nonpayment that the debt should double, / Is twenty hundred kisses such a trouble?" (ll. 521–22). When finally she overpowers him, she feeds "glutton-like" on his lips, we are told, "pitch[ing] the price so high / That she will draw his lips' rich treasure dry" (ll. 548, 51–52). When Adonis protests, "Fie, fie! . . . let me go! / You have no reason to withhold me so" (ll. 611–12), she persists in trying to persuade him with what he disparagingly calls her "over-handled theme" (l. 770) of usury, arguing, "Foul cank'ring rust the hidden treasure frets, / But gold that's put to use more gold begets" (ll. 767–68). Shakespeare, *The Riverside Shakespeare*.

27. Shakespeare, *The Merchant of Venice*, ed. Brown. All references to *Merchant*, unless otherwise specified, are to this edition. In two instances mentioned below, I have slightly emended quotations from the Arden edition where it departs from the Folio text. *The Merchant of Venice* looms large in the New Economic criticism; in one recent collection edited by Linda Woodbridge (*Money and the Age of Shakespeare*), no fewer than five of the essays focus on the play. See also Cohen, "*The Merchant of Venice* and the Possibilities of Historical Criticism."

28. Harry Berger Jr. views Portia as a practitioner of "negative usury," someone who deploys the rhetoric of liberality to install in others a sense of emotional obligation, "a burden of gratitude" ("Marriage and Mercifixion in *the Merchant of Venice*," 161). Lars Engle argues that Portia establishes "mastery of the systems of exchange in the play" and thereby succeeds in protecting her portion ("'Thrift Is Blessing,'" 37).

29. Emphasis added. Le Goff, *Your Money or Your Life*, 33. On the character of the male usurer, see Wright, "Some Conventions Regarding the Usurer in Elizabethan Literature." On Portia as gift-giver, see notes 88 and 111 below.

30. On female creditors in early modern England, see Swain, *Industry Before the Industrial Revolution*, 190–91; P. Earle, *Making of the English Middle Class*, 171; Jordan, *Women and Credit*; Lemire, "Introduction: Women, Credit and the Creation of Opportunity," 6–8; Fontaine, "Women's Economic Spheres and Credit in Pre-Industrial Europe," 28; and McIntosh, *Working Women in English Society*, 85–114. Women's role in the credit economy before the advent of modern banking in England can be traced to the Middle Ages, where manorial court litigation "reveals them as village money-lenders" (Hilton, *English Peasantry in the Later Middle Ages*, 103). On female creditors in medieval London, see Lacey, "Women and Work," 52.

31. Erickson, *Women and Property*, 68–78, 81. On changes to inheritance laws, see Jardine, *Still Harping on Daughters*, 85–86. See also Spicksley, "To Be or Not to Be Married," 92.

32. Spicksley maintains that an early seventeenth-century single woman could support herself "with a more than tolerable living standard" from the interest earned on a loan of £30 ("'Fly with a Duck,'" 206).

33. Froide, *Never Married*, 128–41; Holderness, "Credit in a Rural Community," 100–101. According to Froide, "In the disparate towns of Southampton, Bristol, Oxford, and York a consistent 42–45 percent of urban singlewomen engaged in moneylending during the early modern period." Single women loaned out as much as two-thirds of their estates. In 1601, for example, "Southampton appraisers valued Elizabeth Parkinson's property at a little over £274, of which £210 was in the form of outstanding loans" (*Never Married*, 130, 132).

34. For a general history of the 1571 statute, see N. Jones, *God and the Moneylenders*.

35. Spicksley, "To Be or Not to Be Married," 96, 91, 93. See also Spicksley, "Usury Legislation."

36. Clarkson, *Pre-Industrial Economy in England*, 148; Froide, *Never Married*, 28–30.

37. The wealthy heiress Joyce Jefferies, for example, who lived in the West Midlands in the early seventeenth century and never married, kept an account book covering the period 1638–49, which details a thriving, interest-bearing, moneylending operation that yielded several hundred pounds a year in income. Jefferies loaned money not only to relatives (who made up only 10 percent of her debtors) but to a broad cross-section of her community and beyond, including alehouse keepers, innkeepers, mercers, merchants, tailors, victuallers, vintners, and widows. While approximately 44 percent of her debtors came from within a four-mile radius of her home, close to 20 percent lived over fifteen miles away, some as far away as London. See Tittler, "Money-Lending in the West Midlands."

38. Froide, "Surplus Women with Surplus Money." See also Hill, *Women Alone*, 44.

39. Froide, *Never Married*, 134–45. This was true even of smaller loans. Thus, for example, "When Anne Codner of Abbotskerswell died in 1622, her probate inventory indicates there was due unto her by a bond from her brother Isacke Codner £20" (Cash, *Devon Inventories*, 29). Spicksley argues that during the seventeenth century, "The wills and inventories of single women reveal an increasing preoccupation with formal credit instruments, even on relatively small amounts" ("'Fly with a Duck,'" 195). For other examples of single women lending both small and large sums on bond, see Spicksley, "To Be or Not to Be Married,'" 86–87.

40. Stretton, *Women Waging Law*, 43, 99.

41. Holderness, "Widows in Pre-Industrial Society," 435. The widows' wills examined by Holderness contain "sheaves of promissory notes or bonds of debt owing to them at death" (430). Of the 170 probate inventories of widows who worked as moneylenders, 43.5 percent of their personal estates comprised debts owed to them (436, 440).

42. According to Vivien Brodsky, wealthier widows in London in particular worked "as rentiers and as the facilitators of urban credit," as manifested by the "bills of hand, bonds, and extra leases scattered throughout [their] wills" ("Widows in Late Elizabethan London," 144).

238   Notes to Pages 59–63

43. Holderness, "Widows in Pre-Industrial Society," 439.

44. Ibid., 439–40; Clarkson, *Pre-Industrial Economy in England*, 148; Swain, *Industry Before the Industrial Revolution*, 190–91; Jordan, *Women and Credit*, 68.

45. Cash, *Devon Inventories*, 42.

46. T. Wilson, *A Discourse Uppon Usurye*, fols. 15r–15v. Froide maintains that if we take into account that "female lenders left estates worth less than £10" and that female servants were also known to be moneylenders, it appears that "wealth was not a prerequisite" for women to loan money (*Never Married*, 130–31).

47. Honigmann and Brock, eds., *Playhouse Wills*, 118.

48. Ibid., 187–88.

49. Sisson, "Mr. and Mrs. Browne," 99; Fleay, *A Chronicle History of the London Stage*, 271.

50. Gurr, *The Shakespearean Stage*, 56.

51. Fleay, *A Chronicle History of the London Stage*, 275–76; Gurr, *The Shakespearean Stage*, 56.

52. Fleay, *A Chronicle History of the London Stage*, 278 For other examples of female moneylenders who were accused of charging higher than the legal rate of interest, see McIntosh, *Working Women in English Society*.

53. Honigmann and Brock, eds., *Playhouse Wills*, 125. Although the money Tooley owed may have been for arrears in rent (Tooley was living with Cuthbert and Elizabeth when he died), is it unclear why he would have owed the rent money to Elizabeth rather than her husband; as discussed below, "hostesses" and landladies were known to lend money, as well as extending other forms of credit, to their tenants.

54. See, e.g., H. Smith, *Examination of Usury*, 15; Pie, *Usuries Spright Conjured*, 35.

55. Froide, *Never Married*, 48, 71.

56. In the late seventeenth-century jest-biography *Wanton Tom; or, The Merry History of Tom Stitch the Taylor*, Tom's landlady/hostess is an "Old Rich Woman" whose "purse as well as her heart" were "at his Command." One day, while "Kissing and playing with her," he asks her "to lend him some money to set him up." Not having "the power to deny him," she loaned him "what money he desired." Meanwhile, Tom seduces all of the single women in the town, who bring him gifts and tokens of their affection. His hostess grows jealous of his many young female paramours and threatens to "turn him out of doors," and to arrest him for fifteen shillings he owes her. He quells her "with some sweet loving words, and was into favour again." He then tells her "(if she would lend him five pounds) he would Marry her" and give her a gold ring, "to which his old Landlady agreed." Tom meanwhile goes to his young paramours and promises each one individually that he will marry her, "But yet he requested one thing of every one, and that was, to lend him what Money they could." Each one obliges: "one lent him 5 pounds, some more, some less, according as they could." On the appointed wedding day, his old hostess "dress[es] her self to be marryed" and goes "to the place appointed," where she meets the other girls similarly gussied up and soon realizes her mistake. He, meanwhile, leaves under her pillow the following note: "Farewel old hostess, my smooth flat'ring tongue / Hath prov'd to old for you, tho' I'm but young. / You had me sure, you thought, & that this night / I should with licence grant you much delight.

/ You that oft times claim'd debts of me . . . / Could you so much a fool think me to be, / . . . / No, the case is far more just as it doth stand, / For you too oft had me at your command" (17–22). In Thomas Herbert's *Keep Within Compasse Dick and Robin*, Robin "went so much upon the score" with his hostess "that he could trusted be no more, / Wherefore he ranne out of the doore / Most swiftly" and "away to Sea." The "Hostesse when her guest was gone" moans, "O Robin thou art gone, . . . / And plaid the knave thou hast with me," and swears that "shee her purse would lend no more / To such as would runne on the score, / And cheat her" (6–7). For a hostess who is cheated out of her reckoning with a song, see Chamberlain, *A New Book of Mistakes*, 33–36. See also Peacham, *A Merry Discourse of Meum*, 11–14.

57. Shakespeare, *The Taming of the Shrew*, ed. Morris.
58. Shakespeare, *King Henry IV, Part 1*, ed. Humphreys.
59. Shakespeare, *King Henry IV, Part 2*, ed. Humphreys.
60. Stretton, *Women Waging Law*, 46, 50–51.
61. Marston, *The Plays of John Marston*, ed. Wood , 3:247–302, esp. 298–300.
62. For example, he records a loan of five shillings in March 1598/9 "unto the company for to spend at the Readynge of that boocke at the sonne [a tavern] in new fyshstreate" and a further five shillings "layd owt . . . for good cheare"; a loan of over four pounds in September 1601 "for the company . . . for ower metynge at the tavern when we did eatte ower vensone"; a loan of two shillings in May 1602 "for the companye when they Read the playe of Jeffa for wine at the tavern"; and a loan of nine shillings in August 1602 "for the company at the mermayd when we weare at owre a grement" (Foakes ed., *Henslowe's Diary*, fols. 45r, 93v, 105v, 115r).
63. "As for my lorde a penbrockes wch you desier to knowe wheare they be they are all at home and hauffe ben t⟨his⟩ v or sixe weeackes for they cane not save their carges [i.e. charges] ⟨w⟩th travell as I heare & weare fayne to pane [i.e. pawn] the⟨r⟩ parell for the carge." Foakes ed., *Henslowe's Diary*, appendix 1, article 14, 280.
64. This figure features prominently in several city comedies, in which male debtors marry wealthy usurers' daughters, thereby canceling their debts and gaining access to the usurer's wealth. In addition to Haughton's *Englishmen for My Money*, see also Heywood, *The Fair Maid of the Exchange*, ll. 2479–2506. As Lorna Hutson argues, the figure of the usurer's daughter functions to establish credit between men rather than as a creditor in her own right. See her *Usurer's Daughter*, 224–38.
65. I am grateful to Professor Kermode for providing me with this gloss in advance of the publication of his edition of the play. See Kermode, *Three Renaissance Usury Plays*.
66. See Fenton, *A Treatise of Usurie*, 115; Bolton, *Short and Private Discourse*, 50. Scriptural references to the protection of orphans, widows, and strangers include: Exod. 22:21–24, Deut. 10:18, 14:29, and Psalms 68:5, 94:6, 146:9. See also Jordan, *Women and Credit*, 69.
67. Fenton, *A Treatise of Usurie*, 100.
68. These popular arguments are rehearsed in order to be refuted in the following treatises: T. Wilson, *A Discourse Uppon Usurye*, 70; H. Smith, *Examination of Usury*, 27; Pie, *Usuries Spright Conjured*, 38–39; Fenton, *A Treatise of Usurie*, 41; Bolton, *Short and Private Discourse*, 51.

69. Fenton, *A Treatise of Usurie*, 110.

70. *Decay of Trade*, 3.

71. H. Smith, *Examination of Usury*, 23.

72. *The Bible and Holy Scriptures*, trans. de Beze, fol. 32r.

73. Fenton, *A Treatise of Usurie*, 41, 116. See also Bolton, *Short and Private Discourse*, 48–49.

74. Fenton, *A Treatise of Usurie*, 115. A similar argument is adduced in Caesar, *Damnable Sect of Usurers*, fol. 29.

75. "Christ is *Alpha* and *Omega* unto us, the *first* and the *last,* the *beginning* and the *end;* and shal the *alpha* of our nonage, and the *omega* of our dotage be dedicated unto usurie?" (Fenton, *A Treatise of Usurie*, 116).

76. Muscul[us], *Lawful and Unlawful Usurie*, sig. E2v. See also Fenton, *A Treatise of Usurie*, 110.

77. Caesar, *Damnable Sect of Usurers*, fol. 29 (sig. H1r). See also Fenton, *A Treatise of Usurie*, 115; Bolton, *Short and Private Discourse*, 49.

78. T. Wilson, *A Discourse Uppon Usurye*, fols. 70r–70v. "Ockre" derives from the Old English *wocor* or *wocer*, meaning "increase, offspring, usury," and is also related to the Dutch word for usury, *woeker* (*OED*, "ocker, *n.*" 1). See also T. Wilson, *A Discourse Uppon Usurye*, 87–88; Caesar, *Damnable Sect of Usurers*, fol. 29 (sig. H1r).

79. "If a yonge woman were a wydow, she should be occupied with some honest labor" (Muscul[us], *Lawful and Unlawful Usurie*, sig. E3v). "Let Widowes and Orphans, &c. Eyther imploy their goods in some honest trade, wherein they have as good cause to expect a blessing from God, as any other; or let them deale by partnership; or if other meanes faile, let annuities be bought for their lives, or Lands, or Rents purchased for ever; or let some other honest course be taken, which wise men can easily devise, if they list" (Blaxton, *The English Usurer*, 55).

80. Bell, *The Speculation of Usurie*, sig. G3v. "Usurie," we are told, "requireth more than *her* owne" and "rejoyceth to gather other mens goods to *her* selfe" (H. Smith, *Examination of Usury*, 9; emphasis added).

81. Fenton, *A Treatise of Usurie*, 117–18. In contrast to Mary Poovey's claim that women were invariably associated with risk in commercial discourse, in usury treatises they were often aligned with security, in contrast to the risk associated with male (ad)venture (*History of the Modern Fact*, 63).

82. "[I]f a composition be made, and that be demaunded by covenant," they argued, female creditors "pollute themselves with usurie" (Caesar, *Damnable Sect of Usurers*, fols. 29–29v).

83. Fenton, *A Treatise of Usurie*, 119.

84. Fenton's use of the term "sillie" (*A Treatise of Usurie*, 118) draws on several senses of the term, including "lacking in judgement," "weak or deficient in intellect," and perhaps "deserving of pity, compassion" (*OED*, "silly, *a., n., adv.*" 5a, 4, 1a).

85. The phrase is repeated several times in the text and italicized for emphasis. Fenton, *A Treatise of Usurie*, 118–19. See also Bolton, *Short and Private Discourse*, 49–51.

86. Fenton, *A Treatise of Usurie*, 119. Those "distinctions and interpretations which

seeme to qualifie the matter," he insists, "are but the comments of some few learned men, who differ from the rest, and among themselves; according to the variety of their severall apprehensions" (119–20).

87. Brathwaite, *The English Gentlewoman*, 54–55.

88. See, e.g., Levin, "A Garden in Belmont," 14; Sharp, "Gift Exchange," 252. Jyotsna Singh reads "Portia herself as the gift being offered" in marriage by her dead father in relation to feminist critical paradigms of the "traffic in women." She views this gift economy in more complex terms than have previous critics, arguing that Belmont's gift economy is "a mystification of the transactions of global capital and trade" and that the play "ultimately blurs all distinctions between gift-labors and commodity exchanges—and between Belmont and Venice" ("Gendered 'Gifts' in Shakespeare's Belmont," 149–50, 158). Keith Geary argues that in "asserting her claims as a wife Portia . . . ultimately proves herself the most adept businessman of them all" but does not pursue the cultural implications of this in any detail ("The Nature of Portia's Victory," 68). The only scholar to view Portia as a true creditor does so in extremely negative terms. Karoline Szatek views Belmont as a green world that has been "corrupted" or "tainted" by the commercial values of Venice and Portia's commercialism as exemplifying the "nascent corruption of capitalism." This reading has the unfortunate effect of aligning Portia's agency with moral corruption in a manner not unlike that of anti-usury treatises. Portia's commercial practices are lambasted as "the most offensive" in the play. Jessica is likewise excoriated for exhibiting "Belmont's shallowness and its Machiavellian, means-to-an-end, capitalistic compulsion to exploit significantly the less commercially savvy" and for doing so "out of spite." The play as a whole, Szatek maintains, indicts the "corruption, prejudice, fraudulence, usury, treachery, infidelity, religious mockery, and disregard for human rights" that characterized "Early Modern capitalism" ("*The Merchant of Venice* and the Politics of Commerce," 332–33, 337, 345, 347–49).

89. According to the common law of coverture a wife could not own property in her own name, sue or be sued, or make contracts on her own behalf, and her husband took possession of whatever property was hers prior to her marriage. Under common law, men who were fortunate enough to marry wealthy heiresses or widows would therefore have had access to free capital with which to pay off their debts, purchase lands, start a business, etc. For such men, wives' portions often "constitute[d] the most important infusion of capital they would ever receive" (Hunt, *The Middling Sort*, 152).

90. P. Earle, *Making of the English Middle Class*, 159.

91. Erickson, *Women and Property*, 103–13. Trusts for separate estate were upheld by the Court of Chancery starting in Elizabeth's reign; by the 1630s, one authority stated that it was "no uncommon thing for a wife to have separate property, independent of her husband." Quoted in P. Earle, *Making of the English Middle Class*, 159. See also Cioni, "Elizabethan Chancery."

92. Hunt, *The Middling Sort*, 158. See also Cioni, "Elizabethan Chancery,"161; Prior, "Wives and Wills," 220.

93. Hunt, *The Middling Sort*, 158; Muldrew, *Economy of Obligation*, 97.

94. Erickson, *Women and Property*, 137. Ordinary women were known to mark the

goods they brought into marriage so that they could reclaim them in widowhood (137–38). As Fenton maintains in his *Treatise of Usurie*, "A gift is for ever: [a] loane is only for a time"; during this time, it is the borrower's "to doe withal what he list; only at the time appointed that he returne the like againe" (16).

95. Hunt, *The Middling Sort*, 160.

96. Ibid., 161.

97. Ibid., 158–59.

98. Actor Thomas Downton indicates in his will that his second wife, who was a widow when they married, set aside a separate estate before their marriage, as he refers to property that he "possessed for hir & to her use," and states that he has "not Altered Any Estate of hers since my marriadge to her" (Honigmann and Brock, eds., *Playhouse Wills*, 147). See also the abstract of the will of John Astley, Master of Revels from 1622 to 1640, which instructs his wife to "pay to Bridgett Cherson alias Wainwright during her life £4 per quarter after his decease so that she 'may have the whole benefitt thereof to her selfe with out her husband or any other inter medling with the same'" (199). Agnes Woodward may also have set aside separate property when she married Philip Henslowe. The youngest of four sons, Henslowe appears to have owed his initial investment capital for his business and theatrical ventures largely to his provident marriage to Agnes, who was his former master's widow. According to Susan Cerasano, Agnes was "better than a full generation" older than Henslowe (Greg, *Henslowe's Diary*, 2:4; Cerasano, "Henslowe's Biography," 71). His son-in-law, Edward Alleyn, maintained that at the start of Henslowe's career he was "of small means or abillitie," and through his marriage to Agnes had "gained all or the most parte of her estate to a greate value" (Public Record Office, STAC 8/168/18, cited in Cerasano, "Henslowe's Biography," 71). A clue as to what Alleyn may have meant by "all or the most parte of her estate" appears in the 1591 will of Henslowe's brother John, which bequeaths to Agnes "all suche bondes somm or somms of moneie, leases goodes that I have at London within / her house" (ibid., 68). According to Cerasano, the bequest suggests that "Henslowe's residence was his wife's property, inherited from her former marriage." She further notes that Philip was "the sole member of John's immediate family who received nothing in his will" (68). We can only speculate as to whether Agnes set aside other assets to her own separate use. If so, the entries in Henslowe's "diary" recording Agnes lending money to actors, as well as to friends, family, and other employees of Henslowe's, may point to loans of her own assets; if not, the entries nonetheless demonstrate Agnes's active interest and participation in the business ventures her husband had established using her capital. Foakes ed., *Henslowe's Diary*, fol. 28r; see also fols. 28v, 38v, 42v, 124r.

99. Honigmann and Brock, eds., *Playhouse Wills*, 181. On Susan Greene (a.k.a. Browne and Baskerville) and her relationship to the playhouses and playing companies, see Fleay, *A Chronicle History of the London Stage*, 270–97; Sisson, "Mr. and Mrs. Browne"; and Sisson, "The Importunate Widow."

100. Deposition of Thomas Basse, cited in Sisson, "The Importunate Widow," 65.

101. For other theater women who established such trusts, see Honigmann and Brock eds., *Playhouse Wills*, 70, 143, 188, 193, 202.

102. Such a shift in focus toward the woman with the moneybags is hardly against

the grain of the play itself, which accords Portia 578 lines, as compared with Shylock's 361, Bassanio's 339, and Antonio's mere 188.

103. Muldrew, "'Hard Food for Midas,'" 94, 96. Muldrew estimates that at the end of the sixteenth century, there was "only about £1 15s. in circulation for every household in the country" 88).

104. Such ingenuity may be what Thomas Edgar had in mind in *The Lawes Resolutions of Womens Rights*, when he claims that although women "make no Lawes, they consent to none, they abrogate none," yet "some women can shift it well enough" (6). More recently, Amy Erickson has suggested that the "complex legal maneuvers" adopted by women seeking to ameliorate the effects of coverture, which entailed the use of complex financial and legal instruments such as bonds, contracts, settlements, and trusts, "stimulated financial awareness throughout the population and significantly contributed to the creation of the instruments to move capital" and thereby to the rise of capitalism in England ("Coverture and Capitalism," 3, 8).

105. Jardine, *Still Harping on Daughters*, 60–61. See also Sharp, "Gift Exchange," 254; Oldrieve, "Marginalized Voices," 88.

106. Lisa Jardine argues that Portia "does not commit her 'gentle spirit' to Bassanio's direction (she continues to act with authority, and without his knowledge or permission); and as her accounting imagery reminds us, she retains full control of her financial affairs (even the servants continue to answer to her)" ("Cultural Confusion and Shakespeare's Learned Heroines," 17).

107. I have slightly emended the Arden text here, which renders the Folio's "yours, my Lord" as "yours,—my Lord's!" I also emend the Arden's punctuation of line 169, which ends in a period, and use a comma, as in the Folio.

108. According to the *OED*, "bond" was a phonetic variant of "band" and was "used interchangeably with it in early senses" until the usage of "band" to mean "A moral, spiritual, or legal bond of restraint or union" became obsolete sometime in the nineteenth century, to be replaced by "bond" (*OED*, "bond," *n*.1, etymology; and "band," *n*.1, etymology and branch II, especially definitions 8–11). Shakespeare uses the term "band" to designate both the wedding bond (*Much Ado*, 3.1.114; *As You Like It*, 5.4.129; *3 Henry VI*, 3.3.243; *Hamlet*, 3.2.160) and the bond of credit (*Richard II*, 5.3.65; *1 Henry IV*, 3.2.157; *Comedy of Errors*, 4.2.49–50). Shakespeare, *The Riverside Shakespeare*.

109. In Carol Leventen's words, "Portia doesn't say, despite her 'everything I have is yours' avowal, 'hey, lighten up; just write a cheque; it's a joint account now'; she says, in effect '*I* will write that cheque'" ("Patrimony and Patriarchy," 72). Lars Engle argues that Portia "wisely chooses to follow [Bassanio to Venice] to protect her investment" and that her interventions in the trial scene serve to protect her "endowment from threats" ("'Thrift Is Blessing,'" 34, 36).

110. Karen Newman suggests that we read Portia's "vantage" in structuralist-anthropological terms, as arising from a gift of "more than can be reciprocated," a gift that "short-circuits the system of exchange and the male bonds it creates" ("Portia's Ring," 25–26).

111. This reading has certainly predominated within the critical tradition. E. C. Pettet, for example, argues, "Nothing could be more sharply in contrast with the inhuman self-

interest of Shylock than [Portia's] instinctive, almost blind sense of friendship, [and] self-sacrifice" ("*The Merchant of Venice* and the Problem of Usury," 29). Nancy Elizabeth Hodge similarly asserts that the play contrasts Portia's liberal attitude toward her wealth with Antonio's "carefully calculated shipping" and "the embarrassing excrescence accompanying a usurer's sharp practices," and that her liberality has "no uncomfortable conditionals" ("Making Places at Belmont," 166). Other recent criticism, noting the resemblances between Portia and Shylock, view them as similarly oppressed or marginalized. See, e.g., Oldrieve, "Marginalized Voices," 87. One critic views them as similarly oppressive, if not bloodthirsty, asserting that Portia, like Shylock, will have her pound of flesh insofar as "she cuts Bassanio out of Antonio's heart" (Geary, "The Nature of Portia's Victory," 66).

112. Early modern treatises on arithmetic were commercial in orientation, framing mathematical problems in relation to practical issues of buying and selling, calculating interest rates, converting foreign currencies, and so forth. John Mellis's augmented 1582 edition of Robert Record's popular treatise on arithmetic (*The Grounde of Artes*), for example, instructs readers on the calculation of "forbearance" or interest on loans or goods bought on credit. See also K. Thomas, "Numeracy in Early Modern England," 107. The first known English treatise on double-entry bookkeeping, no longer extant, was Hugh Oldcastle's *A Profitable Treatyce called the Instrument or Boke to Learne to Knowe the Good Order of the Kepyng of the Famouse Reconynge called . . . in Englyshe, Debitor and Creditor*, published in 1543, which was republished in augmented form in 1588. See also Peele, *How to Keep a Perfecte Reconyng* and *The Pathe Waye to Perfectnes*; Weddington, *A Brief Instruction*. For an excellent survey of early treatises on accounting, see Yamey, Edey, and Thomson, eds., *Accounting in England and Scotland*.

113. According to Aristotle's *Metaphysics*, "unity is not a number" (1088a7–8); "to be one is to be indivisible . . . a unity is the principle of number" (1052b15–24). My argument here is indebted to Ostashevsky, "Crooked Figures," 206, 209.

114. On the figure of the cipher in early modern English drama, see S. Fisher, *Econolingua*, 55; Parker, "Temporal Gestation," 37–38; Parker, "Sound Government, Polymorphic Bears," 182–83; and Parker, "Cassio, Cash, and the 'Infidel O.'"

115. Ciphers and ciphering were adopted only slowly and unevenly in England beginning in the mid-sixteenth century, not fully replacing Roman numerals until the late seventeenth or early eighteenth century. K. Thomas, "Numeracy in Early Modern England"; Rotman, *Signifying Nothing*, 7–14; Jaffe, *The Story of O*, 25–81.

116. The new skills of ciphering were not easily acquired: prior to 1660, few grammar schools taught arithmetic, which had to be learned through trade, by private tutoring, or in special ciphering schools. Ciphering was thus viewed with a mixture of fascination and suspicion, and the term "cipher" was frequently associated with concealment, obscurity, and the occult. Many Elizabethan merchants and tradesmen still depended on table books or "ready reckoners which poured out in profusion" and allowed them "to look up rates of simple or compound interest or to work out the price of some commodity." K. Thomas, "Numeracy in Early Modern England," 117; see also 109–10, 120–22.

117. Shakespeare uses it in this sense several times, as in act 1, scene 2 of *The Winter's Tale*, where Polixenes, at the end of his stay in Sicilia, invokes the cipher to express his sense

of indebtedness to Leontes, his inability to thank him enough, when he compares himself to a "cipher" who will "multiply / With one 'We thank you' many thousands moe / That go before it" (6–9). In the Prologue to *Henry V*, the actors are famously figured as "ciphers to this great accompt," who "Attest in little place a million" (16–17) and in so doing are able to fill up or "cram" (12) the feminized, "wooden O" (13) of the stage.

118. E.g., see *Merchant of Venice*, ed. Brown, 3.2.158n, and *Riverside Shakespeare*, 3.2.158.

119. Keith Thomas maintains that by the late sixteenth century these new techniques of (ac)counting began to be embraced not only by merchants but also by members of the gentry and aristocracy such as Portia; thus, we need not view Portia's exactitude as out of keeping with her social status ("Numeracy in Early Modern England," 106).

120. Accounting treatises maintained, for example, that the "negligent kepyng of reconynges" caused "great shame" and "trouble in mynde," "disquietnes of body" (including "fevers & deseases"), as well as "great discencion" and "striefe in lawe" between "frendes or neighbour." To avoid these "discomodities," readers were urged to be "desirous & studious" in learning the new methods, rather than dismissing them as "painfull" and not worth the effort. Christoffels, *How to Kepe a Boke of Acco[m]ptes or Reconynges*, cited in Yamey, Edey, and Thomson eds., *Accounting in England and Scotland*, 6–7. See also Peele, *How to Keep a Perfecte Reconyng*, sig. A5r.

121. Cited in Yamey, Edey, and Thomson, eds., *Accounting in England and Scotland*, 49.

122. Record, *The Ground of Artes*, fol. 3v. See also Peele, *How to Keep a Perfecte Reconyng*, sig. A3r. The juridical value of exactitude had earlier been emphasized in Italian treatises on double-entry bookkeeping; see Aho, "Rhetoric and Double-Entry Bookkeeping," 25.

123. Although numeracy, according to Keith Thomas, was most likely "relatively restricted" among ordinary women, many English women kept account books, and "the daughters of well-to-do families sometimes learned mathematics to great effect" ("Numeracy in Early Modern England," 113).

124. On the trial scene as a contest between the Old Law and the New, see Lewalski, "Biblical Allusion and Allegory in *The Merchant of Venice*"; Roston, *Tradition and Subversion in Renaissance Literature*, 12. On the trial scene as a contest between common law and equity, see, e.g., Spinosa, "Shylock and Debt and Contract in *The Merchant of Venice*."

125. Levin, "A Garden in Belmont," 16. See also Bilello, "Accomplished with What She Lacks," 117; Shakespeare, *The Merchant of Venice*, ed. Furness, 221.

126. Oldcastle, *A Brief Instruction and Manner*, sig. A3r.

127. Weddington, *A Brief Instruction*, cited in Yamey, Edey, and Thomson, eds., *Accounting in England and Scotland*, 48. See also Aho, "Rhetoric and Double-Entry Bookkeeping," 28–29; D. Murray, *History of Bookkeeping*, 205; Nobes, *The Development of Double Entry*, 109; and Sullivan, *The Rhetoric of Credit*, 40, 155. On the problem of (in)fidelity in accounting, see Parker, "Cassio, Cash, and the 'Infidel O.'"

128. "Without exception, Renaissance ledgers open with the following *exordium*: *a nome di dio Guadagnio* (in the name of God and Profit)" (Aho, *Confession and Bookkeeping*, 67).

129. Aho, "Rhetoric and Double-Entry Bookkeeping," 34.

130. Record, *Grounde of Arte . . . Augmented . . . by John Mellis*, sigs. A3v, B3v; see also A6v. On Pythagoreanism in Renaissance thought and poetics, see Heninger, *Touches of Sweet Harmony*.

131. Christoffels, *How to Kepe a Boke of Acco[m]ptes or Reconynges*, cited in Yamey, Edey, and Thomson, eds., *Accounting in England and Scotland*, 126.

132. Brown and Johnston, *Paciolo on Accounting*, 40. See also Aho, "Rhetoric and Double-Entry Bookkeeping," 25.

133. D. Smith, *History of Mathematics*, 188. Palsgrave's 1530 French-English dictionary contains the following entry: "I shall reken it syxe tymes by aulgorisme or you can caste it ones by counters / *Je enchifreray six foys avant que vous le puissiez compter une foys par jectons*" (*Leclarcissement De La Langue Francoyse*, sig. 336v). Pacioli maintained that a merchant must be a "good reckoner and a quick calculator [*buon ragioneri e prompto computista*]" (*Exposition of Double Entry Bookkeeping*, 41).

134. "Fractions or Broken numbers, as they used to be called, presented great difficulty in Roman computation. . . . According to the views of the ancient philosophers, unity, that is absolute or numerical unity, was the principle and element of number, but was in itself indivisible; division could not proceed beyond this point" (Murray, *History of Bookkeeping*, 387).

135. Agrippa, *Three Books of Occult Philosophy*, 174.

136. On Shylock's "inscrutable calculus of hatred" and the problem of excess in the play more generally, see Spencer, "Taking Excess, Exceeding Account," 147.

137. The dangers arising from an obdurate inexactitude in the keeping of accounts likewise appear in *Timon of Athens*, where Timon refuses to heed his Steward's repeated warnings that his credit is cracked. "At many times I brought in my accompts," the Steward says, "Laid them before you; you would throw them off, / And say you found them in mine honesty" (2.2.133–35). Although the Steward is indeed honest and values the keeping of precise accounts, his master willfully refuses to look at them. Contemporary accounting treatises defined the ledger as a mirror or "glasse of a mannes state, wherein all men maie se clerely in what case thei stande." They further emphasized the importance of masters learning the new techniques themselves rather than having to rely on their servants. *Timon* explores the "discomodities" arising from a master's lack of interest in his own accounts and, in Timon's case, from excessive liberality rather than covetousness (Shakespeare, *The Riverside Shakespeare*). See also Christoffels, *How to Kepe a Boke of Acco[m]ptes or Reconynges*, cited in Yamey, Edey, and Thomson, eds., *Accounting in England and Scotland*, 7.

138. On the rhetorical relationship between interrogatory questions and accurate accounts, see Aho, 'Rhetoric and Double-Entry Bookkeeping," 26.

139. On the interpretation of the doctrine of due benevolence or the "marital debt" and the penance for failure to comply, see Tentler, *Sin and Confession on the Eve of the Reformation*, 170–74, esp. 173.

140. "*Paul* saith, *Let the Husband give unto the Wife due benevolence*: here is a commandement to yeeld this duetie: that which is commanded, is lawfull; and not to do it, is a breach of the commandement" (H. Smith, *A Preparative to Mariage*, 18). Dudley Fenner, for example, defines due benevolence as "the honorable possession of their vessels in holines

one towards another, for avoyding of sinne, bringing forth a seede of God, and the honest and proper delight which ought to be betweene the man and the wife" (*The Artes of Logike and Rethorike*, sig. B3v).

141. Gouge, *Of Domesticall Duties*, 221–23.

142. Ibid.

143. The term "willing loan" likewise evokes a common argument rehearsed (and rebutted) in treatises on usury, which maintained that if neither the lender nor the borrower "hath harme but both receive benefites," then "there is none offence committed, but rather great goodnes used" (T. Wilson, *A Discourse Uppon Usurye*, fol. 45v).

144. Jill Phillips Ingram maintains that Portia "shifts the balance of obligation in her favor" in "controlling, to her advantage, the credit of all economic agents by the play's end" (*Idioms of Self-Interest*, 99).

145. When Portia returns to Belmont at the end of the play, Lars Engle observes, she refers to the domicile as her own: "I have not yet / Enter'd *my* house" she says (5.1.272–72, emphasis added; "'Thrift Is Blessing,'" 37). See also Newman, "Portia's Ring," 32.

146. Allegories of vanity frequently draw on the visual iconography of smoke and bubbles as emblems of the transience of wealth or beauty. See Rogers, ed., *Coin and Conscience*.

147. For reproductions of these paintings, and a discussion of their iconographic significance, see Cust, "The Misers at Windsor Castle," 252–58.

148. Wheelock Jr., *Vermeer and the Art of Painting*, 99–100.

149. Alpers, "Describe or Narrate?," 26.

150. Pearls, for example, are a symbol of both purity/salvation and pride/riches, and the woman's apparent pregnancy may be read as a reference to the immaculate birth or the excess of the usuress. See Wheelock Jr., *Dutch Paintings of the Seventeenth Century*, 374; Cunnar, "The Viewer's Share"; and Gaskell, "Vermeer, Judgment and Truth."

151. Although there is no stage direction indicating whether Portia holds the scales in her hands while she gives her verdict in the trial scene as an emblem of just reckoning, it seems likely that Shylock hands them to her earlier when she asks, "—are there balance here to weigh / The flesh?" (4.1.251–52) and he replies, "I have them ready" (l. 252). Whether or not Portia holds the scales or merely exerts her authority over them, however, her verdict transforms them into a symbol of justice and (or *as*) precision.

CHAPTER 3

1. For a concise account of the impact of these religious conflicts on immigration to England, see Luu, *Immigrants and the Industries of London*, 104–9.

2. Moryson, *Itinerary*, 97.

3. Davis, *Society and Culture in Early Modern France*, 124–51.

4. According to Simon Schama, it was not uncommon for Dutch women to "handle business and money affairs," as they were legally empowered to "make commercial contracts and notarized documents and so had all the formal qualifications needed for active commercial or business dealing, an opportunity of which many availed themselves"

(*Embarrassment of Riches*, 407). On Netherlandish women's active role in commerce, see also Ogilvie, *A Bitter Living*, 344–45.

5. Schama discusses similar satires of Dutch women by Dutch writers in *Embarrassment of Riches*, 445–53.

6. Grimeston's history (*A Generall Historie of the Netherlands*, sig. B6r) is largely a translation of François Le Petit's *La Grande Chronique* with additions from Emmanuel Van Meteren's *Historica Belgica*.

7. Ibid., 496.

8. Ibid., 1193.

9. See Franits, *Paragons of Virtue*, 76–110.

10. Both images were reinforced during the seventeenth century by Dutch genre paintings and prints depicting brothel scenes or scenes of virtuous froes engaged in domestic chores, such as sewing, cooking, cleaning, and other commercial activities. See Franits, *Paragons of Virtue*; Schama, "Wives and Wantons."

11. Marx, *Capital*, 114.

12. Ibid., 138.

13. "Commodities," Marx writes, "are simply congealed quantities of human labor.... Human labor-power in its fluid state, or human labor, creates value, but is not itself value. It becomes value in its coagulated state in objective form. The value of the linen as a congealed mass of human labor can be expressed only as an 'objectivity' [*Gegenständlichkeit*], a thing which is materially different from the linen itself and yet common to the linen" (*Capital*, 141–42; see also 130).

14. Arnold, Tiramani, and Levey, *Patterns of Fashion 4*, 10–11, 27; Vincent, *Dressing the Elite*, 32. According to Joan Thirsk, starch making "was laborious work, requiring time and care ... a roomy shed or workhouse, many tubs and barrels, and plenty of water. Bran was steeped in water with rock alum ... for 10 to 14 days, then rinsed through three different tubs, finishing with a rinsing in clear pump water. The resulting fine washed flour then stood in its own water for about a week, more pump water was added, and the smallest bran that settled at the bottom was strained off. The tubs were left for another day, the water was then drawn off entirely, the starch left to dry for two more days, rinsed lightly with more pump water, then cut out of the tubs in great pieces with sharp trowels. It was packed into troughs with holes in the bottom, through which the remaining water drained; it was laid on cold bricks to dry for two days and then on a baker's oven ... where it dried for another few days.... The whole process took over a month to complete." Starching was usually done in outbuildings because of its "unpleasant smell" and fire hazard (*Economic Policy and Projects*, 84–85, 921). Philip Stubbes may be describing the smell produced by seething starch when he facetiously calls starch-houses "farting houses" (*The Second Part of the Anatomie of Abuses*, sig. F2r). He describes the process of starching ruffs as follows: "least they should fall down, they are smeared and starched in the devils liquore, I meane *Starch*: after that dryed with great diligence, streaked, patted and rubbed very nicely." They are then "pleted and creted ful curiously" with iron rods and pins, and "last of all, they are either clogged w^t golde, silver, or silk lace of stately price, wrought all over with needle woork, speckled and sparkled heer & there with the sonne, the moone, the starres and many other antiquities

straunge to beholde. Some are wrought with open woork down to the midst of the ruffe and further, some with purled lace so cloyd and other gewgawes so pestred, as the ruffe is the least parte of it self" (*The Anatomy of Abuses*, sigs. F4v–F5r). On English women's work in the manufacture of linen cloth, made from flax, beginning in the sixteenth century, see McIntosh, *Working Women in English Society*, 221–23.

15. Vincent, *Dressing the Elite*, 33.

16. Arnold, Tiramani, and Levey, *Patterns of Fashion 4*, 15; Vincent, *Dressing the Elite*, 33. Stubbes chides: "if *Aeolus* with his blasts, or *Neptune* with his stormes, chaunce to hit uppon the crasie bark of their brused ruffes, then they goe flip flap in the winde like rags flying abroad, and lye upon their shoulders like the dishcloute of a slutte" (*The Anatomy of Abuses*, sig. D7v).

17. Jones and Stallybrass, *Renaissance Clothing*, 2–3.

18. Ibid., 134.

19. Ibid.

20. Ibid., 103, 110, 133, 111.

21. Ibid., 125–33.

22. "Yellow Starch: Fabrications of the Jacobean Court," in ibid., 59–85.

23. Marx, *Writings*, 400.

24. Luu estimates the peak immigrant population at 12.5 percent (*Immigrants and the Industries of London*, 99). Pettegree gives a lower figure of 8 percent (*Foreign Protestant Communities*, 17–18). The location of the Dutch church at Austin Friars and of the French church in Threadneedle Street likewise gave the immigrants greater visibility within the City walls and thus may also have contributed to contemporary rumors of their vast numbers, which were thought to be roughly ten times what they actually were.

25. On the higher concentrations of immigrants in these suburbs and liberties, see Luu, "Assimilation or Segregation," 164; Luu, *Immigrants and the Industries of London*, 125–26, 194–95; J. Murray, *Flanders and England*, 27, 30, 34–35; and Littleton, "Social Interactions of Aliens," 152. Luu argues that the population of aliens in the suburbs and liberties rose during the late sixteenth century, in response to attempts by the guilds to restrict their labor ("Natural Born Versus Stranger-Born Subjects," 70). For graphs indicating the precise numbers of aliens in each ward, see Yungblut, *Strangers Settled Here*, 26–28. On the locations of the commercial theaters, see Gurr, *The Shakespearean Stage*, 47.

26. In 1567, those identified as "Dutch" made up 74.5 percent of the immigrant population in London and Westminster. Yungblut, *Strangers Settled Here*, 14.

27. According to Luu, the "strangers were concentrated overwhelmingly in the clothing industry" (*Immigrants and the Industries of London*, 119–20). See also Peck, *Consuming Splendor*, esp. chap. 2; J. Murray, *Flanders and England*, 149–75; and Goose, "Immigrants and English Economic Development," 138–44.

28. Plummer, *London Weavers' Company*, 16.

29. Scoville, "The Huguenots and the Diffusion of Technology," 301–3. See also Luu, *Immigrants and the Industries of London*, esp. chap. 6.

30. Luu, *Immigrants and the Industries of London*, 115; J. Murray, *Flanders and England*, 152.

31. Chitty, "Aliens in England in the Sixteenth Century," 131, 133; Holderness, "New Draperies in England," 217.

32. Esser, "Immigrant Cultures in Tudor and Stuart England," 163. On the theaters' dependence on the clothing market, see Jones and Stallybrass, *Renaissance Clothing*.

33. Strype, *A Survey of the Cities of London and Westminster*, 2:5:300, 303. On the "dichotomy of attitudes" of the native population toward foreigners, see Yungblut, *Strangers Settled Here*, 44–46.

34. Pettegree, *Foreign Protestant Communities*, 3. On "projects" involving immigrants, see Thirsk, *Economic Policy and Projects*, 43–47; Luu, *Immigrants and the Industries of London*, esp. chap. 3.

35. Some important recent studies of aliens in early modern English drama include the following: Kastan, "Workshop and/as Playhouse"; Hoenselaars, *Images of Englishmen and Foreigners*; Schrickx, "Elizabethan Drama and Anglo-Dutch Relations"; Arab, "Work, Bodies and Gender in *The Shoemaker's Holiday*"; E. Smith, "'So Much English by the Mother'"; J. Archer, *Citizen Shakespeare*; Hoenselaars and Klein, *Shakespeare and the Low Countries*; J. Howard, *Theater of a City*; and Kermode, *Aliens and Englishness in Elizabethan Drama*. On recent reappraisals of the purported "xenophobia" of the English, see Goose, "'Xenophobia' in Elizabethan and Early Stuart England."

36. Hoenselaars argues that Tudor interludes and morality plays, written during the early influx of refugees, tended to emphasize the economic threat they were thought to pose and to identify that threat with various forms of vice (sloth, drunkenness, dissimulation, fraud, sharp dealing, etc.), as in the anonymous Tudor interlude *An Enterlude of Welth, and Health* (1565), in which the unemployed Flemish drunkard Hance Berepot is told by Good Remedy: "fie on you aliaunts al I say ye can wt craft & subtelti get englishmens welth away." By constrast, Hoenselaars argues, in the citizen and city comedies of the late 1590s and 1600s, when the immigrant population had diminished somewhat and those who remained had reached a more "advanced stage of integration," alien characters are "often presented as free from such vices and deliberately so, in order to sharpen the satire of English characters" (sig. D1v, cited in Hoenselaars, *Images of Englishmen and Foreigners*, 41; see also ibid., 43–48, 109, 111, and Feldman, "Dutch Exiles and Elizabethan Playwrights"). On debates concerning the theory of progressive integration, see Luu, *Immigrants and the Industries of London*, 142.

37. This calculation is based on the total numbers of adult householders and non-householders listed in the alien Returns for that year. Luu, *Immigrants and the Industries of London*, 132.

38. Ibid., 97; Goose, "Introduction: Immigrants in Tudor and Early Stuart England," 16. Yungblut argues that the aldermen suspected "that the aliens were not being entirely truthful in reporting to the authorities, sometimes using language difficulties as a means to escape giving the desired information" (*Strangers Settled Here*, 24).

39. Kirk and Kirk, *Returns of Aliens*, part 1, 388–89.

40. The Flemish invention of button loops changed buttons from decorations to fasteners and resulted in a boom in the button business. See J. Murray, *Flanders and England*, 162.

41. Early modern trade manuals for silk workers stated the advantages of women's

nimble fingers in these processes "because of the delicate nature of the work" (Lacey, "'Narrow Ware,'" 187). Silkwomen's occupations listed in the Returns include "silkwynder," "silk throwster," "sylkworkinge," "maker of silkefringe," and "silk lace worker."

42. See Kirk and Kirk, *Returns of Aliens*, part 1, 424, 426–27, 429, part 2, 13, 15, 18, 25, 30, 33, 50, 53, 60, 66, 119–20, 129, 261–65, 269, 275, 285, 315, 326, 355, and part 3, 224, 229, 339, 345–46, 350, 381, 385; Scouloudi, *Returns of Strangers*, 139, 147, 155, 157, 158, 161–63, 165–68, 170, 172, 174, 176, 179, 180–81, 184–85, 187–91, 200–202, 204, 206, 208–9, 211, 213–14, 217. Other widows worked in non-textile-related occupations including "joiner," "surgeon," "cutler," "chaundler," "tablekeeper," "baker," "seller of Rennish wyne," "Juweller," "shoemakinge," "berebruer," "brushmaker," "stiller," "goldsmith," "midwife," "victualler," "stone carver," and "leather dresser." See Kirk and Kirk, *Returns of Aliens*, part 2, 294, 296, 298, 302, 305, 314, 326, 369, and part 3, 337, 397; Scouloudi, *Returns of Strangers*, 148, 151, 153, 159, 172, 187, 196, 202, 206–7, 213, 216, 220.

43. Schama, *Embarrassment of Riches*, 404–5.

44. See Kirk and Kirk, *Returns of Aliens*, part 1, 431–32, 443, 451, 455, and part 2, 263; Scouloudi, *Returns of Strangers*, 195, 199–200.

45. See Scouloudi, *Returns of Strangers*, 82, 170, 178, 181–82, 184, 197, 199–200, 208, 213, 219. A Frenchman named Jean Rosineall is also known to have had a gold and silver "wyre-drawing" workshop in London in 1596, in which he apprenticed English girls to learn the art of making fine gold and silver thread (Stewart, *History of . . . Gold and Silver Wyre-Drawers*, 22). According to the 1593 Returns, aliens were by then employing almost three times as many English workers as immigrant workers, although they still favored immigrant workers for the more skilled jobs, and the numbers of English workers may have been exaggerated in an effort to ward off criticism about their failure to share trade secrets. Littleton, "Social Interactions of Aliens," 152–53.

46. Kirk and Kirk, *Returns of Aliens*, part 1, 448, and part 2, 6.

47. E.g., "makinge parchment lace," "twysters of sylke," "spynninge and the nedle," "silkweavers," "buing and selling of cruell lace and frindge for garmentes," "botchers," "silkewinders," "silkeworkers," "makinge of sackclothe," and "make knitt lace" (Kirk and Kirk, *Returns of Aliens*, part 2, 20, 25, 40, 52, 260–61, 286, and part 3, 330, 350, 361, 412–13, 424).

48. Kirk and Kirk, *Returns of Aliens*, part 3, 219–20.

49. Lapham, for example, mentions Edie de Man, the wife of a Southwark tailor, who is listed as a Dutch baker ("Industrial Status of Women," 584).

50. Scouloudi, *Returns of Strangers*, 82, 179, 200. It appears that this was the case elsewhere in England as well: complaints of the "Inglish against the Dutch strangers" in Colchester during James I's reign includes one against "Josias Snace, a Bay and Say maker," whose "wife selleth blacke, broune, and white threadd, all sortes of bone lace, valure gardes, and other commodities which they receive out of Holland" (Cooper, *Lists of Foreign Protestants*, 26).

51. Kirk and Kirk, *Returns of Aliens*, part 2, 268–69. "Bonelace" was invented in the Low Countries; thus, it is likely that Anne imported her skills rather than learning them from her husband. On bonelace, see J. Murray, *Flanders and England*, 162.

52. Stow, *Annales*, 867. On the importation of skills, see Schilling, "Innovation

Through Migration"; Pettegree, *Foreign Protestant Communities*, 2; and Luu, *Immigrants and the Industries of London*, 90.

53. Stow, *Annales*, 868.

54. Ibid., 869. As these fees suggest, washing, starching, and ironing linens became a "highly skilled, highly paid occupation" during the period, as I discuss at greater length below. Arnold, Tiramani, and Levey, *Patterns of Fashion 4*, 14.

55. It is worth noting that the painting of these intricate ruffs in miniature was itself a highly skilled and labor-intensive technique, one that Hilliard may have learned from the famed Flemish miniaturist Levina Teerlinc at the Tudor court. In his *Arte of Limning* Hilliard credits women painters with devising "an excellent white" pigment "made of quicksilver" that allowed one to draw the "very fine line" required to render ruffs in miniature. Edmond, "Hilliard, Nicholas"; Strong, "Teerlinc, Levina" (see http://www.oxforddnb.com/view/article/13320 and http://www.oxforddnb.com/view/article/38054, ed. Lawrence Goldman, January 2008 [accessed March 7, 2009]).

56. Philip Stubbes complains of these "monsterous ruffes" that "stand a full quarter of a yarde (and more) from their necks," in many layers, "one beneath another," and of the "supportasse or underpropper" that "beare[s] up the whole frame & body of the ruffe, from falling and hanging down." When they became so large in circumference that even the underpropper could not keep them from falling, he claims, "they [we]re pinned up to their eares" (*The Anatomy of Abuses*, sigs. D7v, F4v–F5r). In the second part of his treatise, he again complains that people "use them bigger than ever they did" (*The Second Part of the Anatomie of Abuses*, sig. F1v).

57. Chapman, *The Revenge of Bussy D'Ambois*, sig. E4r.

58. A second manual in which Erondelle had a hand, *The French Schoole-Maister*, which contained similar dialogues, went into six editions between 1602 and 1632. See Hollyband, *The French Schoole-Maister*. Erondelle contributed to the editions of 1602, 1606, 1612, 1615, 1623, and 1632.

59. Erondell, *The French Garden*, sigs. E1v–E5r.

60. On the tirewoman's trade, see Ribeira, *Dress and Morality*, 72. See also Ashelford, *Dress in the Age of Elizabeth I*, 82.

61. The first Italian, the second French, they provided perukes and head-attires and served as dressers for the Children of the Merchant Taylors' School when they played at Hampton Court in 1573/4 and the Children of the Chapel when they played at Richmond in 1574/5, respectively. Feuillerat, *Office of Revels, Queen Elizabeth*, 15, 33, 73, 96, 134, 156, 180, 207, 219, 241.

62. Cited by Nicholl, *The Lodger*, 158.

63. Chapman, *The Gentleman Usher*, sigs. C2v–C3v.

64. Cited in Greenstreet, "The Whitefriars Theatre in the Time of Shakespeare," 275–76.

65. Foakes and Rickert, *Henslowe's Diary*, fol. 22v and appendix 2, 318.

66. Ibid., fols. 44r, 54v, 104r, 106r, 115r, 108r. The entry on fol. 117r is a duplicate of that on 108r.

67. Ibid., appendix 1, article 30, 293.

68. Ibid., fols. 95v, 104r. On the Dutch clan of Gossons in London, see Nicholl, *The Lodger*, 153.

69. Foakes and Rickert, *Henslowe's Diary*, fol. 118v.

70. The documents of the case are transcribed in Wallace, "Shakespeare and His London Associates," 261–304. Wallace ("New Shakespeare Discoveries," 505–6) argues that Shakespeare resided with the Mountjoys from 1598 until the end of his theatrical career (even using it as a pied-à-terre after his move back to Stratford).

71. Nicholl, *The Lodger*, 143–44. See also Hotson, *Essays*, esp. 178–82.

72. Wallace, "Shakespeare and His London Associates," 272–73.

73. Hotson, *Essays*, 182; Nicholl, *The Lodger*, 143 and plate 23.

74. Nicholl speculates that the collar was manufactured in the Mountjoy workshop, although he assumes that the family trade was practiced by Christopher Mountjoy with little assistance from Marie (*The Lodger*, 171). See also Nevinson, "Shakespeare's Dress in His Portraits," 105.

75. All Shakespeare quotations in this chapter, unless otherwise indicated, are to Shakespeare, *The Riverside Shakespeare*.

76. Scouloudi, *Returns of Strangers*, 208, 219. Widow Stedon emigrated in 1578. There are a number of other Dutch and Flemish widows in London during this period who are listed as "landresses" but who had no employees.

77. McIntosh, *Working Women in English Society*, 72–73.

78. Stow, *Annales*, 869.

79. The yeomen of the Weavers' Company, for example, lodged a complaint against immigrant artisans in 1595 that included the accusation that alien craftswomen were disseminating the skills of silk weaving to others who were not entitled to them, and thereby "open[ing] and discover[ing] the secrete of our Occupacion" to "those that never deserved for it" (Consitt, *London Weavers' Company*, 313–14). The 1593 Alien Returns suggest that their accusation was accurate, albeit exaggerated: out of a total of 127 silk weavers listed, only four were women, yet all four had hired employees, including English apprentices, whom they had trained in their craft. Three of these female silk weavers were widows working independently, while the fourth was the wife of an Antwerp merchant who, together with her husband, "set eleven English persons to work" (Scouloudi, *Returns of Strangers*, 159, 166, 179, 195).

80. Hufton, "Women Without Men," 361.

81. Never-married single women or "maids" are recorded as living and working together, as in the following entry: "two Douche maydes, borne in Flaunders, beinge sempsters, and keape together" (Kirk and Kirk, *Returns of Aliens*, part 2, 87). For widows living together, see ibid., 287, and part 3, 413; Scouloudi, *Returns of Strangers*, 155, 158, 200–201, 206. Several generations of widows living together was also not uncommon, such as "Mary Spekehard, widowe, borne in Flanders, who lyveth b[y] the sellinge of clothe"; Mary Berry, also a "widowe, borne in Flanders" who "sojourneth with the said Mary Spekehard her daughter"; and an unnamed "wydowe, and her mother, and v children, which live by makinge of parchement lace" (Kirk and Kirk, *Returns of Aliens*, part 1, 413, part 2, 265, and part 3, 350). Widows also lived with their daughters, other female relatives, and female servants.

Widows living with their daughters include "Barbara Peters, and Zuzan hir daughter, borne in Andwerp, lyveth by sowynge"; "Agnes Reyman, widow, and Hester, Magdalin, and Susan her daughters the[y] use the winding of silke"; and "Johan Farmer, widowe, and Marie her daughter workers of fringe lace" (Kirk and Kirk, *Returns of Aliens*, part 1, 451, part 2, 53, 60, 265, 273, 296, and part 3, 376; Scouloudi, *Returns of Strangers*, 191). Widows living with children and female servants include: "Antonet Adout, widdowe, and silkweaver, Isaack, John, Sara, Rebecca, Rachell, and Marye, her children, and one Anne Laderea, a mayde servaunt" (Kirk and Kirk, *Returns of Aliens*, part 1, 431, and part 2, 264, 275, 277, 289–90). Groups of widows living together with their children include: "Honor Lebreme, widowe, silkwinder, and Israell and Judithe, her children, Burgonians, in England three weekes . . . and Anne Humayne, widowe, and sempster, which came with her" (Kirk and Kirk, *Returns of Aliens*, part 1, 429; see also part 2, 114). Other combinations include a widow who lived with her children and another kinswoman: "Marye Peck, silkweaver, and widowe, Wiberde and Sysley, her daughters, and Agnes Sastell, her kinswoman" (Kirk and Kirk, *Returns of Aliens*, part 1, 443).

82. Such as "Catron Quense, widowe, borne in Andwerp," who "dwelleth within one Widow Smith, and lyveth by sowing" (Kirk and Kirk, *Returns of Aliens*, part 1, 418; see also part 1, 448, 453, and part 3, 220, 397; Scouloudi, *Returns of Strangers*, 213, 221).

83. Kirk and Kirk, *Returns of Aliens*, part 3, 412, 425.

84. In Thomas Middleton's *A Trick to Catch the Old One* (1608), when Walkadine Hoard discovers that he has been tricked into marrying a courtesan posing as a wealthy widow, he shouts, "A Dutch widow, a Dutch widow, a Dutch widow!" (5.2.98). This punch-punch line is set up earlier in the play, when Hoard is told that "Dutch widow" is a cant term for prostitute and is so tickled by the term that he vows, "I shall remember a Dutch widow the longest day of my life" (3.3.15–16)—as he indeed does when he discovers that he is married to one. In John Marston's *The Dutch Courtesan* (1603), Franceschina, unlike Middleton's courtesan, is in fact "Dutch"—although she has an Italian name, she is described as "a pretty, nible-ey'd Dutch Tanakin . . . a soft plump, round cheek'd froe" (1.1.147–49) and speaks with a Dutch accent—but is accorded a far less felicitous fate, when at the end of the play she walks offstage to face the "extremest whip and gaol" (5.3.58). Although it is made clear from the start that Franceschina is not a "common whore" and that the courtesan's trade is a skilled occupation—she entertains her customers, for example, with her musical skills—her considerable ingenuity is soon focused entirely on her revenge against her former paramour Freevill, rather than on establishing her own economic independence, as does the courtesan in *A Trick*. By the end of Marston's play, Franceschina's voice and agency are obliterated; her last words are: "Ick vill not speak . . . me ha' lost my will" (5.3.56–57). The stereotype of the Dutch prostitute thus works to efface the productive labor of immigrant craftswomen. Rather than manufacturing commodities for the market, "Dutch widows" in plays were frequently depicted as marketable commodities themselves.

85. Mistress Quickly famously comments on (while inadvertently suggesting the justification for) this tendency in *Henry V*, when she claims she "cannot lodge and board a dozen or fourteen gentlewomen that live honestly by the prick of their needles, but it will be thought [she] keep[s] a bawdy-house straight" (Shakespeare, *King Henry V*, 2.1.32–35).

86. It is surprising that critics have accepted the veracity of the Dutch courtesan stereotype, given the skepticism with which male immigrant stereotypes, such as that of the Flemish drunkard, have been scrutinized. Citing Burford, *Bawds and Lodgings*, 78, 145–46, Hoenselaars speaks of an "age-old tradition of Dutch prostitutes in London" (*Images of Englishmen and Foreigners*, 117). Jean Howard likewise refers to the "long-standing centrality of Dutch frows to London's illicit sexual economy" (*Theater of a City*, 152).

87. See Kirk and Kirk, *Returns of Aliens*, part 1, 424, 426–27, 429, part 2, 13, 15, 18, 25, 30, 33, 50, 53, 60, 66, 119–20, 129, 261–65, 269, 275, 285, 315, 326, 355, and part 3, 224, 229, 339, 345–46, 350, 381, 385; Scouloudi, *Returns of Strangers*, 139, 147, 155, 157, 158, 161–63, 165–68, 170, 172, 174, 176, 179, 180–81, 184–85, 187–91, 200–202, 204, 206, 208–9, 211, 213–14, 217.

88. These include a widow brewster, who employed twenty-three men and women, a widow shoemaker, who employed eight people, a widow silk throwster, who employed seventeen people, and the aforementioned Widow Stedon and Dionis Welfes, who ran successful starching businesses, the former employing eight English women and the latter nine. See Scouloudi, *Returns of Strangers*, 82, 170, 178, 181–82, 184, 197, 199–200, 208, 213, 219.

89. Shakespeare, *The Merry Wives of Windsor*, ed. Melchiori. All further references are to this edition.

90. See Wendy Wall, "'Why Does Puck Sweep?': Fairylore, Merry Wives and Social Struggle," *Shakespeare Quarterly* 52:1 (2001): 67–106; Korda, *Shakespeare's Domestic Economies*, 76–110.

91. See, e.g., Karen Newman, "Dressing Up: Sartorial Extravagance in Early Modern London," in *Fashioning Femininity and English Renaissance Drama* (Chicago: University of Chicago Press, 1991), 111–27, esp. 114–18, where Newman discusses the "sartorial extravagance" of starched linen attires.

92. Gosson, *Pleasant Quippes for Upstart Newfangled Gentle-Women*, sigs. A3r–A4r.

93. Ger Luijten, "Frills and Furbelows," 140–60, esp. 145–47.

94. Ibid., 144.

95. The anecdote may be found in Phillip Stubbes, *The Anatomie of Abuses Containing a Discoverie, or Briefe Summarie of Such Notable Vices and Corruptions, as Nowe Raigne in Many Christian Countreyes of the Worlde, but (Especially) in the Countrey of Ailgna* (London, 1584), fols. 37r–38r. The 1584 edition reads "Epraurna," which is emended in the 1595 edition as "Antwerp."

96. Foakes and Rickert, *Henslowe's Diary*, fol. 95r. The full title of the play was apparently *Friar Rush and the Proud Woman of Antwerp* (see fols. 91r and 91v), "Friar Rush" being a medieval German folktale about a disguised devil sent to corrupt a convent of monks with his culinary skills. See also fols. 94r and 94v. The conjecture that Stubbes's tale was a source for this lost play was first made by Creizenach. See Creizenach, *The English Drama in the Age of Shakespeare*, 213.

97. Foakes and Rickert, *Henslowe's Diary*, fol. 104r.

98. Rich, *Greenes Newes Both from Heaven and Hell*, sigs. F2–F2v.

99. Her name suggests nearsightedness, perhaps caused by her work (*OED*, "pinkany, n."), and recalls the bespectacled, turd-headed demon in the Nützel print.

100. Marston, *The Plays of John Marston*, 3:243–302, esp. 272–73.

256   Notes to Pages 124–127

101. Hayman, *Quodlibets Lately Come Over from New Britaniola*, 28.

102. Brathwaite, *The English Gentlewoman*, 9, 20, 92.

103. Philip Stubbes describes very similar starch-houses in London: "they have their starching houses made of purpose, to that use and end only, the better to trimme and dresse their ruffes to please the divels eies withal . . . for to that end only were they erected" (*The Second Part of the Anatomie of Abuses*, sig. F2r).

104. Sharpham, *Cupids Whirligig*, sig. F4r.

105. In Dekker's *Satiro-Mastix*, we find the same joke when Sir Vaughan claims, "[L]ove is a Rebato indeede: a Rebato must be poaked; now many women weare Rebatos, and many that weare Rebatos—" and Sir Adam provides the punch line, "Must be poakt." Sir Vaughan replies, "Sir Adam Prickshaft has hit the cloute" (sig. D3v).

106. Stubbes, *The Second Part of the Anatomie of Abuses*, sig. F2v; Nashe, "The Choise of Valentines," 3: 413. See also Arnold, Tiramani, and Levey, *Patterns of Fashion 4*, 14–15.

107. The print is reproduced in Luijten, "Frills and Furbelows," 145. The translation of the Dutch caption is Luijten's.

108. Translation in Arnold, Tiramani, and Levey, *Patterns of Fashion 4*, 14.

109. Stubbes, *The Second Part of the Anatomie of Abuses*, sig. F2v.

110. On laundering as women's work, see McIntosh, *Working Women in English Society*, 72–73; Lapham, "Industrial Status of Women," 585. While the making and laundering of linen accessories and underclothing in England had always been done by women, the introduction of new materials and technologies by alien artisans transformed such work into a highly skilled and lucrative enterprise. According to the eminent fashion historian Janet Arnold (whose extensive work on linen clothing and accessories was completed posthumously by Jenny Tiramani and Santina M. Levey), the "workforce dedicated to the making and ornamenting of linen clothing" was "[a]lmost exclusively female," encompassing "both amateurs and professionals" who worked "outside the guild system," establishing "their own, usually small-scale apprenticeship schemes." This workforce included the sempstress, who cut and sewed together the component parts of linen clothes, hemmed, applied facings, and attached linen neck and wristbands, and whose "range of skills expanded as the decoration of linen clothing became more important." Silkwomen provided the sempstress with "raw or semi-processed silk, which they finished and wove into ribbons, or converted, using a variety of techniques, into narrow trimmings, fringes, tassels, fancy buttons and netted cauls," and other ornaments. The cutwork maker and bonelace (or bobbin lace) maker manufactured the lace with which ruffs, cuffs, bands, coifs, shirts, and smocks were adorned, beginning in the 1560s. The embroidery of linen clothing was also done by women (Arnold, Tiramani, and Levey, *Patterns of Fashion 4*, 5–9).

111. With the industrialization of the laundering trade over the course of the seventeenth and early eighteenth centuries came an increasing awareness that the hot, moist atmosphere of laundry- and starch-houses caused occupational diseases. Bernardino Ramazzini's *De Morbis Artificum Diatriba* (1700), translated into English as *A Treatise of the Diseases of Tradesmen* in 1705, contains chapters on the diseases of starchmakers, laundresses, and washerwomen: "Diseases of Starch-makers, or Those who are employed about the making of Starch," and "Diseases of Laundresses and Washerwomen." Of starch, he

warns that "the Smell that exhales from that frothy Matter is so heavy" that those who work with it "complain much of the Headach, of a difficulty of Breathing, and of a Cough that's so troublesome, as to force 'em to intermit for fear of Choaking." Ramazzini himself professes to find the smell of seething starch "downright unsufferable." He "recommend[s] the Contrivance of some Women, who, to avoid the corrosive Influence of Starch, mix Gum Arabick with it." Laundresses are similarly prone to "various Disorders contracted by the Nature of the Work. These Women being confin'd to moist Places, and their Hands and their Feet being always wet, they turn Cachectick; and if they spend their Life time in the Business, they come at last to a Dropsie; of which I have seen many Instances. They are likewise generally affected with a Paucity or Deficiency of the Menstrua, which loads them with many inconveniences." He concludes, "In fine, the moist Air in which they always Breath, and the constant Bath that bedews their Body, is the Cause of all these Disorders: For the Pores of the Skin being by this Means obstructed, and Transpiration impair'd, the whole Mass of Blood is thereupon stuffed with gross Juices. . . . Add to this, that in washing all sorts of foul Sheets and Linnen, some perhaps of Pocky Persons, other of Women under a menstrual Purgation, &c. they receive at Mouth and Nostrils a strange Medley and Composition of heavy noisome Steams, which pollute the Brain and Animal Spirits." He advises them "to turn away their Faces as much as they can from the Smoak of the hot Lye." Bernardino Ramazzini, *A Treatise of the Diseases of Tradesmen, Shewing the Various Influence of Particular Trades Upon the State of Health* (London, 1705), 159–62, 168–70.

112. Woolley, *The Compleat Servant-Maid*, 61–71, 164–65. In 1594, the Countess of Bath wrote to the sister of Sir George Cary, "Good Mris Kircum: I perceve by my Lo[rdship's] man Shapton that you are very desirous to have a searvant that hath served me," and offered the following recommendation: "She can washe and sterch very well, and what else you will employ her to." Cited in Lapham, "Industrial Status of Women," 566.

113. "Haddest thou nothing but of thyne owne travayle," she chides the idle gentlewoman, "Thou mightest go as naked as my nayle." Heywood, *The Playe of the Weather*, sigs. E1v–E3v.

114. Brathwaite, *Whimzies*, 87.

115. Taylor, *All the Workes of John Taylor the Water-Poet*, 164–70. All further references are to this edition; page numbers will be cited parenthetically.

116. E.g., "as the dier, blecher, or the laundresse washeth, beateth, lompeth and clappeth the foule, uncleanly and defiled clothes, that they may be white and pure and cleane: Even so doeth God sometime handle and deale with us, to make us pure and cleane" (Werdmüller, *A Spirituall, and Most Precious Pearle*, 75).

117. Thomas Dekker, William Haughton, and Henry Chettle, *The Pleasant Comodie of Patient Grissil*, in vol. 1 of *The Dramatic Works of Thomas Dekker*. All further references are to this edition.

118. Thomas Churchyard speaks of "mery gyrls" who are "Bedeckt with works" or embroidery and "roefs of pyrls" or ruffs decorated with pearls that have been "starcht full tryme" with "fine froes pasts" and held in place with "silver pyns" (*The First Parte of Churchyardes Chippes*, 24).

119. The threat starch posed to domestic economy was reinforced by the charge that

its manufacture wasted huge quantities of good, wholesome foodstuffs that would otherwise have been consumed by impoverished subjects who were starving in consequence. Such complaints were particularly vociferous during the food shortages of the 1590s. Thus, Thomas Nashe complains that due to the trend in starched neckware (made of lawn), the "lawne of licentiousnesse hath consumed all the wheat of hospitalitie" (*Pierce Penniless*, sig. C2v). John Norden similarly complains of "the consuming of corne, the meere earthly blessing of God to preserve man, about the strengthening of pride, in making of starch. A to[l]eration intolerable. Woe unto him that brought the devise first into our land. For it crieth out mainly to God, who will not abide that about our neckes, in pride, that should bee consumed which should feede our bodies in penurie" (*A Christian Familiar Comfort*, 17).

120. The term "starch" is derived from the Old English term *strcan*, "to make rigid" (the past participle of which is found in the term *strcedferh*, an adjective meaning "fixed or resolute of mind"). It is the formal equivalent of the Dutch term *sterken*, meaning "to strengthen" (*OED*, "starch, v." etymology).

121. Jones-Davies, *Un peintre de la vie Londonienne*, 374–75.

122. Gasper, *The Dragon and the Dove*, 20.

123. All references to *The London Prodigall* are to the only modern edition, found in Brooke, *The Shakespeare Apocrypha*, 191–218.

124. The term "outlandish" is used in the play to describe Tanikin (Civet asks, "[S]he is outlandish, is she not?"), and by extension her head-attires. Beginning in the eleventh century, the term was used synonymously with the term "alien" and meant "Of or belonging to a foreign country; foreign, alien; not native or indigenous" (*OED*, "outlandish, *adj.* and *n.*" 1a). Beginning in the late sixteenth century, however, it began to have the pejorative sense of "Looking or sounding foreign; unfamiliar, strange. Hence, in extended use: odd, bizarre; going beyond what is considered normal or acceptable; outrageous, extravagant" (*OED*, ibid., 2). Ironically, the term derived from the Dutch *uitlandig*, but in its English usage was ultimately turned against the Dutch. With the increasing tensions and commercial competition between the Dutch and English during the seventeenth century, the term "Dutch" itself became pejorative (*OED*, "Dutch, *a., n.* [*adv.*]" 4).

125. Cunningham, Cunningham, and Beard, *A Dictionary of English Costume*, 49.

126. Thus, Philip Stubbes argues, "if these women wold seek after the bewtie of the mind, they wold not affect apparell so much, for if they be faire in body alredy, than need they not gorgeous apparel to make them fairer . . . so cannot the garments make them fayre, whome God, & nature hath made otherwise" (*The Anatomie of Abuses* [1584], sigs. G4–G4v).

127. See Luu, "Assimilation or Segregation"; Littleton, "Social Interactions of Aliens"; and Pettegree, "'Thirty Years On.'"

128. E.g., "they are a common wealth within themselves" and "keep themselves severed from us in church, in government, in trade, in language and marriage" and even in "their apparel." "A complaynt of the Cytizens of London against the great number of strangers in and about this cytty" ([1571] Public Record Office, SP 12/81/29) and "The inconveniences and damage that the English nation suffer by *the* multitude of strangers w*hich* inhabit in this land" (early seventeenth century; Huntington Library, Ellesmere, MS 2516), cited in Luu, "Assimilation or Segregation," 160.

129. Pettegree, "'Thirty Years On,'" 303–12.

130. Littleton, "Social Interactions of Aliens," 157.

131. The Returns suggest that the number of aliens employed as servants and laborers in English households gradually declined over time and that immigrant artisans conversely began hiring greater numbers of English servants and laborers. Luu, "Assimilation or Segregation," 164–66.

132. An Act of Common Council of 1602 in the London Metropolitan Archives (Journals 26:6v–7v) makes clear that by the early seventeenth century, starched linen wares were among the merchandise commonly sold on the streets of London by female hawkers and hucksters. Royal proclamations in 1607 and 1610 attempted to license and restrict the starch-making trade, complaining that even "inferior persons" were now using, making, and selling starch. Thirsk, *Economic Policy and Projects*, 89.

133. *Band, Cuffe and Ruffe*, sigs. A3r–A4v.

134. Ibid., sig. A4r.

135. Ibid., sig. A4v.

136. Ibid., sigs. B1r–B1v.

137. Ibid., sig. B2v.

138. Ibid., sig. B1v.

139. A contemporary letter dated March 4, 1614/15, from Sir John Holles to his son Denzil, then studying at Clare Hall, Cambridge, reprimands Denzil for having "goodfelloed it more then yow have studdied, which is neither the end of your beeing at Cambridge, neither will that provide for hereafter." At the same time, Sir John informs Denzil, "I have sent yow by this carier a sute of black silk grogram as you desired, & your moyer hath sent yow a band, & cuffs, stockins, garters, & roses" for his "Clare Hall part," and chides that if he had come home to visit he might have been fitted for a much finer suit, such "as all your showes can not affoard the like" (Nelson, *Records of Early English Drama*, 536).

140. On the skit's popularity, see Wiggins, "Copies for Ruff and Cuff."

141. *Exchange Ware at the Second Hand*, sig. A4r.

142. Ibid., sigs. A4r–B1r.

143. Ibid., sig. B1v.

144. Ibid., sig. B1r.

145. Henry Peacham, for example, describes sized paper as "with starch thinne laid on." Peacham, *The Gentlemans Exercise*, 94.

146. *Exchange Ware at the Second Hand*, sig. B2v.

147. Ibid., sig. B2r.

CHAPTER 4

1. Lodge, *Wits Miserie, and the Worlds Madnesse*, 56. All references to *Hamlet*, unless otherwise indicated, are to The Arden Shakespeare edition (2006), ed. Thompson and Taylor.

2. Hibbard, "General Introduction," 13.

3. Hart, *An Orthographie*, sig. H2v.

4. B. Smith, *The Acoustic World*, 206, 209, 211, 214.

5. In Bruce Smith's words, "The *there*ness of sound becomes the *here*ness of sound in the ear of the receiver" (*The Acoustic World*, 8).

6. Platter, *Thomas Platter's Travels in England*, 166. See also Gurr, *Playgoing in Shakespeare's London*, 43, 272–73, 286, 299–300.

7. Bowsher and Miller, *The Rose and the Globe*, 146–52. The finds also include remains of ceramic and glass ale bottles and drinking vessels, hops, tobacco seeds, and tobacco pipes, remnants of the commerce of tobacco and alewives (152–57).

8. Historians have argued that women predominated in the huckstering trade since the Middle Ages; see Hilton, "Lords, Burgesses and Hucksters," 10–11, 15; Hutton, "Women in Fourteenth-Century Shrewsbury," 95–97; Lacey, "Women and Work in Fourteenth and Fifteenth Century London," 51; R. H. Britnell, *Growth and Decline in Colchester, 1300–1525* (Cambridge: Cambridge University Press, 1986), 40–41; Goldberg, "Female Labor, Service and Marriage in the Late Medieval Urban North," 29; and Jordan, *Women and Credit*, 27–28. On female hucksters in the sixteenth and early seventeenth centuries, see S. Wright, "'Churmaids, Huswyfes and Hucksters,'" 108–9; Gowing, "'The Freedom of the Streets,'" 141–42. On female hawkers and hucksters in the late seventeenth and eighteenth centuries, see Lemire, *Dress, Culture and Commerce*, 102, 179nn29, 30.

9. Gurr, *Playgoing in Shakespeare's London*, 43. See also Lawrence, *Those Nut-Cracking Elizabethans*, 1–7.

10. Bentley, *The Jacobean and Caroline Stage*, 6:42, 1:315.

11. See, e.g., J. Smith, *The Cries of London*; Hindley, *A History of the Cries of London*; Bridge, *The Olde Cryes of London*; and W. Roberts, *The Cries of London*.

12. Fox, *Oral and Literate Culture*, 6.

13. I. Archer, *The Pursuit of Stability*, 62. See also Muldrew, *The Economy of Obligation*, 48.

14. Finlay, *Population and Metropolis*, 51.

15. Archer, Barron, and Harding, "Introduction," 11. On the continuation of this trend in the late seventeenth, eighteenth, and early nineteenth centuries, see C. Smith, "The Wholesale and Retail Markets of London," 39–40, 44–47.

16. I. Archer, *The Pursuit of Stability*, 245.

17. Archer, Barron, and Harding, *Hugh Alley's Caveat*, 35.

18. Cited in Archer, Barron, and Harding, "Hugh Alley," 15.

19. For acts, orders, and other reports concerning women hawkers and "brokers" of apparel in the late sixteenth and early seventeenth centuries, see Corporation of London Record Office (temporarily held at the London Metropolitan Archives), Repertories of the Court of Aldermen (hereafter Repertories), 20:237r, 21:274r, 26/2:506r, 29:163v, 30:68r, and Journals of the Court of Common Council (hereafter Journals), 26:6r–7v; for the same concerning fishwives, see Repertories, 21:115r, 22:172r, 24:48r, 30:175r, 31ov, and Journals, 18:117v, 21:418r, 22:378v–380v, 389r, 406r, 28:300r–302r; for the same concerning herb-wives, see Journals, 21:93v, 35:440r; for the same concerning hawkers of dairy products, see 19:325v; for the same concerning forestallers, engrossers, and regraters, see Journals, 25:150v–152r.

20. Journals, 26:7r.

21. Ibid., 22:378v; see also 28:300r–302r.

22. Ibid., 24:98v.
23. Repertories, 24:68r.
24. Journals 26:7r.
25. Archer, Barron, and Harding, "Hugh Alley," 25.
26. Cited in ibid., 23.
27. Watt, *Cheap Print and Popular Piety*, 141. For scholarly studies of street-cries in print culture, see also Beall, *Cries and Itinerant Trades*; Shesgreen, *Criers and Hawkers of London*; Shesgreen, "The First London Cries"; and Shesgreen, *Images of the Outcast*.
28. Shesgreen, *Images of the Outcast*, 19.
29. Ibid., 24.
30. Fox, *Oral and Literate Culture*, 5; Shesgreen, *Images of the Outcast*, 25.
31. The criers in this woodcut are evenly divided by gender, a notable fact given that most continental prints from the sixteenth century depict only male criers. An exception to this is an engraving published by Franz Hogenberg in Cologne in 1589, which depicts both male and female criers. Hogenberg is known to have spent time in England between 1568 and 1587, and both Beall and Shesgreen credit the earliest engraved English cries to him or his influence. Beall, *Cries and Itinerant Trades*, 19; Shesgreen, *Images of the Outcast*, 19–21.
32. Shesgreen, *Criers and Hawkers of London*, 15.
33. Shesgreen, *Images of the Outcast*, 3, 19.
34. Oysterwives and fishwives, for example, frequently clashed with the Company of Fishmongers, who accused them of driving up prices and selling bad fish. A letter of the Lord Mayor of the City of London to the Lord Treasurer in 1595 describes "a riot in Southwark, caused by certain City apprentices, who being sent by their masters to purchase mackerel at Billingsgate, and finding that some fishwives had purchased the whole store and carried them to Southwark, followed them, and took the fish from them," accusing them of charging prices higher than those set by the regulated markets. Corporation of London, *Analytical Index*, 475.
35. Shesgreen, *Images of the Outcast*, 27–28.
36. One male crier sells a condiment ("Worsterchyr salt") used in cooking, one collects "Bread and meat" for the poor prisoners, a familiar cry in other prints and ballads. None of the male criers in the print is selling foodstuffs and only three sell textile-related wares, e.g., "Buy any garters," "Buy any points," "Buy any markingstones [used to identify clothes sent out to laundresses]." The only female crier who sells a commodity unrelated to theatrical commerce is the hawker of "tosting Iron[s]."
37. Lupton, *London and the Countrey Carbonadoed and Quartered into Severall Characters*, sigs. G5r–G6r.
38. It is precisely because printed ballads and cries were so widely disseminated in the late sixteenth and early seventeenth centuries, as Adam Fox and others have argued, that oral and print culture were so thoroughly intertwined: "Everyone who spoke the language, uttered its habitual sayings, sang its popular songs, inherited its commonplace assumptions and adhered to its normative beliefs," he argues, "was absorbed in a world governed by text"—text that was increasingly disseminated via popular print. According to Fox's estimate, "three or four million broadside ballads were printed in the second half of the

sixteenth century alone" (*Oral and Literate Culture*, 10, 15; see also Watt, *Cheap Print and Popular Piety*, 11).

39. Arber, *Transcript*, 1:238.

40. MS Rawlinson poet, 185, reprinted in Clark, *The Shirburn Ballads*, appendix 1, 335–36. According to Clark, the manuscript was "written in 1589 or 1590" and was copied from a "perishable printed Broad-sheet to the more lasting MS. notebook" (334). Other wares cried in this ballad include: brooms, brushes, pudding-pies, neat's feet, hog's cheeks, milk, sausages, oranges, cunny-skins, aqua-vita, shirt laces, and buttons.

41. Rollins, *A Pepysian Garland*, 30–38; Collier, *Roxburghe Ballads*, 207–16.

42. Rollins, *The Pepys Ballads*, 1:47–50.

43. Mithal, *Robert Wilson's Three Ladies*. All further references are to this edition; line numbers will be cited parenthetically.

44. Listed in the Stationer's Register on May 2, 1595, and January 16, 1595, respectively. See Arber, *Transcript*, 1:238, cited in Baskervill, *The Elizabethan Jig*, 290; on Kempe's popular performances of jigs for the Chamberlain's Men during the 1590s, see also 105.

45. Gurr, *The Shakespearean Stage*, 175.

46. Bradbrook, *The Rise of the Common Player*, 38.

47. Ibid., 37.

48. Ibid., 17.

49. Ibid., 41.

50. Weimann, *Author's Pen and Actor's Voice*, 5, 8.

51. Ibid., 110.

52. Ibid., 156.

53. Ibid., 88.

54. Ibid., 166, 85.

55. Ibid., 161.

56. See Graves, "Women on the Pre-Restoration Stage"; Thompson, "Women/'Women' and the Stage," 104–5.

57. Douglas and Greenfield, *Records of Early English Drama: Cumberland, Westmoreland, Gloucestershire*, 359; Wasson, *Records of Early English Drama: Devon*, 223; Galloway, *Records of Early English Drama: Norwich*, 142. See also Somerset Record Office QSR 76, part 1, fol. 45r, cited in Stokes, "Women and Mimesis," 179.

58. 14 Eliz. c. 5. [1572], "An Acte for the Punishment of Vacabondes, and for the Relief of the Poore & Impotent," in Luders et al., *Statutes of the Realm*, 4:592.

59. Weimann, *Author's Pen and Actor's Voice*, 23.

60. Professional musicians of the period likewise intermixed the town crier's call with those of male and female street vendors in consort music. Collected in Brett, *Consort Songs*.

61. The second is headed by a man crying "Bread and Meat for the poor Prisoners," who is therefore likewise serving a civic function by providing for the poor.

62. The bellman at the center of Figure 23 likewise appears to address the female criers who surround him with "Mayds in your smocks. Loocke / Wel to your lock," etc.

63. Bloom, *Voice in Motion*, 10–11.

64. Ibid., 8–9, 11.
65. Ibid., 6–7.
66. Ibid., 10–11.
67. *A Warning for Faire Women*, sigs. A2r–A3r.
68. For a concise account of scholarship on the War of the Theaters, see Knutson, *Playing Companies and Commerce in Shakespeare's Time*, 1–20.
69. "Seneca in Elizabethan Translation," in Eliot, *Essays on Elizabethan Drama*, 22.
70. Marston, *Histrio-Mastix*, sigs. B4v–C1r, D4v.
71. Dekker, *The Dramatic Works of Thomas Dekker*, vol. 1, *Satiromastix*.
72. Gayton, *Pleasant Notes Upon Don Quixot*, 72.
73. B. Smith, *The Acoustic World*, 229.
74. Bloom, *Voice in Motion*, 38.

75. Bloom shows that Marston and others who wrote for the boy-companies were themselves aware of and attempted to manage, and thereby reassert mastery over, the instability of the boy-actor's voice: "Marston's narrative builds up pressure around this moment of potential vocal instability, preparing audiences for its inevitability by scripting characters' vocal failure" (*Voice in Motion*, 48–59, esp. 58).

76. Guazzo, *Civile Conversation*, 129.

77. Guazzo's discussion of *actio* is based on Quintilian's *Institutio Oratoria*, book 11, chapter 3, which argues that the "extraordinary force and power" of *actio* is exemplified in the art of "stage actors" (87).

78. Guazzo, *Civile Conversation*, 123.
79. Ibid., 128–29.
80. Ibid., 130, 132.
81. Ibid., 125. On the increasing emphasis placed on stirring the emotions in English rhetorical manuals of the late sixteenth century, see William G. Crane's introduction to Peacham, *The Garden of Eloquence*, 23. On the way in which this emphasis may have influenced Elizabethan acting styles, see Beckerman, *Shakespeare at the Globe*, 113–21.
82. Guazzo, *Civile Conversation*, 131–32.
83. Ibid., 129, 131, 126, 125.
84. Bevington, *Action Is Eloquence*, 81.

85. "My fate cries out" (1.4.82), Hamlet cries when he first sees the ghost. Laertes, too, evokes the cry as the mode of articulation that can best capture his own father's fate: "His means of death, his obscure funeral . . . / Cry to be heard, as 'twere from heaven to earth" (4.5.205, 208). A stage direction in both Q2 and F suggests that *Hamlet*'s Ghost, like that of the *Ur-Hamlet*, and in spite of Hamlet's advice to the players, cries out miserably, informing us that the "*Ghost cries under the Stage*" (Furness, *Hamlet*, 1:113). The staging of this scene likewise emphasizes the fugitive quality of the ghost's nocturnal cries: like those of the town crier and itinerant street vendors, they are heard "*Hic et ubique*" (l. 156), as the ghost shifts ground no fewer than four times beneath the stage. To liken the voice of the ghost of King Hamlet to that of a town crier is to risk rendering the sublime somewhat ridiculous in precisely the manner that Hamlet aims to prevent in his advice

to the players. That the ghost is *necessarily* somewhat ridiculous has been suggested by Ann Rosalind Jones and Peter Stallybrass in their examination of the problem of staging a ghost who returns in an ungainly, full suit of armor. Jones and Stallybrass, *Renaissance Clothing*, 245–68, esp. 246.

86. The exigency of resorting to such aural violence is emphasized throughout the play: "let us once again assail your ears, / That are so fortified against our story" (1.1.30–31), Barnardo tells Horatio at the start of the play. Warning Hamlet that "the whole ear of Denmark / Is by a forged process of my death / Rankly abused" (1.5.36–38), the ghost pleads for a better hearing from his son: "List, list, O list!" (l.22).

87. For the textual history of the line's emendations, see Furness, *Hamlet*, 1:454.

88. Shakespeare, *King Lear*, ed. Muir.

89. Hecuba's cry likewise transports her into this vocal register, when Q1 and Q2 describe her as "the mobled queen" (2.2.440). The verb "mob" or "moble" meant "to muffle the head or face" or "to dress untidily" (*OED*, "mob, $v.^1$" and "mobble, $v.$") and was suggestive not only of commonality but of sexual vulgarity, for it was also a cant term for "A wench, a slattern; a promiscuous woman; a prostitute" (*OED*, "mob, $n.^1$" 1), perhaps because it was suggestive of female dishabille and because prostitutes were known to wear hoods. Insofar as the term "quean" was also cant for "prostitute" (*OED*, "quean, $n.$" 1), the clamorous cry of the "mobled queen" would appear to draw on the same repertoire of articulations as Hamlet's vociferous drab or scullion, Lodge's rattling oysterwife, and Dekker's screeching rouncival.

90. In *Venus and Adonis* (Shakespeare, *The Riverside Shakespeare*), for example, the owl is associated with predatory female lust when Adonis pleads, "The owl (night's herald) shrieks, 'tis very late" (l. 531), but the sexually voracious Venus refuses to relent.

91. Corporation of London, *An Act of Common Councell*. Like other "unruly" female criers, herb-women were frequently accused of sexual promiscuity, as in *Pericles* (Shakespeare, *The Riverside Shakespeare*), where Lysimachus likens herb-women to bawds and prostitutes, who sow the "seeds and roots of shame and iniquity" (4.6.86).

92. Dekker, *The Dramatic Works of Thomas Dekker*, vol. 2, *The Honest Whore, Part I*.

93. Chettle, *The Tragedy of Hoffman*, ed. H. Jenkins and C. Sisson. All references are to this edition.

94. Jonson, *Epicoene, or The Silent Woman*, ed. R. V. Holdsworth. All references are to this edition.

CHAPTER 5

1. On market regulation and efforts to control informal commerce, see Berlin, "'Broken All in Pieces'"; Kellet, "The Breakdown of Gild and Corporation Control"; I. Archer, *The Pursuit of Stability*, 124–31; and Rappaport, *Worlds Within Worlds*, 45–46, 111–17, 187–88, 225. On the moral ethos of the craft guilds, see Black, *Guilds and Civil Society*, 26–27.

2. Berlin, "'Broken All in Pieces'"; I. Archer, *The Pursuit of Stability*, 127.

3. Berlin, "'Broken All in Pieces,'" 80–81.

4. Thrupp, *A Short History of Bakers*, 42–43, 58. In 1609, a goldsmith named John Brooke, accused of practicing deceit in the manufacture of bowls, was likewise put in the stocks with his faulty bowls hung around his neck. Prideaux, *Memorials of the Goldsmith's Company*, 113.

5. Thrupp, *A Short History of Bakers*, 43.

6. M. Ingram, "Ridings, Rough Music and the 'Reform of Popular Culture,'" 81–82, 86–87

7. Drapers' Company Repertory G, 198ff. Cited in A. Johnson, *History of the Worshipful Company of the Drapers of London*, 2:488–89.

8. Thrupp, *A Short History of Bakers*, 44.

9. Ibid., 44, 58.

10. According to Judith Bennett, as beer began to compete more effectively with ale, "alewives were depicted not only as disorderly and dishonest but also as producers of adulterated, disgusting, and unhealthy drink" (*Ale, Beer, and Brewsters in England*, 155).

11. Jones and Stallybrass, *Renaissance Clothing*.

12. Forestalling was buying up goods before they reached the markets; engrossing was buying up the entire stock of a commodity, so as to resell it at an inflated price; regrating was buying goods in one market for resale elsewhere.

13. See Elton, "Informing for Profit"; Davies, *The Enforcement of English Apprenticeship*; Beresford, "Common Informer"; and McMullan, "Criminal Organization in Sixteenth and Seventeenth Century London."

14. Beresford, "Common Informer"; Elton, "Informing for Profit," 151.

15. Elton, "Informing for Profit," 150.

16. One promoter collected fees at the exorbitant rate of 20 shillings for each promise not to inform. Beresford, "Common Informer," 229; Davies, *The Enforcement of English Apprenticeship*, 58–60.

17. Sir Edward Coke complained that promoters informed "for malice or private ends and never for love of justice." Cited in Beresford, "Common Informer," 221. Barnabe Rich's *My Ladies Looking Glasse* (1616) describes the vices of the city, complaining, "*Knavery* hath taken phisicke, and is growne so strong and lustie, that he walkes the streetes at pleasure, but yet disguised, sometimes like a promoter, sometimes like a broker" (60). In Rich's view, promoters epitomize "vice, masked under the vizard of vertue" (the subtitle of his treatise); they are not the scourge of middlemen and regratresses but rather their unacknowledged twins, for they too earn their living as go-betweens. Sir John Harington, in an epigram of 1618, likewise includes the promoter in a list of "lewd trades" taken up by those who practice "every fraude." Harington, *The Most Elegant and Witty Epigrams*, sig. H7v.

18. Beresford, "Common Informer," 226, 228.

19. Gosson, *Plays Confuted in Five Actions*, sig. E2r.

20. Ibid., sig. B3r.

21. Ibid., sig. G6v.

22. Ibid., sig. E2r. The notion that "ydlenes is the Mother of vice" was commonly held by puritan writers of the period. See Stubbes, *The Anatomy of Abuses*, sig. L8r.

23. According to Gosson, "these outward spectacles effeminate, & soften the heartes

of men" (*Plays Confuted in Five Actions*, sig. G4r). Thomas Beard similarly maintained that playing makes "people idle, effeminate, and voluptuous" (*The Theater of Gods Judgements*, 374).

24. Petition concerning "The inconveniences that grow by Stage playes abowt the Citie of London" sent by the Lord Mayor and aldermen to the Privy Council in July 1597. Chambers, *The Elizabethan Stage*, 4:322.

25. Letter from Nathan Field to Revd. Mr. Sutton, 1616, cited in Pollard, *Shakespeare's Theater*, 277.

26. Chambers, *The Elizabethan Stage*, 4:257.

27. On the playing companies as pseudo-guilds, see Orgel, *Impersonations*, 67.

28. Chambers, *The Elizabethan Stage*, 4:255, 257.

29. Heywood, *Thomas Heywood's Art of Love*.

30. Gosson, *Plays Confuted in Five Actions*, sig. E7v.

31. Ibid., sigs. C6r, G5v.

32. Crosse, *Vertues Common-Wealth*, sig. Q1r.

33. Chambers, *The Elizabethan Stage*, 4:258.

34. Heywood, *Apology for Actors*, sig. A2v; I. G., *Refutation of the Apology for Actors*, 55.

35. Howard, *Theater of a City*, 27–28. On the emergence of new forms of masculinity in early modern England, see Shepard, *Meanings of Manhood*.

36. All references are to Middleton, *A Chaste Maid in Cheapside*, ed. Brissenden.

37. Stow, *Survey of London*, 345.

38. Harding, "Cheapside," 78–79, 85.

39. Ibid., 87.

40. Archer, Barron, and Harding, *Hugh Alley's Caveat*, 90. In 1592 the inhabitants of Cheapside lodged a complaint about disorder in the market, street congestion, uncleared rubbish, and vendors' refusal to adhere to official marketing hours, selling on the Sabbath and until late in the night, sometimes by candlelight. Archer, Barron, and Harding, "Introduction," 12.

41. Harding, "Cheapside," 87–88.

42. Howard, *Theater of a City*, 137. See also Griffiths, "Politics Made Visible."

43. Archer, Barron, and Harding, *Hugh Alley's Caveat*.

44. Ibid., 35.

45. Reddaway, *Early History of the Goldsmiths' Company*, 212, 249.

46. Harding, "Cheapside," 83.

47. Reddaway, *Early History of the Goldsmiths' Company*, 232.

48. Paster, "Leaky Vessels." Although Paster centers her analysis of incontinent women in city comedy on *A Chaste Maid in Cheapside* and *Bartholomew Fair*, she does not draw the connection between female incontinence and false or "leaky" female merchandise, the subject of the present chapter.

49. J. Ford, *Fancies* (1638), cited in *OED*, "dildo, *n*.¹."

50. All references are to Jonson, *Bartholomew Fair*, ed. Hibbard.

51. Barish, *The Antitheatrical Prejudice*, 132.

52. Ibid., 153–54.

53. The Revels Office accounts refer to "Canvas for the Boothes and other necessaries for a play called Bartholomewe Faire" when the play was staged at court. Chambers, *The Elizabethan Stage*, 4:183.

54. *Bartholomew Faire*, 1.

55. Jonson, *Ben Jonson*, 11:305.

56. *Discoveries*, in ibid., 8:635.

57. Sidney, *An Apologie for Poetrie*, sigs. G4r, I2r.

58. *Discoveries*, in Jonson, *Ben Jonson*, 8:626.

59. "To My Old Faithfull Servant: and (by his Continu'd Vertue) my Loving Friend: the Author of the Work, M. Rich. Brome," in ibid., 8:410.

60. Ibid., 8:409.

61. *Discoveries* and "On Poet-Ape," in ibid., 8:315, 44.

62. *Discoveries*, in ibid., 8:635.

63. Horace, *The Art of Poetrie*, trans. Ben Jonson, in ibid., 8:317.

64. Jonson, *Ben Jonson*, 7:209–10.

65. Greenwood, *Bouleuterion*, 393.

66. Ibid., 396.

67. In his dedicatory poem to his friend Christopher Brooke's book on Richard III, George Chapman refers to "Pageant Orsadine / That goes for gold" (Brooke, *The Ghost of Richard the Third*, sig. A2r). As we have seen, the professional players were notorious for their gilded wares more generally, including copper lace.

68. For references to apple-wives in playhouses, see Bentley, *The Jacobean and Caroline Stage*, 1:315, 6:42.

69. In 1661, Pepys described the play as being "so satyricall against Puritanism" that it had not been performed "these forty years." Cited in Jonson, *Bartholomew Fair*, xv.

70. See, e.g., Gosson, *Plays Confuted in Five Actions*, sig. E8; Stubbes, *The Anatomy of Abuses*, sig. L5v.

71. Dekker, *The Guls Horne-Booke*, 28–29.

EPILOGUE

1. Honeyman and Goodman, "Women's Work," 610.

2. Jonson, *Ben Jonson: The Complete Masques*, 233–44.

3. "An Expostulation with Inigo Jones," in *Ben Jonson*, ed. Herford, Simpson, and Simpson, 8:402–5.

4. Crowston, "Women, Gender, and Guild in Early Modern Europe," 39.

5. McIntosh, *Working Women in English Society*, 137–38.

6. See, for example, the history of the Merchant Taylors' Company and female mantua makers of York. S. Smith, "Women's Admission to Guilds."

7. Highfill, Burnim, and Langhans, *Biographical Dictionary of Actors*, 2:368.

8. See, for example, Mr. and Mrs. Francis Heath at Drury Lane. Ibid., 7:229–30.

9. Ibid., 3:84.

10. Ibid., 2:380.

11. Ibid., 6: 286. For other examples of female dressers and wardrobe keepers, see ibid., 5:81, 13:289, 14:111, 14:132, 14:135, 14:140, 14:158, 14:410 and below.

12. Ibid., 2:309. See also 14:141 and 14:324.

13. Ibid., 10:167.

14. Ibid., 6:455–58; Graham Hopkins, *Nell Gwynne* (London: Robson Books, 2000), 21.

15. Highfill, Burnim, and Langhans, *Biographical Dictionary of Actors*, 7:229.

16. Ibid., 6:455.

17. Ibid., 8: 286.

18. Ibid., 9:53.

19. Ibid., 14:244.

20. Ibid., 14:370.

21. Another example is that of Mrs. Carne, who worked as the candlewoman at Covent Garden, collecting tallow drippings and candle ends for resale (amounting to some £120 per season) and was married to the theater's box office keeper; like the Heaths, the couple lived in the theater (ibid., 3:76). Among the many other examples are Mrs. Buchan, a female dresser at Drury Lane, who appears to have been the wife of the theater's watchman and stage sweeper (ibid., 2:381).

22. Cerasano, "Women as Theatrical Investors," 87–94.

23. Highfill, Burnim, and Langhans, *Biographical Dictionary of Actors*, 4:167; Bush-Bailey, *Treading the Bawds*, 29.

24. Shugg, "Prostitution in Shakespeare's London"; Griffiths, "The Structure of Prostitution in Elizabethan England"; Dawson and Yachnin, *The Culture of Playgoing in Shakespeare's England*; Varholy, "Representing Prostitution in Tudor and Stuart England"; Ungerer, "Prostitution in Late Elizabethan London."

25. Book-length studies of cosmetics in early modern England include Drew-Bear, *Painted Faces on the Renaissance Stage*; Karim-Cooper, *Cosmetics in Shakespeare and Renaissance Drama*; and Phillippy, *Painting Women*.

26. Snook, "'The Beautifying Part of Physic,'" 20. See also Margaret Pelling, *The Common Lot: Sickness, Medical Occupations and the Urban Poor in Early Modern England* (London: Longman, 1998), 203–29; Pelling, "Thoroughly Resented?"; and Pelling, *Medical Conflicts in Early Modern London*.

Bibliography

Bibliographic information on manuscript sources is provided in the notes and is not repeated here.

PRIMARY SOURCES

The Actors Remonstrance or Complaint for the Silencing of Their Profession and Banishment from Their Severall Play-Houses. London, 1643.
Advice to the Women and Maidens of London Shewing, That Instead of Their Usual Pastime, and Education in Needlework . . . It Were Far More Necessary and Profitable to Apply Themselves to the Right Understanding and Practice of the Method of Keeping Books of Account. London, 1678.
Agrippa of Nettesheim. *Three Books of Occult Philosophy.* Trans. John French. London, 1651.
Arber, Edward, ed. *A Transcript of the Registers of the Company of Stationers of London, 1554–1640.* 5 vols. London: Privately printed, 1875–94.
Aristotle. *Aristotle's Metaphysics.* Trans. Hippocrates G. Apostle. Bloomington: Indiana University Press, 1966.
———. *Aristotle's Politics.* Trans. Benjamen Jowett. Ed. H[enry] W[illiam] Carless Davis. Oxford: Clarendon Press, 1908.
Bacon, Francis. *The Essays.* Ed. John Pitcher. New York: Penguin, 1985.
Bartholomew Faire, or, Variety of Fancies, Where You May Find a Faire of Wares, and All to Please Your Mind with the Severall Enormityes and Misdemeanours Which are Seene and Acted. London, 1641.
Beard, Thomas. *The Theatre of Gods Judgements.* London, 1597.
Bell, Thomas. *The Speculation of Usurie.* London, 1596.
The Bible and Holy Scriptures Conteined in the Olde and Newe Testament. Trans. Theodore de Beze. London, 1576.
Blaxton, John. *The English Usurer; or Usury Condemned.* London, 1634.
Bohun, William. *Privilegia Londini: or, The Laws, Customs and Priviledges of the City of London.* London, 1702.
Bolton, Robert. *A Short and Private Discourse Betweene Mr. Bolton and One M. S. Concerning Usury.* London, 1637.

Brathwaite, Richard. *The English Gentlewoman, Drawne out to the Full Body Expressing, What Habilliments Doe Best Attire Her, What Ornaments Doe Best Adorne Her, What Complements Doe Best Accomplish Her*. London, 1631.

———. *Whimzies; or, A New Cast of Characters*. London, 1631.

Brett, Philip, ed. *Consort Songs*. Vol. 22. Musica Britannica. London: Royal Musical Association, 1967.

Brooke, C. F. Tucker, ed. *The Shakespeare Apocrypha: Being a Collection of Fourteen Plays Which Have Been Ascribed to Shakespeare*. Oxford: Clarendon Press, 1918.

Brooke, Christopher. *The Ghost of Richard the Third . . . Containing More of Him Then Hath Been Heretofore Shewed, Either in Chronicles, Playes, or Poems*. London, 1614.

Caesar, Philipp. *A General Discourse Against the Damnable Sect of Usurers*. London, 1578.

Cash, Margaret, ed. *Devon Inventories of the Sixteenth and Seventeenth Centuries*. Torquay: Devon and Cornwall Record Society, 1966.

Castiglione, Baldesar. *The Book of the Courtier*. Trans. Charles S. Singleton. Garden City, N.Y.: Anchor Books, 1959.

Chamberlain, Robert. *A New Book of Mistakes*. London, 1637.

Chapman, George. *The Gentleman Usher*. London, 1606.

———. *The Revenge of Bussy D'Ambois A Tragedie. As it Hath Beene Often Presented at the Private Play-House in the White-Fryers*. London, 1613.

Chettle, Henry. *The Tragedy of Hoffman*. Ed. Harold Jenkins and Charles Sisson. Malone Society Reprints. Oxford: Oxford University Press, 1950.

———. *The Tragedy of Hoffman or A Revenge for a Father As it Hath Bin Divers Times Acted with Great Applause, at the Phenix in Druery-Lane*. London, 1631.

Christoffels, Jan Ympyn. *A Notable and Very Excellente Woorke: Expressyng and Declaryng the Maner and Forme How to Kepe a Boke of Acco[m]ptes or Reconynges, Verie Expedient and Necessary to All Marchantes, Receivers, Auditors, Notaries, and All Other*. London, 1547.

Churchyard, Thomas. *The Firste Parte of Churchyardes Chippes Contayning Twelve Severall Labours*. London, 1575.

Clark, Andrew, ed. *The Shirburn Ballads, 1585–1616*. Oxford: Clarendon Press, 1907.

Cleaver, Robert, and John Dod. *A Godly Forme of Houshold Government for the Ordering of Private Families, According to the Direction of Gods Word . . . Newly Perused, Amended and Augmented*. London, 1621.

The Cloath-Worker Caught in a Trap: or, A Fool and his Mony Soon Parted. London, 1670.

Collier, John Payne, ed. *Roxburghe Ballads*. London: Longman, 1847.

Cooper, William Durrant, ed. *Lists of Foreign Protestants and Aliens Resident in England, 1618–1688*. Westminster: John Bowyer Nichols and Sons, 1862.

Corporation of London. *Analytical Index, to the Series of Records Known as the Remembrancia. Preserved Among the Archive of the City of London, A.D. 1579–1664*. London: E. J. Francis, 1878.

———. *An Act of Common Councell for the Reformation of Sundry Abuses Practised by Divers Persons Upon the Common Markets, and Streets of the City of London*. London, 1631.

Cotgrave, Randle. *A Dictionarie of the French and English Tongues*. London, 1611.

Cranmer, Thomas. *Certaine Sermons or Homilies Appointed to Be Read in Churches, in the*

Time of the Late Queene Elizabeth of Famous Memory. And Now Thought Fit to Bee Reprinted by Authority from the Kings Most Excellent Majestie. London, 1623.

Crosse, Henry. *Vertues Common-Wealth: or The High-Way to Honour Wherin Is Discovered, That Although by the Disguised Craft of This Age, Vice and Hypocrisie May Be Concealed: Yet by Tyme (the Triall of Truth) It Is Most Plainly Revealed*. London, 1603.

Culpeper, Sir Thomas. *A Tract Against Usurie Presented to the High Court of Parliament*. London, 1621.

The Death of Usury, or, The Disgrace of Usurers. Cambridge, 1594.

Decay of Trade, A Treatise Against the Abating of Interest. London, 1641.

Dekker, Thomas. *The Dead Tearme*. London, 1608.

———. *The Dramatic Works of Thomas Dekker*. Ed. Fredson Bowers. 4 vols. Cambridge: Cambridge University Press, 1953–61.

———. *The Guls Horne-Booke*. London, 1609.

———. *Satiro-Mastix. Or the Untrussing of the Humorous Poet as it Hath Bin Presented Publikely, by the Right Honorable, the Lord Chamberlaine His Servants; and Privately, by the Children of Paules*. London, 1602.

Deloney, Thomas. *The Pleasant and Princely History of the Gentle-Craft*. London, 1696.

———. *The Works of Thomas Deloney*. Ed. Francis Oscar Mann. Oxford: Clarendon Press, 1912.

A Description of Devils. London, n.d. [1678?].

The Devil and Broker, or, A Character of a Pawn Broker in a Merry Dialogue With Their Manifold Frauds and Deceits Discovered. London, 1677.

Donne, John. "Satire IV." In *John Donne*, ed. John Carey. Oxford: Oxford University Press, 1990. 36–42.

Douglas, Audrey, and Peter Greenfield, eds. *Records of Early English Drama: Cumberland, Westmoreland, Gloucestershire*. Toronto: University of Toronto Press, 1986.

Earle, John. *Micro-Cosmographie. Or, A Peece of the World Discovered in Essayes and Characters*. London, 1628.

Edgar, Thomas. *The Lawes Resolutions of Womens Right:s or, The Lawes Provision for Woemen*. London, 1632.

An Enterlude of Welth, and Health . . . Newly . . . Imprinted. London, 1565.

Erondelle, Pierre. *The French Garden: For English Ladyes and Gentlewomen to Walke In*. London, 1605.

Exchange Ware at the Second Hand Viz. Band, Ruffe, and Cuffe, Lately Out, and Now Newly Dearned Up. Or a Dialogue, Acted in a Shew in the Famous Universitie of Cambridge. London, 1615.

Fenner, Dudley. *The Artes of Logike and Rethorike . . . Togither with Examples for the Practise of the Same for Methode, in the Governement of the Familie*. Middelburg, 1584.

Fenton, Roger. *A Treatise of Usurie*. London, 1611.

Feuillerat, Albert, ed. *Documents Relating to the Office of the Revels in the Time of Queen Elizabeth*. London: David Nutt, 1908.

———, ed. *Documents Relating to the Revels at Court in the Time of King Edward VI and Queen Mary*. London: David Nutt, 1914.

Firmin, Thomas. *Some Proposals for the Imploying of the Poor, Especially in and About the City of London.* London, 1678.
Fitzgeffrey, Henry. *Satyres: and Satyricall Epigrams: with Certaine Observations at Black-Fryers?* London, 1617.
Foakes, R. A, ed. *The Henslowe Papers.* 2 vols. New York: British Book Centre, 1977.
———. *Henslowe's Diary.* 2nd ed. Cambridge: Cambridge University Press, 2002.
Furness, Henry Howard, ed. *Hamlet.* 2 vols. The New Variorum Edition of Shakespeare. Philadelphia: J. B. Lippincott, 1877.
G., I. *A Refutation of the Apology for Actors.* London, 1615.
Galloway, David, ed. *Records of Early English Drama: Norwich, 1540–1642.* Toronto: University of Toronto Press, 1984.
Gascoigne, George. *A Hundreth Sundrie Flowres Bounde Up in One Small Poesie.* London, 1573.
———. *The Spoyle of Antwerpe. Faithfully Reported, by a True Englishman, Who Was Present at the Same.* London, 1576.
Gayton, Edmund. *Pleasant Notes Upon Don Quixot.* London, 1654.
Gosson, Stephen. *Plays Confuted in Five Actions.* London, 1582.
———. *Pleasant Quippes for Upstart Newfangled Gentle-Women. Containing a Pleasant Invective Against the Fantastical Foreigne Toyes, Daylie Used in Womens Apparell.* London, 1595.
———. *The Schoole of Abuse, Conteining a Pleasaunt Invective Against Poets, Pipers, Plaiers, Jesters, and Such Like Caterpillers of a Co[m]monwelth.* London, 1579.
Gouge, William. *Of Domesticall Duties.* London, 1622.
Greenwood, Will[iam]. *Bouleuterion, or, A Practical Demonstration of County Judicatures . . . Together with the Original, Jurisdiction, and Method of Keeping All Countrey Courts.* London, 1659.
Greg, Sir Walter W., ed. *Henslowe Papers: Being Documents Supplementary to Henslowe's Diary.* London: A. H. Bullen, 1907.
———, ed. *Henslowe's Diary.* 2 vols. London: A. H. Bullen, 1904–8.
Griffith, Mathew. *Bethel: or, A Forme for Families in Which All Sorts, of Both Sexes, Are So Squared, and Framed by the Word of God, as They May Best Serve in Their Severall Places, for Usefull Pieces in God's Building.* London, 1633.
Grimeston, Edward. *A Generall Historie of the Netherlands . . . out of the Best Authors That Have Written of That Subject.* London, 1608.
Guazzo, Stephano. *The Civile Conversation of M. Steeven Guazzo.* Trans. George Pettie (Books I–III) and Bartholomew Young (Book IV). New York: A. A. Knopf, 1925 [1581].
Hardinge, Stanley Giffard, Earl of Halsbury. *The Laws of England, Being a Complete Statement of the Whole Law of England.* 31 vols. London: Butterworth, 1907–17.
Harington, Sir John. *The Most Elegant and Witty Epigrams of Sir John Harrington.* London, 1618.
Hart, John. *An Orthographie Conteyning the Due Order and Reason, Howe to Write or Paint Th[']image of Mannes Voice, Most Like to the Life or Nature.* London, 1569.

Haughton, William. *English-men for My Money: or, A Pleasant Comedy, Called, A Woman Will Have Her Will*. Ed. W. W. Greg. Malone Society Reprints. Oxford: Oxford University Press, 1912 [1616].

Hayman, Robert. *Quodlibets Lately Come over from New Britaniola, Old Newfound-Land Epigrams and Other Small Parcels, Both Morall and Divine*. London, 1628.

Herbert, Thomas. *Keep Within Compasse Dick and Robin*. London, 1641.

Heywood, John. *The Playe of the Weather: A Newe and a Very Merye Enterlude of All Maner Wethers*. London, 1573.

Heywood, Thomas. *An Apology for Actors*. London, 1612.

———. *The Fair Maid of the Exchange*. Ed. Peter H. Davison. Malone Society Reprints. Oxford: Oxford University Press, 1962.

Highfill, Philip H., Kalman A. Burnim, and Edward A. Langhans. *A Biographical Dictionary of Actors, Actresses, Musicians, Dancers, Managers & Other Stage Personnel in London, 1660–1800*. 16 vols. Carbondale: Southern Illinois University Press, 1973–93.

Holinshed, Raphael. *The Third Volume of Chronicles . . . Augmented, and Continued . . . To the Yeare 1586*. London, 1587.

Hollyband, Claudius. *The French Schoole-Maister . . . Now Newly Corrected and Amended by P. Erondelle*. London, 1606.

Honigmann, E. A. J., and Susan Brock, eds. *Playhouse Wills, 1558–1642: An Edition of Wills by Shakespeare and His Contemporaries in the London Theatre*. Manchester: Manchester University Press, 1993.

Jewel, John. *The Second Tome of Homilies of Such Matters as Were Promised, and Entituled in the Former Part of Homilies. Set out by the Authority of the Late Queenes Majestie: And to Be Read in Every Parish Church Agreeablie*. London, 1623.

Jonson, Ben. *Bartholomew Fair*. Ed. G. R. Hibbard. The New Mermaids. London: A. C. Black, 1994.

———. *Ben Jonson*. Ed. C. H. Herford, Percy Simpson, and Evelyn Simpson. 11 vols. Oxford: Clarendon Press, 1925–52.

———. *Ben Jonson: The Complete Masques*. Ed. Stephen Orgel. New Haven, Conn.: Yale University Press, 1969.

———. *Chloridia Rites to Chloris and Her Nymphs. Personated in a Masque, at Court. By the Queenes Majesty and Her Ladies*. London, 1631.

———. *The Complete Plays of Ben Jonson, Based on the Edition Edited by C. H. Herford and Percy and Evelyn Simpson*. Ed. G. A. Wilkes. 4 vols. Oxford: Clarendon Press, 1981.

———. *Epicoene, or The Silent Woman*. Ed. R. V. Holdsworth. The New Mermaids. New York: W. W. Norton, 1990.

———. *Poetaster*. Ed. Tom Cain. The Revels Plays. Manchester: Manchester University Press, 1995.

Justices of the Peace, Quarter Sessions. *Middlesex County Records: Calendar of Sessions Rolls*. London: [British Library Typescript], 1925.

Kermode, Lloyd Edward. *Three Renaissance Usury Plays: The Three Ladies of London, Englishmen for My Money, The Hog Hath Lost His Pearl*. Manchester: Manchester University Press, 2009.

The Kind Beleeving Hostesse. London, 1632.

Kirk, R. E. G, and Ernest F. Kirk, eds. *Returns of Aliens Dwelling in the City and Suburbs of London from the Reign of Henry VIII to That of James I, 1523–1571*. Vol. 10, Part 1. Publications of the Huguenot Society of London. Aberdeen: University Press, 1900.

———. *Returns of Aliens Dwelling in the City and Suburbs of London from the Reign of Henry VIII to That of James I, 1571–97*. Vol. 10, Part 2. Publications of the Huguenot Society of London. Aberdeen: University Press, 1902.

———. *Returns of Aliens Dwelling in the City and Suburbs of London from the Reign of Henry VIII to That of James I, 1598–1625*. Vol. 10, Part 3. Publications of the Huguenot Society of London. Aberdeen: University Press, 1907.

Klausner, David N., ed. *Records of Early English Drama: Herefordshire and Worcester*. Toronto: University of Toronto Press, 1990.

Kyd, Thomas. *The Spanish Tragedy*. Ed. J. R. Mulryne. 2nd ed. The New Mermaids. London: A. C. Black, 1989.

Lambarde, William. *A Perambulation of Kent Containing the Description, History and Customs of That County*. London, 1596.

Le Hardy, William, ed. *County of Middlesex: Calendar to the Sessions Records*. 3 vols. Vol. 1: 1600–1800. London: Guildhall, 1935.

Lenton, Francis. *Characterismi: or, Lentons Leasures Expressed in Essayes and Characters, Never Before Written on*. London, 1631.

Lodge, Thomas. *An Alarum against Usurers*. London, 1584.

———. *Wits Miserie, and the Worlds Madnesse: Discovering the Devils Incarnat of This Age*. London, 1596.

Luders, Alexander, Sir Thomas Edlyne Tomlins, John France, Sir William Elias Taunton, and John Raithby, eds. *Statutes of the Realm, 1225–1713, Printed by Command of His Majesty King George the Third in Pursuance of an Address of the House of Commons of Great Britain, from Original Records and Authentic Manuscripts*. 9 vols. London: G. Eyre and A. Strahan, 1810–22.

Lupton, Donald. *London and the Countrey Carbonadoed and Quartred into Severall Characters*. London, 1632.

Machin, Lewis and Gervase Markham. *The Dumbe Knight A Historicall Comedy, Acted Sundry Times by the Children of His Majesties Revels*. London, 1608.

Maitland, William. *The History and Survey of London, from Its Foundation to the Present Time*. 2 vols. London, 1756.

Marston, John. *Antonio and Mellida*. Ed. W. Reavley Gair. The Revels Plays. Manchester: Manchester University Press, 1991.

———. *Antonio's Revenge: The Second Part of Antonio and Mellida*. Ed. G. K. Hunter. Regents Renaissance Drama Series. Lincoln: University of Nebraska Press, 1965.

———. *The Dutch Courtesan*. Ed. Martin L. Wine. Regents Renaissance Drama Series. Lincoln: University of Nebraska Press, 1965.

———. *Histrio-Mastix. Or, The Player Whipt*. London, 1610.

———. *The Plays of John Marston*. Ed. Harvey Wood. London: Oliver and Boyd, 1939.

A Merrie Dialogue, Betweene Band, Cuffe, and Ruffe: Done by an Excellent Wit, and Lately Acted in a Shew in the Famous University of Cambridge. London, 1615.

Middleton, Thomas. *A Chaste Maid in Cheapside*. Ed. Alan Brissenden. The New Mermaids. New York: W. W. Norton, 1994.

———. *Thomas Middleton: The Collected Works*. Ed. Gary Taylor and John Lavagnino. Oxford: Oxford University Press, 2007.

———. *A Trick to Catch the Old One*. Ed. G. J. Watson. The New Mermaids. London: Ernest Benn, 1968.

Middleton, Thomas, and Thomas Dekker. *The Roaring Girl*. Ed. Paul Mulholland. The Revels Plays. Manchester: Manchester University Press, 1987.

Mithal, H. S. D., ed. *An Edition of Robert Wilson's Three Ladies of London and Three Lords and Three Ladies of London*. London: Garland Press, 1988.

Moffett, Thomas. *The Silkewormes, and Their Flies: Lively Described in Verse . . . For the Great Benefit and Enriching of England*. London, 1599.

Moore, Sir Jonas. *A Mathematical Compendium . . . Collected out of the Notes and Papers of Sir Jonas Moore, By Nicholas Stephenson*. London, 1674.

Moryson, Fynes. *An Itinerary Written by Fynes Moryson Gent*. London, 1617.

The Mother and Daughter; or, A Dialogue Betwixt Them Composed in Verse. London, 1670–96.

Muggins, William. *Londons Mourning Garment*. London, 1603.

Munday, Anthony. *A Second and Third Blast of Retrait from Plaies and Theatres*. London, 1580.

Munday, Anthony, and Others. *Sir Thomas More*. Ed. Vittorio Gabrielli and Giorgio Melchiori. The Revels Plays. Manchester: Manchester University Press, 1990.

Muscul[us], Wolfgang. *Of the Lawful and Unlawful Usurie Amo[n]gest Christians*. Wesel, 1556.

Nashe, Thomas. "The Choise of Valentines." In *The Works of Thomas Nashe*, ed. Ronald B. McKerrow. 3 vols. Oxford: Oxford University Press, 1958. 3: 403–16.

———. *Pierce Penilesse His Supplication to the Divell*. London, 1592.

Nelson, Alan H. *Records of Early English Drama: Cambridge*. Toronto: University of Toronto Press, 1989.

The Newe Testament of Our Lorde Jesus Christ. Trans. Theodore de Beze. London, 1578.

Norden, John. *A Christian Familiar Comfort and Incouragement Unto All English Subjects*. London, 1596.

Norris, Ralph. *A Warning to London by the Fall of Antwerp*. London, n.d. [1577?].

Northbrooke, John. *A Treatise Wherein Dicing, Dauncing, Vaine Playes or Enterluds with Other Idle Pastimes &c. Commonly Used on the Sabboth Day, Are Reproved by the Authoritie of the Word of God and Auntient Writers*. London, 1577.

Oldcastle, Hugh. *A Briefe Instruction and Maner How to Keepe Bookes of Accompts After the Order of Debitor and Creditor*. London, 1588.

Pacioli, Luca. *Exposition of Double Entry Bookkeeping*. Trans. Antonia Von Gebsattel. Ed. Basil Yamey. Venice: Albrizzi Editore, 1994.

Palsgrave, John. *Leclarcissement De La Langue Francoyse*. London, 1530.

P.[arker], M.[artin]. *Have Among You Good Women or, A High-Way Discourse Betweene Old William Starket, and Robin Hobs, Going to Maydstone Market*. London, 1634.

Peacham, Henry. *The Garden of Eloquence*. Gainesville, Fla.: Scholars' Facsimiles and Reprints, 1954.

———. *The Gentlemans Exercise Or, An Exquisite Practise, as Well for Drawing All Manner of Beasts in Their True Portraitures: As Also the Making of All Kinds of Colours . . . With Divers Others Most Delightfull and Pleasurable Observations, for All Yong Gentlemen and Others*. London, 1612.

———. *A Merry Discourse of Meum, and Tuum, or, Mine and Thine*. London, 1639.

Peele, James. *The Maner and Fourme How to Kepe a Perfecte Reconyng after the Order of the Most Worthie and Notable Accompte, of Debitour and Creditour*. London, 1554.

———. *The Pathe Waye to Perfectnes, in Th'Accomptes of Debitour, and Creditour in Manner of a Dialogue, Very Pleasaunte and Proffitable for Marchauntes and All Other That Minde to Frequente the Same*. London, 1569.

Pepys, Samuel. *The Diary of Samuel Pepys: A New and Complete Transcription*. Ed. Robert Latham and Robert Matthews. 11 vols. Berkeley: University of California Press, 1970.

Perkins, William. *A Treatise of the Vocations, or, Callings of Men, with the Sorts and Kinds of Them, and the Right Use Thereof*. London, 1603.

Petri, Nicolaus. *The Pathway to Knowledge Conteyning . . . The Order of Keeping of a Marchants Booke, after the Italian Manner, by Debitor and Creditor*. Trans. W[illiam] P[hillip]. London, 1596.

Pie, Thomas. *Usuries Spright Conjured: or A Scholasticall Determination of Usury*. London, 1604.

Platter, Thomas. *Thomas Platter's Travels in England, 1599*. Trans. Clare Williams. London: Jonathan Cape, 1959.

Pollard, Tanya, ed. *Shakespeare's Theater: A Sourcebook*. Oxford: Blackwell, 2004.

Powel, Gabriel. *Theologicall and Scholasticall Positions, Concerning Usurie*. Oxford, 1602.

Quintilian. *Institutio Oratoria*. Trans. and ed. Donald A. Russell. Vol. 5. Loeb Classical Library. Cambridge, Mass.: Harvard University Press, 2001.

Ramazzini, Bernardino. *A Treatise of the Diseases of Tradesmen, Shewing the Various Influence of Particular Trades Upon the State of Health*. London, 1705.

Rankins, William. *A Mirrour of Monsters Wherein Is Plainely Described the Manifold Vices, & Spotted Enormities, That are Caused by the Infectious Sight of Playes*. London, 1587.

Record, Robert. *The Ground of Artes Teachyng the Worke and Practise of Arithmetike, Moch Necessary for All States of Men. After a More Easyer & Exacter Sorte, Then Any Lyke Hath Hytherto Ben Set Forth*. London, 1543.

———. *The Grounde of Artes Teaching the Perfect Worke and Practise of Arithmetike . . . Augmented by M. John Dee, And Now Lately Diligently Corrected, [and] Beautified . . . By John Mellis*. London, 1582.

———. *The Ground of Arts . . . Whereunto Is Added a Compendium of Interest*. London, 1618.

The Revenger's Tragedy. Ed. Brian Gibbons. New York: W. W. Norton, 1991.

Rich, Barnabe. *Greenes Newes Both from Heaven and Hell.* London, 1593.

———. *The Honestie of This Age.* London, 1614.

———. *My Ladies Looking Glasse Wherein May be Discerned a Wise Man from a Foole, a Good Woman from a Bad: and the True Resemblance of Vice, Masked under the Vizard of Vertue.* London, 1616.

Rollins, Hyder Edward, ed. *The Pepys Ballads.* 8 vols. Cambridge, Mass.: Harvard University Press, 1929–32.

———, ed. *A Pepysian Garland: Black-Letter Broadside Ballads of the Years 1595–1639.* Cambridge: Cambridge University Press, 1922.

Sander, Nicholas. *A Briefe Treatise of Usurie.* Louanii, 1568.

Scott, William. *An Essay of Drapery: or, The Compleate Citizen Trading Justly. Pleasingly. Profitably.* London, 1635.

Scouloudi, Irene. *Returns of Strangers in the Metropolis, 1593, 1627, 1635, 1639: A Study of an Active Minority.* London: Huguenot Society of London, 1985.

Serres, Olivier de. *The Perfect Use of Silk-Wormes, and Their Benefit.* London, 1607.

Shakespeare, William [attrib.]. *The London Prodigall. As it Was Plaide by the Kings Majesties Servants. By William Shakespeare.* London, 1605.

Shakespeare, William. *Hamlet.* Ed. G. R. Hibbard. The Oxford Shakespeare. New York: Oxford University Press, 1987.

———. *Hamlet.* Ed. Ann Thompson and Neil Taylor. The Arden Shakespeare. London: Thomson Learning, 2006.

———. *King Henry IV, Part 1.* Ed. A. R. Humphreys. The Arden Shakespeare. New York, Routledge, 1996.

———. *King Henry IV,* Part 2. Ed. A. R. Humphreys. The Arden Shakespeare. New York: Routledge, 1996.

———. *King Henry V.* Ed. J. H. Walter. The Arden Shakespeare. London: Routledge, 1990.

———. *King Lear.* Ed. Kenneth Muir. The Arden Shakespeare. London Routledge, 1972.

———. *The Merchant of Venice.* Ed. John Russell Brown. The Arden Shakespeare. London: Routledge, 1991.

———. *The Merchant of Venice.* Ed. Horace Howard Furness. Vol. 7. A New Variorum Edition of Shakespeare. Philadelphia: J. B. Lippincott, 1888.

———. *The Merry Wives of Windsor.* Ed. Giorgio Melchiori. The Arden Shakespeare. Walton-on-Thames: Thomas Nelson and Sons, 2000.

———. *The Riverside Shakespeare.* Ed. G. Blakemore Evans et al. Boston: Houghton Mifflin, 1997.

———. *Shakespeare's Sonnets.* Ed. Stephen Booth. New Haven, Conn.: Yale University Press, 1977.

———. *Shakespeare's Sonnets.* Ed. Katherine Duncan-Jones. The Arden Shakespeare. London: Thomas Nelson, 1997.

———. *The Taming of the Shrew.* Ed. Brian Morris. The Arden Shakespeare. New York: Routledge, 1995.

———. *The Winter's Tale*. Ed. J. H. P. Pafford. The Arden Shakespeare. London: Methuen, 1984.
Sharpham, Edward. *Cupids Whirligig As it Hath Bene Sundry Times Acted by the Children of the Kings Majesties Revels*. London, 1607.
Sidney, Sir Philip. *An Apologie for Poetrie*. London, 1595.
Smith, Henry. *The Examination of Usury in Two Sermons*. London, 1591.
———. *A Preparative to Mariage*. London, 1591.
Spottiswood, James. *The Execution of Neschech and the Confyning of His Kinsman Tarbith. Or A Short Discourse, Shewing the Difference Betwixt Damned Usurie, and That Which Is Lawfull*. Edinburgh, 1616.
Stout, William. *The Autobiography of William Stout of Lancaster, 1665–1752*. Ed. J. D. Marshall. Manchester: Manchester University Press, 1967.
Stow, John. *The Annales, or A Generall Chronicle of England . . . Continued and Augmented . . . Unto the Ende of This Present Yeere 1614, by Edmund Howes, gentleman*. London, 1615.
———. *A Survey of London*. Ed. Charles Lethbridge Kingford. Oxford: Clarendon Press, 1908.
Strype, John. *A Survey of the Cities of London and Westminster . . . Corrected, Improved, and Very Much Enlarged by John Strype*. 2 vols. London, 1720.
Stubbes, Philip. *The Anatomie of Abuses Containing a Discoverie, or Briefe Summarie of Such Notable Vices and Corruptions, as Nowe Raigne in Many Christian Countreyes of the Worlde, but (Especially) in the Countrey of Ailgna*. London, 1584.
———. *The Anatomie of Abuses Containing a Description of Such Notable Vices and Enormities, As Raigne in Many Countries of the World, but Especiallie in the Realme of England*. London, 1595.
———. *The Second Part of the Anatomie of Abuses*. London, 1583.
Tawney, Richard H., and Eileen Power, eds. *Tudor Economic Documents: Being Selected Documents Illustrating the Economic and Social History of Tudor England*. 3 vols. London: Longmans, Green and Company, 1924.
Taylor, John. *All the Workes of John Taylor the Water-Poet Beeing Sixty and Three in Number. Collected into One Volume by the Author: With Sundry New Additions Corrected, Revised, and Newly Imprinted*. London, 1630.
Tilley, Morris Palmer. *Dictionary of the Proverbs in England in the Sixteenth and Seventeenth Centuries*. Ann Arbor: University of Michigan Press, 1950.
Tomkis, Thomas. *Lingua: or The Combat of the Tongue, and the Five Senses for Superiority A Pleasant Comoedie*. London, 1607.
Tusser, Thomas. *Five Hundreth Points of Good Husbandry United to as Many of Good Huswiferie*. London, 1573.
———. *A Hundreth Good Pointes of Husbandry Lately Maried Unto a Hundreth Good Poynts of Huswifery: Newly Corrected and Amplified*. London, 1570.
Twelve Ingenious Characters, or, Pleasant Descriptions of the Properties of Sundry Persons & Things. London, 1686.
Usurie Araigned and Condemned. Or, A Discoverie of the Infinite Injuries This Kingdome Endureth by the Unlawfull Trade of Usurie. London, 1625.

Wanton Tom: or, The Merry History of Tom Stitch the Taylor. London, 1685.
A Warning for Faire Women. London, 1599.
Wasson, John M., ed. *Records of Early English Drama: Devon*. Toronto: University of Toronto Press, 1984.
Weddington, John. *A Brief Instruction and Manner, How to Keep Merchants' Books of Accompts after the Order of Debitor and Creditor*. Antwerp, 1567.
Werdmüller, Otto. *A Spirituall, and Most Precious Pearle Teaching All Men to Love and Imbrace the Crosse . . . According to the Word of God. Written for thy Comfort by a Learned Preacher Otho Wermulierus. And Translated into English by M. Miles Coverdale*. Trans. Miles Coverdale. London, 1593.
Wheeler, John. *A Treatise of Commerce*. London, 1601.
Whetstone, George. *The Right Excellent and Famous Historye, of Promos and Cassandra Devided into Two Commicall Discourses*. London, 1578.
Wilson, Thomas. *A Discourse Uppon Usurye by Waye of Dialogue and Oracions, for the Better Varietye, and More Delite of All Those, That Shall Reade Thys Treatise*. London, 1572.
Wither, George. *A Collection of Emblemes, Ancient and Moderne Quickened With Metricall Illustrations, Both Morall and Divine: And Disposed into Lotteries, That Instruction, and Good Counsell, May bee Furthered by an Honest and Pleasant Recreation*. London, 1635.
A Womans Work Is Never Done. London, 1660 [c.1629].
Woolley, Hannah. *The Compleat Servant-Maid; or, The Young Maidens Tutor Directing Them How They May Fit, and Qualifie Themselves for Any of These Employments. Viz. Waiting Woman, House-Keeper, Chamber-Maid, Cook-Maid, Under Cook-Maid, Nursery-Maid, Dairy-Maid, Laundry-Maid, House-Maid, Scullery-Maid, Composed for the Great Benefit and Advantage of All Young Maidens*. London, 1677.
Yamey, B. S., H. C. Edey, and Hugh W. Thomson, eds. *Accounting in England and Scotland, 1543–1800*. New York: Garland, 1982.

SECONDARY SOURCES

Acheson, Katherine O. "'Outrage Your Face': Anti-Theatricality and Gender in Early Modern Closet Drama by Women." *Early Modern Literary Studies* 6:3 (2001): 16 paragraphs.
Agnew, Jean-Christophe. "Coming up for Air: Consumer Culture in Historical Perspective." In *Consumption and the World of Goods*, ed. John Brewer and Roy Porter. London: Routledge, 1993. 19–39.
———. *Worlds Apart: The Market and the Theater in Anglo-American Thought, 1550–1750*. Cambridge: Cambridge University Press, 1986.
Aho, James A. *Confession and Bookkeeping: The Religious, Moral, and Rhetorical Roots of Modern Accounting*. Albany: State University of New York Press, 2005.
———. "Rhetoric and the Invention of Double-Entry Bookkeeping." *Rhetorica* 3:1 (1985): 21–43.

Alexander, Sally, Anna Davin, and Eve Hostettler. "Laboring Women: A Reply to Eric Hobsbawm." *History Workshop Journal* 8 (1979): 174–82.

Alpers, Svetlana. "Describe or Narrate? A Problem in Realistic Representation." *New Literary History* 8:1 (1976): 15–41.

Amussen, Susan. *An Ordered Society: Gender and Class in Early Modern England*. New York: Columbia University Press, 1988.

Arab, Ronda A. "Work, Bodies and Gender in *The Shoemaker's Holiday*." *Medieval and Renaissance Drama in England* 13 (2001): 182–212.

Archer, Ian. *The History of the Haberdashers' Company*. Chichester: Phillmore, 1991.

———. *The Pursuit of Stability: Social Relations in Elizabethan London*. Cambridge: Cambridge University Press, 1991.

Archer, Ian, Caroline Barron, and Vanessa Harding. "Hugh Alley, Law Enforcement, and Market Regulation in the Later Sixteenth Century." In *Hugh Alley's Caveat: The Markets of London in 1598*, ed. Ian Archer, Caroline Barron, and Vanessa Harding. London: London Topographical Society, 1988. 15–29.

———. Introduction to *Hugh Alley's Caveat: The Markets of London in 1598*, ed. Ian Archer, Caroline Barron, and Vanessa Harding. London: London Topographical Society, 1988. 3–15.

———, eds. *Hugh Alley's Caveat: The Markets of London in 1598*. London: London Topographical Society, 1988.

Archer, John Michael. *Citizen Shakespeare: Freemen and Aliens in the Language of the Plays*. New York: Palgrave Macmillan, 2005.

Arnold, Janet. *Queen Elizabeth's Wardrobe Unlock'd*. Leeds: W. S. Maney and Son, 1988.

Arnold, Janet, Jenny Tiramani, and Santina M. Levey. *Patterns of Fashion 4: The Cut and Construction of Linen Shirts, Smocks, Neckwear, Headwear and Accessories for Men and Women c. 1540–1660*. London: Macmillan, 2008.

Ashelford, Jane. *Dress in the Age of Elizabeth I*. London: Holmes and Meier, 1988.

———. *A Visual History of Costume: The Sixteenth Century*. London: Batsford, 1983.

Ashton, Robert. "Usury and High Finance in the Age of Shakespeare and Jonson." *Renaissance and Modern Studies* 4 (1960): 14–53.

Bady, David. "The Sum of Something: Arithmetic in *The Merchant of Venice*." *Shakespeare Quarterly* 36:1 (1985): 10–30.

Baker, William, and Brian Vickers, eds. *The Merchant of Venice*. New York: Thoemmes Continuum, 2005.

Baldwin, T. W. *The Organization and Personnel of the Shakespearean Company*. Princeton, N.J.: Princeton University Press, 1927.

Barasch, Frances. "Italian Actresses in Shakespeare's World: Flaminia and Vincenza." *Shakespeare Bulletin* 18:4 (2000): 17–21.

———. "Italian Actresses in Shakespeare's World: Vittoria and Isabella." *Shakespeare Bulletin* 19:3 (2001): 5–9.

Bardsley, Sandy. "Women's Work Reconsidered: Gender and Wage Differentiation in Late Medieval England." *Past & Present* 165 (1999): 3–29.

Barish, Jonas. *The Antitheatrical Prejudice*. Berkeley: University of California Press, 1981.

Barnard, Francis Pierrepont. *The Casting-Counter and the Counting-Board: A Chapter in the History of Numismatics and Early Arithmetic*. Oxford: Clarendon Press, 1916.

Barroll, Leeds. *Anna of Denmark, Queen of England: A Cultural Biography*. Philadelphia: University of Pennsylvania Press, 2001.

Barron, Caroline. "The 'Golden Age' of Women in Medieval London." *Reading Medieval Studies* 15 (1989): 35–58.

Barron, Caroline M., and Anne F. Sutton. *Medieval London Widows, 1300–1500*. London: Hambledon Press, 1994.

Baskerville, Charles Read. *The Elizabethan Jig and Related Song Drama*. New York: Dover, 1965 [1929].

Beall, Karen. *Cries and Itinerant Trades: A Bibliography*. Hamburg: Hauswedell, 1975.

Bearman, Robert. "John Shakespeare: A Papist or Just Penniless?" *Shakespeare Quarterly* 56:4 (2005): 411–33.

Beckerman, Bernard. *Shakespeare at the Globe, 1599–1609*. New York: Macmillan, 1962.

Beier, A. L. "Social Problems in Elizabethan London." *Journal of Interdisciplinary History* 9:2 (1978): 203–21.

Beier, A. L., and Roger Finlay, eds. *London, 1500–1700: The Making of the Metropolis*. New York: Longman, 1986.

Belsey, Catherine. "Love in Venice." *Shakespeare Survey* 44 (1992): 41–53.

Ben-Amos, Ilana Krausman. *Adolescence and Youth in Early Modern England*. New Haven, Conn.: Yale University Press, 1994.

———. "Failure to Become Freemen: Urban Apprentices in Early Modern England." *Social History* 16:2 (1991): 155–72.

———. "Women Apprentices in the Trades and Crafts of Early Modern Bristol." *Continuity and Change* 6:2 (1991): 227–52.

Benedict, Robert Russell. *The Mystery of Hamlet: Prince of Darkness*. Philadelphia: J. B. Lippincott, 1910.

Bennett, Judith M. *Ale, Beer, and Brewsters in England: Women's Work in a Changing World, 1300–1600*. Oxford: Oxford University Press, 1996.

———. "'History That Stands Still': Women's Work in the European Past." *Feminist Studies* 14: 2 (1988): 269–83.

———. "Misogyny, Popular Culture, and Women's Work." *History Workshop* 31 (1991): 166–88.

Bentley, Gerald Eades. "The Grateful Dead: Actor's Testamentary Bequests to Women, 1580–1651." *Proceedings of the American Philosophical Society* 135:2 (1991): 382–87.

———. *The Jacobean and Caroline Stage*. 7 vols. Oxford: Oxford University Press, 1941–68.

———. *The Profession of Dramatist in Shakespeare's Time, 1590–1642*. Princeton, N.J.: Princeton University Press, 1971.

Beresford, M. W. "The Common Informer, the Penal Statutes and Economic Regulation." *Economic History Review*, n.s., 10:2 (1957): 221–38.

Berger, Harry Jr. "Marriage and Mercifixion in *The Merchant of Venice*: The Casket Scene Revisited." *Shakespeare Quarterly* 32:2 (1981): 155–62.

Bergeron, David. *English Civic Pageantry, 1558–1642*. Columbia: University of South Carolina Press, 1971.

———. "Women as Patrons of English Renaissance Drama." In *Patronage in the Renaissance*, ed. Guy Fitch Lytle and Stephen Orgel. Princeton, N.J.: Princeton University Press, 1981. 274–90.

Berlin, Michael. "'Broken All in Pieces': Artisans and the Regulation of Workmanship in Early Modern London." In *The Artisan and the European Town, 1500–1900*, ed. Geoffrey Crossick. Aldershot: Ashgate, 2000. 75–91.

Berry, Herbert. *The First Public Playhouse: The Theatre in Shoreditch, 1576–98*. Montreal: McGill-Queen's University Press, 1979.

Bethell, S. L. *Shakespeare and the Popular Dramatic Tradition*. London: Staples Press, 1948.

Bevington, David. *Action Is Eloquence: Shakespeare's Language of Gesture*. Cambridge, Mass.: Harvard University Press, 1984.

———. *From Mankind to Marlowe: Growth of Structure in the Popular Drama of Tudor England*. Cambridge, Mass.: Harvard University Press, 1962.

———. *Tudor Drama and Politics: A Critical Approach to Topical Meaning*. Cambridge, Mass.: Harvard University Press, 1968.

Bilello, Thomas C. "Accomplished with What She Lacks: Law, Equity and Portia's Con." In *The Law in Shakespeare*, ed. Constance Jordan and Karen Cunningham. Basingstoke: Palgrave Macmillan, 2007. 109–26.

Black, Anthony. *Guilds and Civil Society in European Political Thought from the Twelfth Century to the Present*. Ithaca, N.Y.: Cornell University Press, 1984.

Bland, A. E., P. A. Brown, and R. H. Tawney, eds. *English Economic History: Select Documents*. London, 1914.

Bloom, Gina. *Voice in Motion: Staging Gender, Shaping Sound in Early Modern England*. Philadelphia: University of Pennsylvania Press, 2007.

Bly, Mary. *Queer Virgins and Virgin Queans on the Early Modern Stage*. Oxford: Oxford University Press, 2000.

Boose, Lynda E. "The Comic Contract and Portia's Golden Ring." *Shakespeare Studies* 20 (1988): 241–54.

Boulton, Jeremy. *Neighborhood and Society: A London Suburb in the Seventeenth Century*. Cambridge: Cambridge University Press, 1987.

Bowers, Fredson. *Elizabethan Revenge Tragedy, 1587–1642*. Princeton, N.J.: Princeton University Press, 1940.

Bowsher, Julian, and Pat Miller. *The Rose and the Globe: Playhouses of Shakespeare's Bankside, Southwark*. London: Museum of London Archaeology, 2009.

Boyce, Benjamin. *The Theophrastan Character in England to 1642*. Cambridge, Mass.: Harvard University Press, 1947.

Bradbrook, Muriel C. *The Rise of the Common Player: A Study of Actor and Society in Shakespeare's England*. London: Chatto and Windus, 1962.

Breeze, Andrew. "Welsh Tradition and the Baker's Daughter in Hamlet." *Notes and Queries* 49:2 (2002): 199–200.

Brenner, Robert. *Merchants and Revolution: Commercial Change, Political Conflict and London's Overseas Traders, 1550–1653*. Princeton, N.J.: Princeton University Press, 1993.

Bridenbaugh, Carl. *Vexed and Troubled Englishmen, 1590–1642*. Oxford: Oxford University Press, 1968.

Bridge, Sir Frederick. *The Olde Cryes of London: With Numerous Illustrations and Musical Examples*. London: Novello, 1921.

Briggs, Chris. "Empowered or Marginalized? Rural Women and Credit in Later Thirteenth- and Fourteenth-Century England." *Continuity and Change* 19 (2004): 13–43.

Bristol, Michael D. *Big-Time Shakespeare*. New York: Routledge, 1996.

———. "Carnival and the Institutions of Theater in Elizabethan England." *English Literary History* 50:4 (1983): 637–54.

———. "Shamelessness in Arden: Early Modern Theater and the Obsolescence of Popular Theatricality." In *Print, Manuscript and Performance*, ed. Arthur F. Marotti and Michael D. Bristol. Columbus: Ohio State University Press, 2000. 279–306.

Brodsky, Vivien. "Widows in Late Elizabethan London: Remarriage, Economic Opportunity and Family Orientations." In *The World We Have Gained: Histories of Population and Social Structure*, ed. Lloyd Bonfield, Richard M. Smith, and Keith Wrightson. Oxford: Basil Blackwell, 1986. 122–54.

Brown, Bill. "Thing Theory." *Critical Inquiry* 28:1 (2001): 1–22.

Brown, Gene R., and Kenneth S. Johnston. *Paciolo on Accounting*. New York: McGraw-Hill, 1963.

Brown, Judith C., and Jordan Goodman. "Women and Industry in Florence." *Journal of Economic History* 40 (1980): 73–80.

Brown, Pamela Allen. *Better a Shrew than a Sheep: Women, Drama, and the Culture of Jest in Early Modern England*. Ithaca, N.Y.: Cornell University Press, 2003.

———. "The Counterfeit Innnamorata, or, the Diva Vanishes." *Shakespeare Yearbook* 10 (1999): 402–26.

Brown, Pamela Allen, and Peter Parolin. Introduction to *Women Players in Early Modern England, 1500–1660: Beyond the All-Male Stage*, ed. Pamela Allen Brown and Peter Parolin. Aldershot: Ashgate, 2005. 1–21.

———, eds. *Women Players in England, 1500–1660: Beyond the All-Male Stage*. Aldershot: Ashgate, 2005.

Bruster, Douglas. *Drama and the Market in the Age of Shakespeare*. Cambridge: Cambridge University Press, 1992.

———. *Shakespeare and the Question of Culture: Early Modern Literature and the Cultural Turn*. New York: Palgrave Macmillan, 2003.

Burke, Peter. *Popular Culture in Early Modern Europe*. New York: New York University Press, 1978.

Burnett, Mark Thornton. "Apprentice Literature and the 'Crisis' of the 1590s." *Yearbook of English Studies* 21 (1991): 27–38.

———. "Ophelia's 'False Steward' Contextualized." *Review of English Studies* 46:181 (1995): 48–56.

Bush-Bailey, Gilli. *Treading the Bawds: Actresses and Playwrights on the Late-Stuart Stage*. Manchester: Manchester University Press, 2006.

Callaghan, Dympna. Introduction to *The Impact of Feminism in English Renaissance Studies*, ed. Dympna Callaghan. Basingstoke: Palgrave Macmillan, 2007. 1–29.

———. *Shakespeare Without Women: Representing Gender and Race on the Renaissance Stage*. New York: Routledge, 2000.

Camden, Caroll. "On Ophelia's Madness." *Shakespeare Quarterly* 15:2 (1964): 247–55.

Camp, Charles W. *The Artisan in Elizabethan Literature*. New York: Columbia University Press, 1924.

Campbell, Julie D. "'Merry, Nimble, Stirring Spirit[s]': Academic, Salon and Commedia dell'Arte Influence on the *Innamorate* in *Love's Labour's Lost*." In *Women Players in Early Modern England, 1500–1660: Beyond the All-Male Stage*, ed. Pamela Allen Brown and Peter Parolin. Aldershot: Ashgate, 2005. 145–70.

Capp, Bernard. *When Gossips Meet: Women, Family, and Neighborhood in Early Modern England*. Oxford: Oxford University Press, 2003.

Carlin, Martha. "The Urban Development of Southwark, c. 1200–1550." Ph.D. diss., University of Toronto, 1983.

Carroll, William. *Fat King, Lean Beggar: Representations of Poverty in the Age of Shakespeare*. Ithaca, N.Y.: Cornell University Press, 1996.

Carruthers, Bruce G. *City of Capital: Politics and Markets in the English Financial Revolution*. Princeton, N.J.: Princeton University Press, 1996.

Carson, Neil. *A Companion to Henslowe's Diary*. Cambridge: Cambridge University Press, 1988.

Castells, Manuel, and Alejandro Portes. "World Underneath: The Origins, Dynamics, and Effects of the Informal Economy." In *The Informal Economy: Studies in Advanced and Less Developed Countries*, ed. Alejandro Portes, Manuel Castells, and Lauren A. Benton. Baltimore: Johns Hopkins University Press, 1989. 11–37.

Cerasano, Susan P. "'Borrowed Robes,' Costume Prices and the Drawing of *Titus Andronicus*." *Shakespeare Studies* 22 (1994): 45–57.

———. "Edward Alleyn: His Brothel's Keeper?" *Medieval and Renaissance Drama in England* 13 (2001): 93–100.

———. "The Patronage Network of Philip Henslowe and Edward Alleyn." *Medieval and Renaissance Drama in England* 13 (2001): 82–92.

———. "Revising Philip Henslowe's Biography." *Notes and Queries*, n.s., 32 (1985): 66–71.

———. "Women as Theatrical Investors: Three Shareholders in the Second Fortune Playhouse." In *Readings in Renaissance Women's Drama: Criticism, History, and Performance, 1594–1998*, ed. S. P. Cerasano and Marion Wynne-Davies. London: Routledge, 1998. 87–94.

Cerasano, S. P., and Marion Wynne-Davies, eds. *Readings in Renaissance Women's Drama: Criticism, History and Performance, 1594–1998*. London: Routledge, 1998.

———. *Renaissance Drama by Women*. London: Routledge, 1996.

Chambers, E. K. *The Elizabethan Stage*. 4 vols. Oxford: Clarendon Press, 1923.

———. *William Shakespeare: A Study of Facts and Problems.* 2 vols. Oxford: Clarendon Press, 1930.
Charles, Lindsey. Introduction to *Women and Work in Pre-Industrial England*, ed. Charles Lindsey and Lorna Duffin. London: Croom Helm, 1985. 1–23.
Charles, Lindsey, and Lorna Duffin, eds. *Women and Work in Pre-Industrial England.* London: Croom Helm, 1985.
Charney, Maurice, and Hanna Charney. "The Language of the Madwoman in Shakespeare and His Fellow Dramatists." *Signs* 3:2 (1977): 451–60.
Chedgzoy, Kate, Melanie Hansen, and Suzanne Trill, eds. *Voicing Women: Gender and Sexuality in Early Modern Writing.* Keele: Keele University Press, 1996.
Chitty, C. W. "Aliens in England in the Sixteenth Century." *Race* 8 (1966–67): 129–45.
Chojnacka, Monica. *Working Women of Early Modern Venice.* Baltimore: Johns Hopkins University Press, 2001.
Cioni, Maria L. "The Elizabethan Chancery and Women's Rights." In *Tudor Rule and Revolution: Essays for G. R. Elton from His American Friends*, ed. Delloyd J. Guth and John W. McKenna. Cambridge: Cambridge University Press, 1982. 159–82.
Clark, Alice. *Working Life of Women in the Seventeenth Century.* New York: A. M. Kelley, 1919.
Clark, Peter, and Paul Slack. *The English Alehouse: A Social History, 1200–1830.* Cambridge: Cambridge University Press, 1983.
Clark, Sandra. "The Broadside Ballad and the Woman's Voice." In *Debating Gender in Early Modern England*, ed. Cristina Malcolmson and Mihoko Suzuki. Basingstoke: Palgrave Macmillan, 2002. 103–20.
Clarkson, L. A. *The Pre-Industrial Economy in England, 1500–1700.* London: B. T. Batsford, 1971.
Clay, C. G. A. *Economic Expansion and Social Change.* Cambridge: Cambridge University Press, 1984.
Clough, Wilson O. "The Broken English of Foreign Characters of the Elizabethan Stage." *Philological Quarterly* 12 (1933): 255–68.
Clubb, Louise George. *Italian Drama in Shakespeare's Time.* New Haven, Conn.: Yale University Press, 1989.
Cohen, Walter. "*The Merchant of Venice* and the Possibilities of Historical Criticism." *English Literary History* 49 (1982): 765–89.
Cole, Mary Hill. *The Portable Queen: Elizabeth I and the Politics of Ceremony.* Amherst: University of Massachusetts Press, 1999.
Coleman, D. C. "An Innovation and Its Diffusion: The 'New Draperies.'" *Economic History Review*, n.s., 22:3 (1969): 417–29.
Consitt, Frances. *The London Weavers' Company.* Vol. 1. Oxford: Clarendon, 1933.
Cook, Ann Jennalie. *The Privileged Playgoers of Shakespeare's London, 1576–1642.* Princeton, N.J.: Princeton University Press, 1981.
Coote, Stephen. *The Innholders: A History of the Worshipful Company of Innholders.* Kemble: Collectors Books, 2002.

Corbin, John. *Elizabethan Hamlet: A Study of the Sources, and of Shakespeare's Environment.* New York: C. Scribner's Sons, 1895.
Cotton, Nancy. *Women Playwrights in England, c. 1363–1750.* Lewisburg, Pa.: Bucknell University Press, 1980.
Cox, John D., and David Scott Kastan, eds. *A New History of Early English Drama.* New York: Columbia University Press, 1997.
Cox, Nancy. *The Complete Tradesman: A Study of Retailing, 1550–1820.* Aldershot: Ashgate, 2000.
Creizenach, Wilhelm. *The English Drama in the Age of Shakespeare.* New York: Haskell House, 1964 [1916].
Crosby, Alfred W. *The Measure of Reality: Quantification and Western Society, 1250–1600.* Cambridge: Cambridge University Press, 1997.
Crossick, Geoffrey, ed. *The Artisan and the European Town, 1500–1900.* Aldershot: Ashgate, 1997.
Crowston, Clare. "Women, Gender, and Guild in Early Modern Europe: An Overview of Recent Research." *International Review of Social History* 53 (2008): 19–44.
Cunnar, Eugene R. "The Viewer's Share: Three Sectarian Readings of Vermeer's Woman with a Balance." *Exemplaria* 2 (1990): 501–36.
Cunningham, Cecil W., Phillis E. Cunningham, and Charles Beard. *A Dictionary of English Costume, 900–1900.* London: Black, 1960.
Cunningham, W. *Alien Immigrants to England.* New York: Macmillan, 1897.
Cust, Lionel. "The Misers at Windsor Castle Attributed to Quentin Matsys." *Burlington Magazine for Connoisseurs* 20:107 (1912): 252–58.
Dale, Marion K. "The London Silkwomen of the Fifteenth Century." *Economic History Review* 4 (1932–34): 324–35.
Davidson, Clifford. *Technology, Guilds and Early English Drama.* Kalamazoo, Mich.: Medieval Institute Publications, 1997.
Davies, Margaret Gay. *The Enforcement of English Apprenticeship: A Study in Applied Mercantilism, 1563–1642.* Cambridge, Mass.: Harvard University Press, 1956.
Davies, Matthew, and Ann Saunders. *The History of the Merchant Taylors' Company.* Leeds: Maney Publishing, 2004.
Davis, Natalie Zemon. *Society and Culture in Early Modern France.* Stanford, Calif.: Stanford University Press, 1975.
———. "Women in Crafts in Sixteenth-Century Lyons." *Feminist Studies* 8 (1972): 49–53.
Dawson, Anthony B., and Paul Yachnin. *The Culture of Playgoing in Shakespeare's England: A Collaborative Debate.* Cambridge: Cambridge University Press, 2001.
Demaray, John. *Shakespeare and the Spectacles of Strangeness: The Tempest and the Transformation of Renaissance Theatrical Forms.* Pittsburgh: Duquesne University Press, 1998.
Dickson, Peter G. M. *The Financial Revolution in England: A Study in the Development of Public Credit, 1688–1786.* London: Macmillan, 1967.
Dillon, Janet. *Theatre, Court and City, 1595–1610: Drama and Social Space in London.* Cambridge: Cambridge University Press, 2000.

Dobb, Maurice. *Studies in the Development of Capitalism*. New York: New York International Publishers, 1964.
Dolan, Neil. "Shylock in Love: Economic Metaphors in Shakespeare's Sonnets." *Raritan* 22:2 (2002): 26–51.
Donald, Moira, and Linda Hurcombe. *Gender and Material Culture in Historical Perspective*. New York: St. Martin's, 2000.
Donohue, Joseph W., ed. *The Theatrical Manager in England and America*. Princeton, N.J.: Princeton University Press, 1971.
Dowd, Michelle. *Women's Work in Early Modern English Literature and Culture*. New York: Palgrave Macmillan, 2009.
Dowling, Margaret. "A Note on Moll Cutpurse—'the Roaring Girl.'" *Review of English Studies* 10 (1934): 67–71.
Draper, John W. "Usury in *The Merchant of Venice*." *Modern Philology* 33:1 (1935): 37–47.
Drew-Bear, Annette. *Painted Faces on the Renaissance Stage: The Moral Significance of Face-Painting Conventions*. Lewisburg, Pa.: Bucknell University Press, 1994.
Dunlop, Jocelyn O. *English Apprenticeship and Child Labor*. London: Unwin, 1912.
Dunn, Leslie C. "The Lady Sings in Welsh: Women's Songs as Marginal Discourse on the Shakespearean Stage." In *Place and Displacement in the Renaissance*, ed. Alvin Vos. Binghamton, N.Y.: Medieval and Renaissance Texts and Studies, 1995. 51–67.
———. "Ophelia's Songs in Hamlet: Music, Madness and the Feminine." In *Embodied Voices: Representing Female Vocality in Western Culture*, ed. Leslie C. Dunn and Nancy A. Jones. Cambridge: Cambridge University Press, 1994. 50–64.
Earle, Peter. "The Female Labor Market in London in the Late Seventeenth and Early Eighteenth Centuries." *Economic History Review*, n.s., 42:3 (1989): 328–53.
———. *The Making of the English Middle Class, 1660–1730*. London: Methuen, 1989.
"Early Elizabethan Stage Music." *Musical Antiquary* 1:1 (1909): 30–40.
Eccles, Mark. "Elizabethan Actors II: E–J." *Notes and Queries* 237 (1991): 454–61.
———. "George Wilkins." *Notes and Queries* 220 (1975): 250–52.
———. "Mary Frith, the Roaring Girl." *Notes and Queries*, n.s., 32 (1985): 65–66.
Edmond, Mary. "Hilliard, Nicholas (1547?–1619)." In *Oxford Dictionary of National Biography*, ed. H. C. G. Matthew and Brian Harrison. Oxford: Oxford University Press, 2008.
Eliot, T. S. *Essays on Elizabethan Drama*. New York: Harcourt, Brace, 1932.
Ellinghausen, Laurie. *Labor and Writing in Early Modern England, 1567–1667*. Aldershot: Ashgate, 2008.
Elliot, Vivien Brodsky. "Single Women in the London Marriage Market: Age, Status and Mobility, 1598–1619." In *Marriage and Society: Studies in the Social History of Marriage*, ed. R. B. Outhwaite. New York: St. Martin's, 1981. 81–100.
Elton, G. R. "Informing for Profit: A Sidelight on Tudor Methods of Law-Enforcement." *Cambridge Historical Journal* 11:2 (1954): 149–67.
Empson, William. "*Hamlet* When New." *Sewanee Review* 61 (1953): 15–42.
Enck, John J. "The Peace of the Poetomachia." *PMLA* 77:4 (1962): 386–96.

Engle, Lars. *Shakespearean Pragmatism: Market of His Time*. Chicago: University of Chicago Press, 1993.

———. "'Thrift Is Blessing': Exchange and Explanation in *The Merchant of Venice*." *Shakespeare Quarterly* 37:1 (1986): 20–37.

Erickson, Amy. "Coverture and Capitalism." *History Workshop Journal* 59:1 (2005): 1–16.

———. Introduction to Alice Clark, *Working Life of Women in the Seventeenth Century*, ed. Amy Erickson. New York: Routledge, 1992. vii–lv.

———. *Women and Property in Early Modern England*. New York: Routledge, 1993.

Erler, Mary C. "'Chaste Sports, Juste Prayses, & All Softe Delight': Harefield 1602 and Ashby 1607, Two Female Entertainments." In *The Elizabethan Theater*, ed. A. L. Magnuson and C. E. McGee. Toronto: P. A. Meany, 1991. 1–25.

Esser, Raingard. "Immigrant Cultures in Tudor and Stuart England." In *Immigrants in Tudor and Early Stuart England*, ed. Nigel Goose and Lien Luu. Brighton: Sussex Academic Press, 2005. 161–74.

Everitt, Alan Milner. "The English Urban Inn, 1560–1760." In *Perspectives in English Urban History*, ed. Alan Milner Everitt. London: Macmillan, 1973. 91–137.

———. "The Marketing of Agricultural Produce." In *The Agrarian History of England and Wales*, ed. Joan Thirsk. Cambridge: Cambridge University Press, 1967. 466–592.

Feldman, Abraham. "Dutch Exiles and Elizabethan Playwrights." *Notes and Queries* 196 (1951): 530–33.

———. "Hans Ewouts, Artist of the Tudor Court Theater." *Notes and Queries* 195 (1950): 257–58.

Ferman, L. A., S. Henry, and M. Hoyman. "Preface: The Informal Economy." *Annals of the American Academy of Political and Social Science* 493 (1987): 10–14.

Findlay, Allison, Stephanie Hodgson-Wright, and Gweno Williams. *Women and Dramatic Production, 1550–1700*. Harlow: Pearson, 2000.

Finlay, Roger. *Population and Metropolis: The Demography of London, 1580–1650*. Cambridge: Cambridge University Press, 1981.

Fisch, Harold. "Shakespeare and the Language of Gesture." *Shakespeare Studies* 19 (1987): 239–51.

Fisher, F. J. "Commercial Trends and Policy in Sixteenth-Century England." *Economic History Review* 10:2 (1940): 95–117.

———. "The Development of the London Food Market, 1540–1640." *Economic History Review* 5:2 (1935): 46–64.

———. "Some Experiments in Company Organization in the Early Seventeenth Century." *Economic History Review* 4:2 (1933): 177–94.

Fisher, Sandra K. *Econolingua: A Glossary of Coins and Economic Language in Renaissance Drama*. Newark: University of Delaware Press, 1985.

———. "Hearing Ophelia: Gender and Tragic Discourse in *Hamlet*." *Renaissance and Reformation* 14 (1990): 1–11.

Fleay, Frederick G. *A Biographical Chronicle of the English Drama, 1559–1642*. London: Reeves and Turner, 1891.

———. *A Chronicle History of the London Stage, 1559–1642*. New York: G. E. Stechert & Co., 1909 [1890].

Fontaine, Laurence. "Women's Economic Spheres and Credit in Pre-Industrial Europe." In *Women and Credit: Researching the Past, Reconfiguring the Future*, ed. Beverly Lemire, Ruth Pearson, and Gail Campbell. New York: Berg, 2001. 15–32.
Forse, James H. *Art Imitates Business: Commercial and Political Influences in Elizabethan Theatre*. Bowling Green: Bowling Green State University Popular Press, 1993.
Fox, Adam. *Oral and Literate Culture in England, 1500–1700*. Oxford: Clarendon Press, 2000.
Fox-Good, Jacquelyn. "Ophelia's Mad Songs: Music, Gender, Power." In *Subjects on the World's Stage: Essays on British Literature of the Middle Ages and the Renaissance*, ed. David Allen and Robert White. Newark: University of Delaware Press, 1995. 217–38.
Franits, Wayne E. *Paragons of Virtue: Women and Domesticity in Seventeenth-Century Dutch Art*. Cambridge: Cambridge University Press, 1993.
Freeman, Arthur. "Marlowe, Kyd, and the Dutch Church Libel." *English Literary Renaissance* 3 (1973): 44–52.
Froide, Amy M. "Marital Status as a Category of Difference: Singlewomen and Widows in Early Modern England." In *Singlewomen in the European Past, 1250–1800*, ed. Judith M. Bennett and Amy M. Froide. Philadelphia: University of Pennsylvania Press, 1999. 236–69.
———. *Never Married: Singlewomen in Early Modern England*. Oxford: Oxford University Press, 2005.
———. "Surplus Women with Surplus Money: Singlewomen as Creditors in Early Modern England." Paper presented at the North American Conference on British Studies, Boston, 1999.
Frost, David. *The School of Shakespeare: The Influence of Shakespeare on English Drama, 1600–1642*. Cambridge: Cambridge University Press, 1968.
Fumerton, Patricia. *Cultural Aesthetics: Renaissance Literature and the Practice of Social Ornament*. Chicago: University of Chicago Press, 1991.
———. *Unsettled: The Culture of Mobility and the Working Poor in Early Modern England*. Chicago: University of Chicago Press, 2006.
Gabrielli, Vittorio, and Giorgio Melchiori. Introduction to *Sir Thomas More*, ed. Vittorio Gabrielli and Giorgio Melchiori. Manchester: Manchester University Press, 1990. 1–41.
Gair, Reavley. *The Children of Paul's: The Story of a Theatre Company, 1553–1608*. Cambridge: Cambridge University Press, 1982.
Gaskell, Ivan. "Vermeer, Judgment and Truth." *Burlington Magazine* 126 (1984): 557–61.
Gasper, Julia. *The Dragon and the Dove: The Plays of Thomas Dekker*. Oxford: Clarendon Press, 1990.
Gaughan, J. P., and L. A. Ferman. "Toward an Understanding of the Informal Economy." *Annals of the American Academy of Political and Social Science* 493 (1987): 15–25.
Geary, Keith. "The Nature of Portia's Victory: Turning to Men in *The Merchant of Venice*." *Shakespeare Survey* 37 (1984): 55–68.
Gibbs, Kristine Forney. "A Study of the Cries of London as Found in the Works of English Renaissance Composers." M.A. thesis, University of Kentucky, 1974.

Gieskes, Edward. *Representing the Professions: Administration, Law and Theater in Early Modern England*. Newark: University of Delaware Press, 2006.

Gildersleeve, Virginia Crocheron. *Government Regulation of Elizabethan Drama*. New York: Columbia University Press, 1908.

Girouard, Mark. "Some Alien Craftsmen in Sixteenth- and Seventeenth-Century England." *Proceedings of the Huguenot Society of London* 20 (1958): 26–35.

Glass, D. V. "Socio-Economic Status and Occupations in the City of London at the End of the Seventeenth Century." In *Studies in London History*, ed. A. E. J. Hallaender and W. A. Kenaway. London: Hodder and Stoughton, 1969. 373–89.

Glimp, David, and Michelle R. Warren. Introduction to *Arts of Calculation: Quantifying Thought in Early Modern Europe*, ed. David Glimp and Michelle R. Warren. Basingstoke: Palgrave, 2004. xv–xxix.

Godelier, Maurice. "Work and Its Representations: A Research Proposal." *History Workshop* 10 (1980): 164–74.

Goldberg, P. J. P. "Female Labor, Service and Marriage in the Late Medieval Urban North." *Northern History* 22 (1986): 18–38.

Goose, Nigel. "Immigrants and English Economic Development in the Sixteenth and Early Seventeenth Centuries." In *Immigrants in Tudor and Early Stuart England*, ed. Nigel Goose and Lien Luu. Brighton: Sussex Academic Press, 2005. 136–60.

———. "Introduction: Immigrants in Tudor and Early Stuart England." In *Immigrants in Tudor and Early Stuart England*, ed. Nigel Goose and Lien Luu. Brighton: Sussex Academic Press, 2005. 1–38.

———. "'Xenophobia' in Elizabethan and Early Stuart England: An Epithet Too Far?" In *Immigrants in Tudor and Early Stuart England*, ed. Nigel Goose and Lien Luu. Brighton: Sussex Academic Press, 2005. 110–35.

Goose, Nigel, and Lien Luu, eds. *Immigrants in Tudor and Early Stuart England*. Brighton: Sussex Academic Press, 2005.

Gossett, Suzanne. "'Man-Maid, Begone!': Women in Masques." *English Literary Renaissance* 18 (1998): 96–113.

Gough, Melinda J. "Courtly *Comediantes*: Henrietta Maria and Amateur Women's Stage Plays in France and England." In *Women Players in Early Modern England, 1500–1660: Beyond the All-Male Stage*, ed. Pamela Allen Brown and Peter Parolin. Aldershot: Ashgate, 2005. 193–215.

———. "'Not as Myself': The Queen's Voice in *Tempe Restored*." *Modern Philology* 101:1 (2003): 48–67.

Gowing, Laura. "'The Freedom of the Streets': Women and Social Space, 1560–1640." In *Londinopolis: Essays in the Cultural and Social History of Early Modern London*, ed. Paul Griffiths and Mark S. R. Jenner. Manchester: Manchester University Press, 2000. 130–51.

Graves, Thornton Shirley. "Women on the Pre-Restoration Stage." *Studies in Philology* 22 (1925): 184–97.

Greenstreet, James. "The Whitefriars Theatre in the Time of Shakespeare." *New Shakespeare Society Transactions* 1:3 (1889): 269–84.

Greer, Germaine. *Shakespeare's Wife*. New York: Harper Collins, 2007.

Grell, Ole Peter. *Calvinist Exiles in Tudor and Stuart England*. Aldershot: Scolar Press, 1996.
Griffin, William J. "Notes on Early Tudor Control of the Stage." *Modern Language Notes* 58:1 (1943): 50–54.
Griffiths, Paul. "Politics Made Visible: Order, Residence and Uniformity in Cheapside, 1600–45." In *Londinopolis: Essays in the Cultural and Social History of Early Modern London*, ed. Paul Griffiths and Mark S. R. Jenner. Manchester: Manchester University Press, 2000. 176–96.
———. "The Structure of Prostitution in Elizabethan England." *Continuity and Change* 8 (1993): 39–64.
———. *Youth and Authority: Formative Experiences in England, 1560–1640*. Oxford: Oxford University Press, 1996.
Gross, Kenneth. *Shylock Is Shakespeare*. Chicago: University of Chicago Press, 2006.
Gurr, Andrew. *Playgoing in Shakespeare's London*. 3rd ed. Cambridge: Cambridge University Press, 2004 [1987].
———. *The Shakespearean Stage, 1574–1642*. 3rd ed. Cambridge: Cambridge University Press, 1992.
Guth, Delloyd J. "The Age of Debt, the Reformation and English Law." In *Tudor Rule and Revolution: Essays for G. R. Elton from His American Friends*, ed. Delloyd J. Guth and John W. McKenna. Cambridge: Cambridge University Press, 1982. 69–86.
Gwynn, Robin D. *Huguenot Heritage: The History and Contribution of the Huguenots in Britain*. London: Routledge and Kegan Paul, 1985.
Hafter, Daryl M. Introduction to *European Women and Preindustrial Craft*, ed. Daryl M. Hafter. Bloomington: Indiana University Press, 1995. vii–xv.
Hailey, R. Carter. "The Dating Game: New Evidence for the Dates of Q4 *Romeo and Juliet* and Q4 *Hamlet*." *Shakespeare Quarterly* 58:3 (2007): 367–87.
Halio, Jay L. *Understanding "The Merchant of Venice."* Westport, Conn.: Greenwood, 2000.
Hamilton, A. H. A. *Quarter Sessions from Queen Elizabeth to Queen Anne*. London: Sampson Low, Marston, Searle, & Rivington, 1878.
Harbage, Alfred. *Annals of English Drama, 975–1700: An Analytical Record of All Plays, Extant or Lost, Chronologically Arranged and Indexed by Authors, Titles, Dramatic Companies, &c*. Rev. Samuel Schoenbaum. 3rd ed. Rev. Sylvia Stoler Wagonheim. London and New York: Routledge, 1989.
Hardaker, Alfred. *A Brief History of Pawnbroking*. London: Jackson, Ruston and Keeson, 1892.
Harding, Vanessa. "Cheapside: Commerce and Commemoration." *Huntington Library Quarterly* 71:1 (2008): 77–96.
Harris, Jonathan Gil. *Sick Economies: Drama, Mercantilism, and Disease in Shakespeare's England*. Philadelphia: University of Pennsylvania Press, 2004.
Harris, Jonathan Gil, and Natasha Korda. "Introduction: Towards a Materialist Account of Stage Properties." In *Staged Properties in Early Modern English Drama*, ed. Jonathan Gil Harris and Natasha Korda. Cambridge: Cambridge University Press, 2002. 1–31.
Harris, Tim. *London Crowds in the Reign of Charles II: Propaganda and Politics from the Restoration until the Exclusion Crisis*. Cambridge: Cambridge University Press, 1987.

Harte, N. B. "State Control of Dress and Social Change in Pre-Industrial England." In *Trade, Government and Economy in Pre-Industrial England: Essays Presented to F. J. Fisher*, ed. D. C. Coleman and A. H. John. London: Weidenfeld and Nicolson, 1976.
Hawkes, David. "Sodomy, Usury, and the Narrative of Shakespeare's Sonnets." *Renaissance Studies* 14 (2000): 344–61.
Hawkins, John. "The Cries of London in the Sixteenth and Seventeenth Centuries." *Musical World* 34:51 (1856): 811–12.
Henderson, Edith G. "Relief from Bonds in the English Chancery: Mid-Sixteenth Century." *American Journal of Legal History* 18:4 (1974): 298–306.
Henderson, Tony. *Disorderly Women in Eighteenth-Century London: Prostitution and Control in the Metropolis, 1730–1830*. New York: Longman, 1999.
Heninger, S. K. *Touches of Sweet Harmony: Pythagorean Cosmology and Renaissance Poetics*. San Marino, Calif.: Huntington Library, 1974.
Henry, S. "The Political Economy of Informal Economies." *Annals of the American Academy of Political and Social Science* 493 (1987): 137–43.
Hentschell, Roze. "The Question of Nation: Foreign Clothes on the English Subject." In *Clothing Culture, 1350–1650*, ed. Catherine Richardson. Aldershot: Ashgate Press, 2004. 49–62.
Herbert, William. *The History of the Twelve Great Livery Companies of London*. London: William Herbert, 1887.
Herlihy, David. *Opera Muliebra: Women and Work in Medieval Europe*. New York: McGraw-Hill, 1990.
Herman, Peter C. "What's the Use? Or, the Problematic of Economy in Shakespeare's Procreation Sonnets." In *Shakespeare's Sonnets: Critical Essays*, ed. James Schiffer. New York: Garland, 1999. 263–83.
Hibbard, G. R. "General Introduction." In *Hamlet*, ed. G. R. Hibbard. Oxford: Oxford University Press, 1987. 1–66.
Hill, Bridget. *Women Alone: Spinsters in England, 1660–1850*. New Haven, Conn.: Yale University Press, 2001.
Hilton, Rodney H. *The English Peasantry in the Later Middle Ages*. Oxford: Clarendon Press, 1975.
———. "Lords, Burgesses and Hucksters." *Past and Present* 97 (1982): 3–15.
Hindley, Charles. *A History of the Cries of London (Ancient & Modern)*. 2nd ed. London: Reeves & Turner, 1884.
Hodge, Nancy Elizabeth. "Making Places at Belmont: 'You Are Welcome Notwithstanding.'" *Shakespeare Studies* 21 (1993): 155–74.
Hodgen, Margaret T. "Fairs of Elizabethan England." *Economic Geography* 18:4 (1942): 389–400.
Hoenselaars, A. J. *Images of Englishmen and Foreigners in the Drama of Shakespeare and His Contemporaries: A Study of Stage Characters and National Identity in English Renaissance Drama, 1558–1642*. Rutherford, N.J.: Fairleigh Dickinson University Press, 1992.

Hoenselaars, Ton, and Holger Klein, eds. *Shakespeare and the Low Countries*. Vol. 15. The Shakespeare Yearbook. Lewiston, N.Y.: Edwin Mellen Press, 2005.

Holderness, B. A. "Credit in a Rural Community, 1660–1800: Some Neglected Aspects of Probate Inventories." *Midland History* 3 (1975): 94–115.

———. "The Reception and Distribution of the New Draperies in England." In *The New Draperies in the Low Countries and England, 1300–1800*, ed. N. B. Harte. Oxford: Oxford University Press, 1997. 217–43.

———. "Widows in Pre-Industrial Society: An Essay Upon Their Economic Functions." In *Land, Kinship and Life Cycle*, ed. Richard M. Smith. Cambridge: Cambridge University Press, 1984. 423–42.

Holmer, Joan Ozark. "Miles Mosse's *The Arraignment and Conviction of Usurie* (1595): A New Source for *The Merchant of Venice*." *Shakespeare Studies* 21 (1993): 11–54.

Holmes, Martin. *Elizabethan London*. New York: F. A. Praeger, 1969.

Honan, Park. *Shakespeare: A Life*. Oxford: Oxford University Press, 1998.

Honeyman, Katrina, and Jordan Goodman. "Women's Work, Gender Conflict, and Labor Markets in Europe, 1500–1900." *Economic History Review* 44:4 (1991): 608–28.

Honigmann, E. A. J. "Shakespeare, *Sir Thomas More* and the Asylum Seekers." *Shakespeare Survey* 57 (2004): 225–35.

———. "Shakespeare and London's Immigrant Community." In *Elizabethan and Modern Studies: Presented to Professor Willem Schrickx on the Occasion of His Retirement*, ed. J. P. Vander Motten. Gent: Seminarie voor Engelse en Amerikaanse Literatuur, R. U. G., 1985. 143–51.

———. "Shakespeare's Life." In *The Cambridge Companion to Shakespeare*, ed. Margreta de Grazia and Stanley Wells. Cambridge: Cambridge University Press, 2001. 1–12.

———. *Shakespeare's Impact on His Contemporaries*. London: Macmillan, 1982.

Hooper, Wilfred. "The Tudor Sumptuary Laws." *English Historical Review* 30:119 (1915): 433–49.

Hotson, Leslie. *Shakespeare's Sonnets Dated, and Other Essays*. New York: Oxford University Press, 1949.

Howard, Jean E. *The Stage and Social Struggle in Early Modern England*. London: Routledge, 1994.

———. *Theater of a City: The Places of London Comedy, 1598–1642*. Philadelphia: University of Pennsylvania Press, 2007.

Howard, Skiles. "In Praise of Margaret Brayne." Paper presented at the Shakespeare Association of America Conference, Cleveland, 1998.

Hoy, Cyrus. *Introductions, Notes, and Commentaries to Texts in "The Dramatic Works of Thomas Dekker," Edited by Fredson Bowers*. 4 vols. Cambridge: Cambridge University Press, 1979–80.

Hoyman, M. "Female Participation in the Informal Economy: A Neglected Issue." *Annals of the American Academy of Political and Social Science* 493 (1987): 64–82.

Hudson, Kenneth. *Pawnbroking: An Aspect of British Social History*. London: The Bodley Head, 1982.

Hufton, Olwen. *The Poor of Eighteenth-Century France, 1750–1789*. Oxford: Clarendon Press, 1974.
———. "Women in History: Early Modern Europe." *Past and Present* 101 (1983): 125–41.
———. "Women Without Men: Widows and Spinsters in Britain and France in the Eighteenth Century." *Journal of Family History* 9 (1984): 355–76.
Hughes, Paul L., and James F. Larkin, eds. *Tudor Royal Proclamations*. New Haven, Conn.: Yale University Press, 1969.
Hunt, Margaret. *The Middling Sort: Commerce, Gender and the Family in England, 1680–1780*. Berkeley: University of California Press, 1996.
Hutson, Lorna. *The Usurer's Daughter: Male Friendship and Fictions of Women in Sixteenth-Century England*. London: Routledge, 1997.
Hutton, Diana. "Women in Fourteenth-Century Shrewsbury." In *Women and Work in Pre-Industrial England*, ed. Lindsey Charles and Lorna Duffin. London: Croom Helm, 1985. 83–121.
Ingram, Jill Phillips. *Idioms of Self-Interest: Credit, Identity and Property in English Renaissance Literature*. New York: Routledge, 2006.
Ingram, Martin. "Ridings, Rough Music and the 'Reform of Popular Culture' in Early Modern England." *Past and Present* 105 (1984): 79–113.
Ingram, William. *The Business of Playing: The Beginnings of the Adult Professional Theater in Elizabethan London*. Ithaca, N.Y.: Cornell University Press, 1992.
———. "The Economics of Playing." In *A Companion to Shakespeare*, ed. David Scott Kastan. Oxford: Blackwell, 1999. 313–27.
Inwood, Stephen. *A History of London*. New York: Carroll and Graf, 1998.
Ioppolo, Grace. *Revising Shakespeare*. Cambridge, Mass.: Harvard University Press, 1991.
Jaffe, Michele Sharon. *The Story of O: Prostitutes and Other Good-for-Nothings in the Renaissance*. Harvard Studies in Comparative Literature 45. Cambridge, Mass.: Harvard University Press, 1999.
Jardine, Lisa. "Cultural Confusion and Shakespeare's Learned Heroines: 'These Are Old Paradoxes.'" *Shakespeare Quarterly* 38:1 (1987): 1–18.
———. *Still Harping on Daughters: Women and Drama in the Age of Shakespeare*. Brighton: Harvester Press, 1983.
Johnson, Arthur Henry. *The History of the Worshipful Company of the Drapers of London*. 5 vols. Oxford: Clarendon Press, 1914–22.
Johnson, David J. *Southwark and the City*. Oxford: Oxford University Press, 1969.
Jones, Ann Rosalind, and Peter Stallybrass. *Renaissance Clothing and the Materials of Memory*. Cambridge: Cambridge University Press, 2000.
Jones, Norman. *God and the Moneylenders: Usury and Law in Early Modern England*. Oxford: Basil Blackwell, 1989.
Jones-Davies, Marie-Thérèse. *Un peintre de la vie Londonienne: Thomas Dekker*. Paris: Librairie Marcel Didier, 1958.
Jordan, William Chester. *Women and Credit in Pre-Industrial and Developing Societies*. Philadelphia: University of Pennsylvania Press, 1993.

Karim-Cooper, Farah. *Cosmetics in Shakespearean and Renaissance Drama*. Edinburgh: Edinburgh University Press, 2006.

Kastan, David Scott. "Workshop and/as Playhouse: *The Shoemaker's Holiday* (1599)." In *Staging the Renaissance: Reinterpretations of Elizabethan and Jacobean Drama*, ed. David Scott Kastan and Peter Stallybrass. New York: Routledge, 1991. 151–63.

Kastan, David Scott, and Peter Stallybrass, eds. *Staging the Renaissance: Reinterpretations of Elizabethan and Jacobean Drama*. New York: Routledge, 1991.

Kathman, David. "Alice Layston and the Cross Keys." *Medieval and Renaissance Drama in England* 22 (2009): 144–78.

———. "Grocers, Goldsmiths, and Drapers: Freemen and Apprentices in the Elizabethan Theater." *Shakespeare Quarterly* 55:1 (2004): 1–49.

Katritzky, M. A. "Reading the Actress in Commedia Imagery." In *Women Players in Early Modern England, 1500–1660: Beyond the All-Male Stage*, ed. Pamela Allen Brown and Peter Parolin. Aldershot: Ashgate, 2005. 109–43.

Kellet, J. R. "The Breakdown of Guild and Corporation Control over the Handicraft and Retail Trade in London." *Economic History Review*, n.s., 10:3 (1958): 381–94.

Kermode, Lloyd Edward. "After Shylock: The 'Judaiser' in England." *Renaissance and Reformation* 20:4 (1996): 5–26.

———. *Aliens and Englishness in Elizabethan Drama*. Cambridge: Cambridge University Press, 2009.

Kinney, Arthur. *Markets of Bawdrie: The Dramatic Criticism of Stephen Gosson*. Salzburg: Salzburg Studies in English Literature, 1974.

Knutson, Rosalyn L. "Falconer to the Little Eyases: A New Date and Commercial Agenda for the 'Little Eyases' Passage in *Hamlet*." *Shakespeare Quarterly* 46:1 (1995): 1–31.

———. *Playing Companies and Commerce in Shakespeare's Time*. Cambridge: Cambridge University Press, 2001.

Korda, Natasha. "The Case of Moll Frith: Women's Work and the 'All-Male Stage.'" In *Women Players in Early Modern England, 1500–1660: Beyond the All-Male Stage*, ed. Pamela Allen Brown and Peter Parolin. Aldershot: Ashgate, 2005. 71–87.

———. "Gender at Work in the Cries of London." In *Oral Traditions and Gender in Early Modern Literary Texts*, ed. Mary Ellen Lamb and Karen Bamford. Aldershot: Ashgate, 2008. 117–35.

———. "Household Property/Stage Property: Henslowe as Pawnbroker." *Theatre Journal* 48 (1996): 185–95.

———. "Labors Lost: Women's Work and Early Modern Theatrical Commerce." In *From Script to Stage in Early Modern England*, ed. Peter Holland and Stephen Orgel. Basingstoke: Palgrave Macmillan, 2004. 195–230.

———. *Shakespeare's Domestic Economies: Gender and Property in Early Modern England*. Philadelphia: University of Pennsylvania Press, 2002.

———. "Women's Theatrical Properties." In *Staged Properties in Early Modern English Drama*, ed. Jonathan Gil Harris and Natasha Korda. Cambridge: Cambridge University Press, 2002.

Kowaleski, Maryanne. "Singlewomen in Medieval and Early Modern Europe: The Demographic Perspective." In *Singlewomen in the European Past, 1250–1800*, ed. Judith M. Bennett and Amy M. Froide. Philadelphia: University of Pennsylvania Press, 1999. 38–81.

Kowaleski, Maryanne, and Judith M. Bennett. "Crafts, Guilds, and Women in the Middle Ages: Fifty Years After Marion K. Dale." *Signs* 14:2 (1989): 474–501.

Kramer, Stella. *The English Craft Gilds and the Government*. New York: Columbia University Press, 1905.

———. *The English Craft Gilds: Studies in Their Progress and Decline*. New York: Columbia University Press, 1927.

Lacey, Kay. "The Production of 'Narrow Ware' by Silkwomen in Fourteenth and Fifteenth Century England." *Textile History* 18:2 (1987): 187–204.

———. "Women and Work in Fourteenth and Fifteenth Century London." In *Women and Work in Pre-Industrial England*, ed. Lindsey Charles and Lorna Duffin. London: Croom Helm, 1985. 24–78.

Lapham, Ella Caroline. "The Industrial Status of Women in Elizabethan England." *Journal of Political Economy* 9:4 (1901): 562–99.

Lawrence, W. J. "Elizabethan Players as Tradesfolk." *Modern Language Notes* 41 (1926): 363–64.

———. *Those Nut-Cracking Elizabethans: Studies in the Early Theatre and Drama*. London: Argonaut, 1935.

Le Goff, Jacques. *Your Money or Your Life: Economy and Religion in the Middle Ages*. New York: Zone Books, 1988.

Leinwandt, Theodore. *Theatre, Finance and Society in Early Modern England*. Cambridge: Cambridge University Press, 1999.

Lemire, Beverly. *Dress, Culture and Commerce: The English Clothing Trade Before the Factory, 1600–1800*. New York: St. Martin's, 1997.

———. "Introduction: Women, Credit and the Creation of Opportunity: A Historical Overview." In *Women and Credit: Researching the Past, Refiguring the Future*, ed. Beverly Lemire, Ruth Pearson, and Gail Campbell. Oxford: Berg, 2001. 3–14.

———. "Petty Pawns and Informal Lending: Gender and the Transformation of Small-Scale Credit in England, c. 1600–1800." In *From Family Firms to Corporate Capitalism*, ed. Kristine Bruland and Patrick O'Brien. Oxford: Oxford University Press, 1998. 112–38.

Lemire, Beverly, Ruth Pearson, and Gail Campbell, eds. *Women and Credit: Researching the Past, Refiguring the Future*. Oxford: Berg, 2001.

Leventen, Carol. "Patrimony and Patriarchy in *The Merchant of Venice*." In *The Matter of Difference: Materialist Feminist Criticism of Shakespeare*, ed. Valerie Wayne. Ithaca, N.Y.: Cornell University Press, 1991. 59–79.

Levin, Carole. "'We Princes, I Tell You, Are Set on Stages': Elizabeth I and Dramatic Self-Representation." In *Readings in Renaissance Women's Drama: Criticism, History and Performance, 1594–1998*, ed. S. P. Cerasano and Marion Wynne-Davies. London: Routledge, 1998. 113–24.

Levin, Harry. "A Garden in Belmont: *The Merchant of Venice*, 5.1." In *Shakespeare and Dramatic Tradition: Essays in Honor of S. F. Johnson*, ed. W. R. Elton and William B. Long. Newark: University of Delaware Press, 1989. 13–31.

Levin, Richard. "The Structure of Bartholomew Fair." *PMLA* 80:3 (1965): 172–79.

———. "Women in the Renaissance Theater Audience." *Shakespeare Quarterly* 40 (1989): 165–74.

Lewalski, Barbara. "Biblical Allusion and Allegory in *The Merchant of Venice*." *Shakespeare Quarterly* 13:3 (1962): 327–43.

Littleton, Charles. "Social Interactions of Aliens in Late Elizabethan London: Evidence from the 1593 Returns and the French Church Consistory 'Actes.'" In *The Strangers' Progress: Integration and Disintegration of the Huguenot and Walloon Refugee Community, 1567–1889: Essays in Memory of Irene Scouloudi*, ed. Randolph Vigne and Graham C. Gibbs. London: Huguenot Society, 1995. 147–59.

"London Street Cries Set to Music." *New York Musical World* 12:15 (1855): 174–75.

Lowenstein, Joseph. "Plays Agonistic and Competitive: The Textual Approach to Elsinore." *Renaissance Drama* 19 (1988): 63–96.

Lucking, D. "Standing for Sacrifice: The Casket and Trial Scenes in *The Merchant of Venice*." *University of Toronto Quarterly* 58:3 (1989): 355–75.

Luijten, Ger. "Frills and Furbelows: Satires on Fashion and Pride around 1600. *Simiolus: Netherlands Quarterly for the History of Art* 24:2–3 (1996): 140–60.

Luu, Lien Bich. "Assimilation or Segregation: Colonies of Alien Craftsmen in Elizabethan London." In *The Strangers' Progress: Integration and Disintegration of the Huguenot and Walloon Refugee Community, 1567–1889: Essays in Memory of Irene Scouloudi*, ed. Randolph Vigne and Graham C. Gibbs. London: Huguenot Society, 1995. 160–72.

———. *Immigrants and the Industries of London, 1500–1700*. Aldershot: Ashgate Press, 2005.

———. "Natural Born Versus Stranger-Born Subjects: Aliens and Their Status in Elizabethan London." In *Immigrants in Tudor and Early Stuart England*, ed. Nigel Goose and Lien Luu. Brighton: Sussex Academic Press, 2005. 57–75.

Lyons, Bridget G. "The Iconography of Ophelia." *English Literary History* 44:1 (1977): 60–74.

Macfarlane, Stephen. "Social Policy and the Poor in the Later Seventeenth Century." In *London, 1500–1700: The Making of the Metropolis*, ed. A. L. Beier and Roger Finlay. New York: Longman, 1986. 252–77.

MacIntyre, Jean. *Costumes and Scripts in the Elizabethan Theatres*. Edmonton: University of Alberta Press, 1992.

Marcus, Leah S. *Unediting the Renaissance: Shakespeare, Marlowe, Milton*. New York: Routledge, 1996.

Marino, John A. "Economic Idylls and Pastoral Realities: The 'Trickster Economy' in the Kingdom of Naples." *Comparative Studies in Society and History* 24:2 (1982): 211–34.

Marx, Karl. *Capital: A Critique of Political Economy*. Trans. Ben Fowkes. Vol. 1. New York: Penguin, 1990 [1867].

———. *Writings of the Young Karl Marx on Philosophy and Society*. Trans. Lloyd D. Easton and Kurt H. Guddat. New York: Doubleday, 1967.

Mattera, Philip. *Off the Books: The Rise of the Underground Economy*. New York: St. Martin's, 1985.

Matthew, H. C. G., and Brian Harrison, eds. *Oxford Dictionary of National Biography . . . From the Earliest Times to the Year 2000*. 60 vols. Oxford: Oxford University Press, 2004.

Mauss, Marcel. *The Gift: Forms and Functions of Exchange in Archaic Societies*. Trans. Ian Cunnison. New York: Norton, 1967 [1925].

McGinn, Donald J. *Shakespeare's Influences on the Drama of His Age, Studied in "Hamlet."* New Brunswick, N.J.: Rutgers University Press, 1938.

McIntosh, Marjorie K. "Money Lending on the Periphery of London." *Albion* 20:4 (1988): 557–71.

———. "Women, Credit and Family Relationships in England, 1300–1620." *Journal of Family History* 30:2 (2005): 143–63.

———. *Working Women in English Society, 1300–1620*. Cambridge: Cambridge University Press, 2005.

McLuskie, Kathleen. "The Patriarchal Bard: Feminist Criticism and Shakespeare: *King Lear* and *Measure for Measure*." In *Political Shakespeare: New Essays in Cultural Materialism*, ed. Jonathan Dollimore and Alan Sinfield. Ithaca, N.Y.: Cornell University Press, 1985. 88–108.

McManus, Clare. *Women on the Renaissance Stage: Anna of Denmark and Female Masquing in the Stuart Court, 1590–1619*. Manchester: Manchester University Press, 2002.

McMullan, John L. "Criminal Organization in Sixteenth and Seventeenth Century London." *Social Problems* 29:3 (1982): 311–23.

McNeill, Fiona. "Free and Bound Maids: Women's Work Songs and Industrial Change in the Age of Shakespeare." In *Oral Traditions and Gender in Early Modern Literary Texts*, ed. Mary Ellen Lamb and Karen Bamford. Aldershot: Ashgate, 2008. 101–16.

Mendelson, Sara, and Patricia Crawford. *Women in Early Modern England, 1550–1720*. Oxford: Clarendon Press, 1998.

Miller, John. "Town Governments and Protestant Strangers, 1560–1690." *Proceedings of the Huguenot Society* 26:5 (1997): 577–89.

Milliot, Vincent, and Pascal Benoist. "Cultural Exchanges and Auditory Sensibilities: The Street Cries in the Sixteenth and Seventeenth Century." In *Le Chant, Acteur De L'histoire*, ed. Jean Quéniart. Rennes: University of Rennes, 1999. 201–14.

Mirabella, Bella. " 'Quacking Delilahs': Female Mountebanks in Early Modern England and Italy." In *Women Players in Early Modern England, 1500–1660: Beyond the All-Male Stage*, ed. Pamela Allen Brown and Peter Parolin. Aldershot: Ashgate, 2005. 89–105.

Mischo, John B. " 'That Use Is Not Forbidden Usury': Shakespeare's Procreation Sonnets and the Problem of Usury." In *Subjects on the World's Stage: Essays on British Literature of the Middle Ages and the Renaissance*, ed. David G. Allen and Robert A. White. Newark: University of Delaware Press, 1995. 262–79.

Moison, Thomas. "'Which Is the Merchant Here? And Which the Jew?': Subversion and Recuperation in *The Merchant of Venice*." In *Shakespeare Reproduced: The Text in History and Ideology*, ed. Jean E. Howard and Marion F. O'Connor. New York: Methuen, 1987. 188–206.
Mueller, Sara. "Domestic Work in Progress Entertainments." In *Working Subjects in Early Modern English Drama*, ed. Michelle M. Dowd and Natasha Korda. Burlington, Vt.: Ashgate, 2011. 145–60.
Muldrew, Craig. "Credit and Courts: Debt Litigation in a Seventeenth-Century Urban Community." *Economic History Review* 46 (1993): 23–38.
———. "The Culture of Reconciliation: Community and Settlement of Economic Disputes in Early Modern England." *Historical Journal* 39:4 (1996): 915–42.
———. *The Economy of Obligation: The Culture of Credit and Social Relations in Early Modern England*. New York: St. Martin's, 1998.
———. "'Hard Food for Midas': Cash and Its Social Value in Early Modern England." *Past & Present* 170 (2001): 78–120.
———. "Interpreting the Market: The Ethics of Credit and Community Relations in Early Modern England." *Social History* 18 (1993): 163–83.
———. "'A Mutual Assent of Her Mind?' Women, Debt, Litigation and Contract in Early Modern England." *History Workshop Journal* 55 (2003): 47–72.
Murray, David. *Chapters in the History of Bookkeeping, Accountancy, & Commercial Arithmetic*. New York: Arno Press, 1978.
Murray, John J. "The Cultural Impact of the Flemish Low Countries on Sixteenth- and Seventeenth-Century England." *American Historical Review* 62:4 (1957): 837–54.
———. *Flanders and England: A Cultural Bridge: The Influence of the Low Countries on Tudor-Stuart England*. Antwerp: Fonds Mercator, 1985.
Nathan, Norman. "Belmont and the Monte Di Pieta in *The Merchant of Venice*." *Cahiers Elisabethains* 18 (1980): 69–70.
Neely, Carol Thomas. "Documents in Madness: Reading Madness and Gender in Shakespeare's Tragedies and Early Modern Culture." *Shakespeare Quarterly* 42:3 (1991): 315–38.
Neill, Michael. "'Wit's Most Accomplished Senate': The Audience of the Caroline Private Theaters." *Studies in English Literature* 18 (1978): 341–60.
Nelson, Alan H. "Women in the Audience of Cambridge Plays." *Shakespeare Quarterly* 41 (1990): 333–36.
Nevinson, J. L. "Shakespeare's Dress in His Portraits." *Shakespeare Quarterly* 18:2 (1967): 101–6.
Newman, Karen. *Cultural Capitals: Early Modern London and Paris*. Princeton, N.J.: Princeton University Press, 2007.
———. *Fashioning Femininity and English Renaissance Drama*. Chicago: University of Chicago Press, 1991.
———. "Portia's Ring: Unruly Women and Structures of Exchange in *The Merchant of Venice*." *Shakespeare Quarterly* 38:1 (1987): 19–33.

Newman, Lucille. "Ophelia's Herbal." *Economic Botany* 33:1 (1979): 227–32.
Nicholl, Charles. *The Lodger: Shakespeare on Silver Street*. New York: Penguin, 2007.
Nobes, Christopher, ed. *The Development of Double Entry: Selected Essays*. New York: Garland, 1984.
Nungezer, Edwin. *A Dictionary of Actors, and of Other Persons Associated with the Public Representation of Plays in England Before 1642*. New Haven, Conn.: Yale University Press, 1929.
O'Neill, J. J. "Elizabethan Players as Tradesmen." *Times Literary Supplement*, April 8, 1926, 264.
Ogilvie, Sheilagh. *A Bitter Living: Women, Markets, and Social Capital in Early Modern Germany*. New York: Oxford University Press, 2003.
Oldrieve, Susan. "Marginalized Voices in *The Merchant of Venice*." *Cardozo Studies in Law and Literature* 5 (1993): 87–105.
Orgel, Stephen. *Impersonations: The Performance of Gender in Shakespeare's England*. Cambridge: Cambridge University Press, 1996.
Orlin, Lena Cowen, ed. *Material London, ca. 1600*. Philadelphia: University of Pennsylvania Press, 2000.
Osborne, Laurie E. "Staging the Female Playgoer: Gender in Shakespeare's Onstage Audience." In *Enacting Gender on the English Renaissance Stage*, ed. Viviana Comensoli and Anne Russell. Urbana: University of Illinois Press, 1999. 201–17.
Ostashevsky, Eugene. "Crooked Figures: Zero and Hindu-Arabic Notation in Shakespeare's *Henry V*." In *Arts of Calculation: Quantifying Thought in Early Modern Europe*, ed. David Glimp and Michelle R. Warren. Basingstoke: Palgrave Macmillan, 2004. 205–28.
Palliser, D. M. "The Trade Gilds of Tudor York." In *Crisis and Order in English Towns, 1500–1700*, ed. Peter Clark and Paul Slack. Toronto: University of Toronto Press, 1972.
Palmer, Barbara D. "Early Modern Mobility: Players, Payments, and Patrons." *Shakespeare Quarterly* 56:3 (2005): 259–305.
Parker, Patricia. "Cassio, Cash, and the 'Infidel O': Arithmetic, Double-Entry Bookkeeping, and *Othello*'s Unfaithful Accounts." In *A Companion to the Global Renaissance: English Literature and Culture in the Era of Expansion*, ed. Jyotsna Singh. Oxford: Basil Blackwell, 2009.
———. *Literary Fat Ladies: Rhetoric, Gender, Property*. London: Methuen, 1987.
———. "Sound Government, Polymorphic Bears: *The Winter's Tale* and Other Metamorphoses of Eye and Ear." In *The Wordsworthian Enlightenment: Romantic Poetry and the Ecology of Reading*, ed. Helen Regueiro Elam and Frances Ferguson. Baltimore: Johns Hopkins University Press, 2005. 172–90.
———. "Temporal Gestation, Legal Contracts, and the Promissory Economies of *The Winter's Tale*." In *Women, Property, and the Letters of the Law in Early Modern England*, ed. Nancy E. Wright, Margaret W. Ferguson, and A. R. Buck. Toronto: University of Toronto Press, 2004. 25–49.
Parolin, Peter. "'A Strange Fury Entered My House': Italian Actresses and Female Performance in *Volpone*." *Renaissance Drama* 29 (2000): 107–35.

Passingham, W. J. *London's Markets*. London: Sampson, Low, Marston and Company, 1935.
Paster, Gail Kern. "Leaky Vessels: The Incontinent Women of City Comedy." *Renaissance Drama* 18 (1987): 43–65.
Pearl, Valerie. "Change and Stability in Seventeenth Century London." *London Journal* 5:1 (1979): 3–34.
Pearson, Ruth. "Continuity and Change—Towards a Conclusion." In *Women and Credit: Researching the Past, Refiguring the Future*, ed. Beverly Lemire, Ruth Pearson, and Gail Campbell. Oxford: Berg, 2001. 319–24.
Peck, Linda Levy. *Consuming Splendor: Society and Culture in Seventeenth-Century England*. Cambridge: Cambridge University Press, 2005.
Pelling, Margaret. *Medical Conflicts in Early Modern London: Patronage, Physicians and Irregular Practitioners, 1550–1640*. Oxford: Clarendon Press, 2003.
———. "Thoroughly Resented? Older Women and the Medical Role in Early Modern London." In *Women, Science and Medicine, 1500–1700: Mothers and Sisters of the Royal Society*, ed. Lynette Hunter and Sarah Hutton. Phoenix Mill: Sutton, 1997. 63–88.
Penniman, Josiah H. *The War of the Theaters*. Boston: Ginn, 1897.
Pettegree, Andrew. *Foreign Protestant Communities in Sixteenth-Century London*. Oxford: Clarendon Press, 1986.
———. "'Thirty Years On': Progress Towards Integration Amongst the Immigrant Population of Elizabethan London." In *English Rural Society, 1500–1800: Essays in Honor of Joan Thirsk*, ed. John Chartres and David Hey. Cambridge: Cambridge University Press, 1990. 297–312.
Pettet, E. C. "*The Merchant of Venice* and the Problem of Usury." *Essays and Studies* 31 (1946): 19–33.
Phillippy, Patricia. *Painting Women: Cosmetics, Canvases & Early Modern Culture*. Baltimore: Johns Hopkins University Press, 2006.
Pinchbeck, Ivy. *Women Workers and the Industrial Revolution, 1750–1850*. New York: A. M. Kelley, 1930.
Plummer, Alfred. *The London Weavers' Company, 1600–1970*. London: Routledge and Kegan Paul, 1972.
Pogue, Kate Emery. *Shakespeare's Friends*. Westport, Conn.: Praeger, 2006.
Pollitt, Ronald. "'Refuge of the Distressed Nations': Perceptions of Aliens in Elizabethan England." *Journal of Modern History* 52:1 (1980): D1001–19.
Poovey, Mary. "Accommodating Merchants: Accounting, Civility, and the Natural Laws of Gender." *Differences* 8:3 (1996): 1–20.
———. *A History of the Modern Fact: Problems of Knowledge in the Sciences of Wealth and Society*. Chicago: University of Chicago Press, 1998.
Porter, Roy. *London: A Social History*. Cambridge, Mass.: Harvard University Press, 1995.
Portes, Alejandro, Manuel Castells, and Lauren A. Benton. Conclusion to *The Informal Economy: Studies in Advanced and Less Developed Countries*, ed. Alejandro Portes, Manuel Castells, and Lauren A. Benton. Baltimore: Johns Hopkins University Press, 1989. 298–310.

Poulsen, Rachel. "Women Performing Homoerotic Desire in English and Italian Comedy: *La Calandria, Gl'ingannati* and *Twelfth Night*." In *Women Players in Early Modern England, 1500–1660: Beyond the All-Male Stage*, ed. Pamela Allen Brown and Peter Parolin. Aldershot: Ashgate Press, 2005. 171–91.

Power, M. J. "London and the Control of the 'Crisis' of the 1590s." *History* 70:230 (1985): 371–85.

Pratt, S. M. "Antwerp and the Elizabethan Mind." *Modern Language Quarterly* 24 (1963): 53–60.

Prideaux, Sir Walter Sherburne. *Memorials of the Goldsmiths' Company, Being Gleanings from Their Records Between the Years 1335 and 1815*. Vol. 1. [London]: Printed for Private Circulation by Eyre and Spottiswoode, [1896–97].

Prior, Mary. "Wives and Wills, 1558–1700." In *English Rural Society, 1500–1800: Essays in Honor of Joan Thirsk*, ed. John Chartres and David Hey. Cambridge: Cambridge University Press, 1990. 201–25.

———. "Women in the Urban Economy, Oxford 1500–1800." In *Women in English Society, 1500–1800*, ed. Mary Prior. New York: Methuen, 1985.

Prior, Roger. "The Life of George Wilkins." *Shakespeare Survey* 25 (1972): 137–52.

Pujol, Michele A. *Feminism and Anti-Feminism in Early Economic Thought*. Brookfield: E. Elgar, 1992.

Pullan, Brian. "Charity and Usury: Jewish and Christian Lending in Renaissance and Early Modern Italy." *Proceedings of the British Academy* 125 (2003): 19–40.

Pullan, J. M. *The History of the Abacus*. London: Hutchinson, 1968.

Raber, Karen. *Dramatic Difference: Gender, Class and Genre in the Early Modern Closet Drama*. Newark: University of Delaware Press, 2001.

Rackin, Phyllis. *Shakespeare and Women*. Oxford: Oxford University Press, 2005.

Rappaport, Steve. *Worlds Within Worlds: Structures of Life in Sixteenth-Century London*. Cambridge: Cambridge University Press, 1989.

Reddaway, T. F. *The Early History of the Goldsmiths' Company, 1327–1509*. London: Edward Arnold, 1975.

Rendle, William. *Old Southwark and Its People*. London: W. Drewett, 1878.

Ribeira, Aileen. *Dress and Morality*. London: B. T. Batsford, 1986.

Richardson, Catherine, ed. *Clothing Culture, 1350–1650*. Aldershot: Ashgate, 2004.

Righter, Anne. *Shakespeare and the Idea of the Play*. London: Chatto and Windus, 1962.

Risum, Janne. "The Voice of Ophelia." *New Theatre Quarterly* 10 (1994): 174–82.

Roberts, Bryan. *Perspectives on the Informal Economy*. New York: University Press of America, 1990.

Roberts, Michael. "Women and Work in Sixteenth Century English Towns." In *Work in Towns, 850–1850*, ed. Penelope J. Corfield and Derek Keene. Leicester: Leicester University Press, 1990. 86–102.

Roberts, W[illiam]. *The Cries of London*. London: The Connoisseur, 1924.

Robertson, J. M. *The Problem of "Hamlet."* New York: Harcourt, Brace and Howe, 1920.

Robinson, Solveig C. "Of 'Haymakers' and 'City Artisans': The Chartist Poetics of Eliza Cook's *Songs of Labor*." *Victorian Poetry* 39:2 (2001): 229–53.

Roche, Daniel. *The Culture of Clothing: Dress and Fashion in the "Ancien Regime."* Cambridge: Cambridge University Press, 1994.

Rogers, Ruth, ed. *Coin and Conscience: Popular Views of Money, Credit and Speculation, Sixteenth Through Nineteenth Centuries.* Cambridge, Mass.: Harvard Buisness School, Baker Library, 1986.

Rollins, Hyder E. "The Black-Letter Broadside Ballad." *PMLA* 34:2 (1919): 258–339.

Roston, Murray. *Tradition and Subversion in Renaissance Literature: Studies in Shakespeare, Spenser, Jonson and Donne.* Pittsburgh: Duquesne University Press, 2007.

Rotman, Brian. *Signifying Nothing: The Semiotics of Zero.* London: Macmillan, 1987.

Rowse, A. L. *Simon Forman: Sex and Society in Shakespeare's Age.* London: Weidenfeld and Nicolson, 1974.

Rutter, Carol Chillington. *Enter the Body: Women and Representation on Shakespeare's Stage.* London: Routledge, 2001.

Rutter, Tom. *Work and Play on the Shakespearean Stage.* Cambridge: Cambridge University Press, 2008.

Rye, William Brenchley. *England as Seen by Foreigners in the Days of Elizabeth and James the First.* London: John Russell Smith, 1865.

Sale, Carolyn. "Slanderous Aesthetics and the Woman Writer: The Case of *Hole v. White*." In *From Script to Stage in Early Modern England*, ed. Peter Holland and Stephen Orgel. Basingstoke: Palgrave Macmillan, 2004. 181–94.

Sams, Eric. *The Real Shakespeare: Retrieving the Early Years, 1564–1594.* New Haven, Conn.: Yale University Press, 1995.

———. "Taboo, or Not Taboo? The Text, Dating, and Authorship of *Hamlet*, 1589–1623." *Hamlet Studies* 10 (1988): 12–46.

Schama, Simon. *The Embarrassment of Riches: An Interpretation of Dutch Culture in the Golden Age.* Berkeley: University of California Press, 1988.

———. "Wives and Wantons: Versions of Womanhood in Seventeenth-Century Dutch Art." *Oxford Art Journal* 3 (1980): 5–13.

Schilling, Heinz. "Innovation Through Migration: The Settlements of Calvinistic Netherlands in Sixteenth- and Seventeenth-Century Central and Western Europe." *Histoire Sociale* 16 (1983): 7–33.

Schoenbaum, Samuel. *William Shakespeare: A Documentary Life.* New York: Oxford University Press in Association with the Scholar Press, 1975.

———. *William Shakespeare: Records and Images.* London: Scolar Press, 1981.

Schrickx, Willem. "Elizabethan Drama and Anglo-Dutch Relations." In *Reclamations of Shakespeare*, ed. A. J. Hoenselaars. Amsterdam: Rodopi, 1994. 21–32.

Scoville, Warren C. "The Huguenots and the Diffusion of Technology, Part 1." *Journal of Political Economy* 60:4 (1952): 294–311.

Shaheen, Naseeb. "A Warning for Fair Women and the Ur-Hamlet." *Notes and Queries* 30:2 (1983): 126–27.

Shapiro, Michael. *Children of the Revels: The Boy Companies of Shakespeare's Time and Their Plays.* New York: Columbia University Press, 1977.

———. "The Introduction of Actresses in England: Delay or Defensiveness?" In *Enacting*

Gender on the English Renaissance Stage, ed. Viviana Comensoli and Anne Russell. Urbana: University of Illinois Press, 1999. 177–99.

Sharp, Ronald A. "Gift Exchange and the Economies of Spirit in *The Merchant of Venice*." *Modern Philology* 83:3 (1986): 250–65.

Sharpe, Pamela. *Adapting to Capitalism: Working Women in the English Economy, 1700–1800*. New York: St. Martin's, 1996.

———. "Dealing with Love: The Ambiguous Independence of the Single Woman in Early Modern England." *Gender and History* 11 (1999): 209–32.

———, ed. *Women's Work: The English Experience, 1650–1914*. Oxford: Oxford University Press, 1998.

Shell, Marc. *The Economy of Literature*. Baltimore: Johns Hopkins University Press, 1978.

———. *Money, Language and Thought: Literary and Philosophical Economics from the Medieval to the Modern Era*. Berkeley: University of California Press, 1982.

———. "The Wether and the Ewe: Verbal Usury." In *William Shakespeare's "The Merchant of Venice": Modern Critical Interpretations*, ed. Harold Bloom. New York: Chelsea House, 1986 [1979]. 107–20.

Shepard, Alexandra. *Meanings of Manhood in Early Modern England*. Ed. Keith Thomas. Oxford Studies in Social History. Oxford: Oxford University Press, 2003.

Sheppard, F. H. W. *London: A History*. Oxford: Oxford University Press, 1998.

Shesgreen, Sean. *The Criers and Hawkers of London: Engravings and Drawings by Marcellus Laroon*. Stanford, Calif.: Stanford University Press, 1990.

———. "The First London Cries." *Print Quarterly* 10 (1993): 364–73.

———. *Images of the Outcast: The Urban Poor in the Cries of London*. New Brunswick, N.J.: Rutgers University Press, 2002.

———. "'The Manner of Crying Things in London': Style, Authorship, Chalcography, and History." *Huntington Library Quarterly* 59:4 (1996): 404–63.

Shugg, W. "Prostitution in Shakespeare's London." *Shakespeare Studies* 10 (1977): 291–313.

Singh, Jyotsna G. "Gendered 'Gifts' in Shakespeare's Belmont: The Economies of Exchange in Early Modern England." In *A Feminist Companion to Shakespeare*, ed. Dympna Callaghan. Oxford: Blackwell, 2000. 144–59.

Sisson, C. J. "Mr. and Mrs. Browne of the Boar's Head." *Life and Letters To-Day* 15:6 (1936): 99–107.

———. "The Red Bull Company and the Importunate Widow." *Shakespeare Survey* 7 (1954): 57–68.

Small, Roscoe Addison. *The Stage-Quarrel Between Ben Jonson and the So-Called Poetasters*. Breslau: M. & H. Marcus, 1899.

Smith, Bruce. *The Acoustic World of Early Modern England: Attending to the O-Factor*. Chicago: University of Chicago Press, 1999.

Smith, Colin. "The Wholesale and Retail Markets of London, 1660–1840." *Economic History Review* 55 (2002): 31–50.

Smith, David Eugene. *History of Mathematics*. Vol. 2. New York: Dover, 1953.

Smith, David L., Richard Strier, and David Bevington, eds. *The Theatrical City: Culture,*

Theatre and Politics in London, 1576–1649. Cambridge: Cambridge University Press, 1995.

Smith, Emma. "Ghost Writing: *Hamlet* and the *Ur-Hamlet*." In *Renaissance Text: Theory, Editing, Textuality*, ed. Andrew Murphy. New York: St. Martin's, 2000. 42–49.

———. "'So Much English by the Mother': Gender, Foreigners and the Mother Tongue in William Houghton's *Englishmen for My Money*." *Medieval and Renaissance Drama in England* 13 (2001): 165–81.

Smith, John Thomas. *The Cries of London: Exhibiting Several of the Itinerant Traders of Antient and Modern Times*. London: Nichols and Son, 1839.

Smith, Joshua Touhnin. *English Guilds*. London: N. Trubner, 1870.

Smith, S. D. "Women's Admission to Guilds in Early-Modern England: The Case of the York Merchant Tailor's Company, 1693–1776." *Gender and History* 17:1 (2005): 99–126.

Smythe, W. Dumville. *An Historical Account of the Worshipful Company of Girdlers, London*. London: Chiswick Press, 1905.

Snell, K. D. M. *Annals of the Laboring Poor: Social Change and Agrarian England, 1660–1900*. Cambridge: Cambridge University Press, 1985.

Snook, Edith. "'The Beautifying Part of Physic': Women's Cosmetic Practices in Early Modern England." *Journal of Women's History* 20:3 (2008): 10–33.

Spencer, Eric. "Taking Excess, Exceeding Account: Aristotle Meets *The Merchant of Venice*." In *Money and the Age of Shakespeare: Essays in New Economic Criticism*, ed. Linda Woodbridge. Basingstoke: Palgrave Macmillan, 2003. 143–58.

Spicksley, Judith M. "'Fly with a Duck in Thy Mouth': Single Women as Sources of Credit in Seventeenth-Century England." *Social History* 32:2 (2007): 187–207.

———. "To Be or Not to Be Married: Single Women, Money-Lending, and the Question of Choice in Late Tudor and Stuart England." In *The Single Woman in Medieval and Early Modern England: Her Life and Representation*, ed. Laurel Amtower and Dorothea Kehler. Tempe: Arizona Center for Medieval and Renaissance Studies, 2003. 65–96.

———. "Usury Legislation, Cash and Credit: The Development of the Female Investor in the Late Tudor and Stuart Periods." *Economic History Review* 61 (2008): 277–301.

Spinosa, Charles. "Shylock and Debt and Contract in *The Merchant of Venice*." *Cardozo Studies in Law and Literature* 5 (1993): 65–85.

Stallybrass, Peter. "Marx's Coat." In *Border Fetishisms: Material Objects in Unstable Spaces*, ed. Patricia Spyer. New York: Routledge, 1998. 183–207.

———. "Worn Worlds: Clothes and Identity on the Renaissance Stage." In *Subject and Object in Renaissance Culture*, ed. Margreta de Grazia, Maureen Quilligan, and Peter Stallybrass. Cambridge: Cambridge University Press, 1996. 289–320.

Stallybrass, Peter, and Ann Rosalind Jones. "Fetishizing the Glove in Renaissance Europe." *Critical Inquiry* 28:1 (2001): 114–32.

Stern, W. M. "The Trade, Art or History of Silk Flowers of the City of London in the Seventeenth Century." *Guildhall Miscellany* 6 (1956): 25–30.

Stevens, Joyce. *A History of International Women's Day in Words and Images*. Sydney: IWD Press, 1985.

Stevenson, Laura Caroline. *Praise and Paradox: Merchants and Craftsmen in Elizabethan Popular Literature*. Cambridge: Cambridge University Press, 1984.
Stewart, Horace. *History of the Worshipful Company of Gold and Silver Wyre-Drawers*. London: Leadenhall Press, 1891.
Stokes, James. "Women and Mimesis in Medieval and Renaissance Somerset (and Beyond)." *Comparative Drama* 27:2 (1993): 176–96.
———. "Women and Performance: Evidence of Universal Cultural Suffrage in Medieval and Early Modern Lincolnshire." In *Women Players in Early Modern England, 1500–1660: Beyond the All-Male Stage*, ed. Pamela Allen Brown and Peter Parolin. Aldershot: Ashgate Press, 2005. 25–43.
Stone, Lawrence. *The Crisis of the Aristocracy, 1558–1641*. Oxford: Clarendon Press, 1965.
Stonex, Arthur Bivins. "The Usurer in Elizabethan Drama." *PMLA* 31:2 (1916): 190–210.
Stopes, Charlotte Carmichael. *Shakespeare's Warwickshire Contemporaries*. Stratford-upon-Avon: Shakespeare Head Press, 1907.
Straznicky, Marta. "Closet Drama." In *A Companion to Renaissance Drama*, ed. Arthur F. Kinney. Malden, Mass.: Blackwell Press, 2002. 416–30.
———. *Privacy, Playreading and Women's Closet Drama, 1550–1700*. Cambridge: Cambridge University Press, 2004.
Streitberger, W. R. "Personnel and Professionalization." In *A New History of Early English Drama*, ed. John D. Cox and David Scott Kastan. New York: Columbia University Press, 1997. 337–55.
Stretton, Tim. *Women Waging Law in Elizabethan England*. Cambridge: Cambridge University Press, 1998.
Strong, Roy. "Teerlinc, Levina (d. 1576)." In *Oxford Dictionary of National Biography*, ed. H. C. G. Matthew and Brian Harrison. Oxford: Oxford University Press, 2008.
Sugden, Edward H. *A Topographical Dictionary to the Works of Shakespeare and His Fellow Dramatists*. New York: Longmans, Green and Company, 1925.
Sullivan, Ceri. *The Rhetoric of Credit: Merchants in Early Modern Writing*. London: Associated University Presses, 2002.
Supple, B. E. *Commercial Crisis and Change in England, 1600–1642*. Cambridge: Cambridge University Press, 1959.
Sutton, Anne F. *The Mercery of London: Trade, Goods, and People, 1130–1578*. Aldershot: Ashgate, 2005.
Swain, John T. *Industry Before the Industrial Revolution: Northeast Lancashire, c. 1500–1640*. Manchester: Chetham Society, 1986.
Swanson, Heather. "The Illusion of Economic Structure: Craft Guilds in Late Medieval English Towns." *Past and Present* 121 (1988): 29–48.
———. *Medieval Artisans: An Urban Class in Late Medieval England*. London: Basil Blackwell, 1989.
Szatek, Karoline. "*The Merchant of Venice* and the Politics of Commerce." In *The Merchant of Venice: New Critical Essays*, ed. John W. Mahon and Ellen Macleod Mahon. New York: Routledge, 2002. 325–52.

Tawney, R. H. Introduction to *A Discourse Upon Usury*, by Thomas Wilson, ed. R. H. Tawney. New York: Harcourt Brace, 1925. 1–172.
Tebbutt, Melanie. *Making Ends Meet: Pawnbroking and Working-Class Credit*. Leicester: Leicester University Press, 1983.
Tennenhouse, Leonard. "The Counterfeit Order of *The Merchant of Venice*." In *The Merchant of Venice: Critical Essays*, ed. Thomas Wheeler. New York: Garland, 1991. 195–215.
Tentler, Thomas N. *Sin and Confession on the Eve of the Reformation*. Princeton: Princeton University Press, 1977.
Thaler, Alwin. "Minor Actors and Employees in the Elizabethan Theater." *Modern Philology* 20 (1922): 49–60.
———. "Playwrights' Benefits and 'Interior Gathering' in the Elizabethan Theatre." *Studies in Philology* 16 (1919): 187–96.
Thirsk, Joan, ed. *The Agrarian History of England and Wales*. Vol. 4. Cambridge: Cambridge University Press, 1967.
———. *Economic Policy and Projects: The Development of a Consumer Society in Early Modern England*. Oxford: Clarendon Press, 1978.
Thomas, David L., and Norman E. Evans. "John Shakespeare in the Exchequer." *Shakespeare Quarterly* 35:3 (1984): 315–18.
Thomas, Keith. "Numeracy in Early Modern England." *Transactions of the Royal Historical Society*, 5th ser., 37 (1987): 103–32.
———. "Work and Leisure in Pre-Industrial Society." *Past and Present* 29 (1964): 50–66.
Thompson, Ann. "Women/'Women' and the Stage." In *Women and Literature in Britain, 1500–1700*, ed. Helen Wilcox. Cambridge: Cambridge University Press, 1996. 100–116.
Thrupp, Silvia. *A Short History of the Worshipful Company of Bakers of London*. Croydon: Galleon Press, 1933.
Tittler, Robert. "Jefferies, Joyce (c. 1570–1650)." In *Oxford Dictionary of National Biography*, ed. H. C. G. Mathew and Brian Harrison. Oxford: Oxford University Press, 2004.
———. "Joyce Jefferies, Spinster, Financial Diary (1638–49)." In *Reading Early Modern Women: An Anthology of Texts in Manuscript and Print, 1550–1700*, ed. Helen Ostovich, Elizabeth Sauer, and Melissa Smith. New York: Routledge, 2004. 265–71.
———. "Money-Lending in the West Midlands: The Activities of Joyce Jeffries, 1638–49." *Historical Research* 67 (1994): 249–63.
———. *Townspeople and Nation: English Urban Experiences, 1540–1640*. Stanford, Calif.: Stanford University Press, 2001.
Todd, Barbara. "Freebench and Free Enterprise: Widows and Their Property in Two Berkshire Villages." In *English Rural Society, 1500–1800: Essays in Honor of Joan Thirsk*, ed. John Chartres and David Hey. Cambridge: Cambridge University Press, 1990. 175–200.
Tomlinson, Sophie. "'She That Plays the King': Henrietta Maria and the Threat of the Actress in Caroline Culture." In *The Politics of Tragicomedy: Shakespeare and After*, ed. Gordon McMullan and Jonathan Hope. London: Routledge, 1992. 189–207.

———. "Theatrical Vibrancy on the Caroline Court Stage: *Tempe Restored* and *The Shepherd's Paradise*." In *Women and Culture at the Courts of the Stuart Queens, 1603–42*, ed. Clare McManus. Basingstoke: Palgrave Macmillan, 2003. 186–203.

———. *Women on Stage in Stuart Drama*. Cambridge: Cambridge University Press, 2005.

Tracy, Robert. "The Owl and the Baker's Daughter: A Note on *Hamlet*, IV.v.42–43." *Shakespeare Quarterly* 17:1 (1966): 83–86.

Ungerer, Gustave. "Mary Frith, Alias Moll Cutpurse, in Life and Literature." *Shakespeare Studies* 28 (2000): 42–84.

———. "Prostitution in Late Elizabethan London: The Case of Mary Newborough." *Medieval and Renaissance Drama in England* 15 (2003): 138–223.

Unwin, George. *The Gilds and Companies of London*. London: Methuen, 1908.

———. *Industrial Organization in the Sixteenth and Seventeenth Centuries*. London: Cass, 1957.

Urkowitz, Steve. "Back to Basics: Thinking About the *Hamlet* First Quarto." In *The Hamlet First Published (Q1, 1603): Origins, Form, Intertextualities*, ed. Tom Clayton. Newark: University of Delaware Press, 1992. 257–91.

———. " 'Well-Sayed Olde Mole': Burying Three Hamlets in Modern Editions." In *Shakespeare Study Today*, ed. Georgianna Ziegler. New York: AMS, 1986. 37–70.

Valeri, Mark. "Religious Discipline and the Market: Puritans and the Issue of Usury." *William and Mary Quarterly* 54:4 (1997): 747–68.

Vann, Richard T. "Toward a New Lifestyle: Women in Preindustrial Capitalism." In *Becoming Visible: Women in European History*, ed. R. Bridenthal and C. Koonz. Boston, 1977. 192–216.

Varholy, Christine. "Representing Prostitution in Tudor and Stuart England." Ph.D. diss., University of Wisconsin, Madison, 2001.

Vicente, Marta V. "Images and Realities of Work: Women and Guilds in Early Modern Barcelona." In *Spanish Women in the Golden Age: Images and Realities*, ed. Magdalena S. Sánchez and Alain Saint-Saens. Westport, Conn.: Greenwood Press, 1996. 127–39.

Vincent, Susan. *Dressing the Elite: Clothes in Early Modern England*. Oxford: Berg, 2003.

Wack, Mary. "Women, Work, and Plays in an English Medieval Town." In *Maids and Mistresses, Cousins and Queens: Women's Alliances in Early Modern England*, ed. Susan Frye and Karen Robertson. New York: Oxford University Press, 1999. 33–51.

Wales, Tim. "Poverty, Poor Relief and the Life Cycle: Some Evidence from Seventeenth-Century Norfolk." In *Land, Kinship, and Life Cycle*, ed. R. M. Smith. Cambridge: Cambridge University Press, 1984. 351–404.

Walford, Cornelius. *Fairs, Past and Present: A Chapter in the History of Commerce*. London: Elliot Stock, 1883.

Walker, Garthine. "Women, Theft and the World of Stolen Goods." In *Women, Crime and the Courts in Early Modern England*, ed. Jennifer Kermode and Garthine Walker. Chapel Hill: University of North Carolina Press, 1994. 81–105.

Wall, Wendy. "Why Does Puck Sweep?: Fairylore, Merry Wives and Social Struggle." *Shakespeare Quarterly* 52:1 (2001): 67–106.

Wallace, Charles William. *The Evolution of the English Drama up to Shakespeare, with a History of the First Blackfriars Theatre*. Berlin: Georg Reimer, 1912.
———. *The First London Theatre: Materials for a History*. London: Benjamin Blom, 1969 [1913].
———. "New Shakespeare Discoveries: Shakespeare as a Man among Men." *Harper's Monthly Magazine* 120:718 (1910): 489–510.
———. "Shakespeare and His London Associates as Revealed in Recently Discovered Documents." *University of Nebraska Studies* 10:4 (1910): 261–360.
Ward, Joseph. "'[I]mployment for All Handes That Will Worke': Immigrants, Guilds and the Labor Market in Early Seventeenth-Century London." In *Immigrants in Tudor and Early Stuart England*, ed. Nigel Goose and Lien Luu. Brighton: Sussex Academic Press, 2005. 76–87.
———. *Metropolitan Communities: Trade Guilds, Identity and Change in Early Modern London*. Stanford, Calif.: Stanford University Press, 1997.
Waswo, Richard. "Crises of Credit: Monetary and Erotic Economies in the Jacobean Theatre." In *Plotting in Early Modern London: New Essays on Jacobean City Comedy*, ed. Dieter Mehl, Angela Stock, and Anne-Julia Zwierlein. Aldershot: Ashgate, 2004. 55–73.
Watt, Tessa. *Cheap Print and Popular Piety, 1550–1640*. Cambridge: Cambridge University Press, 1991.
Weimann, Robert. *Author's Pen and Actor's Voice: Playing and Writing in Shakespeare's Theatre*. Cambridge: Cambridge University Press, 2000.
———. *Shakespeare and the Popular Tradition in the Theatre: Studies in the Social Dimension of Dramatic Form and Function*. Baltimore: Johns Hopkins University Press, 1978.
Werstine, Paul. "The Textual Mystery of *Hamlet*." *Shakespeare Quarterly* 39:1 (1988): 1–26.
Westfall, Susan. "'A Commonty a Christmas Gambold or a Tumbling Trick': Household Theater." In *A New History of Early English Drama*, ed. John D. Cox and David Scott Kastan. New York: Columbia University Press, 1997. 39–58.
———. *Patrons and Performance: Early Tudor Household Revels*. Oxford: Oxford University Press, 1990.
Wheelock, Arthur K., Jr. *Dutch Paintings of the Seventeenth Century*. Washington, D.C.: National Gallery of Art; New York: Cambridge University Press, 1995.
———. *Vermeer and the Art of Painting*. New Haven: Yale University Press, 1995.
Whitebrook, J. C. "Huguenots of Blackfriars, and Its Neighborhood, in Shakespearian Days." *Notes and Queries* 181 (1941): 225, 42–43, 54–56.
Wickham, Glynne. *Early English Stages*. 3 vols. London: Routledge and Kegan Paul, 1959.
Wickham, Glynne, Herbert Berry, and William Ingram, eds. *English Professional Theatre, 1530–1660*. Theater in Europe: A Documentary History. Cambridge: Cambridge University Press, 2000.
Wiesner, Merry. "Spinning out Capital: Women's Work in the Early Modern Economy." In *Becoming Visible: Women in European History*, ed. Renate Bridenthal, Claudia Koonz, and Susan Stuard. Boston: Houghton Mifflin, 1987. 221–49.

———. *Women and Gender in Early Modern Europe*. Cambridge: Cambridge University Press, 1993.

———. *Working Women in Renaissance Germany*. New Brunswick, N.J.: Rutgers University Press, 1986.

Wiggins, Martin. "Copies for Ruff and Cuff." *Around the Globe* 30 (2005): 20–21.

Willen, Diane. "Women in the Public Sphere in Early Modern England: The Case of the Urban Working Poor." *Sixteenth Century Journal* 19:4 (1988): 559–75.

Williams, Gweno, Allison Findlay, and Stephanie Hodgson-Wright. "Payments, Permits and Punishments: Women Performers and the Politics of Place." In *Women Players in Early Modern England, 1500–1660: Beyond the All-Male Stage*, ed. Pamela Allen Brown and Peter Parolin. Aldershot: Ashgate, 2005. 45–67.

Wilson, Charles. "Cloth Production and International Competition in the Seventeenth Century." *Economic History Review* 13:2 (1960): 209–21.

Wilson, Richard. "'A Mingled Yarn': Shakespeare and the Cloth Workers." *Literature and History* 12 (1986): 164–80.

Womack, Peter. "Imagining Communities: Theatres and the English Nation in the Sixteenth Century." In *Culture and History*, ed. David Aers. Detroit: Wayne State University Press, 1992. 91–146.

Wood, Merry Wiesner. "Paltry Peddlers or Essential Merchants? Women in the Distributive Trades in Early Modern Nuremberg." *Sixteenth Century Journal* 12:2 (1981): 3–13.

Woodbridge, Linda. Introduction to *Money and the Age of Shakespeare: Essays in New Economic Criticism*, ed. Linda Woodbridge. Basingstoke: Palgrave Macmillan, 2003. 1–18.

———. *Vagrancy, Homelessness, and English Renaissance Literature*. Urbana: University of Illinois Press, 2001.

———, ed. *Money and the Age of Shakespeare: Essays in New Economic Criticism*. Basingstoke: Palgrave Macmillan, 2003.

Woodmansee, Martha, and Mark Osteen, eds. *The New Economic Criticism: Studies at the Intersection of Literature and Economics*. New York: Routledge, 1999.

Woodward, Donald. "The Background to the Statute of Artificers: The Genesis of Labor Policy, 1558–63." *Economic History Review* 33 (1980): 32–44.

———. *Men at Work: Laborers and Building Craftsmen in the Towns of Northern England, 1450–1750*. Cambridge: Cambridge University Press, 1995.

Wright, Celeste Turner. "Some Conventions Regarding the Usurer in Elizabethan Literature." *Studies in Philology* 31 (1934): 176–97.

———. "The Usurer's Sin in Elizabethan Literature." *Studies in Philology* 35 (1938): 178–94.

Wright, Sue. "'Churmaids, Huswyfes and Hucksters': The Employment of Women in Tudor and Stuart Salisbury." In *Women and Work in Pre-Industrial England*, ed. Lindsey Charles and Lorna Duffin. London: Croom Helm, 1985. 100–121.

Wright, Susan. "'Holding up Half the Sky': Women and Their Occupations in Eighteenth-Century Ludlow." *Midland History* 14 (1989): 53–74.

Wrightson, Keith. *Earthly Necessities: Economic Lives in Early Modern Britain*. New Haven, Conn.: Yale University Press, 2000.

Wrigley, E. A., and R. S. Schofield. *The Population History of England, 1541–1871: A Reconstruction*. Cambridge: Cambridge University Press, 1981.

Wurzbach, Natascha. *The Rise of the English Street Ballad, 1550–1650*. Trans. Gayna Walls. Cambridge: Cambridge University Press, 1990.

Wynne-Davies, Marion. "The Queen's Masque: Renaissance Women and the Seventeenth-Century Court Masque." In *Gloriana's Face: Women, Public and Private, in the English Renaissance*, ed. S. P. Cerasano and Marion Wynne-Davies. New York: Wheatsheaf, 1992. 79–104.

Yates, Julian. *Error, Misuse, Failure: Object Lessons from the English Renaissance*. Minneapolis: University of Minnesota Press, 2003.

Yungblut, Laura. *Strangers Settled Here Amongst Us: Policies, Perceptions, and the Presence of Aliens in Elizabethan England*. London: Routledge, 1996.

Index

Page numbers in italics refer to illustrations. Individual actors; ballads; plays and masques; playwrights; theaters; and theatrical investors are listed under these group headings.

(ac)counting, 10, 29, 54, 67, 78, 80, 82, 87, 92, 94, 130, 230–31n157, 235n24; account books, 8, 39, 56, 78, 80, 87, *88*, 90, 108, 237n37, 245n123; double-entry bookkeeping, 80, 235n24, 244n112, 245n122; ethic of exactitude and fidelity in, 64, 78–83, 92, 235n24, 245nn119–20, 245n127; female practices of, 10, 67, 78, 85, 87, *88*, *89*, 90, *91*, 92–95, 130, 196, 237n37, 245n123; inexactitude or infidelity in, 77–81, 196, 245n120, 245n127, 246n137; Lady Arithmetic, 78, *79*; *Merchant of Venice* (Shakespeare), 10–11, 56–57, 61, 71, 76, 85, 90, 92; Portia's evocation of ciphering and rhetorical exactitude, 76, 78–83, 92, 243n106, 245n119, 247n151; Sonnets (Shakespeare), 10–11, 56–57, 61, 67, 76, 78, 84; *Timon of Athens* (Shakespeare), 246n137; treatises on, 78, 80, 244n112; 245n120. *See also* capitalism, rise of; ciphers and ciphering; credit economy; moneylenders and creditors, female; moneylenders and creditors (visual iconography); numeracy; pawnbroking; theatrical investors/stakeholders; usuresses; usury in early modern England

actors: acting styles, 53, 154, 160–61, 164–65, 168, 263; *actio* (vocal and gestural delivery), 169, 263n77; Alleyn, Edward (or "Ned"), 27, 44–45, 47–48, 66, 109, 225n78, 242n98; Beeston, Christopher, 26; Birde, William, 47–48; boy-actors, 9, 32, 34–35, 37–41, 95, 108–9, 113, 123, 167, 228, 263; Brome, Richard, 198; Browne, Robert, 47; Browne, William, 73; Burbage, Richard, 217, 235n18; as "ciphers," 53, 245; Condell, Henry, 47; as counterfeits or "hypocrites," 180–81, 203; defenses of, 7, 52, 180–82, 209; Downton, Thomas, 242n98; Edmondes, John, 60; effeminacy and idleness (accusations of), 2, 49–52, 54, 158–59, 180, 203; enactment of female labor, 2, 123, 135; Field, Nathan, 52, 180; Greene, Thomas, 47, 60; Hamlet's advice to the players, 144, 160, 162, 164, 168–69, 263n85; Hemminges, John, 217; Hovell, William, 60; Keene, Theophilus, 216; Kempe, Will, 160–61, 262n44; marriage to female theater personnel, 217; occupational backgrounds of, 24, 209; purpose of playing, 194, 210; "quality" or status of, 7, 12, 145, 160–61, 168, 174, 182–83, 195, 208; rhetorical skill of, 145, 160, 163, 168, 263n81; Shank, John, 60; skilled/unskilled, 143, 146, 166, 173, 182, 195, 211, 214, 225n66; sweat of, 116; Swynnerton, John, 60; Tarlton, Richard, 161; Taswell, James, 217; Tooley (a.k.a. Wilkinson), Nicholas, 60, 238n53; trained voices of, 144–46, 160, 163–64, 167–69, 171, 263n75; usage of term, 182; vagabond legislation, 12, 160, 162; widows of, 60, 216; wills of, 26, 45, 47, 60, 73, 242n98; Wilson, Robert, 159–60, 161, 166; wives of, 26, 60, 73, 217, 235n18, 242n98; women's loans to, 26, 53, 60, 65, 84, 242n98. *See also* familial ties in theater; female performers; playing companies

ale, consumed in theaters, 22, 49, 143, 146, 196, 201, 204, 260n7. *See also* alehouses

alehouses: alehouse keepers and female creditors, 64, 237n37; attached to playhouses, 49; and "false wares," 205; play readings in, 65, 239n62; sale of ballads in, 150; theatrical activity in, 17

aliens (immigrants from outside England): assimilation of, 138, 140; attitudes of native population toward, 43, 100, 134, 175; competition between native and alien workers,

314 *Index*

aliens (immigrants from outside England): (*cont'd*)
42; complaints of native population against, 140, 258n128; depiction in dramatic literature, 100, 250n36; employment of/by English, 115, 140, 251n45, 259n131; female occupations, 102–3; influx of, 130, 138, 140; intermarriage of, 140; population in London, 99, 101, 138, 245n25, 250nn37–38; population in suburbs and liberties, 245n25, 249n25; Returns of Aliens, 11, 42, 101–3, 113, 250n38, 251n45, 253n79, 259n131; scholarship on, 100–101, 250n35; Shylock as, 92; single women, 254n81; term "outlandish," 258n124; wares branded as "evil," 13, 175; widows, 43, 102, 254–55n81, 255n82; wives, 102–3; xenophobia, 100, 134, 150n35. *See also* foreigners; immigrants, Netherlandish; immigrant women's textile work
Alley, Hugh, 148, 184–86, *185*, *187*. *See also* markets and market regulation
"all-male stage," paradigm of, 1, 6, 8–10, 13–18, 45, 97, 123, 143, 145, 173, 211–14; and erasure/elision of female labor, 8–9, 13–13, 97, 123, 173, 211–14, 220n4, 221n10. *See also* gendered division of labor in early modern England
Alpers, Svetlana, 90
Anne of Denmark, Queen, 17, 110, *111*
anti-theatrical polemics and satires, 7, 13, 52, 117, 180–82, 198, 202, 207, 214, 221n6, 232n193, 265n23; *Anatomie of Abuses* (Stubbes), 32, 122, 252n56, 255n95, 258n126; *Essayes and Characters* (Stephens), 180; *Refutation of the Apology for Actors* (I. G.), 182; *Vertues Common-Wealth* (Crosse). *See also* Gosson, Stephen
apprentices and apprenticeship, 7, 23–25, 27–29, 42, 50, 149–50, 177, 180, 198, 214–15, 225n66, 225n80, 225n84, 251n45, 256n110, 261n34. *See also* livery companies; playing companies
archaeological artifacts excavated from sites of early modern English playhouses, 2–3, 218; costume accessories worn by boy-actors, 41; costume trimmings, 44–45; glass beads, 2–3, 45; material remains of comestibles consumed in theaters, 146, 260n7; remains of female gatherers' trade, 47, 48
Archer, John, 220n14
Arnold, Janet, 256n110

"arsedine" (or orsedue), wares/props gilded with, 199, 200, 267n67
Ars Poetica (Horace), 197–98
attires (tires for the head and neck and other accessories), 3, 9, 11–12, 22, 27, 29–45, 79, 95–143, 181, 215–16, 252n61, 255n91, 258n124; bands (collars), 27, 40–41, 44, 97, 107, 129, 140–43, 181, 256n110; beads, bugles (cylindrical beads), and spangles (sequins), 2–3, 31, *32*, 33–34, 44–45, 97, 103, 117, 211, 209, 229n143, 230n149, 256n110; busks (whalebone stays used to stiffen corsets), 40; buttons, 2, 40, 43, 102, 141, 229n142, 230n146, 250n40, 256n110, 262n40; caps (women's), 33–34, 197; cauls (netted caps), 34, 117, 227n105, 256n110; changing fashion trends in, 140–44, 259n132; chapes (aglets, used to bind together the ends of points), 40, 226n93; "cheeks and ears" (a type of coif), 138, *139*; coifs (close-fitting caps), 34, 131, 138, 256; cuffs, 27, 31, 39–40, 97, 101, *111*, 117, 133, 140–43, 209, 249n139, 256n110; fans, 31, 40, *111*, 120, 124, 209; farthingales (whalebone hoops for skirts), 39, 109, 115, 123; feathers, *111*, 117, 197, 216; French hoods, 34, 216; handkerchiefs, 98, 117, 128–29, 201; as insubstantial, 3, 9, 13, 39, 95, 101, 133, 136, 181, 209, 211, 214; labor of manufacturing, 95–99, 103–7, 123–25; marker of elite (or would-be elite) social status, 97, 107–8; masks, 100, *121*, 122, 210, 218; pins, 2, 31, 39–40, 104, *106*, 141–42, 211, 248; points (laces used to attach parts or articles of clothing), 31, 40–41, 129, 261n36; purses, 153, 166, 192, 196, 201; rebatos (flat, fan-shaped, standing collars), 12, 40–41, 101, 103–4, *105*, 107–9, 110, *111*, *112*, 117, *118*, 133–36, 256n105; ruffs, 2–3, 9, 11–12, 27, 30–31, 33, 38–41, 95, *96*, 97, 101, 103–4, *106*, 107–8, 112–14, 117, *119*, 120, *121*, 122–25, *126*, 127, *128*, 129, 132–33, *139*, 140–43, 177, 181, 209, 215, 227n104, 248–49n14, 252nn55–56, 256n103, 257n118; scarves, 35, 40, 44, 215–16; stockings, 99, 129, 202, 215; supportasses or underproppers (wire or cardboard supports for neck-attires), 33–34, 103, *105*, 117, 252n56; tape (ribbon), 40, 42, 44, 99, 104, 116, 153, 229n142, 256n110; tools used to make, 40, 104, *106*, 125, *126*, 127, 133, 141–42, 177, *106*; veils, *36*, 39,

Index 315

129; wires used to support, 2, 31, 33, 39–41, 103–4, 211, 228n121; worn by boy-actors, 9, 34–41, 95, 108–9, 113, 123, 209, 228n121; worn in masques, 29–31, *32*, 35, *36*, 38, 41, 44, 108, 116, 200, 214–15, 217, 226n93. *See also* clothing; costumes; dressers and dressing, female labor of theatrical; immigrant women's textile work; laundresses; periwigs and perukes; poking sticks; silkwomen; starch; starchwomen; textile trades; tiremakers; tiremen; tirewomen

Bacon, Francis, 234n11
ballads, 55, 150, 154, 190, 196, 202, 208, 261–62n38; *The Cloath-Worker Caught in a Trap*, 61–63, 66; "The Common Crie[s] of London," 154–55, 262n40; criers/singers of, 171–72; the cries of female hawkers in, 147, 154–59, 261n38, 262n40; "I Have Fresh Cheese and Cream," 156–58; *The Kind Beleeving Hostesse*, 63, 64; *The Mother and Daughter*, 61, 66; "Turners Dish of Lenten Stuff," 155–56, 158–59; *A Womans Work is Never Done*, 4
Barish, Jonas, 195
Bartholomew Fair (Jonson), 13, 174, 182, 194–211; accusations regarding market abuses, 199–200; and legitimacy of playing as a profession, 194–211; opposition between consumerism and overzealous market justice, 200–201, 207–10; sexualization of market women, 196; stage properties as "false wares," 195–97, 199–200; staging of market women's "false wares," 13, 174, 182, 194–211
Baskerville, James, 73
Baskerville (a.k.a. Browne, Greene), Susan, 60, 65, 73–74, 242n99. *See also* familial ties in theater; moneylenders and creditors, female; theatrical investors/stakeholders
baskets: as emblems of chaste wives' honest industry, 136; laundry- or buck-baskets, 115–16, 129, 136; as stage properties, 65, 116, 136; used by market women, 150, 184, 193, 199–201, 208; used to convey costumes. *See also* female occupations, basketweavers; stage properties
Beard, Thomas, 51, 265–66n23. *See also* antitheatrical polemics and satires
Bennett, Judith, 4, 265n10
Berger, Harry, Jr., 236n28

Berlin, Michael, 175–76
Bettes, Mrs. John, 31. *See also* Revels Office; spanglers; tirewomen
Bevington, David, 169
Bloom, Gina, 163–64, 166, 167, 263n75
Bowll, Joan, 43, 229n142. *See also* female occupations, silk weavers; Revels Office
Bowsher, Julian, 2, 44
boy-actors. *See* actors
Bradbrook, Muriel, 160–61
Braithwaite, Richard, 70–71, 124–25, 130
Brandon, Martha, 216. *See also* female occupations, concessionaires; Restoration theater
Brayne, Margaret, 26, 47. *See also* familial ties in theater; female occupations
Bride, Elizabeth, 216. *See also* female performers, *under* dancers; Restoration theater
Brodsky, Vivien, 237n42
Browne, Susan. *See* Baskervile (a.k.a. Browne, Greene), Susan
Bubb, Elizabeth, 215. *See also* dressers and dressing, female labor of theatrical; female occupations, costume suppliers; Restoration theater; tirewomen
Burbage, Elizabeth, 60, 238n53. *See also* familial ties in theater; moneylenders and creditors, female
Bush-Bailey, Gilli, 217

Callaghan, Dympna, 15–16, 18, 220n4
Calle, Mistress, 37, 41, 109. *See also* immigrant women's textile work; tirewomen
capitalism, rise of, 243n104; as eroding women's status, 5, 19; global, 241n88; joint-stock ventures, 213; and *Merchant of Venice*, 241n88; new industries or "projects," 5, 20–21, 23, 25, 42, 50, 100, 103, 113, 143, 215, 229n135, 250n34; nostalgia for England's pre-industrial past, 147, 173; theater and, 5, 25–26, 55–56, 213. *See also* (ac)counting; commodity-form; consumers and consumerism; credit economy in early modern England; investment capital of women; markets and market regulation; moneylenders and creditors, female
carpenters, 24, 27, *28*, 225n82, 226n85; girls apprenticed to wives of, to learn needlework, 27, 225–26n84. *See also* female occupations, carpenters
Cerasano, Susan, 45, 217, 242n98

316 Index

A Chaste Maid in Cheapside (Middleton), 13, 174, 182, 183–94; Cheapside market district, 183–86, 266n40; conflation of sexual and commercial (re)production, 186–88, 191–93; cracked wives and female sexual/bodily incontinence, 189–90, 266n48; illegitimate children as "false wares," 191–93; market women's informal commerce, 184, 193–94; satire of corrupt promoters, 192–93; staging of market women's "false wares," 13, 174, 182, 183–94; women as "leaky vessels," 186–88

ciphers and ciphering, 9–12, 79, 81–82; actors' cries as sonic, 145; adoption in England, 244n115; association with Hindu-Arabic numerals, 77–78, 244n115; bubbles as ciphers of vanity, 86; ciphering schools, 244n116; cryptic/occult associations, 77, 244n116; in early modern English drama, 244n114, 244–45n117; and exactitude in (ac)counting, 78–82, 92, 235n24, 245nn119–20; and starched attires, 11, 13, 97, 133, 143, 197; and usuresses, 10–11, 53, 57, 76–82. *See also* (ac)counting; moneylenders and creditors, female

Citizen Shakespeare (Archer), 220n14

citizenship: citizen wives, 19, 186, 188, 197, 210; conferred by livery companies, 23, 224n65; exclusion from, 19, 154, 174–75, 220n14; and freedom of the city, 188, 224n65; language of, 220n14; rights and privileges of, 23, 153–54. *See also* livery companies

city comedies: credulous female creditors in, 66–67, 239n64; female labor and emergent genre of, 6, 220n14; new forms of civic masculinity, 182–83, 214

Civile Conversation (Guazzo), 168

Clark, Alice, 5, 19, 27, 219n8, 225–26n84

clothing: aristocratic, 30; bodices (quilted corsets stayed with whalebone), 40, 123, 157; bombasting (cotton-wool used as stuffing or padding for clothes), 123–24; "bumrolls" (hip padding or bustles), 39, 120, *121*, 122; cloaks, 65, 201, 207, 230n149; clothing economy, 30; doublets, 230n149; fashionable, 2, 11–12, 32–41, 44, *79*, 94–95, 117, 120, 123–24, 134–38, 140–42, 146, 209, 214, 228n121; foreign, 107, 140, 135–36; gowns, 38–39, 46–47, 65, 230n157, 231n165; hats, 33–34, 116, 201, 207; hose, 215, 230n145; jacket (woman's), 31, *32*, 44, 229n143; luxury, 29, 47, 85, 134–35, 172; and market, 100, 250n32; and "material memory," 98; mending of, 155; outerwear, 107; petticoats, 2, 40, 129; recycling of, 30; and sexual incontinence, 120; shirts, 64, 116, 207, 256n110; shoes, 33, 123, 181; smocks, 116, *128*, 129, 131, 163, 256n110, 262n62; underclothing, 107, 129, 131, 256n110; waistcoats, 156–57. *See also* attires; costumes; immigrant women's textile work; secondhand clothing trade; textile trades

Collection of Emblemes (Wither), 24, 225n66

commodity-form: commodification of women, 156, 188; commodities consumed in theaters, 2, 49, 146, 216; labor congealed in, 11; Marx's analysis of, 95, 248n13; theater and, 7. *See also* capitalism, rise of; consumers and consumerism; "false wares"; starch

The Compleat Servant-Maid; or, The Young Maidens Tutor (Woolley), 129

consumers and consumerism: of luxury attire, 3, 34, 117, 124–25, 127, 134–36, 138, 257–58n119; newly available consumer goods, 5, 179, 213; satire of, 3, 34, 55, 117, 124–25, 134–36, 138, 200–201, 204, 207, 210; scholarship on, 220n13; in theaters, 2, 16, 49, 146, 200–201, 204, 207, 210; women as, 3, 16, 34, 117, 124–25, 134–36, 138. *See also* capitalism, rise of; commodity-form; "false wares"

cosmetics, 2, 40–41, 135, 138, 268n25; trade in, 218

costumes: archaeological remains of, 2, 44; bespoke/secondhand, 29, 45; of boy-actors, 37–41; as draw for audiences, 41, 146, 181, 195; dressing actors, 41, 215; embellishment of, 3, 44; ethnic, 137; as "false wares," 13, 97, 181, 209; fashionable, 2, 11–12, 32–41, 44, 94–95, 117, 120, 123–24, 134–38, 140–42, 146, 209, 214, 228n121; female suppliers of, 26, 215; laundering of, 116–17; masque-, 29–31, *32*, *36*, 43–44, 226n89, 229n143; mending of, 48; pawning of, 47, 65–66, 230n154; as payment for court performances, 30, 45; as pointing to pre- or offstage histories of manufacture, 7, 9; renting, 226n89; secondhand, 45; stage as fashion-driven, 1, 11, 41, 95; "translation"

of, 3, 44; as worked upon by women, 1–3, 29–31, 35, 41, 45, 53, 97–98, 117. *See also* attires; clothing; cosmetics; dressers and dressing, female labor of theatrical; immigrant women's textile work; laundresses; pawnbroking; Revels Office; secondhand clothing trade; textile trades; tiremakers; tiremen; tirewomen; tiring-house
Cotgrave, Randle, 110
Court of Alderman for the City of London, 101, 148–49, 184, 226n24, 250n16, 260n19
Court of Chancery, 60, 72, 241n91
Court of Common Council for the City of London, 148–49, 171, 259n132, 260n19
coverture, law of, 58, 71–76, 241n89; legal maneuvers to ameliorate effects of, 74–76, 241n94, 243n104; and Shakespeare's *Merchant of Venice*, 71–72, 74–76, 84, 243n106, 243n109; and women's separate estates and trusts, 71–73, 241n91, 242n98
credit economy in early modern England: credit networks surrounding theaters, 10, 27, 212; expansion of, 54–56; and rise of commercial stage, 56; and threat of insolvency, 65; women's role in, 1, 10, 27, 71, 235n24, 236n30. *See also* (ac)counting; capitalism, rise of; moneylenders and creditors, female; usuresses; usury in early modern England
"Cries of London," 147–48; in ballads, 154–59; broadsheet engravings and woodcuts of, 150–53, *151*, *152*, 163, 261n32, 261n36. *See also* street-criers and hawkers; street-cries, staged as vocal performances
cuckolds and cuckoldry, 84, 116, 176–178, 190

Dale, Marion K., 41–42
Davenant, Lady Mary, 217. *See also* theatrical investors/stakeholders
Davis, Margaret, 29. *See also* apprentices and apprenticeship
defenses of players and playing: *Apology for Actors* (Heywood), 52, 182; *Apology for Poetrie* (Sidney), 52; *Bartholomew Fair*, 194-211; "An Excellent Actor," 181–82
Dictionarie of the French and English Tongues (Cotgrave), 110
dildos, as "false wares," 190. *See also* "poking sticks"
Discoveries (Jonson), 174, 198
double-entry bookkeeping. *See* (ac)counting

Dowd, Michelle, 6
dressers and dressing, female labor of theatrical, 9, 35, 37, 39–41, 108, 113, 116, 123, 137–38, 215–17, 252n61, 268n11. *See also* costumes; tiremakers; tiremen; tirewomen
Dutch immigrants. *See* immigrants, Netherlandish; immigrant women's textile work

Earle, Peter, 21
Edgar, Thomas, 243n104
Eliot, T. S., 165
Elizabeth I, Queen: patronage of theatrical activity, 17; portraits of, 103, *104*; starch women and starched attires of, 103, *104*; tirewomen and head-attires of, 34–35, 108, 227n105; wardrobe accounts of, 39
Ellinghausen, Laurie, 6, 7, 220n20
Engle, Lars, 236n28, 243n109
The English Gentlewoman (Braithwaite), 70–71, 124–25
engrossing (buying up stock of commodity to resell at inflated price), 179, 260n119, 265n12. *See also* capitalism, rise of; markets and market regulation
Erickson, Amy, 72, 243n104
Erondelle, Pierre, 105–7

"false wares": *Bartholomew Fair* (Jonson), 13, 174, 182, 194–211; ceremonial destruction/confiscation in markets, 175–76, 178–80; *A Chaste Maid in Cheapside* (Middleton), 13, 174, 182, 183–94; gendering of civic virtue and vice, 174–80; market regulation of informal commerce, 174–80; market women stigmatized for sexual, verbal, and moral incontinence, 177–78, 189–90, 265n10, 266n48; and private informers ("promoters"), 179–80, 192–93, 205–7; and public shaming/gendered punishments, 176–78, 265n4, 265n10; staged destruction of, 12–13, 174–211, 214; stage properties as, 181–82, 195–96, 200, 214–15; staging of market women's products as, 180–211; the term "dildo," 190
familial ties in theater: collaboration within theater families, 26; continuities between Renaissance and Restoration theater, 216–17, 268n21; female apprenticeships, 27–29, 225n84; theater wives and widows, 25–27, 47–49, 60, 65, 73, 242nn98–99

female occupations: alewives, 5, 20, 63–64, 178, 265n10; apple-wives, 146–47, 155, 201, 267n68; baize (a New Drapery) retailers, 102; bakers, 103, 251n42; basketweavers, 135–36, 257n119; beautifying physic, practitioners of, 218; beer brewsters, 102–3, 251n42; botchers (menders of old clothes), 102, 251n47; brothel keepers, 22, 218; brush makers, 251n42; candle women, 268n21; carpenters, 225n75; chandlers, 251n42; concessionaires, 216–17; cosmetics manufacturers and retailers, 218; costume suppliers, 26, 45, 215, 217; cutlers, 251n42; dyers, 102–3, 216; embroiderers, 27, 98, 102, 124, 129, 256n110; fishwives, 144, 149, 153, 155–56, 172–73, *187*, 216, 260n19, 261n34; frippers (secondhand clothing dealers), 5, 22, 30, 45–47, 172, 230n150; fruit-wives, 22, 144, 146, 149, 153, 163, 184, 197, 201, 216–17; garland weavers, 227n101; goldsmiths, 251n42; herb-wives, 155, 171, 184, 260n19, 264n91; hostesses, 63–65, 238n53, 238–39n56, 254n85; innkeepers, 222n15; jewelers, 251n42; joiners, 251n42; kitchen-stuff women, 155, 160; kitchen wenches ("scullions"), 170; lace makers and retailers, 2–3, 27, *28*, 29, 43, 96, 99, 102–3, 211, 226n87, 229n142, 251n41, 251n47, 251nn50–51, 253–54n81, 256n110; landladies, 238n53, 238n56; leather dressers, 251n42; linen drapers, retailers and weavers, 30, 102–3, 129, 227n93, 249n14; mercers, 227n93; merchants, 102; milliners, 102–3, 227n93; orange women, 173, 216, 262; oysterwives, 2, 146, 149, 155–58, 162–63, 169, 211, 216, 264n89; painters, 128n127, 252n55; pawnbrokers, 5, 45–47, 230n154, 230nn156–57, 231nn160–61; property makers, 1, 31, 53, 98, 108, 217; rentiers, 5, 222n15; sempstresses (seamstresses; also called "needlewomen" or "workwomen"), 9, 20, 29, 45, 95, 97, 102–3, 108, 113, 125, 127, 129, 141, 143, 216, 225–26n84, 230n153, 251n47, 253–54n81, 254nn81–82, 254n85, 256n110; shoemakers, 102, 251n42, 255n88; silk dyers, throwsters, twisters, weavers, and winders, 3, 41–43, *43*, 44, 99, 102–3, 216, 226–27n93, 228n128, 228–29n132, 250–51n41, 251n47, 253n79, 253–54n81, 255n88, 256n110; stillers, 251n42; tailors, 102; tapestry-makers, 102; thread dyers and sellers, 42, 102, 251n50; turners, 227n93; victuallers, 5, 20, 251n42; wardrobe keepers, 216, 268n11; whitsters (bleachers), 103, 115, 117; wire drawers, 251n45; wool carders, combers, spinners, twisters, 102; yarn twisters, 102. *See also* dressers and dressing, female labor of theatrical; female performers; gatherers, female; gendered division of labor in early modern England; immigrant women's textile work; laundresses; market women; moneylenders and creditors, female; pawnbrokers; playwrights; prostitution; silkwomen; spanglers; starchwomen; street-criers and hawkers; theatrical investors/stakeholders; tirewomen

female performers, 15–17, 222n16: acrobats, jugglers, and tumblers, 15, 161; continental, 17, 223n30; in country house entertainments, 17; in court masques, 6, 17, 31–32, 35, *36*, 38, 44, 108, 116; dancers, 17, 161, 216; exclusion from professional stage, 15–16, 18; in guild plays and civic pageants, 15–17; hidden tradition of, 17; influence on "all-male stage," 161; itinerant, 6, 15, 161–62, 223n30; musicians, 15, 17, 161; patronage of, 17; on Restoration and eighteenth-century stage, 215–17; rope-dancers, 161; singers, 17; and vagabond legislation, 162

Fenton, Roger, 69–70, 71, 234n14, 240n84, 240n86, 241–42n94

food: consumed in theaters, 5, 49, 146, 153; retailing of, 20, 153, 261n36; shortages, 257–58n119. *See also* ale, consumed in theaters; street-criers and hawkers, female

foreigners (non-citizens from other counties), 13, 23, 175, 197

forestalling (buying up goods before they reached the market), 179, 260n19, 265n12. *See also* capitalism, rise of; markets and market regulation

Fox, Adam, 147–48, 261n38

The French Garden (Erondelle), 105–7

Frith, Mary, 17. *See also* female performers

Froide, Amy, 59, 237n33, 238n46

gatherers (collectors of entrance-fees in theaters), female, 2, 9, 37, 47–49

Geary, Keith, 241n88

gendered division of labor in early modern England, 1–3, 18, 25–53, 230n123; and "body"/"soul" of theater, 199, 208–9, 214; continuities between pre-Restoration and Restoration theater, 215–17; devaluation of female labor, 3–5, 199, 211, 213; legitimate/illegitimate trades, 5, 13, 22; among Netherlandish immigrants, 93–95, 247n4; and new opportunities for female employment in and around theaters, 1, 47–49, 53; and players' efforts to establish legitimacy of their profession, 1–2, 7, 13, 49–52, 209, 211; and resentment of alien crafts- and tradeswomen, 114; restrictions on female labor, by civic authorities, 1, 5, 58, 69, 102, 113, 184; restrictions on female labor, by guilds, 1, 5, 19–21, 23–25, 42, 58, 69, 102, 215, 223n34, 223n40, 224n65, 225n66, 249n25; scholarship on, 4–5, 8, 18, 19–25; in theater families, 24–29, 28, 47–49, 242n98; and theatrical labor, 3, 18, 22, 25, 37, 47, 173, 209, 212, 215, 217–18; women's work as "never done," 4, 10–11, 57, 97, 101, 123, 132, 143, 196, 214, 219n2. *See also* familial ties in theater; female occupations; informal economy and female labor

Generall Historie of the Netherlands (Grimeston), 94

Golden Age (Heywood), 166–67

Gossen, Mistress, 37, 41, 109, 123, 133–34. *See also* immigrant women's textile work; tirewomen

Gosson, Stephen, 50, 51, 117, 180, 181, 265n23

Gouge, William, 51, 83–84

Gould, Grace, 215–16. *See also* tirewomen

Greene, Susan. *See* Baskerville (a.k.a. Browne, Greene), Susan

Greer, Germaine, 235n23

Greg, Sir Walter, 45, 46

guilds. *See* livery companies

Gull's Hornbook (Dekker), 207

Gurr, Andrew, 60, 147, 221n6

Gwinn, Lucy, 216. *See also* dressers and dressing, female labor of theatrical; familial ties in theater; Restoration theater

Gwyn, Eleanor ("Nell"), 216. *See also* female performers; Restoration theater

Hafter, Daryl M., 4–5

Hamlet (Shakespeare), 144, 160–71; cries of the ghost, 169, 263n85, 264n86; cries as tragic utterance in, 169–71, 263n85, 264n86, 264n89; Hamlet's advice to the players, 144, 160–71, 263n85; Hamlet's dying utterance, 169–70; Hecuba's cry, 170, 264n89; and professionalization of playing, 160–68; and rhetorical treatises on vocal and gestural delivery, 168–69, 263n77; and satire of the *Ur-Hamlet*'s ghost, 144, 166, 263n85; and staging of cries as vocal performance, 144, 160–71; staging of Ophelia's descent into madness, 164, 167, 170–72; and tradition of lampooning neo-Senecan revenge tragedies, 164–67; and War of the Theaters, 164–67

Harding, Vanessa, 183

Hathaway, Ann, 235n23

Hawkes, David, 235–36n25

Heath, Ann, 216, 267n8, 268n21. *See also* familial ties in theater

Henslowe, Agnes (née Woodward), 26–27, 225n78, 242n98. *See also* familial ties in theater

Henslowe, Mary, 27, 29. *See also* apprentices and apprenticeship

Henslowe, Philip: account book or "diary" and pawn accounts, 26, 37, 45–47, 56, 65–66, 108–9, 230n154, 230nn156–57, 231n157, 239n62; apprenticing of niece, Mary, 27, 29; wife Agnes, 26–27, 225n78, 242n98

Hewes, Joan, 47. *See also* gatherers, female

Hibbard, G. R., 169

Hilliard, Nicholas, 103, 104, 252n55

History of the Cries of London (Ancient & Modern) (Hindley), 147–48

Hodge, Nancy Elizabeth, 243–44n111

Hoenselaars, A. J., 250n36, 255n86

Holderness, B. A., 237n41

Honigmann, Ernst, 56

Hovell, Joan, 60. *See also* familial ties in theater; moneylenders and creditors, female

Howard, Frances, 98

Howard, Jean E., 6, 182, 221n6, 255n88

A Hundreth Good Pointes of Husbandry, Lately Married Unto a Hundreth Good Poyntes of Huswifery (Tusser), 219n2

Hunt, Margaret, 72, 241n89

Hutchinson, Elizabeth, 26–27, 45. *See also* familial ties in theater

Hutson, Lorna, 239n64

"idleness," stigma of: as effeminizing, 190; and female labor, 22, 130, 132, 159; "idle occupations," 50, 180, 191, 194, 198; and labor in informal sector, 22–23; and players, 7, 22, 50–52, 158, 160, 180, 182, 198, 203, 214, 232n193, 255–56n23; and usurers, 54–55. *See also* informal economy and female labor

immigrants, Netherlandish, 99–101, 138–40, 249nn24–26, 259n131; ambivalence of native population toward, 93–95, 100, 140, 250n33, 250n36; 258n128; assimilation/segregation, 140, 250n36, 258n128; economic "projects" of 250n34; in environs of theaters, 99, 133, 249n25; and gendered division of labor, 93–95, 247n4; importation of skills and revitalization of the English clothing market, 99–100, 249n27, 251–52n52; population in London, 99, 101, 249n24, 250nn36–38; recent scholarship on depictions in dramatic literature, 100–101, 250nn35–36; women's active role in commerce, 85, 93–94, 247n4. See also aliens; immigrant women's textile work

immigrant women's textile work, 11–12, 31–41, 93–143, 213; all-female households and widow-run boarding houses, 114–15, 253–54n81, 254nn84–85; complaints of guildsmen against, 253n79; Dutch courtesan stereotype, 114–15, 254nn84–85, 255n86; imported skills, techniques, and technologies, 1, 39, 41, 95, 99, 102–3, 107–8, 114, 117, 122–23, 125, 127, 135, 137–38, 140, 213, 253n79, 256n110; male anxiety surrounding, 114–16, 125–33, *128*, 253n79, 256nn110–11; Returns of the Aliens occupational data concerning, 42, 101–3, 113, 250n38, 251n45, 253n79, 259n131; satirical attacks and moralistic polemics, 117–33, *118, 119, 121, 126*, 138; sexualization of, 38, 39, 114–15, 120, 122, 125–29, *126*, 133, 228n121, 248n10, 254nn84–85, 255n86, 256n105; single women, 102; starching labor, 95–99, 103–8, 123–25, 248n14; widows, 42, 102, 113, 114–15, 251n42, 253n76; wives, 102–3. See also attires; laundresses; silkwomen; starchwomen; tirewomen

immigrant women's textile work (staging of), 11–12, 94–95, 133–43; and changing fashion trends, 140–44, 259n132; in *The London Prodigall*, 136–40; mockery of outlandish attires, 138, *139*, 258n124; in *Patient Grissil*, 133–37, 138; in *The Proud Woman of Antwerp* (Day and Haughton), 122–23. See also attires; laundresses; silkwomen; starchwomen; tirewomen

Impersonations (Orgel), 18

informal economy and female labor, 1, 8, 20–25, 42, 50, 52–53, 148–50, 193–94, 212–14, 218, 223n40, 224n58, 230n150, 256n110; civic authorities' legislative attempts to control, 5, 22–23, 50, 148–50, 174–80, 224n55; concept of "informality," 21–22; evidence of, 2–3, 7–8, 20–21, 29, 45–47, 49, 58, 97, 101–4, 110, 146–50, 230n150; flexibility of, 3, 25–26, 29, 153, 155, 180–82, 193; guild restrictions on female labor, 5, 20–21, 23, 148–50, 215, 223n34, 223n40; and loosening of the guild system, 23–25, 224n65, 225n66; and market regulations, 174–80; and never-married women ("maids"), 20–21; scholarship on, 8–9, 21–22; stigmatization of, 3, 23, 54–55, 155, 175; theatrical commerce, intersection with, 1, 3, 8, 27, 52–53, 212–14, 218; unguilded, 3, 20–21, 23, 25, 54, 175, 212–13, 215, 223n40. See also "false wares"; female occupations; gendered division of labor in early modern England; "idleness," stigma of; immigrant women's textile work; street-criers and hawkers, female

Ingram, Jill Phillips, 247n144

In Praise of Cleane Linnen, With the Commendable Use of the Laundresse (Taylor), 130–33

investment capital of women, 1, 10, 26, 53, 58, 61, 66–67, 71, 73, 75, 241n89, 242n98, 243n104. See also capitalism, rise of

Itinerary (Moryson), 93–94

Jardine, Lisa, 243n106

Jefferies, Joyce, 17, 237n37. See also moneylenders and creditors, female; patronage, female theatrical

Jones, Ann Rosalind, 98–99

Jonson, Ben: and anti-theatricalism, 195, 198, 202–7; and "body"/"soul" of theater, 198, 209, 214–15; references to starched ruffs and rebatos, 112–13; reliance on and derision of tirewomen's wares, 214–15; and tiremakers of Silver Street, 112–13; on virtuous "workmanship" of the poet-playwright, 198. See also *Bartholomew Fair* (Jonson)

Kathman, David, 17
Kermode, Lloyd, 67
Knapton, Anne, 217. See also dressers and dressing, female labor of theatrical; Restoration theater

Labor and Writing in Early Modern England, 1567–1667 (Ellinghausen), 6
lace: adorning linen attires, 110, 248–49n14, 256n110; archaeological remains found on theater sites, 2, 211; bonelace (or bobbin lace), 27, *28*, 29, 43–44, 96, 103, 226n87, 251n51, 256n110; bugle (beaded) lace, 103; copper lace, 29, 44, 181, 229n142, 267n67; cutwork, 141, 256n110; gold lace, 44, 129, 230nn145–46, 230n149, 248–49n14; immigrant innovations in and manufacture of, *28*, 99, 102–3, 251n47; parchment lace, 103, 251n47; silk lace, 43–44, 103, 248–49n14, 250–51n41; silver lace, 44, 129, 230nn145–46, 248–49n14; as women's work, 226n87, 256n110. *See also* attires; female occupations, lace makers and retailers; passementerie
Lacey, Kay, 229n140, 230n150
laundresses, 97, 113–17, 125–33, *126*, *128*, 141–42, 154, 256nn110–11; all-female workspace of laundry, 125, *126*, 127, 133; and bodily/moral filth, 94, 107, 113, 130–31; chaste industry of, 95, 116, 130–32, 135–38, 213; codification of techniques in how-to books, 129; immigrant women, 11, 103, 108, 113–17, 122, 213; incessant labor of, 97, 101, 125, 136; and informal economy, 20; male anxiety surrounding, 127–33, *128*, 256n110, 256–57n111; in *The Merry Wives of Windsor* (Shakespeare), 115–17; occupational diseases of, 256n111; in *The Proud Woman of Antwerp* (Day and Haughton), 122–23; sexualization of, 125–29, *126*, *128*, 129–33; social advancement and upward mobility of, 130–33; Taylor's mock encomium of, 130–33; techniques and technologies of, 127, 153, 231n36; and theatrical production, 9, 22, 95, 108, 116–17, 177, 216; transformation of the profession, 127, 129–31, 256n110. *See also* attires; clothing; costumes; immigrant women's textile work; "poking sticks"; starch; starching, labor of; starchwomen; tirewomen
Lemire, Beverly, 21
Leventen, Carol, 243n109
Levin, Richard, 221n6
livery companies: Bakers' Company, 176–77; Clothworkers' Company, 19–20; complaints against aliens, 43, 100, 114, 229n139, 245n25, 249n25; Cordwainers' Company, 33; decline or loosening of guild system, 21–25, 27, 173, 179, 215, 224n65, 225n66; Drapers' Company, 24, 176; eventual admittance of women, 215; Fishmongers' Company, 261n34; and freedom of the city, 188, 224n65; Goldsmiths' Company, 25, 184, 186, 189, 194; inspection or searching of markets, 13, 175–76, 205; and legitimate trade, 1, 22, 54, 174; London Weavers' Company, 20, 42–43, 102, 139, 223n34, 228–29n131, 229n, 253n79, 265n4; Mercers' Company, 25, 188; Merchant Taylors' Company, 267n6; moral ethos of, 13, 183, 264n1; proscription and punishment of deceptive trade practices and manufacture or sale of "false wares," 13, 33, 50, 175–79, 186, 264n34, 265n4; restrictions on women's work, 5, 19–20, 23, 42–43, 58, 102, 114, 149–50, 212, 215, 228–29n131, 264n34; 267n6; scholarship on, 23; status and privileges of, 153–54, 224n65; wealth of, 224n65; work of wives, daughters, and widows of guildsmen, 20. *See also* apprentices and apprenticeship; citizenship; informal economy and female labor
Lodge, Thomas, 144, 163–64, 166, 169, 264n89
London and the Countrey Carbonadoed (Lupton), 153–54
Luu, Lien Bich, 249nn24–25, 249n27

markets and market regulation, 174–80, *185*, *187*, 192, 264n1; Alley's market reform proposal, 148–49, 184–86, *185*, *187*; as arena of performance, 12, 17, 48, 155, 166, 171, 173, 180, 195; broadsheets depicting architectural sequestration and segregation of street hawkers, 150–53, *151*, *152*, 261n36; growing disorder of, 21, 23, 149, 173, 179, 183, 184, 190, 197, 266n40; market abuses, 150, 155–56, 179, *185*, 186, *187*, 200, 204–6, 265n12; moral imperative of reform, 13, 175–78, 184, 204, 264n1; New Fishstreet Market, *187*; private informers ("promoters"), 179–80, 182–84, 186, 192–93, 194, 202, 203, 205, 206, 265nn16–17; public shaming of offenders, 13, 175–78, 199; theater and, 13, 21–22, 25, 45, 48, 100, 146, 171, 173–74, 180–83, 194–95, 200, 201–2, 207, 210–11, 250n32; and unstable boundary between formal and informal commerce, markets and market regulation, (cont'd) 22–24, 174–80; virtues/vices of, 175, 177, 181, 183, 197. See also *Bartholomew Fair* (Jonson); capitalism, rise of; *A Chaste Maid in Cheapside* (Middleton); Cheapside market district; consumers and consumerism; "false wares"; informal economy and female labor; market women; street-criers and hawkers, female

market women (or "hucksters"), 22, 146, 148, 260n8; accused of market abuses, 50, 149–50, 177, 184, *185*, 186, *187*, 196, 100, 261n34; adulterated products of, 13, 32, 176–78, 185, 190–91, 196, 199, 209, 214; cries of, 12, 148, 166, 173; disorderly commercial practices of, 13, 150, 155, 166, 173, 190, 197, 261n34, 264n91, 265n10; as foil of professional players/playwrights, 13, 195, 198–99, 210–11; incontinence of, 13, 178, 183, 188, 189, 190, 194, 196, 197, 266n48; legislation aimed at reforming/curbing unruly commerce of, 148–50, 171, 184, 259n132, 260n19; marketing techniques of, 48, 145, 148, 153, 155–57, 171, 178, 196, 199, 200, 213, 218, 266n40; and pawnbroking, 45; public punishment of, 13, 177–78, 199; reliance of theaters on wares of, 1, 13, 22, 52, 201, 209, 211; sexualization of, 177, 188, 196; as threat to prerogatives of guildsmen, 149, 183, 261n34; wares defined/destroyed as "trash," 10, 13, 175, 178, 182–83, 196–201, 208–9, 211; wit or ingenuity of, 193. See also *Bartholomew Fair* (Jonson); *A Chaste Maid in Cheapside* (Middleton); "false wares"; markets and market regulation; street-criers and hawkers, female

Marston, John, 48–49, 65–66, 124, 164–66, 254n84, 263n75

Marx, Karl, 95, 99, 238n13, 248n13

masculinity: city comedies and ideal of virtuous, civic masculinity, 13, 182–83, 190, 214; and gendered punishments for hawking of "false wares," 176–77; and legitimacy of playing profession, 13, 174, 211, 214; new forms of, 266n35; and vocal self-restraint, 163–64

Megg, Mary, 216. See also female occupations, concessionaires; female occupations, fruit-wives; Restoration theater

The Merchant of Venice (Shakespeare), 10–11, 57–58, 71–85, 92; and doctrine of "due benevolence," 83–85, 92, 246n140; and economic crisis of the 1590s, 73, 243n103; and emergent ethos of virtuous, Christian exactitude, 57, 75, 78, 92, 213; and female moneylenders and creditors, 10–11, 57–58, 71–85, 92; justice as "just measure"/exactitude, 82–83, 92, 247n151; and law of coverture, 71–72, 74–76, 84, 243n106, 243n109; and married women's separate estates and trusts, 71–73, 241n91; Portia's agency, 71–82; Portia's ciphering and exactitude, 78–82, 92, 245n119, 247n151; Portia's exercise of wit, will, and skill, 73–82; Portia as gift-giver/creditor/usuress, 10, 58, 73, 76–78, 84–85, 236n28, 241n88, 243–44n111, 247n144; Portia's likening of marital bond/band to an "oath of credit," 57–58, 75–76, 83–85, 92, 243n108; Portia's vocabulary/lexicon of (ac)counting, 76–83; Shylock's inexactitude in (ac)counting, 80–82; stage properties (caskets, rings, scales), 85, 90–92; traditional interpretation of Portia as gift-giver, 58, 71–72, 236n28, 241n88; trial scene, 80, 92, 247n151; trope of usuress as "cipherer," 57, 77–82, 245n119. See also (ac)counting; moneylenders and creditors, female; usuresses; usury in early modern England

Middleton, Thomas, 13, 39, 171–72, 180, 183, 193–94, 197, 210, 254n84. See also *A Chaste Maid in Cheapside* (Middleton)

Miller, Pat, 2, 44

moneylenders and creditors, female, 10–11, 53, 54–92; broadside ballads depicting, 61–63; and city comedies, 66–67, 239n64; English anti-usury polemics, 54, 55, 67–71, 234n14, 240n79, 240nn81–82, 240n84, 240n86; evidence/explanations for, 58–59; and exactitude in (ac)counting, 78–82, 92, 235n24, 245nn119–20, 247n151; and excessive/unnatural reproduction, 55, 233n9, 234nn10–11; and law of coverture, 71–76, 84, 241n89, 243n104; lending to kin, 58–59, 237n37, 237n39; litigation ("waging law"), 59, 64; marital bonds/bands, 57–58, 75–76, 83–85, 243n108; and married women's separate estates and trusts, 71–73, 241n91; *Merchant of Venice*, 10–11, 57–58, 71–85, 92; and popular compensatory narratives of male debtors avoiding repayment, 63–67, 238n56, 239n64; power dynamics between female creditors and male debtors, 56–57; propriety of, in conduct manuals for women, 70–71; sexualization of, 61–63, 64, 67; Shakespeare's Sonnets, 10–11, 57, 67, 76–77, 78, 84, 235–36n25, 236n26; single women lending and living off interest, 58–60, 62–63, 237nn32–33, 237n37, 237n39; and theatrical commerce/networks of credit, 27, 59–61, 242n98; usury in early modern England, 54–56, 58, 233n2; usury legislation, 55, 58; vocabulary/lexicon of (ac)counting, 76–83; wealth/earnings of, 59, 237nn32–33, 237n37, 237n41, 238n46; widows, 58–60, 67–71, 237nn41–42. *See also* credit economy in early modern England; moneylenders and creditors (visual iconography); usuresses; usury in early modern England

moneylenders and creditors (visual iconography), 79, 85–92, 86, 88, 89, 91; *Allegory of Vanity* (Bloemart engraving), 86; *Arithmetica* (Glover engraving), 79; engravings of Lady Avarice and Lady Vanity, 85–87, 86; Lady Arithmetic, 78, 79; in *The Moneylender and His Wife* (Matsys painting), 87; scales as emblems of just reckoning/Last Judgment, 90, 91, 92, 247n151; stage properties of *Merchant of Venice* and worldly/spiritual accounting, 85, 90–92; tools used by and shifting attitudes toward, 87–90, 88, 89, 91; *Woman Holding a Balance* (Vermeer painting), 91; *Woman Weighing Gold* (van Hemessen and Woutersz paintings), 88, 89; women weighing gold, 87–90

Moorer, Awdrey, 31. *See also* Revels Office; tirewomen

Morgan, Ellin, 31. *See also* Revels Office; tirewomen

Moryson, Fynes, 93–94

Mountague, Alice, 35, 43. *See also* silkwomen

Mountjoy, Christopher, and Mountjoy family, 109–13, 137, 253n70, 253n74. *See also* tiremakers

Mountjoy, Marie, 110, 253n74. *See also* immigrant women's textile work; tirewomen

Muldrew, Craig, 72, 73, 243n103

My Ladies Looking Glasse (Rich), 265n17

Nashe, Thomas, 127, 166, 257–58n119
Neill, Michael, 221n6
Nelson, Alan H., 221n6

"New Draperies," 99–100, 102
Newes both from Heaven and Hell (Rich), 123–24
Newman, Karen, 243n110
Nicholl, Charles, 110, 253n74
numeracy, 115, 116, 123, 244nn112, 245nn119. *See also* (ac)counting; ciphers and ciphering

Of Domesticall Duties (Gouge), 83–84
Ogilvie, Sheilagh, 223n40
Orgel, Stephen, 18

passementerie (decorative trimmings), 29, 41, 43–44, 251n41, 251n47, 253–54n81, 256n110. *See also* attires; lace
Paster, Gail Kern, 189, 266n48
patronage, female theatrical, 17, 217, 237n37
pawnbroking: Henslowe's pawn accounts, 45–47, 230n154, 230nn156–57, 231n157; illegal use and renting out of attire, 46–47, 226n89, 231nn160–61. *See also* female occupations, pawnbrokers; moneylenders and creditors, female; usuresses
periwigs and perukes, 2, 31, 35, 37, 103, 110, 112–13, 123, 125, 209, 215, 252n61. *See also* attires; starch
Perkins, William, 51, 233n204
Pettegree, Andrew, 249n24
Pettet, E. C., 243n111
Phillips, Mary, 47. *See also* gatherers, female
Pie-Powders, Court of, 199–200, 205, 207
Pilkington, Joan, 31, 227n99. *See also* Revels Office; tiremakers; tirewomen
Pilkington, William, 31. *See also* Revels Office; tiremakers
Platter, Thomas, 30, 47
players. *See* actors
Playgoing in Shakespeare's London (Gurr), 221n6
playing companies: Admiral's Men, 37, 45, 47–48, 108–9, 117, 122–23, 133–34, 144, 172, 232n179, 239n62; adult companies, 41, 108–9, 145–46, 164–65, 171–73; Chamberlain's Men, 112, 116, 144, 160, 164, 262n44; Children of the Chapel or Queen's Revels, 35, 38, 108, 113, 167, 172, 252n61; Children of the King's Revels, 37–38, 113, 125, 167, 228n118; Children of the Merchant Taylors' School, 252n61; children's companies, 35–38, 108, 145–46, 164–65, 167, 172,

324 Index

playing companies: Admiral's Men, (cont'd) 263n75; and cries of female street-criers and hawkers, 12, 144–46, 160–68, 173; Duke's Company, 217; Earl of Leicester's Men, 159-60; Earl of Pembroke's Men, 66; Earl of Worcester's Men, 37, 109; employment of female gatherers, 47–49; exclusion of women, 1, 15, 17–19, 49, 53, 161; and female financiers, 11, 56, 60, 65, 73, 84, 217, 242n99; female patronage of, 17; and gendered division of labor, 1–2, 7, 13, 49–52, 209, 211; and Hamlet's advice to the players, 160–68; as hybrid economic structures, 25, 213; King's Company, 215, 216; King's Men, 47, 112, 217; King's and Queen's Young Company, 26, 45; Lady Elizabeth's Men, 173, 183, 194; patronage and/or employment of tirewomen, 35–39, 41, 108–9, 117, 123, 252n61; post-Restoration admittance of women, 215; Prince Henry's Men, 47, 171–72; and professionalization, 1–2, 7, 12-13, 49–52, 145, 160, 174, 180-82, 195, 210, 214, 218; as pseudo-guilds, 25, 49, 52, 180, 198, 213–14, 266n27; Queen Anne's Men, 47, 60, 73, 110; reliance on second-hand clothing trade, 9, 22, 30, 45, 47; Sir Oliver Owlet's Men in *Histrio-Mastix* (Marston), 65–66, 166, 171; staging of market women's wares, 13, 180-82, 194, 211; staging of tirewomen's work and wares; 37–39; stigma of effeminacy, 49–50, 180–82, 265n23; stigma of illegitimacy and idleness, 7, 50–52, 180–82, 202–7, 232n193, 265n23; traveling companies, 15, 17, 160–62, 166–67, 173, 223n30; War of the Theaters, 12, 144–46, 160, 164–67. *See also* actors; costumes
plays and masques: *Antonio and Mellida* (Marston), 164–65; *Antonio's Revenge* (Marston), 165–66; *Bussy D'Ambois* (Chapman), 104; *Christmas, His Masque* (Jonson), 214–15, 217; closet dramas, 17, 221n10; *Cupids Whirligig* (Sharpham), 37–38, 125–27; *Cynthia's Revels; or, The Fountain of Self-Love* (Jonson), 38–39; *The Dumb Knight* (Machin and Markham), 38; *The Dutch Courtesan* (Marston), 254n84; *English-men for My Money* (Haughton), 66, 73, 85; *Epicoene; or, The Silent Woman* (Jonson), 112–13, 172; *Exchange Ware at the Second Hand Viz. Band, Ruffe, and Cuffe, Lately Out, and Now Newly Dearned Up*, 142–43; *Frederick and Basilea*, 48; *The Gentleman Usher* (Chapman), 108; *Henry IV* (Shakespeare), 64–65; *Henry V* (Shakespeare), 244–45n117, 254n85; *Histrio-Mastix* (Marston), 48–49, 65–66, 124, 166; *The Honest Whore, Part One* (Dekker and Middleton), 171–72; *Hymenai* (Jonson), 198; *Lingua; or, The Combat of the Tongue, and the Five Senses for Superiority: A Pleasant Comœdie* (Tompkis), 40; *The London Prodigall*, 11–12, 136–40; *Measure for Measure* (Shakespeare), 204; *A Merrie Dialogue Between Band, Cuffe, and Ruffe*, 140–43; *The Merry Wives of Windsor* (Shakespeare), 110, 115–17; *Michaelmas Term* (Middleton), 39, 228n121; *Much Ado About Nothing* (Shakespeare), 110; *Patient Grissil* (Dekker, Chettle, and Haughton), 11, 133–37, 138; *Pericles* (Shakespeare), 264n91; *The Playe of the Weather* (Heywood), 129–30; *The Pleasant Comodie of Patient Grissil*, 133–37; *Poetaster* (Jonson), 113, 164; *Proud Woman of Antwerp* (Day and Haughton), 122–23, 255n96; revenge tragedies, 164–66, 167; *Satiro-Mastix* (Dekker), 166, 256n105; *The Shoemakers' Holiday* (Dekkers), 52; *The Spanish Tragedy* (Kyd), 165; *The Taming of the Shrew* (Shakespeare), 63–64; *The Three Ladies of London* (Wilson), 159–60, 166; *Timon of Athens* (Shakespeare), 246n137; *The Tragedy of Hoffman* (Chettle), 172; *A Trick to Catch the Old One* (Middleton), 254n84; *Twelfth Night* (Shakespeare), 226n87; *The Two Gentlemen of Verona* (Shakespeare), 110; *Ur-Hamlet*, 144, 166, 263n85; *A Warning for Faire Women*, 164; *The Winter's Tale* (Shakespeare), 55, 244–45n117. *See also Bartholomew Fair* (Jonson); *A Chaste Maid in Cheapside* (Middleton); city comedies; *The Merchant of Venice* (Shakespeare)
playwrights: Behn, Aphra,109–10; Brome, Richard, 198; Cary, Elizabeth, 17; Chapman, George, 12, 104, 108, 267n67; Chettle, Henry, 11, 133, 172; Day, John, 122–23; Dekker, Thomas, 11, 52, 133, 136–37, 166, 171–72, 207, 233n217, 256n105; female, 17, 221n10; Haughton, William, 11, 66, 73, 122–23, 133; Heywood, John, 129–30, 257n113; Heywood, Thomas, 52, 166–67, 181–82, 239n64; Kyd, Thomas, 144, 165; Machin, Lewis, 38; Markham, Gervase,

38; Sharpham, Edward, 37–38, 125; Sidney, Mary, 17; Tompkis, Thomas, 40; Wilson, Robert, 159–60, 161, 166; Wither, George, 24, 225n66; Wroth, Mary, 17. *See also* Jonson, Ben; Marston, John; Middleton, Thomas; Shakespeare, William

Pleasant Quippes for Upstart Newfangled Gentle-Women (Gosson), 117

"poking sticks" (heated irons used to set ruffs), 40, 104, *106*, 120, 125, *126*, 127, 132–33, 142, 177, 248–49n14, 252n54. *See also* attires; laundresses; starch; starching; starchwomen

Poovey, Mary, 235n24, 240n81

promoters (private informers). *See* markets and market regulation

prostitution: prostitutes, 10, 13, 17, 22, 61, 63, 94, 101, 114, 130, 177, 189, 191–93, 210, 233n2, 254n84, 255n86, 264n89; sex work in commercial networks surrounding theaters, 17, 22, 114–15, 217–18

Rackin, Phyllis, 15–16, 221n10
Rappaport, Steve, 19–20, 23
rebatos. *See* attires
regrating (buying goods for resale elsewhere), 148, 150, 155, 179, 186, *187*, 260n19, 265n12. *See also* capitalism, rise of; markets and market regulation
Restoration theater, 215–17
Returns of Aliens (London), 42, 101–3, 113, 250n38, 251n45, 253n79, 259n131
Revels Office: account books of, 29–31, 226n89, 226–27n93, 227n94, 227n99, 227n101, 266n53; costumes used as payment to actors for court performances, 30, 45; employment of artisans' wives, daughters, and widows, 30–31; employment of crafts- and tradeswomen, 30–31, 226–27n93; employment of female garland weavers, 227n101; employment of female spanglers, 31; employment of immigrant women, 35, 41, 43, 252n61; employment of silkwomen, 41–42, 43, 226–27n93, 229n142; employment of single women, 227n99; employment of tirewomen, 31, 35, 108; recycling or translating of costumes, 30, 44; renting out of costumes, 226n89
Rich, Barnabe, 123–24, 265n17
ruffs. *See* attires
Rutter, Tom, 6, 7, 50, 220n17, 233n217

Schama, Simon, 247n4
Schetz (née Barney), Margaret, 34. *See also* tirewomen
scholarship on women and pre-Restoration theater, 1–14, 15–25; absence/presence dichotomy, 8–9, 15–18, 213–14, 220n4, 221n10; on female patrons, 17; on female "players" or performers, 6, 17–18, 222n16; on female playwrights, 17, 221–22n10; on female spectators, 221n6; feminist, 15–18; future avenues of research, 217–18; hypotheses regarding women's exclusion from professional stage, 18–19, 223n30. *See also* "all-male stage," paradigm of
scholarship on women's labor history, 4–6, 19–23, 219n6, 219n8
secondhand clothing trade, 45–47, 142, 230n150; female "frippers," 20, 22, 45, 172, 230n150, 231n160; theater's reliance on, 9, 22, 30, 45, 47; women's involvement in, 9, 20, 30, 45, 47, 230n150. *See also* pawnbroking
separate estates and trusts, married women's, 71–73, 241n91, 242n98.
Shakespeare, William: Cobbe portrait (attributed), 110; Droeshout portrait, 110, *112*, 253n74; as moneylender, 56, 235n23; and Mountjoy family of Huguenot tiremakers, 109–13, 137, 253n70, 253n74. *See also Hamlet* (Shakespeare); *The Merchant of Venice* (Shakespeare); plays and masques; Sonnets (Shakespeare)
Shakespeare and Women (Rackin), 15–16
Shakespeare Without Women (Callaghan), 15, 16
Shapiro, Michael, 18–19, 223n30
Sidney, Sir Philip, 52, 108, 198, 207–8
silkwomen, 35, 39, 41–45, *43*, 97, 99, 102–3, 108, 226–27n93, 228n128, 229nn139–40, 250–51n41, 253n79, 253–54n81, 256n110. *See also* textile trades
Singh, Jyotsna G., 241n88
single women: all female households, 62, 253n81; economic agency of, 58, 61, 63, 71, 196; labor/occupational identities of, 20, 102, 253n81; moneylenders and creditors, 58–63, 66, 68, 73, 237n33, 238–39n56; sexual virtue/vice of, 61; theatrical commerce/labor of, 27, 29, 227n99. *See also* familial ties in theater; widows; wives
Smith, Bruce, 145, 167

326 Index

Snowe, Joan, 59. See also moneylenders and creditors, female
Sonnets (Shakespeare): and doctrine of "due benevolence," 84; female usurers and usury trope, 10–11, 57, 67, 76–77, 78, 84, 235–36n25, 236n26; usuress and "ciphering," 57, 76–77, 78
spanglers (needlewomen specializing in beadwork), 2–3, 20, 31, 44–45, 108, 117, 229n143
Speckard, Dorothy, 35. See also silkwomen
Spicksley, Judith M., 237n32, 237n39
stage properties: basket in *Patient Grissil* (Dekker, Chettle, and Haughton), 135–36; buck-basket in *The Merry Wives of Windsor* (Shakespeare), 115–16, 136; caskets, rings, and scales in *The Merchant of Venice* (Shakespeare), 85, 90–92; Dutch head-attire in *The London Prodigall*, 137–38; as evoking/eliding pre-histories of production, 7, 9; as "false wares," 13, 181–82, 195–96, 200, 214–15; as metonymies of women's work, 136; and pawnbroking, 47, 230n154; rebato in *Patient Grissil* (Dekker, Chettle, and Haughton), 133–36; scholarship on gendered meanings of, 6–7; women's work in fabrication of, 1, 53, 108, 217, 226n93, 227n94.
Stallybrass, Peter, 98–99
starch, 95, 98–99, 103, 117, 124–25, 131, 136, 141–42, 153; etymology of term, 258n120; and food shortages, 257–58n119; as insubstantial, 3, 9, 39, 95, 101, 133, 136, 214; and Marx on commodity form, 95, 248n13; occupational diseases caused by starching, 256–57n111; sale of, 259n132; smell of seething, 256–57n111; starch-houses, 127, *128*, 129, 248n14, 256n103, 256–57n111; starch-making, 97, 248n14, 256–57n111, 259n132. See also attires; laundresses; starchwomen
starching, labor of, 40, 97, 103, 107, 110, 113–15, 127, 123, 125, *128*, 129, 141–42, 177, 248n14; and the "all-male stage," 97, 123; codification of techniques in how-to books, 129; elision of, 95–97, 123; historical recovery of, 97–99; *Merry Wives of Windsor* (Shakespeare), 115–17; satirized in association with female vanity, 120–22; satirized as "tiresome," 123–25; sexualization of, 120, 122, 125–29, *126*, 130; starched ruffs and rebatos, 95–99, 103–7, 123–25; as threat to domestic economy, 257n119;

and wasteful expenditures on luxury attire, 135–36, 257n119. See also attires; immigrant women's textile work; laundresses; "poking sticks"; starch; starchwomen; tirewomen
starchwomen, 95, 108, 110, 113–15, 117, 123, 127, *128*, 129, 141–42. See also laundresses; immigrant women's textile work; starch; starching, labor of
Stedon of Maastricht, Widow, 113, 116, 253n76. See also immigrant women's textile work; laundresses; starchwomen
Stevens, Joyce, 4
street-criers and hawkers, female, 12, 49, 143, 144–73; antiquarian collectors of the "Cries of London," 147–48; archaeological remains in theater sites of foodstuffs sold by, 146, 260n7; broadsheet prints, engravings, and woodcuts, 150–53, *151, 152*, 163, 261n32, 261n36; in *Epicoene* and *Bartholomew Fair* (Jonson), 172–73; hawking of wares in and around theaters, 49, 146–54, 163; immigrant women selling door to door, 229n139; and informal economy, 153–54; legislation aimed at reforming/curbing commerce of, 148–50; as scapegoats for economic problems, 149–50, 154, 173, 261n34; as threat to prerogatives of guildsmen, 149, 261n34. See also markets and market regulation; street-cries, staged as vocal performances
street-cries, staged as vocal performances, 145, 154–73; acoustics of theaters, 145; and actors' vocal and gestural delivery, 168; adult companies' competition with children's companies, 146, 164–67; ambivalence toward female criers, 155–58; boy-actors' voices, 165–67, 263n75; children's company plays, 164–67, 172–73; contrasted with eloquence of professional male players, 12, 145–46, 160–68, 173; in English ballads, 154–59, 261n38; excessive forcefulness of, 165; ghost of Old Hamlet, 169, 263n85, 264n86; Hamlet's advice to the players, 144, 160–71; Hamlet's dying utterance, 169–70; Hecuba's cry, 170, 264n89; *The Honest Whore, Part One* (Dekker and Middleton), 171–72; lampooning cries of unskilled players, 166–67; lampooning neo-Senecan revenge tragedies, 164–66, 167; Lodge's ridicule of *Ur-Hamlet*'s ghost, 144, 166; and players' quest for profes-

sional legitimacy, 12, 144–46, 160–68, 173; in post-play jigs, 160; Shakespeare and the cry as preferred mode of tragic utterance, 169–71, 263n85, 264n86, 264n89; staging of Ophelia's mad scenes, 170–72; sympathetic depictions of, 159–60; in *The Three Ladies of London* (Wilson), 159–60; in *The Tragedy of Hoffman* (Chettle), 172; and vocal self-restraint, 163–64, 167–68. *See also* street-criers and hawkers, female
Stretton, Tim, 59, 64–65
Stubbes, Philip, 32–34, 122, 127, 248n14, 256n103, 258n126
Szatek, Karoline, 241n88

Taswell, Elizabeth, 217. *See also* dressers and dressing, female labor of theatrical; familial ties in theater; Restoration theater
Taylor, John, 130–33
Teerlinc, Levina, 252n55
textile trades, 3, 5, 9, 20, 22, 29–47, 95, 101, 103, 114, 153, 188, 213, 215, 261n36; and the "all-male stage," 97, 123; and female pawnbrokers, 45–47, 230n154, 230nn156–57, 231nn160–61; innovations revitalizing the clothing market, 98–100, 107, 130, 249n27; tailors, 30, 39, 45, 230n153, 251n49. *See also* attires; clothing; costumes; female occupations; immigrant women's textile work; secondhand clothing trade; silkwomen; spanglers; starching, labor of; starchwomen; tiremakers; tiremen; tirewomen
Theater of a City: The Places of London Comedy, 1598–1642 (Howard), 6
theater personnel, 7, 37, 48, 108, 145, 214, 217. *See also* dressers and dressing, female labor of theatrical; female occupations; gatherers; street-criers and hawkers, female; tiremen; tirewomen
theaters, 100; acoustics of, 145–46; Blackfriars, 38, 47, 99, 108, 147, 167, 252n61; Boar's Head Inn, 47, 99; Cockpit, 26; Covent Garden, 215–17, 268n21; Curtain, 99; Dorset Gardens, 217; Drury Lane, 216, 217, 268n21; Fortune, 99, 147; Globe, 41, 44, 47, 99, 146; Hope, 99, 194; "housekeepers," 48; immigrant population in environs of, 99, 249n25; Lincoln's Inn Fields, 215, 216–17; location of, 1, 24, 25, 50, 99, 173, 212; networks of commerce surrounding, 6, 22, 25, 94, 100–101, 217; Newington Butts, 144; private (indoor) theaters, 1, 6, 37, 49, 99, 108, 146, 172, 221n6; public amphitheaters, 1, 3, 6, 13, 16, 17, 18, 24, 29, 41, 49, 99, 146, 158, 160, 183, 221; purpose-built, 12, 24, 26, 47, 55, 160, 195, 218; Red Bull, 47, 99; Red Lion, 99; Rose, 2–3, 41, 44–45, 47, 48, 99, 146; Swan, 99, 158, 183; The Theatre, 26, 47, 99, 144, 159, 218; Trinity College Cambridge, 140; vending in, 49, 146; Whitefriars, 37, 49, 108, 215. *See also* theater personnel; tiring-house
theatrical investors/stakeholders: Alleyn, Edward (or "Ned"), 27, 44–45, 47, 48, 66, 109, 225n78, 242n98; Baskerville (a.k.a Browne, Greene), Susan, 60, 65, 73–74, 242n99; Beeston, Christopher, 26; Brayne, John, 26, 47; Brayne, Margaret, 26, 47; Burbage, James, 26. *See also* Henslowe, Philip; patronage, female theatrical
Thirsk, Joan, 248n14
Thomas, Keith, 245n119, 245n123
tiremakers: devil as tiremaker, 122; gendered division of labor among, 37, 215–16; immigrant, 140; satirical portrayals of, 120, *121*, 122; Shakespeare and Mountjoy family of tiremakers, 109–13, 137, 253n70, 253n74. *See also* attires; tiremen; tirewomen
tiremen, 37, 214, 215, 232n179. *See also* tiremakers; tirewomen
tirewomen: and the "all-male stage," 97, 123; archaeological remains in theater sites of wares produced/sold by, 2, 44, 211; and continuities between pre-Restoration and Restoration theater, 215–16, 267n7; as cosmetics retailers, 104, 113; elided labor of, 97, 117, *118*, 120; and female vanity/pride, 85, *86*, 117, *118*, 120, *121*, 122–24, 127, 133–34, 141, 209, 257–58n119; head-attires manufactured for the professional stage, 37–39, 108–9; head-attires worn by boy-actors, 9, 35–39, 108–9, 113, 116, 123; head-attires worn by elite/aristocratic women, 34–35, *36*, 107–8, 227n105; hiring of/payments to, 35–39, 43–44, 108–9, 123; as illegitimate calling, 32; immigrant/alien women, 9, 11–12, 22, 31–41, 95–97, 103–10, 115, 117, 122–25, 127, 136–40; insubstantial, "false wares" of, 9–10, 95, 101, 104, 124, 127, 133, 181, 200, 209, 211, 214; labor contrasted with "workmanship" of professional players/playwrights, 143, 209, 214–15; labor of

tirewomen: and the "all-male stage," (cont'd) curling/frizzling/setting hair, 2, 31, 33–34, 122–23; labor of dressing and undressing, 9, 34, 37, 39–41, 108, 116, 123; labor of starching linen attires, 95–97, 103–8, 123–25, 248n14; manufacture/retail of perukes and periwigs, 31, 33–35, 103–5, 110, 112–13, 120, 209, 215; moralistic polemics against and satires of, 32–34, 117–25; novelty/variety of wares, 33–34, 44, 104, 117, 123–25; playing companies' reliance on wares of, 22, 108–10, 112–13, 117, 122–23, 209, 214–15, 267n7; as practicing the "devil's work," 117–23, *118*, *119*, 120, 256n103; scholarship on, 252n60; sexualization of, 38, 39, 120, *121*, 122, 125, *126*, 127, 228n121; skilled labor of, 33–34, 122–23, 125, 127, 137–40, 181; staging of work and wares in plays, 37–39, 108, 110, 113, 116, 122–24, 133–43, 228n121; "tiresome," incessant labors of, 104, 123–25, 154; tools, techniques, and technologies of, 104–5, *106*, 127. *See also* attires; dressers and dressing, female labor of theatrical; immigrant women's textile work; "poking sticks"; starch; starching, labor of; starchwomen

tiring-house, 25, 30, 37, 40, 41, 108, 125

"To My Old Faithfull Servant" (Jonson), 198

trade secrets, 101, 114, 251n45

trade tools, techniques, and technologies used by women, 11, 34–35, 42, *43*, 44, 57, 67, 76, 82, 87, 99, 104, *106*, 107, 113, 117, 125, *126*, 127, 129, 138, 141–42, 177, 190, 213, 218, 235n24, 245n119, 252n55, 256n110

Treatise of the Vocations; or, Callings of Men (Perkins), 51, 233n204

usuresses, 10–11, 53, 57, 76–82. *See also* moneylenders and creditors, female

usury in early modern England, 54–56, 233n2; anti-usury polemics, 54, 55, 67–71, 234n14, 240n79, 240nn81–82, 240n84, 240n86; biblical injunctions against, 68–69; *Discourse Uppon Usurye* (Wilson), 54, 59; *Merchant of Venice* (Shakespeare), 10–11, 57–58, 71–85; pervasiveness and proliferation/diversification of, 55, 234n12, 234n14; and the rise/financing of the first purpose-built London theaters, 55–56, 235n18; Sonnets (Shakespeare), 10–11, 57, 67, 76–77, 78, 84, 235–36n25, 236n26; stigmatized as idle/effeminate occupation, 54–55; theological debate over female moneylending, 67–71; *Treatise of Usurie* (Fenton), 69–70, 241–42n94; and unnatural reproduction, 55, 233n9, 234nn10–11; Usury Act of 1571, 55, 58. *See also* (ac)counting; capitalism, rise of; credit economy in early modern England; moneylenders and creditors, female; usuresses

van den Plasse, Mistress Dinghen, 103, 113–14. *See also* immigrant women's textile work; laundresses; starchwomen

vanity: Bloemaert engraving, 85, *86*; engravings of Lady Avarice and Lady Vanity, 85–87, *86*; and luxury attires, 120–22, *121*

Venus and Adonis (Shakespeare), 236n26, 264n90

Vermeer, Johannes, 90, *91*, 92

vocations or callings, Protestant doctrine of, 7, 32, 50–52, 54, 100, 124, 143, 160, 180, 182, 209, 233n204

War of the Theaters, 12, 144–45, 146, 160, 164–66. *See also Hamlet* (Shakespeare)

Watson, Goody, 46, 230n157, 231n160. *See also* pawnbroking; secondhand clothing trade

Watt, Tessa, 150

Webbe, Ellin, 34. *See also* tirewomen

Weimann, Robert, 161, 162

Welfes, Widow Dionis, 113, 116, 255n88. *See also* immigrant women's textile work; laundresses; starchwomen

Wheelock, Arthur, 90

Whimzies; or, A New Cast of Characters (Braithwaite), 130

widows: *Bartholomew Fair* (Jonson), 203; boarding houses and all-female households, 114–15, 253–54n81, 254nn84–85; economic agency of, 26–27, 65, 67–71, 136, 242n98, 255n88; immigrant crafts- and tradeswomen, 42, 102, 113, 114–15, 253n76; as moneylenders/creditors, 58–60, 67–71, 237nn41–42; silkwomen, 42, 102, 253n79; and textile trades, 42, 102, 113, 114–15, 253n76, 253n79; and theatrical commerce/labor, 1, 9, 22, 26–27, 30, 60, 108, 114, 216. *See also* familial ties in theater; single women; wives

Wilson, Thomas, 54, 55, 59, 69. *See also* usury in early modern England

Wits Miserie, and the Worlds Madnesse (Lodge), 144
wives: doctrine of "due benevolence," 84, 246–47n140; economic agency of, 71–75, 93, 103, 114–16, 133–35, 223n37, 241n88, 241–42n92, 242n98, 253n79; huswifery, 4, 6, 46, 115, 219n2; labor/occupational identities of, 20, 25, 27, 93, 102–3, 149, 177, 225n84, 225–26n84, 253n79; labor proscribed/regulated by guilds, 19–20; and law of coverture, 71–75, 241n89; as moneylenders/creditors, 55, 60–61, 72–76, 83–85, 87, 235n23, 242n98; scolds, punishment of, 176; separate estates of, 71–75, 241n91; sexual virtue/vice of, 136, 176–77, 188–89, 196; and theatrical commerce/labor, 1, 9, 22, 25–27, 30–31, 47, 60–61, 73, 110, 112, 116, 217, 268n21; wife-beaten husbands, 176. *See also* familial ties in theater; single women; widows
"Womens Tyers" (Hayman epigram), 124
women's work: absence/presence dichotomy, 8–9, 15–18, 213–14, 220n4, 221n10; as "never done," 4, 10–11, 57, 97, 101, 123, 132, 143, 178, 196, 214, 218, 219n2. *See also* female occupations; gatherers, female; gendered division of labor in early modern England; immigrant women's textile work; informal economy and female labor; laundresses; moneylenders and creditors, female; scholarship on women's labor history; silkwomen; starchwomen; street-criers and hawkers, female; tirewomen
Women's Work in Early Modern English Literature and Culture (Dowd), 6
Woolley, Hannah, 129
Work and Play on the Shakespearean Stage (Rutter), 6
Working Life of Women in the Seventeenth Century (Clark), 5, 19
"workmanship": contrasted with "unworkmanly" female labor, 13, 145, 166, 175, 183, 209, 214; of crafts- and tradesmen, 5, 120, 155; of God, 32; of players/playwrights, 5, 7, 143, 145–46, 166, 173, 180, 183, 194–95, 198, 207–9, 214. *See also* "false wares"
Worlds Within Worlds (Rappaport), 19, 23
writing, labor of, 7, 220n20
Wyett, Mistris, 43. *See also* silkwomen

Yungblut, Laura, 250n38

Acknowledgments

HAVING WRITTEN A book about the networks of collaboration, commerce, and credit that take place behind the scenes of theatrical production, I want to express my deep gratitude to the many colleagues and institutions whose support has made this book possible.

My work has benefited from the insight of many generous readers, interlocutors, and mentors. I am particularly indebted to Jean Howard for reading the entire manuscript and offering sage, challenging, and uncommonly helpful advice. Other early modernist colleagues and friends who have read all or parts of this book and have offered incisive commentary include Amanda Bailey, Mary Bly, Pamela Allen Brown, Bianca Calabresi, Julie Crawford, Mario di Gangi, Will Fisher, Bella Mirabella, Pat Parker, Gail Kern Paster, Tanya Pollard, Nancy Selleck, Henry Turner, Bronwyn Wallace, and Adam Zucker. Scholars who have generously shared unpublished material, expertise in related fields, translation advice, editorial guidance, and other assistance include Karen Bamford, Crystal Bartolovich, Julian Bowsher, Joshua Calhoun, Dympna Callaghan, Andy Curran, James Davis, Michelle Dowd, Richard Dutton, Valerie Forman, Amy Froide, Emilie Gordenker, Suzanne Gossett, Tara Hamling, Roze Hentschell, Peter Holland, David Kathman, Lloyd Kermode, Mary Ellen Lamb, Eleanor Lowe, Craig Muldrew, Stephen Orgel, Lena Cowen Orlin, Peter Parolin, Phyllis Rackin, Catherine Richardson, Michael Roberts, Christopher Scott, Gary Shaw, and Will Stenhouse.

I am deeply grateful to the Theater Without Borders research group for inviting me to participate in their intellectual and collaborative work. Their influence has been particularly important in my thinking about the issues of performance and about transnational networks of exchange in early modern drama. Thanks are due to Dick Andrews, Christian Billing, Pam Brown, Melinda Gough, Rob Henke, Peg Katritzky, Jacques Lezra, Clare McManus, Eric Nicholson, Michael Armstrong Roche, David Schalkwyk, Jane Tylus, Melissa Walter, Susanne Wofford, and in particular Pavel Drabek for his support and generosity during an unplanned monthlong stay in the Czech Republic.

Wesleyan University has been tremendously supportive of my research through several sabbaticals and research grants for travel to various archives and conferences, as well as through a Faculty Fellowship at its Center for the Humanities (CHUM). Special thanks are due to Jill Morawski, the director of the Center, and to my fellow CHUM fellows, Gretchen Bakke, Joe Fitzpatrick, Jason Harris, Liza McAlister, Marcela Oteiza, Litia Perta, and Joel Pfister. My debt to Wesleyan goes well beyond financial support, as I have rarely encountered the kind of intellectual community I have enjoyed during my many years at this exceptional institution. In particular, I would like to thank my colleagues in the English Department, whose support and encouragement helped bring this project to completion. Special thanks are due to Lisa Cohen, Christina Crosby, Ann duCille, Matthew Garrett, Gertrude Hughes, Indira Karamcheti, Sean McCann, Ashraf Rushdy, Bill Stowe, and Stephanie Weiner. I would also like to thank my colleagues in the Feminist, Gender and Sexuality Studies Program, the Wesleyan Renaissance Seminar, and my "littermates," Ellen Nerenberg and Andy Curran.

The Andrew W. Mellon Foundation and the Folger Shakespeare Library supported this project with financial assistance that enabled me to conduct research at the Huntington and Folger libraries, respectively. At the Huntington, I would particularly like to thank Roy Ritchie, then director of research. The Folger has long provided an intellectual home away from home on the east coast, and I have benefited greatly from the generous assistance of its staff, including Carol Brobeck, fellowships administrator; Kathleen Lynch, executive director of the Folger Institute; Betsy Walsh, head of Reader Services; Heather Wolfe, curator of manuscripts; and Georgianna Ziegler, head of Reference. My thanks also go to Erin Blake, curator of art, and Julie Ainsworth in the Photography Department for assistance with images and to the wonderful reading-room staff. Suzy Taraba, head of Special Collections at Wesleyan's Olin Library, has also provided advice and assistance over the years, as have various librarians, curators, and archivists at the New York Public Library, the Metropolitan Museum of Art, the Museum of London, the National Portrait Gallery in London, the Victoria and Albert Museum, the British Museum Print Room, the British Library, the Guildhall Library, and the Corporation of London Record Office.

The research that grounds this book has taken place over many years, during which time I have published preliminary versions of several essays. I am grateful for permission to reprint material that has appeared in the following: "Labors Lost: Women's Work and Early Modern Theatrical Commerce," in *From Script to Stage in Early Modern England*, ed. Peter Holland and Stephen Orgel (Basingstoke: Palgrave Macmillan, 2004), 195–230; "Gender at Work in the Cries of London," in *Oral Traditions and Gender in Early Modern Literary Texts*, ed. Mary Ellen Lamb and Karen Bamford (Aldershot: Ashgate, 2008), 117–35; "Dame Usury: Gender, Credit and (Ac)counting in the Sonnets and *The Merchant of Venice*," *Shakespeare Quarterly* 60:2 (2009): 129–53; "Women and the Theater," in *Oxford Handbook on Early Modern Theatre*, ed. Richard Dutton (Oxford: Oxford University Press, 2009), 456–73; "Froes, Rebatos and Other 'Outlandish Comodityes': Weaving Alien Women's Work into the Fabric of Early Modern Material Culture," in *Everyday Objects: Medieval and Early Modern Material Culture and Its Meanings*, ed. Tara Hamling and Catherine Richardson (Aldershot: Ashgate, 2010), 95–106; "Accessorizing the Stage: Starched Ruffs," in *Ornamentalism: The Art of Renaissance Accessories*, ed. Bella Mirabela (Ann Arbor: University of Michigan Press, forthcoming). At the University of Pennsylvania Press, Jerry Singerman has been unceasingly supportive, as have his assistant, Caroline Winschel, and my project editor, Erica Ginsburg.

The insightful questions and comments of auditors too numerous to mention by name at conferences and invited lectures where I have presented material from this book have been invaluable, including those I received at the Bates College Renaissance Seminar; the University of Birmingham Centre for Reformation and Early Modern Studies and Shakespeare Institute; the City University of New York Graduate Center; Clemson University English Department and Shakespeare Festival; Columbia University Shakespeare and Early Modern Culture Seminars; the University of Connecticut at Storrs Humanities Center; the Group for Early Modern Cultural Studies; the Huntington Library; Masaryk University, Czech Republic; the University of Massachusetts at Amherst Center for Renaissance Studies; the University of Michigan at Ann Arbor Early Modern Colloquium; the Modern Language Association; New York University; the North American Conference on British Studies; the University of Pennsylvania English Department and Medieval/Renaissance Seminar; the University of Pittsburgh English Department; the Renaissance Society of America; Roehampton University; the Shakespeare Association of America; Theater Without Borders; and the University of Wisconsin at Madison English Department.

Friends and family who have provided emotional and spiritual sustenance include Cameron Anderson, Rebecca Bach, Bob Campbell, Kathy Cherry, Tricia Dailey, Rachel and Jim Dunlap, Sheila Gray and Jason and Sofia Bagdade, Natasha Gray, Jonathan Gil Harris and Madhavi Menon, Traies Johannessen, Josh Korda, Deborah Krohn, Pamela Lawton, Sharon Marcus, Julia and Tim Purinton, Sandy and Pinky Roe, Pat and John Thackray, and Brigitte Young.

    I continue to be inspired by innumerable labors of love that take place behind the scenes at my theatrical home away from home, Metropolitan Playhouse in New York City, and above all by those of its artistic director, my brilliant, tender, witty, dashing collaborator in life and love, Alex Roe, to whom this book is dedicated.